W9-DFN-484

The Philosophical Writings of Descartes

VOLUME II

These two volumes provide a completely new translation of the philosophical works of Descartes, based on the best available Latin and French texts. They are intended to replace the only reasonably comprehensive selection of his works in English, by Haldane and Ross, first published in 1911. All the works included in that edition are translated here, together with a number of additional texts crucial for an understanding of Cartesian philosophy, including important material from Descartes' scientific writings. The result should meet the widespread demand for an accurate and authoritative edition of Descartes' philosophical writings in clear and readable modern English.

Contents

The Philosophical Writings of
DESCARTES

translated by

JOHN COTTINGHAM
ROBERT STOOTHOFF
DUGALD MURDOCH

VOLUME II

CAMBRIDGE
UNIVERSITY PRESS

CAMBRIDGE UNIVERSITY PRESS
Cambridge, New York, Melbourne, Madrid, Cape Town, Singapore,
São Paulo, Delhi, Dubai, Tokyo, Mexico City

Cambridge University Press
32 Avenue of the Americas, New York, NY 10013-2473, USA

www.cambridge.org
Information on this title: www.cambridge.org/9780521288088

First published 1984
20th printing 2008

A catalogue record for this publication is available from the British Library

ISBN 978-0-521-24595-1 Hardback
ISBN 978-0-521-28808-8 Paperback

Contents

Meditations on First Philosophy

Objections and Replies

The Search for Truth

General Introduction

The aim of this two-volume edition is to provide a completely new translation of the philosophical writings of Descartes, based on the original Latin and French texts. Although many of Descartes' philosophical works are now available in English either individually, or in various selections, the only tolerably comprehensive edition remains that of Haldane and Ross, which first appeared in 1911.[1] But although it has come to be regarded as the standard English edition, HR omits many works which are crucial for a full understanding of Descartes' philosophy. The present work, by contrast, aims to be as comprehensive as possible. Considerations of space have prevented us from being as inclusive as some, no doubt, would have wished; we have not, for example, included any of Descartes' letters, partly because an excellent selection is already available in English.[2] But as well as including all the works to be found in Haldane and Ross, *viz.* the *Discourse on the Method, Meditations, Objections and Replies, Rules for the Direction of the Mind, The Search for Truth, Comments on a Certain Broadsheet, The Passions of the Soul* and selections from the *Principles of Philosophy*, we have also provided extracts from Descartes' *Early Writings*, from *The World, Treatise on Man, Optics* and *Description of the Human Body*; our selection from the *Principles*, moreover, includes many articles not translated in Haldane and Ross. In general, we have construed the term 'philosophical' in a fairly generous way, so as to include, as well as Descartes' more celebrated metaphysical and epistemological works, a fair selection of his scientific writings (on physiology, psychology, physics and cosmology), which are likely to be of interest to students of philosophy and allied disciplines.

Descartes wrote with equal fluency in Latin and French, and published in both languages; within his lifetime some of his Latin works were subsequently translated into French, and some of his French works into

---

1 *The Philosophical Works of Descartes*, tr. Elisabeth S. Haldane and G. R. T. Ross (Cambridge: CUP, 1911; repr. 1931).
2 *Descartes, Philosophical Letters*, tr. A. Kenny (Oxford: OUP, 1970; repr. Oxford: Blackwells, 1980).

Latin. Our own translations of Descartes' works are made, in each case, from the original language in which they were composed (for further details see translators' prefaces to the individual works). Where subsequent translations approved by Descartes provide important additional material, this has also been translated, but in footnotes or within diamond brackets 〈. . .〉, to distinguish it from the original material. We have thus firmly rejected the practice of Haldane and Ross, whose translation, e.g. in the case of the *Meditations* and *Principles*, is based on an uneasy amalgam of the original Latin and later French editions, with the result that the reader is frequently left in the dark as to whether a given rendering corresponds to Descartes' original words or to the formulation of one of his contemporary translators.

We have endeavoured to make our translations as accurate as possible, while at the same time attempting to produce readable modern English. Where Descartes employs technical terms which are now obsolete (e.g. 'objective reality') or uses expressions which are liable to cause difficulty to the modern student, we have supplied explanatory footnotes. But apart from this, we have tried to make the translations stand on their own feet. Often we have found that the choice of a particular English word or phrase hinges on a complex chain of philosophical argument which it is impossible to summarize adequately in a brief footnote; to do justice to the issues involved would have required a formidable exegetical apparatus which would greatly have reduced the space available for presenting Descartes' own writings. We have also rejected the device, used sporadically by Haldane and Ross and others, of inserting unexplained original Latin or French phrases when the translation is difficult or problematical; such a proceeding merely tends to puzzle the reader having no French or Latin, and is of doubtful value to those who are able to consult the original texts for themselves. In cases where we have found it necessary to refer to Latin or French terms in our footnotes, we have always explained their meaning.

In dividing the material between the two volumes, we have decided to place the *Meditations* and *Objections and Replies* together, since they are interconnected in the closest possible way, and were originally published by Descartes as a single book. These works comprise the bulk of Volume Two; also included is *The Search for Truth*, whose exact date is uncertain but which was probably composed in the same period as the *Meditations*, and deals with many of the same themes. Volume One contains all the remaining works, arranged in chronological order. Each work is preceded by a preface giving details of its composition and original publication. Comprehensive philosophical indexes are included at the end of each volume, and each volume also contains a brief chronological table of Descartes' life and works.

Our translations are based on the texts to be found in the standard twelve-volume edition of Descartes' works by Adam and Tannery (known as AT).[1] We have, however, consulted many other editions, and where these have been of particular value they are mentioned in the prefaces to individual works. Important departures from the text in AT are recorded in footnotes. Where the text is abridged, omitted material is indicated by dots, thus . . ., and further information is supplied in a footnote. For each work we have supplied, in the margins, running cross-references to the page number of the relevant volume of AT. It should be noted that, unless otherwise indicated, all comments in footnotes are those of the translators, not of Descartes.

The work of translation has been divided as follows: John Cottingham has translated the *Meditations, Objections and Replies, Early Writings, Principles of Philosophy* and *Description of the Human Body*; Robert Stoothoff has translated *The World, Treatise on Man, Discourse on the Method, Optics, The Passions of the Soul* and the first half of *The Search for Truth*; and Dugald Murdoch has translated the *Rules for the Direction of the Mind, Comments on a Certain Broadsheet* and the second half of *The Search for Truth*. All the members of the team have, however, scrutinized each others' work, and made numerous suggestions, many of which have found their way into the final versions.

We are happy to acknowledge our debt to the many previous translators, editors and writers – too numerous to list here – who have contributed to our understanding of Descartes' works. In a project of this size it is no empty formality to acknowledge our own responsibility for the shortcomings that undoubtedly remain; we can only enter as our plea the words with which Descartes himself concluded the *Meditations – naturae nostrae infirmitas est agnoscenda.*

John Cottingham
University of Reading, England

Robert Stoothoff
Dugald Murdoch
University of Canterbury, New Zealand

---

1 *Oeuvres de Descartes,* edited by Ch. Adam and P. Tannery (revised edition, Paris: Vrin/C.N.R.S., 1964–76).

Chronological table of Descartes' life and works

1596   born at La Haye near Tours on 31 March

1606–14   attends Jesuit college of La Flèche in Anjou[1]

1616   takes *Baccalauréat* and *Licence* in law at University of Poitiers

1618   goes to Holland; joins army of Prince Maurice of Nassau; meets Isaac Beeckman; composes a short treatise on music, the *Compendium Musicae*

1619   travels in Germany; 10 November: has vision of new mathematical and scientific system

1622   returns to France; during next few years spends time in Paris, but also travels in Europe

1628   composes *Rules for the Direction of the Mind*; leaves for Holland, which is to be his home until 1649, though with frequent changes of address

1629   begins working on *The World*

1633   condemnation of Galileo; Descartes abandons plans to publish *The World*

1635   birth of Descartes' natural daughter Francine, baptized 7 August (died 1640)

1637   publishes *Discourse on the Method*, with *Optics, Meteorology* and *Geometry*

1641   *Meditations on First Philosophy* published, together with *Objections and Replies* (first six sets)

1642   second edition of *Meditations* published, with all seven sets of *Objections and Replies* and *Letter to Dinet*

1643   Cartesian philosophy condemned at the University of Utrecht; Descartes' long correspondence with Princess Elizabeth of Bohemia begins

1644   visits France; *Principles of Philosophy* published

---

1 Descartes is known to have stayed at La Flèche for eight or nine years, but the exact dates of his arrival and departure are uncertain. Baillet places Descartes' admission in 1604, the year of the College's foundation (A. Baillet, *La vie de Monsieur Des-Cartes* (1691), vol. 1, p. 18).

1647   awarded a pension by King of France; publishes *Comments on a Certain Broadsheet*; begins work on *Description of the Human Body*

1648   interviewed by Frans Burman at Egmond-Binnen (*Conversation with Burman*)

1649   goes to Sweden on invitation of Queen Christina; *The Passions of the Soul* published

1650   dies at Stockholm on 11 February

Meditations on First Philosophy

Translator's preface

Descartes' most celebrated philosophical work was written in Latin during the period 1638–40, when the philosopher was living, for the most part, at Santpoort. This 'corner of north Holland', he wrote to Mersenne on 17 May 1638, was much more suitable for his work than the 'air of Paris' with its 'vast number of inevitable distractions'. The work was completed by April 1640, and was first published in Paris in 1641 by Michel Soly under the title *Meditationes de Prima Philosophiae* (*Meditations on First Philosophy*); the subtitle adds 'in which are demonstrated the existence of God and the immortality of the soul'. In earlier correspondence Descartes had referred to his work as the *Metaphysics*, but he eventually decided that 'the most suitable title is *Meditations on First Philosophy*, because the discussion is not confined to God and the soul but treats in general of all the first things to be discovered by philosophizing' (letter to Mersenne, 11 November 1640).

Descartes was not entirely satisfied with Soly as a publisher, and he arranged for a second edition of the *Meditations* to be brought out in Holland, by the house of Elzevir of Amsterdam. This second edition appeared in 1642, with a new and more appropriate subtitle, *viz.* 'in which are demonstrated the existence of God and the distinction between the human soul and the body'. The second edition contains a number of minor corrections to the text[1] (though in practice the sense is seldom affected), and except where indicated it is this edition that is followed in the present translation.

A French translation of the *Meditations* by Louis-Charles d'Albert, Duc de Luynes (1620–90) appeared in 1647. This is a tolerably accurate version which was published with Descartes' approval; Adrien Baillet, in his biography of Descartes, goes so far as to claim that the philosopher took advantage of the French edition to 'retouch his original work'.[2] In fact, however, the French version generally stays fairly close to the Latin.

---

1 But the strictures in AT against the first edition are not always well founded; for a full discussion see F. Alquié (ed.), *Oeuvres philosophiques de Descartes* (Paris: Garnier, 1963–73), vol. II, pp. 377ff. See also General Introduction, above p. ix.
2 A. Baillet, *Vie de Monsieur Des-Cartes* (1691), vol. II, p. 172.

There are a number of places where phrases in the original are para-phrased or expanded somewhat, but it is impossible to say which of these modifications, if any, were directly initiated by Descartes (some are certainly too clumsy to be his work). There is thus no good case for giving the French version greater authority than the original Latin text, which we know that Descartes himself composed; and the present translation therefore always provides, in the first instance, a direct rendering of the original Latin. But where expansions or modifications to be found in the French version offer useful glosses on, or additions to, the original, these are also translated, but always in diamond brackets, or in footnotes, to avoid confusion.[1] For details of the *Objections and Replies*, which were published together with the *Meditations* in the 1641 and 1642 editions, see below, p. 63.

J.C.

---

1 For detailed comparison between the French and Latin versions see G. Rodis Lewis (ed.), *Descartes, Méditations: texte Latin et traduction du Duc de Luynes* (Paris: Vrin, 1946).

[Dedicatory letter to the Sorbonne]

To those most learned and distinguished men, the Dean and Doctors of 1
the sacred Faculty of Theology at Paris, from René Descartes.

I have a very good reason for offering this book to you, and I am confident that you will have an equally good reason for giving it your protection once you understand the principle behind my undertaking; so much so, that my best way of commending it to you will be to tell you briefly of the goal which I shall be aiming at in the book.

I have always thought that two topics – namely God and the soul – are prime examples of subjects where demonstrative proofs ought to be given with the aid of philosophy rather than theology. For us who are believers, it is enough to accept on faith that the human soul does not die with the 2 body, and that God exists; but in the case of unbelievers, it seems that there is no religion, and practically no moral virtue, that they can be persuaded to adopt until these two truths are proved to them by natural reason. And since in this life the rewards offered to vice are often greater than the rewards of virtue, few people would prefer what is right to what is expedient if they did not fear God or have the expectation of an after-life. It is of course quite true that we must believe in the existence of God because it is a doctrine of Holy Scripture, and conversely, that we must believe Holy Scripture because it comes from God; for since faith is the gift of God, he who gives us grace to believe other things can also give us grace to believe that he exists. But this argument cannot be put to unbelievers because they would judge it to be circular. Moreover, I have noticed both that you and all other theologians assert that the existence of God is capable of proof by natural reason, and also that the inference from Holy Scripture is that the knowledge of God is easier to acquire than the knowledge we have of many created things – so easy, indeed, that those who do not acquire it are at fault. This is clear from a passage in the Book of Wisdom, Chapter 13: 'Howbeit they are not to be excused; for if their knowledge was so great that they could value this world, why did they not rather find out the Lord thereof?' And in Romans, Chapter 1 it is said that they are 'without excuse'. And in the same place, in the passage 'that which is known of God is manifest in them', we seem to be told that everything that may be known of God can be demonstrated by reasoning which has no other source but our own mind. Hence I thought it was quite proper for me to inquire how this may be, and how God may be more easily and more certainly known than the things of this world.

3 As regards the soul, many people have considered that it is not easy to discover its nature, and some have even had the audacity to assert that, as far as human reasoning goes, there are persuasive grounds for holding that the soul dies along with the body and that the opposite view is based on faith alone. But in its eighth session the Lateran Council held under Leo X condemned those who take this position,[1] and expressly enjoined Christian philosophers to refute their arguments and use all their powers to establish the truth; so I have not hesitated to attempt this task as well.

In addition, I know that the only reason why many irreligious people are unwilling to believe that God exists and that the human mind is distinct from the body is the alleged fact that no one has hitherto been able to demonstrate these points. Now I completely disagree with this: I think that when properly understood almost all the arguments that have been put forward on these issues by the great men have the force of demonstrations, and I am convinced that it is scarcely possible to provide any arguments which have not already been produced by someone else. Nevertheless, I think there can be no more useful service to be rendered in philosophy than to conduct a careful search, once and for all, for the best of these arguments, and to set them out so precisely and clearly as to produce for the future a general agreement that they amount to demonstrative proofs. And finally, I was strongly pressed to undertake this task by several people who knew that I had developed a method for resolving certain difficulties in the sciences – not a new method (for nothing is older than the truth), but one which they had seen me use with some success in other areas; and I therefore thought it my duty to make some attempt to apply it to the matter in hand.

4 The present treatise contains everything that I have been able to accomplish in this area. Not that I have attempted to collect here all the different arguments that could be put forward to establish the same results, for this does not seem worthwhile except in cases where no single argument is regarded as sufficiently reliable. What I have done is to take merely the principal and most important arguments and develop them in such a way that I would now venture to put them forward as very certain and evident demonstrations. I will add that these proofs are of such a kind that I reckon they leave no room for the possibility that the human mind will ever discover better ones. The vital importance of the cause and the glory of God, to which the entire undertaking is directed, here compel me to speak somewhat more freely about my own achievements

1 The Lateran Council of 1513 condemned the Averroist heresy which denied personal immortality.

than is my custom. But although I regard the proofs as quite certain and evident, I cannot therefore persuade myself that they are suitable to be grasped by everyone. In geometry there are many writings left by Archimedes, Apollonius, Pappus and others which are accepted by everyone as evident and certain because they contain absolutely nothing that is not very easy to understand when considered on its own, and each step fits in precisely with what has gone before; yet because they are somewhat long, and demand a very attentive reader, it is only comparatively few people who understand them. In the same way, although the proofs I employ here are in my view as certain and evident as the proofs of geometry, if not more so, it will, I fear, be impossible for many people to achieve an adequate perception of them, both because they are rather long and some depend on others, and also, above all, because they require a mind which is completely free from preconceived opinions and which can easily detach itself from involvement with the senses. Moreover, people who have an aptitude for metaphysical studies are certainly not to be found in the world in any greater numbers than those who have an aptitude for geometry. What is more, there is the difference that in 5 geometry everyone has been taught to accept that as a rule no proposition is put forward in a book without there being a conclusive demonstration available; so inexperienced students make the mistake of accepting what is false, in their desire to appear to understand it, more often than they make the mistake of rejecting what is true. In philosophy, by contrast, the belief is that everything can be argued either way; so few people pursue the truth, while the great majority build up their reputation for ingenuity by boldly attacking whatever is most sound.

Hence, whatever the quality of my arguments may be, because they have to do with philosophy I do not expect they will enable me to achieve any very worthwhile results unless you come to my aid by granting me your patronage.[1] The reputation of your Faculty is so firmly fixed in the minds of all, and the name of the Sorbonne has such authority that, with the exception of the Sacred Councils, no institution carries more weight than yours in matters of faith; while as regards human philosophy, you are thought of as second to none, both for insight and soundness and also for the integrity and wisdom of your pronouncements. Because of this, the results of your careful attention to this book, if you deigned to give it, would be threefold. First, the errors in it would be corrected – for when I remember not only that I am a human being, but above all that I am an ignorant one, I cannot claim it is free of mistakes. Secondly, any passages

---

1 Although the title page of the first edition of the *Meditations* carries the words 'with the approval of the learned doctors', Descartes never in fact obtained the endorsement from the Sorbonne which he sought.

which are defective, or insufficiently developed or requiring further explanation, would be supplemented, completed and clarified, either by yourselves or by me after you have given me your advice. And lastly, once the arguments in the book proving that God exists and that the mind is distinct from the body have been brought, as I am sure they can be, to

6 such a pitch of clarity that they are fit to be regarded as very exact demonstrations, you may be willing to declare as much, and make a public statement to that effect. If all this were to happen, I do not doubt that all the errors which have ever existed on these subjects would soon be eradicated from the minds of men. In the case of all those who share your intelligence and learning, the truth itself will readily ensure that they subscribe to your opinion. As for the atheists, who are generally posers rather than people of real intelligence or learning, your authority will induce them to lay aside the spirit of contradiction; and, since they know that the arguments are regarded as demonstrations by all who are intellectually gifted, they may even go so far as to defend them, rather than appear not to understand them. And finally, everyone else will confidently go along with so many declarations of assent, and there will be no one left in the world who will dare to call into doubt either the existence of God or the real distinction between the human soul and body. The great advantage that this would bring is something which you, in your singular wisdom, are in a better position to evaluate than anyone;[1] and it would ill become me to spend any more time commending the cause of God and religion to you, who have always been the greatest tower of strength to the Catholic Church.

7   *Preface to the reader*[2]

I briefly touched on the topics of God and the human mind in my *Discourse on the method of rightly conducting reason and seeking the truth in the sciences*, which was published in French in 1637. My purpose there was not to provide a full treatment, but merely to offer a sample, and learn from the views of my readers how I should handle these topics at a later date. The issues seemed to me of such great importance that I considered they ought to be dealt with more than once; and the route which I follow in explaining them is so untrodden and so remote from the normal way, that I thought it would not be helpful to give a full

---

1 'It is for you to judge the advantage that would come from establishing these beliefs firmly, since you see all the disorders which come from their being doubted' (French version).

2 The French version of 1647 does not translate this preface, but substitutes a brief foreword, *Le Libraire au Lecteur* ('The Publisher to the Reader'), which is probably not by Descartes.

account of it in a book written in French and designed to be read by all and sundry, in case weaker intellects might believe that they ought to set out on the same path.

In the *Discourse* I asked anyone who found anything worth criticizing in what I had written to be kind enough to point it out to me.[1] In the case of my remarks concerning God and the soul, only two objections worth mentioning were put to me, which I shall now briefly answer before embarking on a more precise elucidation of these topics.

The first objection is this. From the fact that the human mind, when directed towards itself, does not perceive itself to be anything other than a thinking thing, it does not follow that its nature or essence consists only in its being a thinking thing, where the word 'only' excludes everything else that could be said to belong to the nature of the soul. My answer to this objection is that in that passage it was not my intention to make those exclusions in an order corresponding to the actual truth of the matter (which I was not dealing with at that stage) but merely in an order corresponding to my own perception. So the sense of the passage was that I was aware of nothing at all that I knew belonged to my essence, except that I was a thinking thing, or a thing possessing within itself the faculty of thinking.[2] I shall, however, show below how it follows from the fact that I am aware of nothing else belonging to my essence, that nothing else does in fact belong to it.

The second objection is this. From the fact that I have within me an idea of a thing more perfect than myself, it does not follow that the idea itself is more perfect than me, still less that what is represented by the idea exists. My reply is that there is an ambiguity here in the word 'idea'. 'Idea' can be taken materially, as an operation of the intellect, in which case it cannot be said to be more perfect than me. Alternatively, it can be taken objectively, as the thing represented by that operation; and this thing, even if it is not regarded as existing outside the intellect, can still, in virtue of its essence, be more perfect than myself. As to how, from the mere fact that there is within me an idea of something more perfect than me, it follows that this thing really exists, this is something which will be fully explained below.

Apart from these objections, there are two fairly lengthy essays which I have looked at,[3] but these did not attack my reasoning on these matters so much as my conclusions, and employed arguments lifted from the standard sources of the atheists. But arguments of this sort can carry no

---

1 See *Discourse*, part 6: vol. 1, p. 149.
2 See *Discourse*, part 4: vol. 1, p. 127.
3 One of the critics referred to here is Petit: see letter to Mersenne of 17 May 1638. The other is unknown.

weight with those who understand my reasoning. Moreover, the judgement of many people is so silly and weak that, once they have accepted a
view, they continue to believe it, however false and irrational it may be,
in preference to a true and well-grounded refutation which they hear
subsequently. So I do not wish to reply to such arguments here, if only to
avoid having to state them. I will only make the general point that all the
objections commonly tossed around by atheists to attack the existence of
God invariably depend either on attributing human feelings to God or on
arrogantly supposing our own minds to be so powerful and wise that we
can attempt to grasp and set limits to what God can or should perform.
So, provided only that we remember that our minds must be regarded as
finite, while God is infinite and beyond our comprehension, such
objections will not cause us any difficulty.

But now that I have, after a fashion, taken an initial sample of people's
opinions, I am again tackling the same questions concerning God and the
human mind; and this time I am also going to deal with the foundations
of First Philosophy in its entirety. But I do not expect any popular
approval, or indeed any wide audience. On the contrary I would not urge
anyone to read this book except those who are able and willing to
meditate seriously with me, and to withdraw their minds from the senses
and from all preconceived opinions. Such readers, as I well know, are few
and far between. Those who do not bother to grasp the proper order of
my arguments and the connection between them, but merely try to carp
10 at individual sentences, as is the fashion, will not get much benefit from
reading this book. They may well find an opportunity to quibble in many
places, but it will not be easy for them to produce objections which are
telling or worth replying to.

But I certainly do not promise to satisfy my other readers straightaway
on all points, and I am not so presumptuous as to believe that I am
capable of foreseeing all the difficulties which anyone may find. So first of
all, in the *Meditations*, I will set out the very thoughts which have
enabled me, in my view, to arrive at a certain and evident knowledge of
the truth, so that I can find out whether the same arguments which have
convinced me will enable me to convince others. Next, I will reply to the
objections of various men of outstanding intellect and scholarship who
had these Meditations sent to them for scrutiny before they went to press.
For the objections they raised were so many and so varied that I would
venture to hope that it will be hard for anyone else to think of any point –
at least of any importance – which these critics have not touched on. I
therefore ask my readers not to pass judgement on the *Meditations* until
they have been kind enough to read through all these objections and my
replies to them.

Synopsis of the following six Meditations

In the First Meditation reasons are provided which give us possible grounds for doubt about all things, especially material things, so long as we have no foundations for the sciences other than those which we have had up till now. Although the usefulness of such extensive doubt is not apparent at first sight, its greatest benefit lies in freeing us from all our preconceived opinions, and providing the easiest route by which the mind may be led away from the senses. The eventual result of this doubt is to make it impossible for us to have any further doubts about what we subsequently discover to be true.

In the Second Meditation, the mind uses its own freedom and supposes the non-existence of all the things about whose existence it can have even the slightest doubt; and in so doing the mind notices that it is impossible that it should not itself exist during this time. This exercise is also of the greatest benefit, since it enables the mind to distinguish without difficulty what belongs to itself, i.e. to an intellectual nature, from what belongs to the body. But since some people may perhaps expect arguments for the immortality of the soul in this section, I think they should be warned here and now that I have tried not to put down anything which I could not precisely demonstrate. Hence the only order which I could follow was that normally employed by geometers, namely to set out all the premisses on which a desired proposition depends, before drawing any conclusions about it. Now the first and most important prerequisite for knowledge of the immortality of the soul is for us to form a concept of the soul which is as clear as possible and is also quite distinct from every concept of body; and that is just what has been done in this section. A further requirement is that we should know that everything that we clearly and distinctly understand is true in a way which corresponds exactly to our understanding of it; but it was not possible to prove this before the Fourth Meditation. In addition we need to have a distinct concept of corporeal nature, and this is developed partly in the Second Meditation itself, and partly in the Fifth and Sixth Meditations. The inference to be drawn from these results is that all the things that we clearly and distinctly conceive of as different substances (as we do in the case of mind and body) are in fact substances which are really distinct one from the other; and this conclusion is drawn in the Sixth Meditation. This conclusion is confirmed in the same Meditation by the fact that we cannot understand a body except as being divisible, while by contrast we cannot understand a mind except as being indivisible. For we cannot conceive of half of a mind, while we can always conceive of half of a body, however small; and this leads us to recognize that the natures of

mind and body are not only different, but in some way opposite. But I
have not pursued this topic any further in this book, first because these
arguments are enough to show that the decay of the body does not imply
the destruction of the mind, and are hence enough to give mortals the
hope of an after-life, and secondly because the premisses which lead to
the conclusion that the soul is immortal depend on an account of the
14   whole of physics. This is required for two reasons. First, we need to know
that absolutely all substances, or things which must be created by God in
order to exist, are by their nature incorruptible and cannot ever cease to
exist unless they are reduced to nothingness by God's denying his
concurrence[1] to them. Secondly, we need to recognize that body, taken in
the general sense, is a substance, so that it too never perishes. But the
human body, in so far as it differs from other bodies, is simply made up
of a certain configuration of limbs and other accidents[2] of this sort;
whereas the human mind is not made up of any accidents in this way, but
is a pure substance. For even if all the accidents of the mind change, so
that it has different objects of the understanding and different desires and
sensations, it does not on that account become a different mind; whereas
a human body loses its identity merely as a result of a change in the shape
of some of its parts. And it follows from this that while the body can very
easily perish, the mind[3] is immortal by its very nature.

In the Third Meditation I have explained quite fully enough, I think,
my principal argument for proving the existence of God. But in order to
draw my readers' minds away from the senses as far as possible, I was not
willing to use any comparison taken from bodily things. So it may be that
many obscurities remain; but I hope they will be completely removed
later, in my Replies to the Objections. One such problem, among others,
is how the idea of a supremely perfect being, which is in us, possesses so
much objective[4] reality that it can come only from a cause which is
supremely perfect. In the Replies this is illustrated by the comparison of a
very perfect machine, the idea of which is in the mind of some engineer.[5]
Just as the objective intricacy belonging to the idea must have some

---

1 The continuous divine action necessary to maintain things in existence; see below, Fifth
   Replies pp. 254f.
2 Descartes here uses this scholastic term to refer to those features of a thing which may
   alter, e.g. the particular size, shape etc. of a body, or the particular thoughts, desires etc.
   of a mind.
3 '. . . or the soul of man, for I make no distinction between them' (added in French
   version).
4 For Descartes' use of this term, see Med. III, below p. 28.
5 First Replies, below p. 75.

cause, namely the scientific knowledge of the engineer, or of someone else who passed the idea on to him, so the idea of God which is in us must 15 have God himself as its cause.

In the Fourth Meditation it is proved that everything that we clearly and distinctly perceive is true, and I also explain what the nature of falsity consists in. These results need to be known both in order to confirm what has gone before and also to make intelligible what is to come later. (But here it should be noted in passing that I do not deal at all with sin, i.e. the error which is committed in pursuing good and evil, but only with the error that occurs in distinguishing truth from falsehood. And there is no discussion of matters pertaining to faith or the conduct of life, but simply of speculative truths which are known solely by means of the natural light.)[1]

In the Fifth Meditation, besides an account of corporeal nature taken in general, there is a new argument demonstrating the existence of God. Again, several difficulties may arise here, but these are resolved later in the Replies to the Objections. Finally I explain the sense in which it is true that the certainty even of geometrical demonstrations depends on the knowledge of God.

Lastly, in the Sixth Meditation, the intellect is distinguished from the imagination; the criteria for this distinction are explained; the mind is proved to be really distinct from the body, but is shown, notwithstanding, to be so closely joined to it that the mind and the body make up a kind of unit; there is a survey of all the errors which commonly come from the senses, and an explanation of how they may be avoided; and, lastly, there is a presentation of all the arguments which enable the existence of material things to be inferred. The great benefit of these arguments is not, in my view, that they prove what they establish – 16 namely that there really is a world, and that human beings have bodies and so on – since no sane person has ever seriously doubted these things. The point is that in considering these arguments we come to realize that they are not as solid or as transparent as the arguments which lead us to knowledge of our own minds and of God, so that the latter are the most certain and evident of all possible objects of knowledge for the human intellect. Indeed, this is the one thing that I set myself to prove in these Meditations. And for that reason I will not now go over the various other issues in the book which are dealt with as they come up.

1 Descartes added this passage after reading the Fourth Set of Objections (see below pp. 151–2). He told Mersenne 'please put the words in brackets so that it can be seen that they have been added' (letter of 18 March 1641).

in which are demonstrated the existence of God and the distinction between the human soul and the body

FIRST MEDITATION

What can be called into doubt

Some years ago I was struck by the large number of falsehoods that I had accepted as true in my childhood, and by the highly doubtful nature of the whole edifice that I had subsequently based on them. I realized that it was necessary, once in the course of my life, to demolish everything completely and start again right from the foundations if I wanted to establish anything at all in the sciences that was stable and likely to last. But the task looked an enormous one, and I began to wait until I should reach a mature enough age to ensure that no subsequent time of life would be more suitable for tackling such inquiries. This led me to put the project off for so long that I would now be to blame if by pondering over it any further I wasted the time still left for carrying it out. So today I have expressly rid my mind of all worries and arranged for myself a clear stretch of free time. I am here quite alone, and at last I will devote myself sincerely and without reservation to the general demolition of my opinions.

But to accomplish this, it will not be necessary for me to show that all my opinions are false, which is something I could perhaps never manage. Reason now leads me to think that I should hold back my assent from opinions which are not completely certain and indubitable just as carefully as I do from those which are patently false. So, for the purpose of rejecting all my opinions, it will be enough if I find in each of them at least some reason for doubt. And to do this I will not need to run through them all individually, which would be an endless task. Once the foundations of a building are undermined, anything built on them collapses of its own accord; so I will go straight for the basic principles on which all my former beliefs rested.

Whatever I have up till now accepted as most true I have acquired either from the senses or through the senses. But from time to time I have found that the senses deceive, and it is prudent never to trust completely those who have deceived us even once.

Yet although the senses occasionally deceive us with respect to objects which are very small or in the distance, there are many other beliefs about which doubt is quite impossible, even though they are derived from the senses – for example, that I am here, sitting by the fire, wearing a winter dressing-gown, holding this piece of paper in my hands, and so on. Again, how could it be denied that these hands or this whole body are mine? Unless perhaps I were to liken myself to madmen, whose brains are 19 so damaged by the persistent vapours of melancholia that they firmly maintain they are kings when they are paupers, or say they are dressed in purple when they are naked, or that their heads are made of earthenware, or that they are pumpkins, or made of glass. But such people are insane, and I would be thought equally mad if I took anything from them as a model for myself.

A brilliant piece of reasoning! As if I were not a man who sleeps at night, and regularly has all the same experiences[1] while asleep as madmen do when awake – indeed sometimes even more improbable ones. How often, asleep at night, am I convinced of just such familiar events – that I am here in my dressing-gown, sitting by the fire – when in fact I am lying undressed in bed! Yet at the moment my eyes are certainly wide awake when I look at this piece of paper; I shake my head and it is not asleep; as I stretch out and feel my hand I do so deliberately, and I know what I am doing. All this would not happen with such distinctness to someone asleep. Indeed! As if I did not remember other occasions when I have been tricked by exactly similar thoughts while asleep! As I think about this more carefully, I see plainly that there are never any sure signs by means of which being awake can be distinguished from being asleep. The result is that I begin to feel dazed, and this very feeling only reinforces the notion that I may be asleep.

Suppose then that I am dreaming, and that these particulars – that my eyes are open, that I am moving my head and stretching out my hands – are not true. Perhaps, indeed, I do not even have such hands or such a body at all. Nonetheless, it must surely be admitted that the visions which come in sleep are like paintings, which must have been fashioned in the likeness of things that are real, and hence that at least these general kinds of things – eyes, head, hands and the body as a whole – are things 20 which are not imaginary but are real and exist. For even when painters try to create sirens and satyrs with the most extraordinary bodies, they cannot give them natures which are new in all respects; they simply jumble up the limbs of different animals. Or if perhaps they manage to think up something so new that nothing remotely similar has ever been seen before – something which is therefore completely fictitious and unreal – at least the colours used in the composition must be real. By similar reasoning, although these general kinds of things – eyes, head,

1 '. . . and in my dreams regularly represent to myself the same things' (French version).

hands and so on – could be imaginary, it must at least be admitted that certain other even simpler and more universal things are real. These are as it were the real colours from which we form all the images of things, whether true or false, that occur in our thought.

This class appears to include corporeal nature in general, and its extension; the shape of extended things; the quantity, or size and number of these things; the place in which they may exist, the time through which they may endure,[1] and so on.

So a reasonable conclusion from this might be that physics, astronomy, medicine, and all other disciplines which depend on the study of composite things, are doubtful; while arithmetic, geometry and other subjects of this kind, which deal only with the simplest and most general things, regardless of whether they really exist in nature or not, contain something certain and indubitable. For whether I am awake or asleep, two and three added together are five, and a square has no more than four sides. It seems impossible that such transparent truths should incur any suspicion of being false.

21   And yet firmly rooted in my mind is the long-standing opinion that there is an omnipotent God who made me the kind of creature that I am. How do I know that he has not brought it about that there is no earth, no sky, no extended thing, no shape, no size, no place, while at the same time ensuring that all these things appear to me to exist just as they do now? What is more, since I sometimes believe that others go astray in cases where they think they have the most perfect knowledge, may I not similarly go wrong every time I add two and three or count the sides of a square, or in some even simpler matter, if that is imaginable? But perhaps God would not have allowed me to be deceived in this way, since he is said to be supremely good. But if it were inconsistent with his goodness to have created me such that I am deceived all the time, it would seem equally foreign to his goodness to allow me to be deceived even occasionally; yet this last assertion cannot be made.[2]

Perhaps there may be some who would prefer to deny the existence of so powerful a God rather than believe that everything else is uncertain. Let us not argue with them, but grant them that everything said about God is a fiction. According to their supposition, then, I have arrived at my present state by fate or chance or a continuous chain of events, or by some other means; yet since deception and error seem to be imperfections, the less powerful they make my original cause, the more likely it is that I am so imperfect as to be deceived all the time. I have no answer to these arguments, but am finally compelled to admit that there is not one of my former beliefs about which a doubt may not properly be

---

1 '... the place where they are, the time which measures their duration' (French version).
2 '... yet I cannot doubt that he does allow this' (French version).

raised; and this is not a flippant or ill-considered conclusion, but is based on powerful and well thought-out reasons. So in future I must withhold my assent from these former beliefs just as carefully as I would from obvious falsehoods, if I want to discover any certainty.[1]

But it is not enough merely to have noticed this; I must make an effort to remember it. My habitual opinions keep coming back, and, despite my wishes, they capture my belief, which is as it were bound over to them as a result of long occupation and the law of custom. I shall never get out of the habit of confidently assenting to these opinions, so long as I suppose them to be what in fact they are, namely highly probable opinions – opinions which, despite the fact that they are in a sense doubtful, as has just been shown, it is still much more reasonable to believe than to deny. In view of this, I think it will be a good plan to turn my will in completely the opposite direction and deceive myself, by pretending for a time that these former opinions are utterly false and imaginary. I shall do this until the weight of preconceived opinion is counter-balanced and the distorting influence of habit no longer prevents my judgement from perceiving things correctly. In the meantime, I know that no danger or error will result from my plan, and that I cannot possibly go too far in my distrustful attitude. This is because the task now in hand does not involve action but merely the acquisition of knowledge.

I will suppose therefore that not God, who is supremely good and the source of truth, but rather some malicious demon of the utmost power and cunning has employed all his energies in order to deceive me. I shall think that the sky, the air, the earth, colours, shapes, sounds and all external things are merely the delusions of dreams which he has devised to ensnare my judgement. I shall consider myself as not having hands or eyes, or flesh, or blood or senses, but as falsely believing that I have all these things. I shall stubbornly and firmly persist in this meditation; and, even if it is not in my power to know any truth, I shall at least do what is in my power,[2] that is, resolutely guard against assenting to any falsehoods, so that the deceiver, however powerful and cunning he may be, will be unable to impose on me in the slightest degree. But this is an arduous undertaking, and a kind of laziness brings me back to normal life. I am like a prisoner who is enjoying an imaginary freedom while asleep; as he begins to suspect that he is asleep, he dreads being woken up, and goes along with the pleasant illusion as long as he can. In the same way, I happily slide back into my old opinions and dread being shaken out of them, for fear that my peaceful sleep may be followed by hard labour when I wake, and that I shall have to toil not in the light, but amid the inextricable darkness of the problems I have now raised.

22

23

1 '. . . in the sciences' (added in French version).
2 '. . . nevertheless it is in my power to suspend my judgement' (French version).

SECOND MEDITATION

The nature of the human mind, and how it is better known than the body

So serious are the doubts into which I have been thrown as a result of yesterday's meditation that I can neither put them out of my mind nor
24 see any way of resolving them. It feels as if I have fallen unexpectedly into a deep whirlpool which tumbles me around so that I can neither stand on the bottom nor swim up to the top. Nevertheless I will make an effort and once more attempt the same path which I started on yesterday. Anything which admits of the slightest doubt I will set aside just as if I had found it to be wholly false; and I will proceed in this way until I recognize something certain, or, if nothing else, until I at least recognize for certain that there is no certainty. Archimedes used to demand just one firm and immovable point in order to shift the entire earth; so I too can hope for great things if I manage to find just one thing, however slight, that is certain and unshakeable.

I will suppose then, that everything I see is spurious. I will believe that my memory tells me lies, and that none of the things that it reports ever happened. I have no senses. Body, shape, extension, movement and place are chimeras. So what remains true? Perhaps just the one fact that nothing is certain.

Yet apart from everything I have just listed, how do I know that there is not something else which does not allow even the slightest occasion for doubt? Is there not a God, or whatever I may call him, who puts into me[1] the thoughts I am now having? But why do I think this, since I myself may perhaps be the author of these thoughts? In that case am not I, at least, something? But I have just said that I have no senses and no body.
25 This is the sticking point: what follows from this? Am I not so bound up with a body and with senses that I cannot exist without them? But I have convinced myself that there is absolutely nothing in the world, no sky, no earth, no minds, no bodies. Does it now follow that I too do not exist?

---

1 '. . . puts into my mind' (French version).

No: if I convinced myself of something[1] then I certainly existed. But there is a deceiver of supreme power and cunning who is deliberately and constantly deceiving me. In that case I too undoubtedly exist, if he is deceiving me; and let him deceive me as much as he can, he will never bring it about that I am nothing so long as I think that I am something. So after considering everything very thoroughly, I must finally conclude that this proposition, *I am, I exist*, is necessarily true whenever it is put forward by me or conceived in my mind.

But I do not yet have a sufficient understanding of what this 'I' is, that now necessarily exists. So I must be on my guard against carelessly taking something else to be this 'I', and so making a mistake in the very item of knowledge that I maintain is the most certain and evident of all. I will therefore go back and meditate on what I originally believed myself to be, before I embarked on this present train of thought. I will then subtract anything capable of being weakened, even minimally, by the arguments now introduced, so that what is left at the end may be exactly and only what is certain and unshakeable.

What then did I formerly think I was? A man. But what is a man? Shall I say 'a rational animal'? No; for then I should have to inquire what an animal is, what rationality is, and in this way one question would lead me down the slope to other harder ones, and I do not now have the time to waste on subtleties of this kind. Instead I propose to concentrate on what came into my thoughts spontaneously and quite naturally whenever I 26 used to consider what I was. Well, the first thought to come to mind was that I had a face, hands, arms and the whole mechanical structure of limbs which can be seen in a corpse, and which I called the body. The next thought was that I was nourished, that I moved about, and that I engaged in sense-perception and thinking; and these actions I attributed to the soul. But as to the nature of this soul, either I did not think about this or else I imagined it to be something tenuous, like a wind or fire or ether, which permeated my more solid parts. As to the body, however, I had no doubts about it, but thought I knew its nature distinctly. If I had tried to describe the mental conception I had of it, I would have expressed it as follows: by a body I understand whatever has a determinable shape and a definable location and can occupy a space in such a way as to exclude any other body; it can be perceived by touch, sight, hearing, taste or smell, and can be moved in various ways, not by itself but by whatever else comes into contact with it. For, according to my judgement, the power of self-movement, like the power of sensation or of thought, was quite foreign to the nature of a body; indeed, it was a

---

1 '. . . or thought anything at all' (French version).

source of wonder to me that certain bodies were found to contain faculties of this kind.

But what shall I now say that I am, when I am supposing that there is some supremely powerful and, if it is permissible to say so, malicious deceiver, who is deliberately trying to trick me in every way he can? Can I now assert that I possess even the most insignificant of all the attributes which I have just said belong to the nature of a body? I scrutinize them, think about them, go over them again, but nothing suggests itself; it is tiresome and pointless to go through the list once more. But what about the attributes I assigned to the soul? Nutrition or movement? Since now I do not have a body, these are mere fabrications. Sense-perception? This surely does not occur without a body, and besides, when asleep I have appeared to perceive through the senses many things which I afterwards realized I did not perceive through the senses at all. Thinking? At last I have discovered it – thought; this alone is inseparable from me. I am, I exist – that is certain. But for how long? For as long as I am thinking. For it could be that were I totally to cease from thinking, I should totally cease to exist. At present I am not admitting anything except what is necessarily true. I am, then, in the strict sense only a thing that thinks;[1] that is, I am a mind, or intelligence, or intellect, or reason – words whose meaning I have been ignorant of until now. But for all that I am a thing which is real and which truly exists. But what kind of a thing? As I have just said – a thinking thing.

What else am I? I will use my imagination.[2] I am not that structure of limbs which is called a human body. I am not even some thin vapour which permeates the limbs – a wind, fire, air, breath, or whatever I depict in my imagination; for these are things which I have supposed to be nothing. Let this supposition stand;[3] for all that I am still something. And yet may it not perhaps be the case that these very things which I am supposing to be nothing, because they are unknown to me, are in reality identical with the 'I' of which I am aware? I do not know, and for the moment I shall not argue the point, since I can make judgements only about things which are known to me. I know that I exist; the question is, what is this 'I' that I know? If the 'I' is understood strictly as we have been taking it, then it is quite certain that knowledge of it does not

1 The word 'only' is most naturally taken as going with 'a thing that thinks', and this interpretation is followed in the French version. When discussing this passage with Gassendi, however, Descartes suggests that he meant the 'only' to govern 'in the strict sense'; see below p. 276.
2 '. . . to see if I am not something more' (added in French version).
3 Lat. *maneat* ('let it stand'), first edition. The second edition has the indicative *manet*: 'The proposition still stands, *viz.* that I am nonetheless something.' The French version reads: 'without changing this supposition, I find that I am still certain that I am something'.

depend on things of whose existence I am as yet unaware; so it cannot 28 depend on any of the things which I invent in my imagination. And this very word 'invent' shows me my mistake. It would indeed be a case of fictitious invention if I used my imagination to establish that I was something or other; for imagining is simply contemplating the shape or image of a corporeal thing. Yet now I know for certain both that I exist and at the same time that all such images and, in general, everything relating to the nature of body, could be mere dreams ⟨and chimeras⟩. Once this point has been grasped, to say 'I will use my imagination to get to know more distinctly what I am' would seem to be as silly as saying 'I am now awake, and see some truth; but since my vision is not yet clear enough, I will deliberately fall asleep so that my dreams may provide a truer and clearer representation.' I thus realize that none of the things that the imagination enables me to grasp is at all relevant to this knowledge of myself which I possess, and that the mind must therefore be most carefully diverted from such things[1] if it is to perceive its own nature as distinctly as possible.

But what then am I? A thing that thinks. What is that? A thing that doubts, understands, affirms, denies, is willing, is unwilling, and also imagines and has sensory perceptions.

This is a considerable list, if everything on it belongs to me. But does it? Is it not one and the same 'I' who is now doubting almost everything, who nonetheless understands some things, who affirms that this one thing is true, denies everything else, desires to know more, is unwilling to be deceived, imagines many things even involuntarily, and is aware of many things which apparently come from the senses? Are not all these things just as true as the fact that I exist, even if I am asleep all the time, 29 and even if he who created me is doing all he can to deceive me? Which of all these activities is distinct from my thinking? Which of them can be said to be separate from myself? The fact that it is I who am doubting and understanding and willing is so evident that I see no way of making it any clearer. But it is also the case that the 'I' who imagines is the same 'I'. For even if, as I have supposed, none of the objects of imagination are real, the power of imagination is something which really exists and is part of my thinking. Lastly, it is also the same 'I' who has sensory perceptions, or is aware of bodily things as it were through the senses. For example, I am now seeing light, hearing a noise, feeling heat. But I am asleep, so all this is false. Yet I certainly *seem* to see, to hear, and to be warmed. This cannot be false; what is called 'having a sensory perception' is strictly just this, and in this restricted sense of the term it is simply thinking.

1 '... from this manner of conceiving things' (French version).

From all this I am beginning to have a rather better understanding of what I am. But it still appears – and I cannot stop thinking this – that the corporeal things of which images are formed in my thought, and which the senses investigate, are known with much more distinctness than this puzzling 'I' which cannot be pictured in the imagination. And yet it is surely surprising that I should have a more distinct grasp of things which I realize are doubtful, unknown and foreign to me, than I have of that which is true and known – my own self. But I see what it is: my mind enjoys wandering off and will not yet submit to being restrained within

30 the bounds of truth. Very well then; just this once let us give it a completely free rein, so that after a while, when it is time to tighten the reins, it may more readily submit to being curbed.

Let us consider the things which people commonly think they understand most distinctly of all; that is, the bodies which we touch and see. I do not mean bodies in general – for general perceptions are apt to be somewhat more confused – but one particular body. Let us take, for example, this piece of wax. It has just been taken from the honeycomb; it has not yet quite lost the taste of the honey; it retains some of the scent of the flowers from which it was gathered; its colour, shape and size are plain to see; it is hard, cold and can be handled without difficulty; if you rap it with your knuckle it makes a sound. In short, it has everything which appears necessary to enable a body to be known as distinctly as possible. But even as I speak, I put the wax by the fire, and look: the residual taste is eliminated, the smell goes away, the colour changes, the shape is lost, the size increases; it becomes liquid and hot; you can hardly touch it, and if you strike it, it no longer makes a sound. But does the same wax remain? It must be admitted that it does; no one denies it, no one thinks otherwise. So what was it in the wax that I understood with such distinctness? Evidently none of the features which I arrived at by means of the senses; for whatever came under taste, smell, sight, touch or hearing has now altered – yet the wax remains.

Perhaps the answer lies in the thought which now comes to my mind; namely, the wax was not after all the sweetness of the honey, or the fragrance of the flowers, or the whiteness, or the shape, or the sound, but was rather a body which presented itself to me in these various forms a little while ago, but which now exhibits different ones. But what exactly

31 is it that I am now imagining? Let us concentrate, take away everything which does not belong to the wax, and see what is left: merely something extended, flexible and changeable. But what is meant here by 'flexible' and 'changeable'? Is it what I picture in my imagination: that this piece of wax is capable of changing from a round shape to a square shape, or from a square shape to a triangular shape? Not at all; for I can grasp that

the wax is capable of countless changes of this kind, yet I am unable to run through this immeasurable number of changes in my imagination, from which it follows that it is not the faculty of imagination that gives me my grasp of the wax as flexible and changeable. And what is meant by 'extended'? Is the extension of the wax also unknown? For it increases if the wax melts, increases again if it boils, and is greater still if the heat is increased. I would not be making a correct judgement about the nature of wax unless I believed it capable of being extended in many more different ways than I will ever encompass in my imagination. I must therefore admit that the nature of this piece of wax is in no way revealed by my imagination, but is perceived by the mind alone. (I am speaking of this particular piece of wax; the point is even clearer with regard to wax in general.) But what is this wax which is perceived by the mind alone?[1] It is of course the same wax which I see, which I touch, which I picture in my imagination, in short the same wax which I thought it to be from the start. And yet, and here is the point, the perception I have of it[2] is a case not of vision or touch or imagination – nor has it ever been, despite previous appearances – but of purely mental scrutiny; and this can be imperfect and confused, as it was before, or clear and distinct as it is now, depending on how carefully I concentrate on what the wax consists in.

But as I reach this conclusion I am amazed at how ⟨weak and⟩ prone to error my mind is. For although I am thinking about these matters within myself, silently and without speaking, nonetheless the actual words bring me up short, and I am almost tricked by ordinary ways of talking. We say that we see the wax itself, if it is there before us, not that we judge it to be there from its colour or shape; and this might lead me to conclude without more ado that knowledge of the wax comes from what the eye sees, and not from the scrutiny of the mind alone. But then if I look out of the window and see men crossing the square, as I just happen to have done, I normally say that I see the men themselves, just as I say that I see the wax. Yet do I see any more than hats and coats which could conceal automatons? I *judge* that they are men. And so something which I thought I was seeing with my eyes is in fact grasped solely by the faculty of judgement which is in my mind. 32

However, one who wants to achieve knowledge above the ordinary level should feel ashamed at having taken ordinary ways of talking as a basis for doubt. So let us proceed, and consider on which occasion my perception of the nature of the wax was more perfect and evident. Was it when I first looked at it, and believed I knew it by my external senses, or

1 '... which can be conceived only by the understanding or the mind' (French version).
2 '... or rather the act whereby it is perceived' (added in French version).

at least by what they call the 'common' sense[1] – that is, the power of imagination? Or is my knowledge more perfect now, after a more careful investigation of the nature of the wax and of the means by which it is known? Any doubt on this issue would clearly be foolish; for what distinctness was there in my earlier perception? Was there anything in it which an animal could not possess? But when I distinguish the wax from its outward forms – take the clothes off, as it were, and consider it naked – then although my judgement may still contain errors, at least my perception now requires a human mind.

33   But what am I to say about this mind, or about myself? (So far, remember, I am not admitting that there is anything else in me except a mind.) What, I ask, is this 'I' which seems to perceive the wax so distinctly? Surely my awareness of my own self is not merely much truer and more certain than my awareness of the wax, but also much more distinct and evident. For if I judge that the wax exists from the fact that I see it, clearly this same fact entails much more evidently that I myself also exist. It is possible that what I see is not really the wax; it is possible that I do not even have eyes with which to see anything. But when I see, or think I see (I am not here distinguishing the two), it is simply not possible that I who am now thinking am not something. By the same token, if I judge that the wax exists from the fact that I touch it, the same result follows, namely that I exist. If I judge that it exists from the fact that I imagine it, or for any other reason, exactly the same thing follows. And the result that I have grasped in the case of the wax may be applied to everything else located outside me. Moreover, if my perception of the wax seemed more distinct[2] after it was established not just by sight or touch but by many other considerations, it must be admitted that I now know myself even more distinctly. This is because every consideration whatsoever which contributes to my perception of the wax, or of any other body, cannot but establish even more effectively the nature of my own mind. But besides this, there is so much else in the mind itself which can serve to make my knowledge of it more distinct, that it scarcely seems worth going through the contributions made by considering bodily things.

34   I see that without any effort I have now finally got back to where I wanted. I now know that even bodies are not strictly perceived by the senses or the faculty of imagination but by the intellect alone, and that this perception derives not from their being touched or seen but from their being understood; and in view of this I know plainly that I can

1 See note p. 59 below.
2 The French version has 'more clear and distinct' and, at the end of this sentence, 'more evidently, distinctly and clearly'.

achieve an easier and more evident perception of my own mind than of anything else. But since the habit of holding on to old opinions cannot be set aside so quickly, I should like to stop here and meditate for some time on this new knowledge I have gained, so as to fix it more deeply in my memory.

THIRD MEDITATION

The existence of God

I will now shut my eyes, stop my ears, and withdraw all my senses. I will eliminate from my thoughts all images of bodily things, or rather, since this is hardly possible, I will regard all such images as vacuous, false and worthless. I will converse with myself and scrutinize myself more deeply; and in this way I will attempt to achieve, little by little, a more intimate knowledge of myself. I am a thing that thinks: that is, a thing that doubts, affirms, denies, understands a few things, is ignorant of many things,[1] is willing, is unwilling, and also which imagines and has sensory perceptions; for as I have noted before, even though the objects of my sensory experience and imagination may have no existence outside me, nonetheless the modes of thinking which I refer to as cases of sensory perception and imagination, in so far as they are simply modes of thinking, do exist within me – of that I am certain.

35

In this brief list I have gone through everything I truly know, or at least everything I have so far discovered that I know. Now I will cast around more carefully to see whether there may be other things within me which I have not yet noticed. I am certain that I am a thinking thing. Do I not therefore also know what is required for my being certain about anything? In this first item of knowledge there is simply a clear and distinct perception of what I am asserting; this would not be enough to make me certain of the truth of the matter if it could ever turn out that something which I perceived with such clarity and distinctness was false. So I now seem to be able to lay it down as a general rule that whatever I perceive very clearly and distinctly is true.[2]

Yet I previously accepted as wholly certain and evident many things which I afterwards realized were doubtful. What were these? The earth, sky, stars, and everything else that I apprehended with the senses. But what was it about them that I perceived clearly? Just that the ideas, or thoughts, of such things appeared before my mind. Yet even now I am

1 The French version here inserts 'loves, hates'.
2 '. . . all the things which we conceive very clearly and very distinctly are true' (French version).

24

not denying that these ideas occur within me. But there was something else which I used to assert, and which through habitual belief I thought I perceived clearly, although I did not in fact do so. This was that there were things outside me which were the sources of my ideas and which resembled them in all respects. Here was my mistake; or at any rate, if my judgement was true, it was not thanks to the strength of my perception.[1]

But what about when I was considering something very simple and straightforward in arithmetic or geometry, for example that two and three added together make five, and so on? Did I not see at least these things clearly enough to affirm their truth? Indeed, the only reason for my later judgement that they were open to doubt was that it occurred to me that perhaps some God could have given me a nature such that I was deceived even in matters which seemed most evident. And whenever my preconceived belief in the supreme power of God comes to mind, I cannot but admit that it would be easy for him, if he so desired, to bring it about that I go wrong even in those matters which I think I see utterly clearly with my mind's eye. Yet when I turn to the things themselves which I think I perceive very clearly, I am so convinced by them that I spontaneously declare: let whoever can do so deceive me, he will never bring it about that I am nothing, so long as I continue to think I am something; or make it true at some future time that I have never existed, since it is now true that I exist; or bring it about that two and three added together are more or less than five, or anything of this kind in which I see a manifest contradiction. And since I have no cause to think that there is a deceiving God, and I do not yet even know for sure whether there is a God at all, any reason for doubt which depends simply on this supposition is a very slight and, so to speak, metaphysical one. But in order to remove even this slight reason for doubt, as soon as the opportunity arises I must examine whether there is a God, and, if there is, whether he can be a deceiver. For if I do not know this, it seems that I can never be quite certain about anything else.

First, however, considerations of order appear to dictate that I now classify my thoughts into definite kinds,[2] and ask which of them can properly be said to be the bearers of truth and falsity. Some of my thoughts are as it were the images of things, and it is only in these cases that the term 'idea' is strictly appropriate – for example, when I think of a man, or a chimera, or the sky, or an angel, or God. Other thoughts have

1 '. . . it was not because of any knowledge I possessed' (French version).
2 The opening of this sentence is greatly expanded in the French version: 'In order that I may have the opportunity of examining this without interrupting the order of meditating which I have decided upon, which is to start only from those notions which I find first of all in my mind and pass gradually to those which I may find later on, I must here divide my thoughts . . .'

various additional forms: thus when I will, or am afraid, or affirm, or deny, there is always a particular thing which I take as the object of my thought, but my thought includes something more than the likeness of that thing. Some thoughts in this category are called volitions or emotions, while others are called judgements.

Now as far as ideas are concerned, provided they are considered solely in themselves and I do not refer them to anything else, they cannot strictly speaking be false; for whether it is a goat or a chimera that I am imagining, it is just as true that I imagine the former as the latter. As for the will and the emotions, here too one need not worry about falsity; for even if the things which I may desire are wicked or even non-existent, that does not make it any less true that I desire them. Thus the only remaining thoughts where I must be on my guard against making a mistake are judgements. And the chief and most common mistake which is to be found here consists in my judging that the ideas which are in me resemble, or conform to, things located outside me. Of course, if I considered just the ideas themselves simply as modes of my thought, without referring them to anything else, they could scarcely give me any material for error.

Among my ideas, some appear to be innate, some to be adventitious,[1] and others to have been invented by me. My understanding of what a thing is, what truth is, and what thought is, seems to derive simply from my own nature. But my hearing a noise, as I do now, or seeing the sun, or feeling the fire, comes from things which are located outside me, or so I have hitherto judged. Lastly, sirens, hippogriffs and the like are my own invention. But perhaps all my ideas may be thought of as adventitious, or they may all be innate, or all made up; for as yet I have not clearly perceived their true origin.

But the chief question at this point concerns the ideas which I take to be derived from things existing outside me: what is my reason for thinking that they resemble these things? Nature has apparently taught me to think this. But in addition I know by experience that these ideas do not depend on my will, and hence that they do not depend simply on me. Frequently I notice them even when I do not want to: now, for example, I feel the heat whether I want to or not, and this is why I think that this sensation or idea of heat comes to me from something other than myself, namely the heat of the fire by which I am sitting. And the most obvious judgement for me to make is that the thing in question transmits to me its own likeness rather than something else.

I will now see if these arguments are strong enough. When I say 'Nature taught me to think this', all I mean is that a spontaneous impulse leads

38

1 '. . . foreign to me and coming from outside' (French version).

me to believe it, not that its truth has been revealed to me by some natural light. There is a big difference here. Whatever is revealed to me by the natural light – for example that from the fact that I am doubting it follows that I exist, and so on – cannot in any way be open to doubt. This is because there cannot be another faculty[1] both as trustworthy as the natural light and also capable of showing me that such things are not 39 true. But as for my natural impulses, I have often judged in the past that they were pushing me in the wrong direction when it was a question of choosing the good, and I do not see why I should place any greater confidence in them in other matters.[2]

Then again, although these ideas do not depend on my will, it does not follow that they must come from things located outside me. Just as the impulses which I was speaking of a moment ago seem opposed to my will even though they are within me, so there may be some other faculty not yet fully known to me, which produces these ideas without any assistance from external things; this is, after all, just how I have always thought ideas are produced in me when I am dreaming.

And finally, even if these ideas did come from things other than myself, it would not follow that they must resemble those things. Indeed, I think I have often discovered a great disparity ⟨between an object and its idea⟩ in many cases. For example, there are two different ideas of the sun which I find within me. One of them, which is acquired as it were from the senses and which is a prime example of an idea which I reckon to come from an external source, makes the sun appear very small. The other idea is based on astronomical reasoning, that is, it is derived from certain notions which are innate in me (or else it is constructed by me in some other way), and this idea shows the sun to be several times larger than the earth. Obviously both these ideas cannot resemble the sun which exists outside me; and reason persuades me that the idea which seems to have emanated most directly from the sun itself has in fact no resemblance to it at all.

All these considerations are enough to establish that it is not reliable 40 judgement but merely some blind impulse that has made me believe up till now that there exist things distinct from myself which transmit to me ideas or images of themselves through the sense organs or in some other way.

But it now occurs to me that there is another way of investigating whether some of the things of which I possess ideas exist outside me. In so far as the ideas are ⟨considered⟩ simply ⟨as⟩ modes of thought, there is no recognizable inequality among them: they all appear to come from

1 '. . . or power for distinguishing truth from falsehood' (French version).
2 '. . . concerning truth and falsehood' (French version).

within me in the same fashion. But in so far as different ideas ⟨are considered as images which⟩ represent different things, it is clear that they differ widely. Undoubtedly, the ideas which represent substances to me amount to something more and, so to speak, contain within themselves more objective[1] reality than the ideas which merely represent modes or accidents. Again, the idea that gives me my understanding of a supreme God, eternal, infinite, ⟨immutable,⟩ omniscient, omnipotent and the creator of all things that exist apart from him, certainly has in it more objective reality than the ideas that represent finite substances.

Now it is manifest by the natural light that there must be at least as much ⟨reality⟩ in the efficient and total cause as in the effect of that cause. For where, I ask, could the effect get its reality from, if not from the cause? And how could the cause give it to the effect unless it possessed it? It follows from this both that something cannot arise from nothing, and also that what is more perfect – that is, contains in itself more reality – cannot arise from what is less perfect. And this is transparently true not only in the case of effects which possess ⟨what the philosophers call⟩ actual or formal reality, but also in the case of ideas, where one is considering only ⟨what they call⟩ objective reality. A stone, for example, which previously did not exist, cannot begin to exist unless it is produced by something which contains, either formally or eminently everything to be found in the stone;[2] similarly, heat cannot be produced in an object which was not previously hot, except by something of at least the same order ⟨degree or kind⟩ of perfection as heat, and so on. But it is also true that the *idea* of heat, or of a stone, cannot exist in me unless it is put there by some cause which contains at least as much reality as I conceive to be in the heat or in the stone. For although this cause does not transfer any of its actual or formal reality to my idea, it should not on that account be supposed that it must be less real.[3] The nature of an idea is such that of itself it requires no formal reality except what it derives from my thought, of which it is a mode.[4] But in order for a given idea to contain such and such objective reality, it must surely derive it from some cause which contains at least as much formal reality as there is objective reality in the

41

---

1 '. . . i.e. participate by representation in a higher degree of being or perfection' (added in French version). According to the scholastic distinction invoked in the paragraphs that follow, the 'formal' reality of anything is its own intrinsic reality, while the 'objective' reality of an idea is a function of its representational content. Thus if an idea *A* represents some object *X* which is *F*, then *F*-ness will be contained 'formally' in *X* but 'objectively' in *A*. See below, Second Replies pp. 74f.

2 '. . . i.e. it will contain in itself the same things as are in the stone or other more excellent things' (added in French version). In scholastic terminology, to possess a property 'formally' is to possess it literally, in accordance with its definition; to possess it 'eminently' is to possess it in some higher form. Cf. below, p. 201.

3 '. . . that this cause must be less real' (French version).

4 '. . . i.e. a manner or way of thinking' (added in French version).

idea. For if we suppose that an idea contains something which was not in its cause, it must have got this from nothing; yet the mode of being by which a thing exists objectively ⟨or representatively⟩ in the intellect by way of an idea, imperfect though it may be, is certainly not nothing, and so it cannot come from nothing.

And although the reality which I am considering in my ideas is merely objective reality, I must not on that account suppose that the same reality need not exist formally in the causes of my ideas, but that it is enough for it to be present in them objectively. For just as the objective mode of being belongs to ideas by their very nature, so the formal mode of being belongs to the causes of ideas – or at least the first and most important ones – by *their* very nature. And although one idea may perhaps originate from another, there cannot be an infinite regress here; eventually one must reach a primary idea, the cause of which will be like an archetype which contains formally ⟨and in fact⟩ all the reality ⟨or perfection⟩ which is present only objectively ⟨or representatively⟩ in the idea. So it is clear to me, by the natural light, that the ideas in me are like ⟨pictures, or⟩ images which can easily fall short of the perfection of the things from which they are taken, but which cannot contain anything greater or more perfect. 42

The longer and more carefully I examine all these points, the more clearly and distinctly I recognize their truth. But what is my conclusion to be? If the objective reality of any of my ideas turns out to be so great that I am sure the same reality does not reside in me, either formally or eminently, and hence that I myself cannot be its cause, it will necessarily follow that I am not alone in the world, but that some other thing which is the cause of this idea also exists. But if no such idea is to be found in me, I shall have no argument to convince me of the existence of anything apart from myself. For despite a most careful and comprehensive survey, this is the only argument I have so far been able to find.

Among my ideas, apart from the idea which gives me a representation of myself, which cannot present any difficulty in this context, there are ideas which variously represent God, corporeal and inanimate things, angels, animals and finally other men like myself. 43

As far as concerns the ideas which represent other men, or animals, or angels, I have no difficulty in understanding that they could be put together from the ideas I have of myself, of corporeal things and of God, even if the world contained no men besides me, no animals and no angels.

As to my ideas of corporeal things, I can see nothing in them which is so great ⟨or excellent⟩ as to make it seem impossible that it originated in myself. For if I scrutinize them thoroughly and examine them one by one, in the way in which I examined the idea of the wax yesterday, I notice that the things which I perceive clearly and distinctly in them are very few in number. The list comprises size, or extension in length, breadth and depth; shape, which is a function of the boundaries of this extension; position, which is a relation between various items possessing shape; and motion, or change in position; to these may be added substance, duration and number. But as for all the rest, including light and colours, sounds, smells, tastes, heat and cold and the other tactile qualities, I think of these only in a very confused and obscure way, to the extent that I do not even know whether they are true or false, that is, whether the ideas I have of them are ideas of real things or of non-things.[1] For although, as I have noted before, falsity in the strict sense, or formal falsity, can occur only in judgements, there is another kind of falsity, material falsity, which occurs in ideas, when they represent non-things as things. For example, the ideas

44   which I have of heat and cold contain so little clarity and distinctness that they do not enable me to tell whether cold is merely the absence of heat or vice versa, or whether both of them are real qualities, or neither is. And since there can be no ideas which are not as it were of things,[2] if it is true that cold is nothing but the absence of heat, the idea which represents it to me as something real and positive deserves to be called false; and the same goes for other ideas of this kind.

Such ideas obviously do not require me to posit a source distinct from myself. For on the one hand, if they are false, that is, represent non-things, I know by the natural light that they arise from nothing – that is, they are in me only because of a deficiency and lack of perfection in my nature. If on the other hand they are true, then since the reality which they represent is so extremely slight that I cannot even distinguish it from a non-thing, I do not see why they cannot originate from myself.

With regard to the clear and distinct elements in my ideas of corporeal things, it appears that I could have borrowed some of these from my idea of myself, namely substance, duration, number and anything else of this kind. For example, I think that a stone is a substance, or is a thing capable of existing independently, and I also think that I am a substance. Admittedly I conceive of myself as a thing that thinks and is not extended, whereas I conceive of the stone as a thing that is extended and does not think, so that the two conceptions differ enormously; but they seem to agree with respect to the classification 'substance'.[3] Again, I perceive that I now exist, and remember that I have existed for some time; moreover, I have various thoughts which I can count; it is in these

1 '. . . chimerical things which cannot exist' (French version).
2 'And since ideas, being like images, must in each case appear to us to represent something' (French version).
3 '. . . in so far as they represent substances' (French version).

ways that I acquire the ideas of duration and number which I can then 45
transfer to other things. As for all the other elements which make up the
ideas of corporeal things, namely extension, shape, position and movement, these are not formally contained in me, since I am nothing but a
thinking thing; but since they are merely modes of a substance,[1] and I am
a substance, it seems possible that they are contained in me eminently.

So there remains only the idea of God; and I must consider whether
there is anything in the idea which could not have originated in myself.
By the word 'God' I understand a substance that is infinite, ⟨eternal,
immutable,⟩ independent, supremely intelligent, supremely powerful, and
which created both myself and everything else (if anything else there be)
that exists. All these attributes are such that, the more carefully I
concentrate on them, the less possible it seems that they[2] could have
originated from me alone. So from what has been said it must be
concluded that God necessarily exists.

It is true that I have the idea of substance in me in virtue of the fact that
I am a substance; but this would not account for my having the idea of an
infinite substance, when I am finite, unless this idea proceeded from some
substance which really was infinite.

And I must not think that, just as my conceptions of rest and darkness
are arrived at by negating movement and light, so my perception of the
infinite is arrived at not by means of a true idea but merely by negating
the finite. On the contrary, I clearly understand that there is more reality
in an infinite substance than in a finite one, and hence that my perception
of the infinite, that is God, is in some way prior to my perception of the
finite, that is myself. For how could I understand that I doubted or 46
desired – that is, lacked something – and that I was not wholly perfect,
unless there were in me some idea of a more perfect being which enabled
me to recognize my own defects by comparison?

Nor can it be said that this idea of God is perhaps materially false and
so could have come from nothing,[3] which is what I observed just a
moment ago in the case of the ideas of heat and cold, and so on. On the
contrary, it is utterly clear and distinct, and contains in itself more
objective reality than any other idea; hence there is no idea which is in
itself truer or less liable to be suspected of falsehood. This idea of a
supremely perfect and infinite being is, I say, true in the highest degree;
for although perhaps one may imagine that such a being does not exist, it
cannot be supposed that the idea of such a being represents something

---

1 '. . . and as it were the garments under which corporeal substance appears to us' (French
  version).
2 '. . . that the idea I have of them' (French version).
3 '. . . i.e. could be in me in virtue of my imperfection' (added in French version).

unreal, as I said with regard to the idea of cold. The idea is, moreover, utterly clear and distinct; for whatever I clearly and distinctly perceive as being real and true, and implying any perfection, is wholly contained in it. It does not matter that I do not grasp the infinite, or that there are countless additional attributes of God which I cannot in any way grasp, and perhaps cannot even reach in my thought; for it is in the nature of the infinite not to be grasped by a finite being like myself. It is enough that I understand[1] the infinite, and that I judge that all the attributes which I clearly perceive and know to imply some perfection – and perhaps countless others of which I am ignorant – are present in God either formally or eminently. This is enough to make the idea that I have of God the truest and most clear and distinct of all my ideas.

But perhaps I am something greater than I myself understand, and all the perfections which I attribute to God are somehow in me potentially, though not yet emerging or actualized. For I am now experiencing a gradual increase in my knowledge, and I see nothing to prevent its increasing more and more to infinity. Further, I see no reason why I should not be able to use this increased knowledge to acquire all the other perfections of God. And finally, if the potentiality for these perfections is already within me, why should not this be enough to generate the idea of such perfections?

47

But all this is impossible. First, though it is true that there is a gradual increase in my knowledge, and that I have many potentialities which are not yet actual, this is all quite irrelevant to the idea of God, which contains absolutely nothing that is potential;[2] indeed, this gradual increase in knowledge is itself the surest sign of imperfection. What is more, even if my knowledge always increases more and more, I recognize that it will never actually be infinite, since it will never reach the point where it is not capable of a further increase; God, on the other hand, I take to be actually infinite, so that nothing can be added to his perfection. And finally, I perceive that the objective being of an idea cannot be produced merely by potential being, which strictly speaking is nothing, but only by actual or formal being.

If one concentrates carefully, all this is quite evident by the natural light. But when I relax my concentration, and my mental vision is blinded by the images of things perceived by the senses, it is not so easy for me to remember why the idea of a being more perfect than myself must

---

1 According to Descartes one can know or understand something without fully grasping it 'just as we can touch a mountain but not put our arms around it. To grasp something is to embrace it in one's thought; to know something, it suffices to touch it with one's thought' (letter to Mersenne, 26 May 1630).
2 '. . . but only what is actual and real' (added in French version).

necessarily proceed from some being which is in reality more perfect. I   48
should therefore like to go further and inquire whether I myself, who
have this idea, could exist if no such being existed.

From whom, in that case, would I derive my existence? From myself
presumably, or from my parents, or from some other beings less perfect
than God; for nothing more perfect than God, or even as perfect, can be
thought of or imagined.

Yet if I derived my existence from myself,[1] then I should neither doubt
nor want, nor lack anything at all; for I should have given myself all the
perfections of which I have any idea, and thus I should myself be God.
I must not suppose that the items I lack would be more difficult to
acquire than those I now have. On the contrary, it is clear that, since I am
a thinking thing or substance, it would have been far more difficult for
me to emerge out of nothing than merely to acquire knowledge of the
many things of which I am ignorant – such knowledge being merely an
accident of that substance. And if I had derived my existence from
myself, which is a greater achievement, I should certainly not have denied
myself the knowledge in question, which is something much easier to
acquire, or indeed any of the attributes which I perceive to be contained
in the idea of God; for none of them seem any harder to achieve. And if
any of them were harder to achieve, they would certainly appear so to
me, if I had indeed got all my other attributes from myself, since I should
experience a limitation of my power in this respect.

I do not escape the force of these arguments by supposing that I have
always existed as I do now, as if it followed from this that there was no
need to look for any author of my existence. For a lifespan can be divided   49
into countless parts, each completely independent of the others, so that it
does not follow from the fact that I existed a little while ago that I must
exist now, unless there is some cause which as it were creates me afresh at
this moment – that is, which preserves me. For it is quite clear to anyone
who attentively considers the nature of time that the same power and
action are needed to preserve anything at each individual moment of its
duration as would be required to create that thing anew if it were not yet
in existence. Hence the distinction between preservation and creation is
only a conceptual one,[2] and this is one of the things that are evident by
the natural light.

I must therefore now ask myself whether I possess some power
enabling me to bring it about that I who now exist will still exist a little
while from now. For since I am nothing but a thinking thing – or at least

---

1 '. . . and were independent of every other being' (added in French version).
2 Cf. *Principles*, Part 1, art. 62: vol. 1, p. 214.

since I am now concerned only and precisely with that part of me which is a thinking thing – if there were such a power in me, I should undoubtedly be aware of it. But I experience no such power, and this very fact makes me recognize most clearly that I depend on some being distinct from myself.

But perhaps this being is not God, and perhaps I was produced either by my parents or by other causes less perfect than God. No; for as I have said before, it is quite clear that there must be at least as much in the cause as in the effect.[1] And therefore whatever kind of cause is eventually proposed, since I am a thinking thing and have within me some idea of God, it must be admitted that what caused me is itself a thinking thing and possesses the idea of all the perfections which I attribute to God. In respect of this cause one may again inquire whether it derives its existence from itself or from another cause. If from itself, then it is clear from what has been said that it is itself God, since if it has the power of existing through its own might,[2] then undoubtedly it also has the power of actually possessing all the perfections of which it has an idea – that is, all the perfections which I conceive to be in God. If, on the other hand, it derives its existence from another cause, then the same question may be repeated concerning this further cause, namely whether it derives its existence from itself or from another cause, until eventually the ultimate cause is reached, and this will be God.

It is clear enough that an infinite regress is impossible here, especially since I am dealing not just with the cause that produced me in the past, but also and most importantly with the cause that preserves me at the present moment.

Nor can it be supposed that several partial causes contributed to my creation, or that I received the idea of one of the perfections which I attribute to God from one cause and the idea of another from another – the supposition here being that all the perfections are to be found somewhere in the universe but not joined together in a single being, God. On the contrary, the unity, the simplicity, or the inseparability of all the attributes of God is one of the most important of the perfections which I understand him to have. And surely the idea of the unity of all his perfections could not have been placed in me by any cause which did not also provide me with the ideas of the other perfections; for no cause could have made me understand the interconnection and inseparability of the perfections without at the same time making me recognize what they were.

---

1 '. . . at least as much reality in the cause as in its effect' (French version).
2 Lat. *per se*; literally 'through itself'.

Lastly, as regards my parents, even if everything I have ever believed about them is true, it is certainly not they who preserve me; and in so far as I am a thinking thing, they did not even make me; they merely placed certain dispositions in the matter which I have always regarded as containing me, or rather my mind, for that is all I now take myself to   51
be. So there can be no difficulty regarding my parents in this context. Altogether then, it must be concluded that the mere fact that I exist and have within me an idea of a most perfect being, that is, God, provides a very clear proof that God indeed exists.

It only remains for me to examine how I received this idea from God. For I did not acquire it from the senses; it has never come to me unexpectedly, as usually happens with the ideas of things that are perceivable by the senses, when these things present themselves to the external sense organs – or seem to do so. And it was not invented by me either; for I am plainly unable either to take away anything from it or to add anything to it. The only remaining alternative is that it is innate in me, just as the idea of myself is innate in me.

And indeed it is no surprise that God, in creating me, should have placed this idea in me to be, as it were, the mark of the craftsman stamped on his work – not that the mark need be anything distinct from the work itself. But the mere fact that God created me is a very strong basis for believing that I am somehow made in his image and likeness, and that I perceive that likeness, which includes the idea of God, by the same faculty which enables me to perceive myself. That is, when I turn my mind's eye upon myself, I understand that I am a thing which is incomplete and dependent on another and which aspires without limit to ever greater and better things; but I also understand at the same time that he on whom I depend has within him all those greater things, not just indefinitely and potentially but actually and infinitely, and hence that he is God. The whole force of the argument lies in this: I recognize that it would be impossible for me to exist with the kind of nature I have – that   52
is, having within me the idea of God – were it not the case that God really existed. By 'God' I mean the very being the idea of whom is within me, that is, the possessor of all the perfections which I cannot grasp, but can somehow reach in my thought, who is subject to no defects whatsoever.[1]
It is clear enough from this that he cannot be a deceiver, since it is manifest by the natural light that all fraud and deception depend on some defect.

But before examining this point more carefully and investigating other

---

1 '. . . and has not one of the things which indicate some imperfection' (added in French version).

truths which may be derived from it, I should like to pause here and spend some time in the contemplation of God; to reflect on his attributes, and to gaze with wonder and adoration on the beauty of this immense light, so far as the eye of my darkened intellect can bear it. For just as we believe through faith that the supreme happiness of the next life consists solely in the contemplation of the divine majesty, so experience tells us that this same contemplation, albeit much less perfect, enables us to know the greatest joy of which we are capable in this life.

FOURTH MEDITATION

Truth and falsity

During these past few days I have accustomed myself to leading my mind away from the senses; and I have taken careful note of the fact that there is very little about corporeal things that is truly perceived, whereas much more is known about the human mind, and still more about God. The result is that I now have no difficulty in turning my mind away from imaginable things[1] and towards things which are objects of the intellect alone and are totally separate from matter. And indeed the idea I have of the human mind, in so far as it is a thinking thing, which is not extended in length, breadth or height and has no other bodily characteristics, is much more distinct than the idea of any corporeal thing. And when I consider the fact that I have doubts, or that I am a thing that is incomplete and dependent, then there arises in me a clear and distinct idea of a being who is independent and complete, that is, an idea of God. And from the mere fact that there is such an idea within me, or that I who possess this idea exist, I clearly infer that God also exists, and that every single moment of my entire existence depends on him. So clear is this conclusion that I am confident that the human intellect cannot know anything that is more evident or more certain. And now, from this contemplation of the true God, in whom all the treasures of wisdom and the sciences lie hidden, I think I can see a way forward to the knowledge of other things.[2]

To begin with, I recognize that it is impossible that God should ever deceive me. For in every case of trickery or deception some imperfection is to be found; and although the ability to deceive appears to be an indication of cleverness or power, the will to deceive is undoubtedly evidence of malice or weakness, and so cannot apply to God.

Next, I know by experience that there is in me a faculty of judgement which, like everything else which is in me, I certainly received from God. And since God does not wish to deceive me, he surely did not give me the

53

54

1 '. . . from things which can be perceived by the senses or imagined' (French version).
2 '. . . of the other things in the universe' (French version).

37

kind of faculty which would ever enable me to go wrong while using it correctly.

There would be no further doubt on this issue were it not that what I have just said appears to imply that I am incapable of ever going wrong. For if everything that is in me comes from God, and he did not endow me with a faculty for making mistakes, it appears that I can never go wrong. And certainly, so long as I think only of God, and turn my whole attention to him, I can find no cause of error or falsity. But when I turn back to myself, I know by experience that I am prone to countless errors. On looking for the cause of these errors, I find that I possess not only a real and positive idea of God, or a being who is supremely perfect, but also what may be described as a negative idea of nothingness, or of that which is farthest removed from all perfection. I realize that I am, as it were, something intermediate between God and nothingness, or between supreme being and non-being: my nature is such that in so far as I was created by the supreme being, there is nothing in me to enable me to go wrong or lead me astray; but in so far as I participate in nothingness or non-being, that is, in so far as I am not myself the supreme being and am lacking in countless respects, it is no wonder that I make mistakes. I understand, then, that error as such is not something real which depends on God, but merely a defect. Hence my going wrong does not require me to have a faculty specially bestowed on me by God; it simply happens as a result of the fact that the faculty of true judgement which I have from God is in my case not infinite.

55   But this is still not entirely satisfactory. For error is not a pure negation,[1] but rather a privation or lack of some knowledge which somehow should be in me. And when I concentrate on the nature of God, it seems impossible that he should have placed in me a faculty which is not perfect of its kind, or which lacks some perfection which it ought to have. The more skilled the craftsman the more perfect the work produced by him; if this is so, how can anything produced by the supreme creator of all things not be complete and perfect in all respects? There is, moreover, no doubt that God could have given me a nature such that I was never mistaken; again, there is no doubt that he always wills what is best. Is it then better that I should make mistakes than that I should not do so?

As I reflect on these matters more attentively, it occurs to me first of all that it is no cause for surprise if I do not understand the reasons for some of God's actions; and there is no call to doubt his existence if I happen to find that there are other instances where I do not grasp why or how

---

1 '. . . i.e. not simply the defect or lack of some perfection to which I have no proper claim' (added in French version).

certain things were made by him. For since I now know that my own nature is very weak and limited, whereas the nature of God is immense, incomprehensible and infinite, I also know without more ado that he is capable of countless things whose causes are beyond my knowledge. And for this reason alone I consider the customary search for final causes to be totally useless in physics; there is considerable rashness in thinking myself capable of investigating the ⟨impenetrable⟩ purposes of God.

It also occurs to me that whenever we are inquiring whether the works of God are perfect, we ought to look at the whole universe, not just at one created thing on its own. For what would perhaps rightly appear very imperfect if it existed on its own is quite perfect when its function as 56 a part of the universe is considered. It is true that, since my decision to doubt everything, it is so far only myself and God whose existence I have been able to know with certainty; but after considering the immense power of God, I cannot deny that many other things have been made by him, or at least could have been made, and hence that I may have a place in the universal scheme of things.

Next, when I look more closely at myself and inquire into the nature of my errors (for these are the only evidence of some imperfection in me), I notice that they depend on two concurrent causes, namely on the faculty of knowledge which is in me, and on the faculty of choice or freedom of the will; that is, they depend on both the intellect and the will simultaneously. Now all that the intellect does is to enable me to perceive[1] the ideas which are subjects for possible judgements; and when regarded strictly in this light, it turns out to contain no error in the proper sense of that term. For although countless things may exist without there being any corresponding ideas in me, it should not, strictly speaking, be said that I am deprived of these ideas,[2] but merely that I lack them, in a negative sense. This is because I cannot produce any reason to prove that God ought to have given me a greater faculty of knowledge than he did; and no matter how skilled I understand a craftsman to be, this does not make me think he ought to have put into every one of his works all the perfections which he is able to put into some of them. Besides, I cannot complain that the will or freedom of choice which I received from God is not sufficiently extensive or perfect, since I know by experience that it is not restricted in any way. Indeed, I think it is very noteworthy that there 57 is nothing else in me which is so perfect and so great that the possibility of a further increase in its perfection or greatness is beyond my understanding. If, for example, I consider the faculty of understanding, I

1 '. . . without affirming or denying anything' (added in French version).
2 '. . . it cannot be said that my understanding is deprived of these ideas, as if they were something to which its nature entitles it' (French version).

immediately recognize that in my case it is extremely slight and very finite, and I at once form the idea of an understanding which is much greater – indeed supremely great and infinite; and from the very fact that I can form an idea of it, I perceive that it belongs to the nature of God. Similarly, if I examine the faculties of memory or imagination, or any others, I discover that in my case each one of these faculties is weak and limited, while in the case of God it is immeasurable. It is only the will, or freedom of choice, which I experience within me to be so great that the idea of any greater faculty is beyond my grasp; so much so that it is above all in virtue of the will that I understand myself to bear in some way the image and likeness of God. For although God's will is incomparably greater than mine, both in virtue of the knowledge and power that accompany it and make it more firm and efficacious, and also in virtue of its object, in that it ranges over a greater number of items, nevertheless it does not seem any greater than mine when considered as will in the essential and strict sense. This is because the will simply consists in our ability to do or not do something (that is, to affirm or deny, to pursue or avoid); or rather, it consists simply in the fact that when the intellect puts something forward for affirmation or denial or for pursuit or avoidance, our inclinations are such that we do not feel we are determined by any external force. In order to be free, there is no need for me to be inclined both ways; on the contrary, the more I incline in one direction – either because I clearly understand that reasons of truth and goodness point that way, or because of a divinely produced disposition of my inmost thoughts – the freer is my choice. Neither divine grace nor natural knowledge ever diminishes freedom; on the contrary, they increase and strengthen it. But the indifference I feel when there is no reason pushing me in one direction rather than another is the lowest grade of freedom; it is evidence not of any perfection of freedom, but rather of a defect in knowledge or a kind of negation. For if I always saw clearly what was true and good, I should never have to deliberate about the right judgement or choice; in that case, although I should be wholly free, it would be impossible for me ever to be in a state of indifference.

From these considerations I perceive that the power of willing which I received from God is not, when considered in itself, the cause of my mistakes; for it is both extremely ample and also perfect of its kind. Nor is my power of understanding to blame; for since my understanding comes from God, everything that I understand I undoubtedly understand correctly, and any error here is impossible. So what then is the source of my mistakes? It must be simply this: the scope of the will is wider than that of the intellect; but instead of restricting it within the same limits, I extend its use to matters which I do not understand. Since the will is indifferent in such cases, it easily turns aside from what is true and good, and this is the source of my error and sin.

For example, during these past few days I have been asking whether anything in the world exists, and I have realized that from the very fact of my raising this question it follows quite evidently that I exist. I could not but judge that something which I understood so clearly was true; but this was not because I was compelled so to judge by any external force, but because a great light in the intellect was followed by a great inclination in the will, and thus the spontaneity and freedom of my belief was all the greater in proportion to my lack of indifference. But now, besides the knowledge that I exist, in so far as I am a thinking thing, an idea of corporeal nature comes into my mind; and I happen to be in doubt as to whether the thinking nature which is in me, or rather which I am, is distinct from this corporeal nature or identical with it. I am making the further supposition that my intellect has not yet come upon any persuasive reason in favour of one alternative rather than the other. This obviously implies that I am indifferent as to whether I should assert or deny either alternative, or indeed refrain from making any judgement on the matter.

What is more, this indifference does not merely apply to cases where the intellect is wholly ignorant, but extends in general to every case where the intellect does not have sufficiently clear knowledge at the time when the will deliberates. For although probable conjectures may pull me in one direction, the mere knowledge that they are simply conjectures, and not certain and indubitable reasons, is itself quite enough to push my assent the other way. My experience in the last few days confirms this: the mere fact that I found that all my previous beliefs were in some sense open to doubt was enough to turn my absolutely confident belief in their truth into the supposition that they were wholly false.

If, however, I simply refrain from making a judgement in cases where I do not perceive the truth with sufficient clarity and distinctness, then it is clear that I am behaving correctly and avoiding error. But if in such cases I either affirm or deny, then I am not using my free will correctly. If I go for the alternative which is false, then obviously I shall be in error; if I take the other side, then it is by pure chance that I arrive at the truth, and I shall still be at fault since it is clear by the natural light that the perception of the intellect should always precede the determination of the will. In this incorrect use of free will may be found the privation which constitutes the essence of error. The privation, I say, lies in the operation of the will in so far as it proceeds from me, but not in the faculty of will which I received from God, nor even in its operation, in so far as it depends on him.

59

60

And I have no cause for complaint on the grounds that the power of understanding or the natural light which God gave me is no greater than it is; for it is in the nature of a finite intellect to lack understanding of many things, and it is in the nature of a created intellect to be finite. Indeed, I have reason to give thanks to him who has never owed me anything for the great bounty that he has shown me, rather than thinking myself deprived or robbed of any gifts he did not bestow.[1]

Nor do I have any cause for complaint on the grounds that God gave me a will which extends more widely than my intellect. For since the will consists simply of one thing which is, as it were, indivisible, it seems that its nature rules out the possibility of anything being taken away from it. And surely, the more widely my will extends, then the greater thanks I owe to him who gave it to me.

Finally, I must not complain that the forming of those acts of will or judgements in which I go wrong happens with God's concurrence. For in so far as these acts depend on God, they are wholly true and good; and my ability to perform them means that there is in a sense more perfection in me than would be the case if I lacked this ability. As for the privation involved – which is all that the essential definition of falsity and wrong consists in – this does not in any way require the concurrence of God, since it is not a thing; indeed, when it is referred to God as its cause, it should be called not a privation but simply a negation.[2] For it is surely no imperfection in God that he has given me the freedom to assent or not to assent in those cases where he did not endow my intellect with a clear and distinct perception; but it is undoubtedly an imperfection in me to misuse that freedom and make judgements about matters which I do not fully understand. I can see, however, that God could easily have brought it about that without losing my freedom, and despite the limitations in my knowledge, I should nonetheless never make a mistake. He could, for example, have endowed my intellect with a clear and distinct perception of everything about which I was ever likely to deliberate; or he could simply have impressed it unforgettably on my memory that I should never make a judgement about anything which I did not clearly and distinctly understand. Had God made me this way, then I can easily understand that, considered as a totality,[3] I would have been more perfect than I am now. But I cannot therefore deny that there may in some way be more perfection in the universe as a whole because some of

---

1 '. . . rather than entertaining so unjust a thought as to imagine that he deprived me of, or unjustly withheld, the other perfections which he did not give me' (French version).
2 '. . . understanding these terms in accordance with scholastic usage' (added in French version).
3 '. . . as if there were only myself in the world' (added in French version).

its parts are not immune from error, while others are immune, than there would be if all the parts were exactly alike. And I have no right to complain that the role God wished me to undertake in the world is not the principal one or the most perfect of all.

What is more, even if I have no power to avoid error in the first way just mentioned, which requires a clear perception of everything I have to deliberate on, I can avoid error in the second way, which depends merely on my remembering to withhold judgement on any occasion when the truth of the matter is not clear. Admittedly, I am aware of a certain weakness in me, in that I am unable to keep my attention fixed on one and the same item of knowledge at all times; but by attentive and repeated meditation I am nevertheless able to make myself remember it as often as the need arises, and thus get into the habit of avoiding error.

It is here that man's greatest and most important perfection is to be found, and I therefore think that today's meditation, involving an investigation into the cause of error and falsity, has been very profitable. The cause of error must surely be the one I have explained; for if, whenever I have to make a judgement, I restrain my will so that it extends to what the intellect clearly and distinctly reveals, and no further, then it is quite impossible for me to go wrong. This is because every clear and distinct perception is undoubtedly something,[1] and hence cannot come from nothing, but must necessarily have God for its author. Its author, I say, is God, who is supremely perfect, and who cannot be a deceiver on pain of contradiction; hence the perception is undoubtedly true. So today I have learned not only what precautions to take to avoid ever going wrong, but also what to do to arrive at the truth. For I shall unquestionably reach the truth, if only I give sufficient attention to all the things which I perfectly understand, and separate these from all the other cases where my apprehension is more confused and obscure. And this is just what I shall take good care to do from now on.

1 '. . . something real and positive' (French version).

62

FIFTH MEDITATION

The essence of material things, and the existence of God considered a second time

There are many matters which remain to be investigated concerning the attributes of God and the nature of myself, or my mind; and perhaps I shall take these up at another time. But now that I have seen what to do and what to avoid in order to reach the truth, the most pressing task seems to be to try to escape from the doubts into which I fell a few days ago, and see whether any certainty can be achieved regarding material objects.

But before I inquire whether any such things exist outside me, I must consider the ideas of these things, in so far as they exist in my thought, and see which of them are distinct, and which confused.

Quantity, for example, or 'continuous' quantity as the philosophers commonly call it, is something I distinctly imagine. That is, I distinctly imagine the extension of the quantity (or rather of the thing which is quantified) in length, breadth and depth. I also enumerate various parts of the thing, and to these parts I assign various sizes, shapes, positions and local motions; and to the motions I assign various durations.

Not only are all these things very well known and transparent to me when regarded in this general way, but in addition there are countless particular features regarding shape, number, motion and so on, which I perceive when I give them my attention. And the truth of these matters is so open and so much in harmony with my nature, that on first discovering them it seems that I am not so much learning something new as remembering what I knew before; or it seems like noticing for the first time things which were long present within me although I had never turned my mental gaze on them before.

But I think the most important consideration at this point is that I find within me countless ideas of things which even though they may not exist anywhere outside me still cannot be called nothing; for although in a sense they can be thought of at will, they are not my invention but have their own true and immutable natures. When, for example, I imagine a triangle, even if perhaps no such figure exists, or has ever existed, anywhere outside my thought, there is still a determinate nature, or essence, or form of the triangle which is immutable and eternal, and not invented by me or dependent on my mind. This is clear from the fact that various properties can be demonstrated of the triangle, for example that its three angles equal two right angles, that its greatest side subtends its greatest angle, and the like; and since these properties are ones which I now clearly recognize whether I want to or not, even if I never thought of them at all when I previously imagined the triangle, it follows that they cannot have been invented by me.

It would be beside the point for me to say that since I have from time to time seen bodies of triangular shape, the idea of the triangle may have come to me from external things by means of the sense organs. For I can think up countless other shapes which there can be no suspicion of my ever having encountered through the senses, and yet I can demonstrate 65 various properties of these shapes, just as I can with the triangle. All these properties are certainly true, since I am clearly aware of them, and therefore they are something, and not merely nothing; for it is obvious that whatever is true is something; and I have already amply demonstrated that everything of which I am clearly aware is true. And even if I had not demonstrated this, the nature of my mind is such that I cannot but assent to these things, at least so long as I clearly perceive them. I also remember that even before, when I was completely preoccupied with the objects of the senses, I always held that the most certain truths of all were the kind which I recognized clearly in connection with shapes, or numbers or other items relating to arithmetic or geometry, or in general to pure and abstract mathematics.

But if the mere fact that I can produce from my thought the idea of something entails that everything which I clearly and distinctly perceive to belong to that thing really does belong to it, is not this a possible basis for another argument to prove the existence of God? Certainly, the idea of God, or a supremely perfect being, is one which I find within me just as surely as the idea of any shape or number. And my understanding that it belongs to his nature that he always exists[1] is no less clear and distinct than is the case when I prove of any shape or number that some property belongs to its nature. Hence, even if it turned out that not everything on which I have meditated in these past days is true, I ought still to regard the existence of God as having at least the same level of certainty as I 66 have hitherto attributed to the truths of mathematics.[2]

At first sight, however, this is not transparently clear, but has some

[1] '... that actual and eternal existence belongs to his nature' (French version).
[2] '... which concern only figures and numbers' (added in French version).

appearance of being a sophism. Since I have been accustomed to
distinguish between existence and essence in everything else, I find it easy
to persuade myself that existence can also be separated from the essence
of God, and hence that God can be thought of as not existing. But when I
concentrate more carefully, it is quite evident that existence can no more
be separated from the essence of God than the fact that its three angles
equal two right angles can be separated from the essence of a triangle, or
than the idea of a mountain can be separated from the idea of a valley.
Hence it is just as much of a contradiction to think of God (that is, a
supremely perfect being) lacking existence (that is, lacking a perfection),
as it is to think of a mountain without a valley.

However, even granted that I cannot think of God except as existing,
just as I cannot think of a mountain without a valley, it certainly does not
follow from the fact that I think of a mountain with a valley that there is
any mountain in the world; and similarly, it does not seem to follow from
the fact that I think of God as existing that he does exist. For my thought
does not impose any necessity on things; and just as I may imagine a
winged horse even though no horse has wings, so I may be able to attach
existence to God even though no God exists.

But there is a sophism concealed here. From the fact that I cannot think
of a mountain without a valley, it does not follow that a mountain and
67 valley exist anywhere, but simply that a mountain and a valley, whether
they exist or not, are mutually inseparable. But from the fact that I
cannot think of God except as existing, it follows that existence is
inseparable from God, and hence that he really exists. It is not that my
thought makes it so, or imposes any necessity on any thing; on the
contrary, it is the necessity of the thing itself, namely the existence of
God, which determines my thinking in this respect. For I am not free to
think of God without existence (that is, a supremely perfect being
without a supreme perfection) as I am free to imagine a horse with or
without wings.

And it must not be objected at this point that while it is indeed
necessary for me to suppose God exists, once I have made the supposition
that he has all perfections (since existence is one of the perfections),
nevertheless the original supposition was not necessary. Similarly, the
objection would run, it is not necessary for me to think that all
quadrilaterals can be inscribed in a circle; but given this supposition, it
will be necessary for me to admit that a rhombus can be inscribed in a
circle – which is patently false. Now admittedly, it is not necessary that I
ever light upon any thought of God; but whenever I do choose to think of
the first and supreme being, and bring forth the idea of God from the
treasure house of my mind as it were, it is necessary that I attribute all

perfections to him, even if I do not at that time enumerate them or attend to them individually. And this necessity plainly guarantees that, when I later realize that existence is a perfection, I am correct in inferring that the first and supreme being exists. In the same way, it is not necessary for me ever to imagine a triangle; but whenever I do wish to consider a rectilinear figure having just three angles, it is necessary that I attribute to it the properties which license the inference that its three angles equal no 68
more than two right angles, even if I do not notice this at the time. By contrast, when I examine what figures can be inscribed in a circle, it is in no way necessary for me to think that this class includes all quadrilaterals. Indeed, I cannot even imagine this, so long as I an willing to admit only what I clearly and distinctly understand. So there is a great difference between this kind of false supposition and the true ideas which are innate in me, of which the first and most important is the idea of God. There are many ways in which I understand that this idea is not something fictitious which is dependent on my thought, but is an image of a true and immutable nature. First of all, there is the fact that, apart from God, there is nothing else of which I am capable of thinking such that existence belongs[1] to its essence. Second, I cannot understand how there could be two or more Gods of this kind; and after supposing that one God exists, I plainly see that it is necessary that he has existed from eternity and will abide for eternity. And finally, I perceive many other attributes of God, none of which I can remove or alter.

But whatever method of proof I use, I am always brought back to the fact that it is only what I clearly and distinctly perceive that completely convinces me. Some of the things I clearly and distinctly perceive are obvious to everyone, while others are discovered only by those who look more closely and investigate more carefully; but once they have been discovered, the latter are judged to be just as certain as the former. In the case of a right-angled triangle, for example, the fact that the square on 69
the hypotenuse is equal to the square on the other two sides is not so readily apparent as the fact that the hypotenuse subtends the largest angle; but once one has seen it, one believes it just as strongly. But as regards God, if I were not overwhelmed by preconceived opinions, and if the images of things perceived by the senses did not besiege my thought on every side, I would certainly acknowledge him sooner and more easily than anything else. For what is more self-evident than the fact that the supreme being exists, or that God, to whose essence alone existence belongs,[2] exists?

1 '... necessarily belongs' (French version).
2 '... in the idea of whom alone necessary and eternal existence is comprised' (French version).

Although it needed close attention for me to perceive this, I am now just as certain of it as I am of everything else which appears most certain. And what is more, I see that the certainty of all other things depends on this, so that without it nothing can ever be perfectly known.

Admittedly my nature is such that so long as[1] I perceive something very clearly and distinctly I cannot but believe it to be true. But my nature is also such that I cannot fix my mental vision continually on the same thing, so as to keep perceiving it clearly; and often the memory of a previously made judgement may come back, when I am no longer attending to the arguments which led me to make it. And so other arguments can now occur to me which might easily undermine my opinion, if I were unaware of God: and I should thus never have true and certain knowledge about anything, but only shifting and changeable opinions. For example, when I consider the nature of a triangle, it appears most evident to me, steeped as I am in the principles of geometry, that its three angles are equal to two right angles; and so long as I attend to the proof, I cannot but believe this to be true. But as soon as I turn my mind's eye away from the proof, then in spite of still remembering that I perceived it very clearly, I can easily fall into doubt about its truth, if I am unaware of God. For I can convince myself that I have a natural disposition to go wrong from time to time in matters which I think I perceive as evidently as can be. This will seem even more likely when I remember that there have been frequent cases where I have regarded things as true and certain, but have later been led by other arguments to judge them to be false.

Now, however, I have perceived that God exists, and at the same time I have understood that everything else depends on him, and that he is no deceiver; and I have drawn the conclusion that everything which I clearly and distinctly perceive is of necessity true. Accordingly, even if I am no longer attending to the arguments which led me to judge that this is true, as long as I remember that I clearly and distinctly perceived it, there are no counter-arguments which can be adduced to make me doubt it, but on the contrary I have true and certain knowledge of it. And I have knowledge not just of this matter, but of all matters which I remember ever having demonstrated, in geometry and so on. For what objections can now be raised?[2] That the way I am made makes me prone to frequent error? But I now know that I am incapable of error in those cases where my understanding is transparently clear. Or can it be objected that I have in the past regarded as true and certain many things which I afterwards recognized to be false? But none of these were things which I clearly and

1 '... as soon as' (French version).
2 '... to oblige me to call these matters into doubt' (added in French version).

distinctly perceived: I was ignorant of this rule for establishing the truth, and believed these things for other reasons which I later discovered to be less reliable. So what is left to say? Can one raise the objection I put to myself a while ago, that I may be dreaming, or that everything which I am now thinking has as little truth as what comes to the mind of one who is asleep? Yet even this does not change anything. For even though I might be dreaming, if there is anything which is evident to my intellect, then it is wholly true.

Thus I see plainly that the certainty and truth of all knowledge depends uniquely on my awareness of the true God, to such an extent that I was incapable of perfect knowledge about anything else until I became aware of him. And now it is possible for me to achieve full and certain knowledge of countless matters, both concerning God himself and other things whose nature is intellectual, and also concerning the whole of that corporeal nature which is the subject-matter of pure mathematics.[1]

71

1 '. . . and also concerning things which belong to corporeal nature in so far as it can serve as the object of geometrical demonstrations which have no concern with whether that object exists' (French version).

SIXTH MEDITATION

The existence of material things, and the real distinction between mind and body[1]

It remains for me to examine whether material things exist. And at least I now know they are capable of existing, in so far as they are the subject-matter of pure mathematics, since I perceive them clearly and distinctly. For there is no doubt that God is capable of creating everything that I am capable of perceiving in this manner; and I have never judged that something could not be made by him except on the grounds that there would be a contradiction in my perceiving it distinctly. The conclusion that material things exist is also suggested by the faculty of imagination, which I am aware of using when I turn my mind to material things. For when I give more attentive consideration to what imagination is, it seems to be nothing else but an application of the cognitive faculty to a body which is intimately present to it, and which therefore exists.

To make this clear, I will first examine the difference between imagination and pure understanding. When I imagine a triangle, for example, I do not merely understand that it is a figure bounded by three lines, but at the same time I also see the three lines with my mind's eye as if they were present before me; and this is what I call imagining. But if I want to think of a chiliagon, although I understand that it is a figure consisting of a thousand sides just as well as I understand the triangle to be a three-sided figure, I do not in the same way imagine the thousand sides or see them as if they were present before me. It is true that since I am in the habit of imagining something whenever I think of a corporeal thing, I may construct in my mind a confused representation of some figure; but it is clear that this is not a chiliagon. For it differs in no way from the representation I should form if I were thinking of a myriagon, or any figure with very many sides. Moreover, such a representation is useless for recognizing the properties which distinguish a chiliagon from other polygons. But suppose I am dealing with a pentagon: I can of course understand the figure of a pentagon, just as I can the figure of a

1 '... between the soul and body of man' (French version).

chiliagon, without the help of the imagination; but I can also imagine a pentagon, by applying my mind's eye to its five sides and the area contained within them. And in doing this I notice quite clearly that imagination requires a peculiar effort of mind which is not required for understanding; this additional effort of mind clearly shows the difference between imagination and pure understanding.

Besides this, I consider that this power of imagining which is in me, differing as it does from the power of understanding, is not a necessary constituent of my own essence, that is, of the essence of my mind. For if I lacked it, I should undoubtedly remain the same individual as I now am; from which it seems to follow that it depends on something distinct from myself. And I can easily understand that, if there does exist some body to which the mind is so joined that it can apply itself to contemplate it, as it were, whenever it pleases, then it may possibly be this very body that enables me to imagine corporeal things. So the difference between this mode of thinking and pure understanding may simply be this: when the mind understands, it in some way turns towards itself and inspects one of the ideas which are within it; but when it imagines, it turns towards the body and looks at something in the body which conforms to an idea understood by the mind or perceived by the senses. I can, as I say, easily understand that this is how imagination comes about, if the body exists; and since there is no other equally suitable way of explaining imagination that comes to mind, I can make a probable conjecture that the body exists. But this is only a probability; and despite a careful and comprehensive investigation, I do not yet see how the distinct idea of corporeal nature which I find in my imagination can provide any basis for a necessary inference that some body exists.

But besides that corporeal nature which is the subject-matter of pure mathematics, there is much else that I habitually imagine, such as colours, sounds, tastes, pain and so on – though not so distinctly. Now I perceive these things much better by means of the senses, which is how, with the assistance of memory, they appear to have reached the imagination. So in order to deal with them more fully, I must pay equal attention to the senses, and see whether the things which are perceived by means of that mode of thinking which I call 'sensory perception' provide me with any sure argument for the existence of corporeal things.

To begin with, I will go back over all the things which I previously took to be perceived by the senses, and reckoned to be true; and I will go over my reasons for thinking this. Next, I will set out my reasons for subsequently calling these things into doubt. And finally I will consider what I should now believe about them.

First of all then, I perceived by my senses that I had a head, hands, feet and other limbs making up the body which I regarded as part of myself, or perhaps even as my whole self. I also perceived by my senses that this body was situated among many other bodies which could affect it in various favourable or unfavourable ways; and I gauged the favourable effects by a sensation of pleasure, and the unfavourable ones by a sensation of pain. In addition to pain and pleasure, I also had sensations within me of hunger, thirst, and other such appetites, and also of physical propensities towards cheerfulness, sadness, anger and similar emotions.

75 And outside me, besides the extension, shapes and movements of bodies, I also had sensations of their hardness and heat, and of the other tactile qualities. In addition, I had sensations of light, colours, smells, tastes and sounds, the variety of which enabled me to distinguish the sky, the earth, the seas, and all other bodies, one from another. Considering the ideas of all these qualities which presented themselves to my thought, although the ideas were, strictly speaking, the only immediate objects of my sensory awareness, it was not unreasonable for me to think that the items which I was perceiving through the senses were things quite distinct from my thought, namely bodies which produced the ideas. For my experience was that these ideas came to me quite without my consent, so that I could not have sensory awareness of any object, even if I wanted to, unless it was present to my sense organs; and I could not avoid having sensory awareness of it when it was present. And since the ideas perceived by the senses were much more lively and vivid and even, in their own way, more distinct than any of those which I deliberately formed through meditating or which I found impressed on my memory, it seemed impossible that they should have come from within me; so the only alternative was that they came from other things. Since the sole source of my knowledge of these things was the ideas themselves, the supposition that the things resembled the ideas was bound to occur to me. In addition, I remembered that the use of my senses had come first, while the use of my reason came only later; and I saw that the ideas which I formed myself were less vivid than those which I perceived with the senses and were, for the most part, made up of elements of sensory ideas. In this way I easily convinced myself that I had nothing at all in the intellect which I had not previously

76 had in sensation.[1] As for the body which by some special right I called 'mine', my belief that this body, more than any other, belonged to me had some justification. For I could never be separated from it, as I could from other bodies; and I felt all my appetites and emotions in, and on account of, this body; and finally, I was aware of pain and pleasurable ticklings in parts of this body, but not in other bodies external to it. But why should that curious sensation of pain give rise to a particular distress of mind; or

1 See note 3, p. 186 below.

why should a certain kind of delight follow on a tickling sensation? Again, why should that curious tugging in the stomach which I call hunger tell me that I should eat, or a dryness of the throat tell me to drink, and so on? I was not able to give any explanation of all this, except that nature taught me so. For there is absolutely no connection (at least that I can understand) between the tugging sensation and the decision to take food, or between the sensation of something causing pain and the mental apprehension of distress that arises from that sensation. These and other judgements that I made concerning sensory objects, I was apparently taught to make by nature; for I had already made up my mind that this was how things were, before working out any arguments to prove it.

Later on, however, I had many experiences which gradually undermined all the faith I had had in the senses. Sometimes towers which had looked round from a distance appeared square from close up; and enormous statues standing on their pediments did not seem large when observed from the ground. In these and countless other such cases, I found that the judgements of the external senses were mistaken. And this applied not just to the external senses but to the internal senses as well. For what can be more internal than pain? And yet I had heard that those who had had a leg or an arm amputated sometimes still seemed to feel pain intermittently in the missing part of the body. So even in my own case it was apparently not quite certain that a particular limb was hurting, even if I felt pain in it. To these reasons for doubting, I recently added two very general ones.[1] The first was that every sensory experience I have ever thought I was having while awake I can also think of myself as sometimes having while asleep; and since I do not believe that what I seem to perceive in sleep comes from things located outside me, I did not see why I should be any more inclined to believe this of what I think I perceive while awake. The second reason for doubt was that since I did not know the author of my being (or at least was pretending not to), I saw nothing to rule out the possibility that my natural constitution made me prone to error even in matters which seemed to me most true. As for the reasons for my previous confident belief in the truth of the things perceived by the senses, I had no trouble in refuting them. For since I apparently had natural impulses towards many things which reason told me to avoid, I reckoned that a great deal of confidence should not be placed in what I was taught by nature. And despite the fact that the perceptions of the senses were not dependent on my will, I did not think that I should on that account infer that they proceeded from things

---

1 Cf. Med. 1, above pp. 13–15.

distinct from myself, since I might perhaps have a faculty not yet known to me which produced them.[1]

But now, when I am beginning to achieve a better knowledge of myself and the author of my being, although I do not think I should heedlessly
78   accept everything I seem to have acquired from the senses, neither do I think that everything should be called into doubt.

\ First, I know that everything which I clearly and distinctly understand is capable of being created by God so as to correspond exactly with my understanding of it. Hence the fact that I can clearly and distinctly understand one thing apart from another is enough to make me certain that the two things are distinct, since they are capable of being separated, at least by God. The question of what kind of power is required to bring about such a separation does not affect the judgement that the two things are distinct. Thus, simply by knowing that I exist and seeing at the same time that absolutely nothing else belongs to my nature or essence except that I am a thinking thing, I can infer correctly that my essence consists solely in the fact that I am a thinking thing. It is true that I may have (or, to anticipate, that I certainly have) a body that is very closely joined to me. But nevertheless, on the one hand I have a clear and distinct idea of myself, in so far as I am simply a thinking, non-extended thing; and on the other hand I have a distinct idea of body,[2] in so far as this is simply an extended, non-thinking thing. And accordingly, it is certain that I[3] am really distinct from my body, and can exist without it.\

Besides this, I find in myself faculties for certain special modes of thinking,[4] namely imagination and sensory perception. Now I can clearly and distinctly understand myself as a whole without these faculties; but I cannot, conversely, understand these faculties without me, that is, without an intellectual substance to inhere in. This is because there is an intellectual act included in their essential definition; and hence I perceive that the distinction between them and myself corresponds to the distinction between the modes of a thing and the thing itself.[5] Of course I also recognize that there are other faculties (like those of changing position, of taking on various shapes, and so on) which, like sensory perception and
79   imagination, cannot be understood apart from some substance for them

1 Cf. Med. III, above p. 27.
2 The Latin term *corpus* as used here by Descartes is ambiguous as between 'body' (i.e. corporeal matter in general) and 'the body' (i.e. this particular body of mine). The French version preserves the ambiguity.
3 '... that is, my soul, by which I am what I am' (added in French version).
4 '... certain modes of thinking which are quite special and distinct from me' (French version).
5 '... between the shapes, movements and other modes or accidents of a body and the body which supports them' (French version).

to inhere in, and hence cannot exist without it. But it is clear that these other faculties, if they exist, must be in a corporeal or extended substance and not an intellectual one; for the clear and distinct conception of them includes extension, but does not include any intellectual act whatsoever. Now there is in me a passive faculty of sensory perception, that is, a faculty for receiving and recognizing the ideas of sensible objects; but I could not make use of it unless there was also an active faculty, either in me or in something else, which produced or brought about these ideas. But this faculty cannot be in me, since clearly it presupposes no intellectual act on my part,[1] and the ideas in question are produced without my cooperation and often even against my will. So the only alternative is that it is in another substance distinct from me – a substance which contains either formally or eminently all the reality which exists objectively[2] in the ideas produced by this faculty (as I have just noted). This substance is either a body, that is, a corporeal nature, in which case it will contain formally ⟨and in fact⟩ everything which is to be found objectively ⟨or representatively⟩ in the ideas; or else it is God, or some creature more noble than a body, in which case it will contain eminently whatever is to be found in the ideas. But since God is not a deceiver, it is quite clear that he does not transmit the ideas to me either directly from himself, or indirectly, via some creature which contains the objective reality of the ideas not formally but only eminently. For God has given me no faculty at all for recognizing any such source for these ideas; on the contrary, he has given me a great propensity to believe that 80 they are produced by corporeal things. So I do not see how God could be understood to be anything but a deceiver if the ideas were transmitted from a source other than corporeal things. It follows that corporeal things exist. They may not all exist in a way that exactly corresponds with my sensory grasp of them, for in many cases the grasp of the senses is very obscure and confused. But at least they possess all the properties which I clearly and distinctly understand, that is, all those which, viewed in general terms, are comprised within the subject-matter of pure mathematics.

What of the other aspects of corporeal things which are either particular (for example that the sun is of such and such a size or shape), or less clearly understood, such as light or sound or pain, and so on? Despite the high degree of doubt and uncertainty involved here, the very fact that God is not a deceiver, and the consequent impossibility of there being any falsity in my opinions which cannot be corrected by some other

---

1 '... cannot be in me in so far as I am merely a thinking thing, since it does not presuppose any thought on my part' (French version).
2 For the terms 'formally', 'eminently' and 'objectively', see notes, p. 28 above.

faculty supplied by God, offers me a sure hope that I can attain the truth even in these matters. Indeed, there is no doubt that everything that I am taught by nature contains some truth. For if nature is considered in its general aspect, then I understand by the term nothing other than God himself, or the ordered system of created things established by God. And by my own nature in particular I understand nothing other than the totality of things bestowed on me by God.

There is nothing that my own nature teaches me more vividly than that I have a body, and that when I feel pain there is something wrong with the body, and that when I am hungry or thirsty the body needs food and drink, and so on. So I should not doubt that there is some truth in this.

81   Nature also teaches me, by these sensations of pain, hunger, thirst and so on, that I am not merely present in my body as a sailor is present in a ship,[1] but that I am very closely joined and, as it were, intermingled with it, so that I and the body form a unit. If this were not so, I, who am nothing but a thinking thing, would not feel pain when the body was hurt, but would perceive the damage purely by the intellect, just as a sailor perceives by sight if anything in his ship is broken. Similarly, when the body needed food or drink, I should have an explicit understanding of the fact, instead of having confused sensations of hunger and thirst. For these sensations of hunger, thirst, pain and so on are nothing but confused modes of thinking which arise from the union and, as it were, intermingling of the mind with the body.

I am also taught by nature that various other bodies exist in the vicinity of my body, and that some of these are to be sought out and others avoided. And from the fact that I perceive by my senses a great variety of colours, sounds, smells and tastes, as well as differences in heat, hardness and the like, I am correct in inferring that the bodies which are the source of these various sensory perceptions possess differences corresponding to them, though perhaps not resembling them. Also, the fact that some of the perceptions are agreeable to me while others are disagreeable makes it quite certain that my body, or rather my whole self, in so far as I am a combination of body and mind, can be affected by the various beneficial or harmful bodies which surround it.

82   There are, however, many other things which I may appear to have been taught by nature, but which in reality I acquired not from nature but from a habit of making ill-considered judgements; and it is therefore quite possible that these are false. Cases in point are the belief that any space in which nothing is occurring to stimulate my senses must be empty; or that the heat in a body is something exactly resembling the idea of heat which is in me; or that when a body is white or green, the

1 '. . . as a pilot in his ship' (French version).

selfsame whiteness or greenness which I perceive through my senses is present in the body; or that in a body which is bitter or sweet there is the selfsame taste which I experience, and so on; or, finally, that stars and towers and other distant bodies have the same size and shape which they present to my senses, and other examples of this kind. But to make sure that my perceptions in this matter are sufficiently distinct, I must more accurately define exactly what I mean when I say that I am taught something by nature. In this context I am taking nature to be something more limited than the totality of things bestowed on me by God. For this includes many things that belong to the mind alone – for example my perception that what is done cannot be undone, and all other things that are known by the natural light;[1] but at this stage I am not speaking of these matters. It also includes much that relates to the body alone, like the tendency to move in a downward direction, and so on; but I am not speaking of these matters either. My sole concern here is with what God has bestowed on me as a combination of mind and body. My nature, then, in this limited sense, does indeed teach me to avoid what induces a feeling of pain and to seek out what induces feelings of pleasure, and so on. But it does not appear to teach us to draw any conclusions from these sensory perceptions about things located outside us without waiting until the intellect has examined[2] the matter. For knowledge of the truth about such things seems to belong to the mind alone, not to the combination of mind and body. Hence, although a star has no greater effect on my eye than the flame of a small light, that does not mean that there is any real or positive inclination in me to believe that the star is no bigger than the light; I have simply made this judgement from childhood onwards without any rational basis. Similarly, although I feel heat when I go near a fire and feel pain when I go too near, there is no convincing argument for supposing that there is something in the fire which resembles the heat, any more than for supposing that there is something which resembles the pain. There is simply reason to suppose that there is something in the fire, whatever it may eventually turn out to be, which produces in us the feelings of heat or pain. And likewise, even though there is nothing in any given space that stimulates the senses, it does not follow that there is no body there. In these cases and many others I see that I have been in the habit of misusing the order of nature. For the proper purpose of the sensory perceptions given me by nature is simply to inform the mind of what is beneficial or harmful for the composite of which the mind is a part; and to this extent they are sufficiently clear and distinct. But I misuse them by treating them as reliable touchstones for immediate

83

1 '... without any help from the body' (added in French version).
2 '... carefully and maturely examined' (French version).

judgements about the essential nature of the bodies located outside us; yet this is an area where they provide only very obscure information.

I have already looked in sufficient detail at how, notwithstanding the goodness of God, it may happen that my judgements are false. But a further problem now comes to mind regarding those very things which nature presents to me as objects which I should seek out or avoid, and also regarding the internal sensations, where I seem to have detected errors[1] – e.g. when someone is tricked by the pleasant taste of some food

84   into eating the poison concealed inside it. Yet in this case, what the man's nature urges him to go for is simply what is responsible for the pleasant taste, and not the poison, which his nature knows nothing about. The only inference that can be drawn from this is that his nature is not omniscient. And this is not surprising, since man is a limited thing, and so it is only fitting that his perfection should be limited.

And yet it is not unusual for us to go wrong even in cases where nature does urge us towards something. Those who are ill, for example, may desire food or drink that will shortly afterwards turn out to be bad for them. Perhaps it may be said that they go wrong because their nature is disordered, but this does not remove the difficulty. A sick man is no less one of God's creatures than a healthy one, and it seems no less a contradiction to suppose that he has received from God a nature which deceives him. Yet a clock constructed with wheels and weights observes all the laws of its nature just as closely when it is badly made and tells the wrong time as when it completely fulfils the wishes of the clockmaker. In the same way, I might consider the body of a man as a kind of machine equipped with and made up of bones, nerves, muscles, veins, blood and skin in such a way that, even if there were no mind in it, it would still perform all the same movements as it now does in those cases where movement is not under the control of the will or, consequently, of the mind.[2] I can easily see that if such a body suffers from dropsy, for example, and is affected by the dryness of the throat which normally produces in the mind the sensation of thirst, the resulting condition of the nerves and other parts will dispose the body to take a drink, with the result that the disease will be aggravated. Yet this is just as natural as the body's being stimulated by a similar dryness of the throat to take a drink

85   when there is no such illness and the drink is beneficial. Admittedly, when I consider the purpose of the clock, I may say that it is departing from its nature when it does not tell the right time; and similarly when I consider the mechanism of the human body, I may think that, in relation to the movements which normally occur in it, it too is deviating from its nature if the throat is dry at a time when drinking is not beneficial to its

1 '... and thus seem to have been directly deceived by my nature' (added in French version).
2 '... but occurs merely as a result of the disposition of the organs' (French version).

continued health. But I am well aware that 'nature' as I have just used it has a very different significance from 'nature' in the other sense. As I have just used it, 'nature' is simply a label which depends on my thought; it is quite extraneous to the things to which it is applied, and depends simply on my comparison between the idea of a sick man and a badly-made clock, and the idea of a healthy man and a well-made clock. But by 'nature' in the other sense I understand something which is really to be found in the things themselves; in this sense, therefore, the term contains something of the truth.

When we say, then, with respect to the body suffering from dropsy, that it has a disordered nature because it has a dry throat and yet does not need drink, the term 'nature' is here used merely as an extraneous label. However, with respect to the composite, that is, the mind united with this body, what is involved is not a mere label, but a true error of nature, namely that it is thirsty at a time when drink is going to cause it harm. It thus remains to inquire how it is that the goodness of God does not prevent nature, in this sense, from deceiving us.

The first observation I make at this point is that there is a great difference between the mind and the body, inasmuch as the body is by its very nature always divisible, while the mind is utterly indivisible. For when I consider the mind, or myself in so far as I am merely a thinking thing, I am unable to distinguish any parts within myself; I understand myself to be something quite single and complete. Although the whole mind seems to be united to the whole body, I recognize that if a foot or arm or any other part of the body is cut off, nothing has thereby been taken away from the mind. As for the faculties of willing, of understanding, of sensory perception and so on, these cannot be termed parts of the mind, since it is one and the same mind that wills, and understands and has sensory perceptions. By contrast, there is no corporeal or extended thing that I can think of which in my thought I cannot easily divide into parts; and this very fact makes me understand that it is divisible. This one argument would be enough to show me that the mind is completely different from the body, even if I did not already know as much from other considerations.

My next observation is that the mind is not immediately affected by all parts of the body, but only by the brain, or perhaps just by one small part of the brain, namely the part which is said to contain the 'common' sense.[1] Every time this part of the brain is in a given state, it presents the

1 The supposed faculty which integrates the data from the five specialized senses (the notion goes back ultimately to Aristotle). 'The seat of the common sense must be very mobile, to receive all the impressions coming from the senses, but must be moveable only by the spirits which transmit these impressions. Only the *conarion* [pineal gland] fits these conditions' (letter to Mersenne, 21 April 1641).

same signals to the mind, even though the other parts of the body may be
in a different condition at the time. This is established by countless
observations, which there is no need to review here.

I observe, in addition, that the nature of the body is such that whenever
any part of it is moved by another part which is some distance away, it
can always be moved in the same fashion by any of the parts which lie in
between, even if the more distant part does nothing. For example, in a
87 cord ABCD, if one end D is pulled so that the other end A moves, the
exact same movement could have been brought about if one of the
intermediate points B or C had been pulled, and D had not moved at all.
In similar fashion, when I feel a pain in my foot, physiology tells me that
this happens by means of nerves distributed throughout the foot, and
that these nerves are like cords which go from the foot right up to the
brain. When the nerves are pulled in the foot, they in turn pull on inner
parts of the brain to which they are attached, and produce a certain
motion in them; and nature has laid it down that this motion should
produce in the mind a sensation of pain, as occurring in the foot. But
since these nerves, in passing from the foot to the brain, must pass
through the calf, the thigh, the lumbar region, the back and the neck, it
can happen that, even if it is not the part in the foot but one of the
intermediate parts which is being pulled, the same motion will occur in
the brain as occurs when the foot is hurt, and so it will necessarily come
about that the mind feels the same sensation of pain. And we must
suppose the same thing happens with regard to any other sensation.

My final observation is that any given movement occurring in the part
of the brain that immediately affects the mind produces just one
corresponding sensation; and hence the best system that could be devised
is that it should produce the one sensation which, of all possible
sensations, is most especially and most frequently conducive to the
preservation of the healthy man. And experience shows that the sensations which nature has given us are all of this kind; and so there is
absolutely nothing to be found in them that does not bear witness to the
88 power and goodness of God. For example, when the nerves in the foot
are set in motion in a violent and unusual manner, this motion, by way of
the spinal cord, reaches the inner parts of the brain, and there gives the
mind its signal for having a certain sensation, namely the sensation of a
pain as occurring in the foot. This stimulates the mind to do its best to get
rid of the cause of the pain, which it takes to be harmful to the foot. It is
true that God could have made the nature of man such that this
particular motion in the brain indicated something else to the mind; it
might, for example, have made the mind aware of the actual motion
occurring in the brain, or in the foot, or in any of the intermediate

regions; or it might have indicated something else entirely. But there is nothing else which would have been so conducive to the continued well-being of the body. In the same way, when we need drink, there arises a certain dryness in the throat; this sets in motion the nerves of the throat, which in turn move the inner parts of the brain. This motion produces in the mind a sensation of thirst, because the most useful thing for us to know about the whole business is that we need drink in order to stay healthy. And so it is in the other cases.

It is quite clear from all this that, notwithstanding the immense goodness of God, the nature of man as a combination of mind and body is such that it is bound to mislead him from time to time. For there may be some occurrence, not in the foot but in one of the other areas through which the nerves travel in their route from the foot to the brain, or even in the brain itself; and if this cause produces the same motion which is generally produced by injury to the foot, then pain will be felt as if it were in the foot. This deception of the senses is natural, because a given motion in the brain must always produce the same sensation in the mind; and the origin of the motion in question is much more often going to be something which is hurting the foot, rather than something existing elsewhere. So it is reasonable that this motion should always indicate to 89 the mind a pain in the foot rather than in any other part of the body. Again, dryness of the throat may sometimes arise not, as it normally does, from the fact that a drink is necessary to the health of the body, but from some quite opposite cause, as happens in the case of the man with dropsy. Yet it is much better that it should mislead on this occasion than that it should always mislead when the body is in good health. And the same goes for the other cases.

This consideration is the greatest help to me, not only for noticing all the errors to which my nature is liable, but also for enabling me to correct or avoid them without difficulty. For I know that in matters regarding the well-being of the body, all my senses report the truth much more frequently than not. Also, I can almost always make use of more than one sense to investigate the same thing; and in addition, I can use both my memory, which connects present experiences with preceding ones, and my intellect, which has by now examined all the causes of error. Accordingly, I should not have any further fears about the falsity of what my senses tell me every day; on the contrary, the exaggerated doubts of the last few days should be dismissed as laughable. This applies especially to the principal reason for doubt, namely my inability to distinguish between being asleep and being awake. For I now notice that there is a vast difference between the two, in that dreams are never linked by memory with all the other actions of life as waking experiences are. If, while I am

awake, anyone were suddenly to appear to me and then disappear immediately, as happens in sleep, so that I could not see where he had
90 come from or where he had gone to, it would not be unreasonable for me to judge that he was a ghost, or a vision created in my brain,[1] rather than a real man. But when I distinctly see where things come from and where and when they come to me, and when I can connect my perceptions of them with the whole of the rest of my life without a break, then I am quite certain that when I encounter these things I am not asleep but awake. And I ought not to have even the slightest doubt of their reality if, after calling upon all the senses as well as my memory and my intellect in order to check them, I receive no conflicting reports from any of these sources. For from the fact that God is not a deceiver it follows that in cases like these I am completely free from error. But since the pressure of things to be done does not always allow us to stop and make such a meticulous check, it must be admitted that in this human life we are often liable to make mistakes about particular things, and we must acknowledge the weakness of our nature.

1 '. . . like those that are formed in the brain when I sleep' (added in French version).

Objections and Replies

Translator's preface

As soon as he had completed the *Meditations*, Descartes began to circulate them among his friends, asking for comments and criticisms. He also sent the manuscript to Friar Marin Mersenne (1588–1648), his friend and principal correspondent, asking him to obtain further criticisms. He wrote to Mersenne in a letter of 28 January 1641: 'I shall be glad if people make me as many objections as possible – and the strongest ones they can find. For I hope that in consequence the truth will stand out all the better.' The resulting six sets of Objections (the first set collected by Descartes himself, the remainder by Mersenne) were published in Latin, together with Descartes' Replies, in the same volume as the first (1641) edition of the *Meditations*. The second edition of the *Meditations* (1642) contained in addition the Seventh Set of Objections together with Descartes' Replies, and also the Letter to Dinet (all in Latin). The terms 'Objections' and 'Replies' were suggested by Descartes himself, who asked that his own comments should be called 'Replies' rather than 'Solutions' in order to leave the reader to judge whether his replies contained solutions to the difficulties offered (letter to Mersenne, 18 March 1641).

The volume containing the French translation of the *Meditations* (by de Luynes), which appeared in 1647, also contained a French version of the first six sets of *Objections and Replies* by Descartes' disciple Claude Clerselier (1614–84). Although it is frequently said that Descartes saw and approved of this translation,[1] there is, as with the *Meditations* proper, no good case for preferring the French version to the original Latin which Descartes himself composed.[2] It should also be remembered that all the objectors wrote in Latin, and had before them only the Latin text of the *Meditations* when they wrote. The present translation is therefore based entirely on the original Latin.

---

1 Descartes visited Clerselier in 1644 and saw some of his work; he did not, however, wish the Fifth Set of Objections and Replies to be included in the translation (see Author's Note, below p. 268). Clerselier's version of the Seventh Set of Objections and Replies did not appear till after Descartes' death, in the second French edition of 1661.
2 See Translator's preface to *Meditations*, above p. 1.

The First Set of Objections is by a Catholic theologian from Holland, Johannes Caterus (Johan de Kater), who was priest in charge of the church of St Laurens at Alkmaar from 1632–56. Caterus had been asked to comment on the *Meditations* by two fellow priests who were friends of Descartes, Bannius and Bloemaert; and it is to these two intermediaries that both Caterus' Objections and Descartes' Replies are addressed. Descartes wrote to Mersenne on 24 December 1640 that Caterus himself wished to remain anonymous.

The Second Set of Objections is simply attributed to 'theologians and philosophers' in the index to the first edition, but the French version of 1647 announces that they were 'collected by the Reverend Father Mersenne'. In fact they are largely the work of Mersenne himself.

The Third Set of Objections ('by a celebrated English philosopher', says the 1647 edition) is by Thomas Hobbes (1588–1679) who had fled to France, for political reasons, in 1640. Although many of Hobbes' points are of considerable philosophical interest, Descartes' comments are mostly curt and dismissive in the extreme.

The Fourth Set of Objections is by the French theologian and logician Antoine Arnauld (1612–94), who became Doctor of Theology at the Sorbonne in 1641. Both the Objections and Replies are addressed to Mersenne as intermediary, and the tone of both authors is courteous and respectful throughout.

The Fifth Set of Objections is by the philosopher Pierre Gassendi (1592–1655). His comments are very lengthy and come near to being a paragraph by paragraph commentary on the *Meditations*. Gassendi's tone is often acerbic, and Descartes frequently reacts with bristly defensiveness. For the further prolonged debate between Descartes and Gassendi which followed the publication of the Fifth Objections and Replies, see the Appendix, pages 268ff below.

The Sixth Set of Objections was printed with no indication of the author in the first and second editions, and is described in the 1647 French edition as being 'by various theologians and philosophers'. The compiler, as in the case of the Second Objections, is Mersenne.

The Seventh Set of Objections is by the Jesuit, Pierre Bourdin (1595–1653). Descartes had been eager to obtain the support of the Jesuits for his philosophy, but he was very disappointed with what he called 'the quibbles of Father Bourdin'; he wrote to Mersenne 'I have treated him as courteously as possible but I have never seen a paper so full of faults' (letter of March 1642). Descartes' Replies take the form of comments or annotations which are interspersed with Bourdin's Objections.

The Letter to Father Dinet, in which Descartes describes his reaction to Bourdin's Objections, was printed at the end of the Seventh Set of

Objections and Replies in the second (1642) edition. Dinet was Bourdin's superior in the Jesuit order, and had taught Descartes at the College of La Flèche. An abridged version of the letter to Dinet is translated below; the Objections and Replies are translated in full.

NOTE ON TYPOGRAPHY AND QUOTATIONS

The time-honoured practice in presenting the *Objections and Replies* (one which goes back to the earliest editions) has been to use italic type for the objectors' words and Roman type for those of Descartes. This convention has been abandoned in the present edition. It is unnecessary, since there is (with the exception of the exchange with Bourdin, where an alternative device is used) never any doubt about who is speaking; and it is potentially confusing, since the use of roman type in quotations from the *Meditations* can mislead the reader into supposing he has before him the exact words of Descartes. In fact, however, the objectors are often cavalier about quotations, paraphrasing and altering the syntax to suit their purposes. Because of this, readers referring back to the *Meditations* should not always expect to find that quotations in the *Objections and Replies* correspond word for word with the relevant passages in the *Meditations*.

J.C.

*Objections raised by several men of learning against the
preceding Meditations together with the author's Replies*

FIRST SET OF OBJECTIONS[1]

Gentlemen,

Observing your enthusiastic desire for me to make a detailed examination of the writings of M. Descartes, I felt myself obliged, in this matter, to go along with the wishes of such very good friends. In complying with your request I hope to make you realize the great regard which I have for you, and also to establish the inadequacy of my own intellectual powers, so that in future you may show me a little more indulgence, if I require it, and not press me so hard if my performance here turns out to be inadequate.

M. Descartes is in my judgement a man of the highest intellect and the utmost modesty – a man such as even Momus,[2] were he now with us, would approve of. 'I am thinking', he says, 'therefore I exist; indeed, I am thought itself – I am a mind.' Granted. 'But in virtue of thinking, I 92 possess within me ideas of things, and in particular an idea of a supremely perfect and infinite being.' True again. 'However I am not the cause of this idea, since I do not measure up to its objective reality; hence something more perfect than myself is its cause, and accordingly there exists something besides myself, something more perfect than I am. This is someone who is not a being in any ordinary sense but who simply and without qualification embraces the whole of being within himself, and is as it were the ultimate original cause, as Dionysius[3] says in chapter eight of the *Divina Nomina*.'

But here I am forced to stop for a while to avoid becoming exhausted. My mind ebbs and flows like the Euripus with its violent tides: first I accept, but then I deny; I give my approval but then I withdraw it; I am unwilling to disagree with the author, but I am unable to agree with him. My question is this: what sort of cause does an idea need? Indeed, what *is* an idea? It is the thing that is thought of, in so far as it has objective being in the intellect. But what is 'objective being in the intellect'? According to what I was taught, this is simply the determination of an act of the

1 By Caterus. For details of the author and the addressees, see Translator's preface, above p. 64.
2 In Greek mythology the personification of criticism and fault-finding.
3 Dionysius the Areopagite, a fifth-century writer who sought to introduce certain neoplatonic elements into Christianity.

intellect by means of an object. And this is merely an extraneous label which adds nothing to the thing itself. Just as 'being seen' is nothing other than an act of vision attributable to myself, so 'being thought of', or having objective being in the intellect, is simply a thought of the mind which stops and terminates in the mind. And this can occur without any movement or change in the thing itself, and indeed without the thing in question existing at all. So why should I look for a cause of something which is not actual, and which is simply an empty label, a non-entity?

'Nevertheless', says our ingenious author, 'in order for a given idea to contain such and such objective reality it must surely derive it from some cause.'[1] On the contrary, this requires no cause; for objective reality is a pure label, not anything actual. A cause imparts some real and actual 93 influence; but what does not actually exist cannot take on anything, and so does not receive or require any actual causal influence. Hence, though I have ideas, there is no cause for these ideas, let alone some cause which is greater than I am, or which is infinite.

'But if you do not grant that ideas have a cause, you must at least explain why a given idea contains such and such objective reality.' Certainly; I do not normally stint my friends, but am as lavish as possible. I take the same general view about all ideas as M. Descartes takes of a triangle. He says: 'even if perhaps no such figure exists, or has ever existed, anywhere outside my thought, there is still a determinate nature or essence or form which is immutable and eternal'.[2] What we have here is an eternal truth, which does not require a cause. A boat is a boat and nothing else. Davus is Davus and not Oedipus.[3] But if you insist on having an explanation, the answer lies in the imperfection of our intellect, which is not infinite. For since it does not comprehend in one single grasp that totality that is all at once and once for all, it divides and separates out the universal good, and being unable to bring forth the totality, it conceives of it piecemeal, or, as they say, inadequately.

The author goes on to say, 'And yet the mode of being by which a thing exists objectively in the intellect by way of an idea, imperfect though it may be, is certainly not nothing, and so it cannot come from nothing.'[4] There is an equivocation here. If *nothing* is the same as an entity which does not actually exist, then this, since it is not actual, is nothing at all, and hence comes from nothing, that is, does not come from any cause. 94 But if 'nothing' means something imaginary, or what they commonly call a 'conceptual entity'[5] then this is not 'nothing' but something real which

---

1 Med. III, above p. 28.   2 Med. V, above p. 45.
3 A reference to Terence, *Andria* I, ii, where the slave Davus, on being asked a question, replies 'I am Davus, not Oedipus' (alluding to the fact that Oedipus alone was able to solve the riddle of the Sphinx).
4 Med. III, above p. 29.   5 Lat. *ens rationis*, literally 'entity of reason'.

is distinctly conceived. Nevertheless, since it is merely conceived and is not actual, although it can be conceived, it cannot in any way be caused.

But he goes on: 'I should like to go further and inquire whether I myself who have this idea could exist if no such being existed' (that is, as he says just before this, if there did not exist a being from whom my idea of a being more perfect than myself proceeds). He goes on: 'From whom, in that case, would I derive my existence? From myself, presumably, or from my parents or from others etc. Yet if I derived my existence from myself, then I should neither doubt nor want, nor lack anything at all; for I should have given myself all the perfections of which I have any idea, and thus I should myself be God.'[1] But if I derive my existence from some other, then if I trace the series back I will eventually come to a being which derives its existence from itself; and so the argument here becomes the same as the argument based on the supposition that I derive my existence from myself.[2] This is exactly the same approach as that taken by St Thomas: he called this way 'the way based on the causality of the efficient cause'.[3] He took the argument from Aristotle, although neither he nor Aristotle was bothered about the causes of ideas. And perhaps they had no need to be; for can I not take a much shorter and more direct line of argument? 'I am thinking, therefore I exist; indeed, I am thought itself, I am a mind. But this mind and thought derives its existence either from itself, or from another. If the latter, then we continue to repeat the question – where does this other being derive its existence from? And if the former, if it derives its existence from itself, it is God. For what derives existence from itself will without difficulty have endowed itself with all things.'

95   I beg and beseech our author not to hide his meaning from a reader who, though perhaps less intelligent, is eager to follow. The phrase 'from itself' has two senses. In the first, positive, sense, it means 'from itself as from a cause'. What derives existence from itself in this sense bestows its own existence on itself; so if by an act of premeditated choice it were to give itself what it desired, it would undoubtedly give itself all things, and so would be God. But in the second, negative, sense, 'from itself' simply means 'not from another'; and this, as far as I remember, is the way in which everyone takes the phrase.

But now, if something derives its existence from itself in the sense of 'not from another', how can we prove that this being embraces all things and is infinite? This time I shall not listen if you say 'If it derives its existence from itself it could easily have given itself all things.' For it does

---

1 Med. III, above p. 32f.   2 Cf. Med. III, above p. 34.

3 This is the second of Aquinas' 'Five Ways': *Summa Theologiae*, Pars 1, Quaestio 2, art. 3. Cf. Aristotle, *Physics* VIII, 251ff; *Metaphysics* Λ, 1072ff.

not derive existence from itself as a cause, nor did it exist prior to itself so that it could choose in advance what it should subsequently be. Admittedly, I am sure I have heard somewhere that Suarez[1] argued as follows: 'Every limitation proceeds from some cause; therefore if something is limited and finite this is because its cause was either unable or unwilling to endow it with more greatness or perfection; and hence if something derives its existence from itself, and not from some cause, it is indeed unlimited and infinite.'

I do not entirely accept this, however. For what happens if the limitation arises from the thing's internal constitutive principles, that is, from its essence or form? Remember that you have not yet proved this essence to be infinite, even though the thing derives its existence from itself, in the sense of 'not from another'. That which is hot, for example, if you suppose there to be such a thing, will be hot as opposed to cold in virtue of its internal constitutive principles, and this will be true even if you imagine that its being what it is does not depend on anything else. I am sure that M. Descartes has plenty of arguments to support a thesis that others have not perhaps defended with sufficient clarity.

At last I find myself in agreement with the author. He has laid it down as a general rule that 'everything of which I am clearly and distinctly aware is a true entity'.[2] Indeed, to go further: 'whatever I think of is true'. For from our boyhood onwards we have totally outlawed all chimeras 96 and similar 'conceptual entities'. No faculty can be diverted from its proper object. The will, if it moves at all, tends towards the good. Even the senses do not in themselves go astray: sight sees what it sees; the ears hear what they hear; and even if you see fool's gold, there is nothing wrong with your vision. The error arises from your judgement, when you decide that what you see is gold. Hence M. Descartes most properly puts all error down to the judgement and the will.

But now use this rule to make the inference you wanted. 'I am clearly and distinctly aware of an infinite being; hence this is a true entity and something real.' Yet will not someone ask '*Are* you clearly and distinctly aware of an infinite being? What, in that case, is the meaning of that well-worn maxim which is common knowledge: *the infinite qua infinite is unknown?*' When I think of a chiliagon, and construct for myself a confused representation of some figure, I do not distinctly imagine the chiliagon itself, since I do not distinctly see the thousand sides. And if this is so, then the question obviously arises as to how the infinite can be thought of in a distinct as opposed to a confused manner, given that the

1 Francisco Suarez (1548–1617). Commentator on, and critic of, Aristotle; author of the *Metaphysical Disputations*.
2 Cf. Med. III, above p. 24, and Med. V, above p. 45.

infinite perfections that make it up cannot be seen clearly 'before the eyes' as it were.

This is perhaps what St Thomas meant when he denied that the proposition 'God exists' is self-evident.[1] He considers an objection to this put by Damascene: 'The knowledge of the existence of God is naturally implanted in all men; hence the existence of God is self-evident.' His reply is that the knowledge that God exists is naturally implanted in us only in a general sense, or 'in a confused manner', as he puts it, that is, in so far as God is the ultimate felicity of man. But this, he says, is not straightforward knowledge of the existence of God, just as to know that someone is coming is not the same as to know Peter, even though it is Peter who is coming. He is in effect saying that God is known under some general conception, as an ultimate end or as the first and most perfect being, or even under the concept of that which includes all things in a confused and general manner; but he is not known in terms of the precise concept of his own proper essence, for in essence God is infinite and so unknown to us. I know that M. Descartes will have a ready answer to this line of questioning. Yet I trust that these objections, which I am putting forward purely for discussion, will remind him of the dictum of Boethius: 'There are certain common conceptions of the mind which are self-evident only to the wise.'[2] Hence, it should be no surprise if those who desire to increase their wisdom ask many questions and spend rather a long time on these topics. For they know that these matters have been laid down as the fundamental basis of the whole subject; and if they are to understand them, intensive scrutiny is required.

Let us then concede that someone does possess a clear and distinct idea of a supreme and utterly perfect being. What is the next step you will take from here? You will say that this infinite being exists, and that his existence is so certain that 'I ought to regard the existence of God as having at least the same level of certainty as I have hitherto attributed to the truths of mathematics. Hence it is just as much of a contradiction to think of God (that is, a supremely perfect being) lacking existence (that is, lacking a perfection), as it is to think of a mountain without a valley.'[3] This is the lynchpin of the whole structure; to give in on this point is to be obliged to admit defeat. But since I am taking on an opponent whose strength is greater than my own, I should like to have a preliminary skirmish with him, so that, although I am sure to be beaten in the end, I may at least put off the inevitable for a while.

I know we are basing our argument on reason alone and not on appeals to authority. But to avoid giving the impression that I am wilfully

---

1 *Summa Theologiae*, Pars I, Q. 2, art. 1.   2 Quoted by Aquinas, *loc. cit.*
3 Med. v, above pp. 45f.

taking issue with such an outstanding thinker as M. Descartes, let me nevertheless begin by asking you to listen to what St Thomas says. He raises the following objection to his own position:

As soon as we understand the meaning of the word 'God', we immediately grasp that God exists. For the word 'God' means 'that than which nothing greater can be conceived'. Now that which exists in reality as well as in the intellect is greater than that which exists in the intellect alone. Hence, since God immediately exists in the intellect as soon as we have understood the word 'God', it follows that he also exists in reality.[1]

This argument may be set out formally as follows. 'God is that than which nothing greater can be conceived. But that than which nothing greater can be conceived includes existence. Hence God, in virtue of the very word or concept of "God", contains existence; and hence he cannot lack, or be conceived of as lacking, existence.' But now please tell me if this is not the selfsame argument as that produced by M. Descartes? St Thomas defines God as 'that than which nothing greater can be conceived'. M. Descartes calls him 'a supremely perfect being'; but of course nothing greater than this can be conceived. St Thomas's next step is to say 'that than which nothing greater can be conceived includes existence', for otherwise something greater could be conceived, namely a being conceived of as also including existence. Yet surely M. Descartes' next step is identical to this. God, he says, is a supremely perfect being; and a supremely perfect being includes existence, for otherwise it would not be a supremely perfect being. St Thomas's conclusion is that 'since God immediately exists in the intellect as soon as we have understood the word "God", it follows that he also exists in reality'. In other words, since the very concept or essence of 'a being than which nothing greater can be conceived' implies existence, it follows that this very being exists. M. Descartes' conclusion is the same: 'From the very fact that I cannot think of God except as existing, it follows that existence is inseparable from God and hence that he really exists.'[2] But now let St Thomas reply both to himself and to M. Descartes. 'Let it be granted', he says,

that we all understand that the word 'God' means what it is claimed to mean, namely 'that than which nothing greater can be thought of'. However, it does not follow that we all understand that what is signified by this word exists in the real world. All that follows is that it exists in the apprehension of the intellect. Nor can it be shown that this being really exists unless it is conceded that there really

99

1 *Loc. cit.* In the passage cited Aquinas is in fact criticizing St Anselm's version of the ontological argument.
2 Above p. 46.

is something such that nothing greater can be thought of; and this premiss is denied by those who maintain that God does not exist.

My own answer to M. Descartes, which is based on this passage, is briefly this. Even if it is granted that a supremely perfect being carries the implication of existence in virtue of its very title, it still does not follow that the existence in question is anything actual in the real world; all that follows is that the concept of existence is inseparably linked to the concept of a supreme being. So you cannot infer that the existence of God is anything actual unless you suppose that the supreme being actually exists; for then it will actually contain all perfections, including the perfection of real existence.

Pardon me, gentlemen: I am now rather tired and propose to have a little fun. The complex 'existing lion' includes both 'lion' and 'existence', and it includes them essentially, for if you take away either element it will not be the same complex. But now, has not God had clear and distinct knowledge of this composite from all eternity? And does not the idea of this composite, as a composite, involve both elements essentially? In other words, does not existence belong to the essence of the composite 'existing lion'? Nevertheless the distinct knowledge of God, the distinct knowledge he has from eternity, does not compel either element in the composite to exist, unless we assume that the composite itself exists (in which case it will contain all its essential perfections including actual existence). Similarly even if I have distinct knowledge of a supreme being, and even if the supremely perfect being includes existence as an essential part of the concept, it still does not follow that the existence in question is anything actual, unless we suppose that the supreme being exists (for in that case it will include actual existence along with all its other perfections). Accordingly we must look elsewhere for a proof that the supremely perfect being exists.

With regard to the essence of the soul and its distinction from the body, I have only a little to say. For I confess that our highly gifted author has already so exhausted me that I can hardly add one word more. His proof of the supposed distinction between the soul and the body appears to be based on the fact that the two can be distinctly conceived apart from each other. Here I refer the learned gentleman to Scotus, who says that for one object to be distinctly conceived apart from another, there need only be what he calls a *formal and objective* distinction between them (such a distinction is, he maintains, intermediate between a *real* distinction and a *conceptual* distinction). The distinction between God's justice and his mercy is of this kind. For, says Scotus, 'The formal concepts of the two are distinct prior to any operation of the intellect, so that one is not the same as the other. Yet it does not follow that because justice and mercy can be conceived apart from one another they can therefore exist apart.'[1]

But I see that I have gone far beyond the normal limits of a letter. These, gentlemen, are the matters which I thought needed to be raised on this subject, and I leave it to your judgement to pick out the more important points. If you take my side, then M. Descartes will easily be prevailed upon, out of friendship, not to think too badly of me for having contradicted him on a few points. But if you take his side, I shall submit and own myself beaten; indeed, I shall be only too happy to avoid a second defeat. And so I conclude with my good wishes to you both.

101

1 Duns Scotus, *Opus Oxoniense* 1. 8. 4.

AUTHOR'S REPLIES TO THE FIRST SET OF
OBJECTIONS

Gentlemen,[1]

You have indeed called up a mighty opponent to challenge me, and his intelligence and learning could well have caused me serious difficulty had he not been a good and kind theologian who preferred to befriend the cause of God, and its humble champion, rather than to mount a serious attack. But though it was extremely kind of him to pull his punches, it would not be so acceptable for me to keep up the pretence; and hence I would rather expose his carefully disguised assistance to me than answer him as if he were an adversary.

First of all he summarizes my chief argument for proving the existence of God, thus helping to fix it all the more firmly in the reader's memory. And after briefly conceding the claims which he considers to have been demonstrated with sufficient clarity, thereby adding the weight of his own authority to them, he raises the one question which gives rise to the most important difficulty, namely the question of what should be understood by the term 'idea' in this context, and of whether such an idea requires a cause of any sort.

Now I wrote that an idea is the thing which is thought of in so far as it has objective being in the intellect.[2] But to give me an opportunity of explaining these words more clearly the objector pretends to understand them in quite a different way from that in which I used them. 'Objective being in the intellect', he says, 'is simply the determination of an act of the intellect by means of an object, and this is merely an extraneous label which adds nothing to the thing itself.'[3] Notice here that he is referring to the thing itself as if it were located outside the intellect, and in this sense 'objective being in the intellect' is certainly an extraneous label; but I was speaking of the idea, which is never outside the intellect, and in this sense 'objective being' simply means being in the intellect in the way in which objects are normally there. For example, if anyone asks what happens to the sun through its being objectively in my intellect, the best answer is that nothing happens to it beyond the application of an extraneous label

102

1 For the addressees, see above p. 64.   2 Above pp. 66f; Cf. Med. III, above pp. 28f.
3 Above p. 67.

74

which does indeed 'determine an act of the intellect by means of an object'. But if the question is about what the *idea* of the sun is, and we answer that it is the thing which is thought of, in so far as it has objective being in the intellect, no one will take this to be the sun itself with this extraneous label applied to it. 'Objective being in the intellect' will not here mean 'the determination of an act of the intellect by means of an object', but will signify the object's being in the intellect in the way in which its objects are normally there. By this I mean that the idea of the sun is the sun itself existing in the intellect – not of course formally existing, as it does in the heavens, but objectively existing, i.e. in the way in which objects normally are in the intellect. Now this mode of being is of course much less perfect than that possessed by things which exist outside the intellect; but, as I did explain, it is not therefore simply nothing.[1]

When the learned theologian says that there is an equivocation in what I say here,[2] he apparently means to remind me of the point I have just made, in case I should forget it. He says, first of all, that when a thing exists in the intellect by means of an idea, it is not an actual entity, that is, it is not a being located outside the intellect; and this is quite true. Next he goes on to say that 'it is not something fictitious or a conceptual entity but something real which is distinctly conceived'; here he concedes everything which I have assumed. But he then adds 'since it is merely conceived and is not actual' – i.e. since it is merely an idea, and not a thing located outside the intellect – 'although it can be conceived it cannot in any way be caused'. This is to say that it does not require a cause enabling it to exist outside the intellect. This I accept; but it surely needs a cause enabling it to be conceived, which is the sole point at issue. Thus if someone possesses in his intellect the idea of a machine of a highly intricate design, it is perfectly fair to ask what is the cause of this idea. And it will not be an adequate reply to say that the idea is not anything outside the intellect and hence that it cannot be caused but can merely be conceived. For the precise question being raised is what is the cause of its being conceived. Nor will it suffice to say that the intellect itself is the cause of the idea, in so far as it is the cause of its own operations; for what is at issue is not this, but the cause of the objective intricacy which is in the idea. For in order for the idea of the machine to contain such and such objective intricacy, it must derive it from some cause; and what applies to the objective intricacy belonging to this idea also applies to the objective reality belonging to the idea of God. Now admittedly there could be various causes of the intricacy contained in the idea of the machine. Perhaps the cause was a real machine of this design

1 Med. III, above p. 29.   2 Above p. 67.

which was seen on some previous occasion, thus producing an idea resembling the original. Or the cause might be an extensive knowledge of mechanics in the intellect of the person concerned, or perhaps a very subtle intelligence which enabled him to invent the idea without any previous knowledge. But notice that all the intricacy which is to be found merely objectively in the idea must necessarily be found, either formally or eminently,[1] in its cause, whatever this turns out to be. And the same must apply to the objective reality in the idea of God. Yet where can the corresponding reality be found, if not in a really existing God? But my shrewd critic sees all this quite well, and he therefore concedes that we can ask why a given idea contains such and such objective reality. His answer is that, in the case of all ideas, what I wrote in connection with the idea of a triangle holds good, namely that 'even if perhaps a triangle does not exist anywhere, it still has a determinate nature or essence or form which is immutable and eternal'. And this, he says, does not require a cause. But he is well aware that this is not an adequate reply; for even if the nature of the triangle is immutable and eternal, it is still no less appropriate to ask why there is an idea of it within us. Hence he adds 'If you insist on having an explanation, the answer lies in the imperfection of our intellect', etc.[2] In making this reply he simply means, I think, that those who have tried to take a different view from mine on this issue have 105 no plausible reply to make. For surely to claim that the imperfection of our intellect is the cause of our having the idea of God is as implausible as claiming that lack of experience in mechanics is the cause of our imagining some very intricate machine as opposed to a more imperfect one. On the contrary, if someone possesses the idea of a machine, and contained in the idea is every imaginable intricacy of design, then the correct inference is plainly that this idea originally came from some cause in which every imaginable intricacy really did exist, even though the intricacy now has only objective existence in the idea. By the same token, since we have within us the idea of God, and contained in the idea is every perfection that can be thought of, the absolutely evident inference is that this idea depends on some cause in which all this perfection is indeed to be found, namely a really existing God. The latter inference would not present any more problems than the former, were it not the case that we all have the same ability to conceive of the idea of God, whereas everyone is not equally experienced in mechanics, and so not everyone can have an idea of a very intricate machine. Because the idea of God is implanted in the same way in the minds of all, we do not notice it coming into our minds from any external source, and so we suppose it belongs to the nature of our own intellect. This is correct enough, but we

1 See above p. 28, note 2.　　2 Above p. 67.

forget something else which is a most important consideration – indeed one on which the entire luminous power of the argument depends – namely that this ability to have within us the idea of God could not belong to our intellect if the intellect were simply a finite entity (as indeed it is) and did not have God as its cause. Hence I went on to inquire 'whether I could exist if God did not exist'.[1] But my purpose here was not to produce a different proof from the preceding one, but rather to take the same proof and provide a more thorough explanation of it.

At this point my critic has, through his excessive desire to be kind to me, put me in an unfortunate position. For in comparing my argument with one taken from St Thomas and Aristotle, he seems to be demanding an explanation for the fact that, after starting on the same road as they do, I have not kept to it in all respects. However, I hope he will allow me to avoid commenting on what others have said, and simply give an account of what I have written myself.

Firstly, then, I did not base my argument on the fact that I observed there to be an order or succession of efficient causes among the objects perceived by the senses. For one thing, I regarded the existence of God as much more evident than the existence of anything that can be perceived by the senses; and for another thing, I did not think that such a succession of causes could lead me anywhere except to a recognition of the imperfection of my intellect, since an infinite chain of such successive causes from eternity without any first cause is beyond my grasp. And my inability to grasp it certainly does not entail that there must be a first cause, any more than my inability to grasp the infinite number of divisions in a finite quantity entails that there is an ultimate division beyond which any further division is impossible. All that follows is that my intellect, which is finite, does not encompass the infinite. Hence I preferred to use my own existence as the basis of my argument, since it does not depend on any chain of causes and is better known to me than anything else could possibly be. And the question I asked concerning myself was not what was the cause that originally produced me, but what is the cause that preserves me at present. In this way I aimed to escape the whole issue of the succession of causes.

Next, in inquiring about what caused me, I was asking about myself, not in so far as I consist of mind and body, but only and precisely in so far as I am a thinking thing. This point is, I think, of considerable relevance. For such a procedure made it much easier for me to free myself from my preconceived opinions, to attend to the light of nature, to ask myself questions, and to affirm with certainty that there can be nothing within me of which I am not in some way aware. This is plainly a quite

1 Above pp. 32ff.

different approach from observing that my father begot me, inferring that my grandfather begot my father, and in view of the impossibility of going on *ad infinitum* in the search for parents of parents, bringing the inquiry to a close by deciding that there is a first cause.

Moreover, in inquiring about what caused me I was not simply asking about myself as a thinking thing; principally and most importantly I was asking about myself in so far as I observe, amongst my other thoughts, that there is within me the idea of a supremely perfect being. The whole force of my proof depends on this one fact. For, firstly, this idea contains the essence of God, at least in so far as I am capable of understanding it; and according to the laws of true logic, we must never ask about the existence of anything until we first understand its essence.[1] Secondly, it is this idea which provides me with the opportunity of inquiring whether I derive my existence from myself, or from another, and of recognizing my defects. And, lastly, it is this same idea which shows me not just that I have a cause, but that this cause contains every perfection, and hence that it is God.

Finally, I did not say that it was impossible for something to be the efficient cause of itself. This is obviously the case when the term 'efficient' is taken to apply only to causes which are prior in time to their effects, or different from them. But such a restriction does not seem appropriate in the present context. First, it would make the question trivial, since everyone knows that something cannot be prior to, or distinct from, itself. Secondly, the natural light does not establish that the concept of an efficient cause requires that it be prior in time to its effect. On the contrary, the concept of a cause is, strictly speaking, applicable only for as long as the cause is producing its effect, and so it is not prior to it. However, the light of nature does establish that if anything exists we may always ask why it exists; that is, we may inquire into its efficient cause, or, if it does not have one, we may demand why it does not need one. Hence, if I thought that nothing could possibly have the same relation to itself as an efficient cause has to its effect, I should certainly not conclude that there was a first cause. On the contrary, I should go on to ask for the cause of the so-called 'first' cause, and thus I would never reach anything which was the first cause of everything else. However, I do readily admit that there can exist something which possesses such great and inexhaustible power that it never required the assistance of anything else in order to exist in the first place, and does not now require any assistance for its preservation, so that it is, in a sense, its own cause; and I understand God to be such a being. Now I regard the divisions of time as being separable from each other, so that the fact that I now exist does not imply that I

1 Literally: 'we must never ask *if* it is (*an est*) until we first understand *what* it is (*quid est*)'.

shall continue to exist in a little while unless there is a cause which, as it were, creates me afresh at each moment of time. Hence, even if I had existed from eternity, and thus nothing had existed prior to myself, I should have no hesitation in calling the cause which preserves me an 'efficient' cause. By the same token, although God has always existed, since it is he who in fact preserves himself, it seems not too inappropriate to call him 'the cause of himself'. It should however be noted that 'preservation' here must not be understood to be the kind of preservation that comes about by the positive influence of an efficient cause; all that is implied is that the essence of God is such that he must always exist.

These considerations make it easy for me to answer the point about the ambiguity in the phrase 'from itself' which, as the learned theologian has reminded me, needs to be explained. There are some who attend only to the literal and strict meaning of the phrase 'efficient cause' and thus think it is impossible for anything to be the cause of itself. They do not see that there is any place for another kind of cause analogous to an efficient cause, and hence when they say that something derives its existence 'from itself' they normally mean simply that it has no cause. But if they would look at the facts rather than the words, they would readily observe that the negative sense of the phrase 'from itself' comes merely from the imperfection of the human intellect and has no basis in reality. But there is a positive sense of the phrase which is derived from the true nature of things, and it is this sense alone which is employed in my argument. For example, if we think that a given body derives its existence from itself, we may simply mean that it has no cause; but our claim here is not based on any positive reason, but merely arises in a negative way from our ignorance of any cause. Yet this is a kind of imperfection in us, as we will easily see if we consider the following. The separate divisions of time do not depend on each other; hence the fact that the body in question is supposed to have existed up till now 'from itself', that is, without a cause, is not sufficient to make it continue to exist in future, unless there is some power in it that as it were recreates it continuously. But when we see that no such power is to be found in the idea of a body, and immediately conclude that the body does not derive its existence from itself, we shall then be taking the phrase 'from itself' in the positive sense. Similarly, when we say that God derives his existence 'from himself', we can understand the phrase in the negative sense, in which case the meaning will simply be that he has no cause. But if we have previously inquired into the cause of God's existing or continuing to exist, and we attend to the immense and incomprehensible power that is contained within the idea of God, then we will have recognized that this power is so exceedingly great that it is plainly the cause of his continuing existence, and nothing but this can be the cause. And if we say as a result that God derives his existence from himself, we will not be using the phrase in its negative sense but in an absolutely positive sense. There is no need to say that God is the efficient cause of himself, for this might give rise to a verbal dispute. But the fact that God derives his existence from himself, or has no cause apart from himself, depends not on nothing but on the real immensity of his power; hence, when we perceive this, we are quite entitled to think that in a sense he stands in the same relation to himself as an efficient cause does to its effect, and hence that he derives his existence from himself in the positive sense. And each one of us may ask himself whether he derives his existence from himself in this same sense. Since he will find no power within himself which suffices to preserve him even for one moment of time, he will be right to conclude that he derives his existence from another being, and indeed that this other being derives its existence from itself (there is no possibility of an infinite regress here, since the question concerns the present, not the past or the future). Indeed, I will now add something which I have not put down in writing before, namely that the cause we arrive at cannot merely be a secondary cause; for a cause which possesses such great power that it can preserve something situated outside itself must, *a fortiori*, preserve itself by its own power, and hence derive its existence from itself.

As for the dictum 'Every limitation proceeds from some cause',[1] I think that what is meant here is something true, but that it is inappropriately expressed, and that the underlying difficulty is not solved. Strictly speaking, a limitation is merely a negation or denial of any further perfection, and such a negation does not proceed from a cause, though the thing itself which is so limited does. But even if it is true that everything which is limited proceeds from a cause, this is not self-evident and needs to be proved from other premisses. For, as the subtle theologian points out, a thing can be regarded as limited in various ways; for example, it can be limited because this is part of its nature, just as it belongs to the nature of a triangle that it consists of no more than three lines. What does seem to me self-evident is that whatever exists either derives its existence from a cause or derives its existence from itself as from a cause. For since we understand not only what is meant by existence but also what is meant by its negation, it is impossible for us to imagine anything deriving existence from itself without there being some reason why it should exist rather than not exist. So in such a case we are bound to interpret 'from itself' in a causal sense, because of the superabundance of power involved – a superabundance which, as is very easily demonstrated, can exist in God alone.

1 Above p. 69.

My opponent goes on to grant me a principle[1] which, though it does not admit of any doubt, commonly receives very little attention. But so great is its importance for rescuing the whole of philosophy from darkness that, by adding the weight of his authority to it, he has greatly helped me in my enterprise.

At this point, however, he shrewdly asks whether I am 'clearly and distinctly aware of the infinite'.[2] I did try to anticipate this objection, but it is one which occurs so spontaneously to everyone that it is worthwhile replying to it at some length. So let me say first of all that the infinite, *qua* infinite, can in no way be grasped. But it can still be understood,[3] in so far as we can clearly and distinctly understand that something is such that no limitations can be found in it, and this amounts to understanding clearly that it is infinite.

Now I make a distinction here between the *indefinite* and the *infinite*. I   113 apply the term 'infinite', in the strict sense, only to that in which no limits of any kind can be found; and in this sense God alone is infinite. But in cases like the extension of imaginary space, or the set of numbers, or the divisibility of the parts of a quantity, there is merely some respect in which I do not recognize a limit; so here I use the term 'indefinite' rather than 'infinite', because these items are not limitless in every respect.

Moreover, I distinguish between the formal concept of the infinite, or 'infinity', and the thing which is infinite. In the case of infinity, even if we understand it to be positive in the highest degree, nevertheless our way of understanding it is negative, because it depends on our not noticing any limitation in the thing. But in the case of the thing itself which is infinite, although our understanding is positive, it is not adequate, that is to say, we do not have a complete grasp of everything in it that is capable of being understood. When we look at the sea, our vision does not encompass its entirety, nor do we measure out its enormous vastness; but we are still said to 'see' it. In fact if we look from a distance so that our vision almost covers the entire sea at one time, we see it only in a confused manner, just as we have a confused picture of a chiliagon when we take in all its sides at once. But if we fix our gaze on some part of the sea at close quarters, then our view can be clear and distinct, just as our picture of a chiliagon can be, if it is confined to one or two of the sides. In the same way, God cannot be taken in by the human mind, and I admit   114 this, along with all theologians. Moreover, God cannot be distinctly known by those who look from a distance as it were, and try to make their minds encompass his entirety all at once. This is the sense in which

1 'Everything of which I am clearly and distinctly aware is a true entity'; above p. 69.
2 *Ibid.*
3 See footnote 1, above p. 32.

St Thomas says, in the passage quoted, that the knowledge of God is within us 'in a somewhat confused manner'.[1] But those who try to attend to God's individual perfections and try not so much to take hold of them as to surrender to them, using all the strength of their intellect to contemplate them, will certainly find that God provides much more ample and straightforward subject-matter for clear and distinct knowledge than does any created thing.

St Thomas did not deny this in the passage quoted, as is clear from the fact that in the following article he insists that the existence of God is demonstrable.[2] But when I said that God can be clearly and distinctly known, I was referring merely to knowledge of the finite kind just described, which corresponds to the small capacity of our minds. Indeed there was no need to construe it in any other way in order to establish the truth of the claims I made, as will be readily apparent if one recalls that I made the statement about clear and distinct knowledge of God in only two places. The first was where the question arose as to whether the idea which we form of God contains something real or only the negation of the real (as, for example, the idea of cold contains no more than the negation of heat) – a point on which there can be no doubt.[3] And the second place was where I asserted that existence belongs to the concept of a supremely perfect being just as much as three sides belong to the concept of a triangle;[4] and this point can be understood without adequate knowledge of God.

The author of the objections here again compares one of my arguments with one of St Thomas',[5] thus as it were forcing me to explain how one argument can have any greater force than the other. I think I can do this without too much unpleasantness. For, first, St Thomas did not use the argument which he then puts forward as an objection to his own position conclusion as I do; and lastly, on this issue I do not differ from the Angelic Doctor in any respect. St Thomas asks whether the existence of God is self-evident as far as we are concerned, that is, whether it is obvious to everyone; and he answers, correctly, that it is not. The argument which he then puts forward as an objection to his own position can be stated as follows. 'Once we have understood the meaning of the word "God", we understand it to mean "that than which nothing greater can be conceived". But to exist in reality as well as in the intellect is greater than to exist in the intellect alone. Therefore, once we have understood the meaning of the word "God" we understand that God exists in reality as well as in the understanding.' In this form the argument is manifestly invalid, for the only conclusion that should have

1 Above p. 70. 2 *Summa Theologiae*, Pars 1, Q. 2, art. 2. 3 Med. III, above p. 31
4 Med. v, above p. 45. 5 Above pp. 71ff.

been drawn is: 'Therefore, once we have understood the meaning of the word "God" we understand that what is conveyed is that God exists in reality as well as in the understanding.' Yet because a word conveys something, that thing is not therefore shown to be true. My argument however was as follows: 'That which we clearly and distinctly understand to belong to the true and immutable nature, or essence, or form of something, can truly be asserted of that thing. But once we have made a 116 sufficiently careful investigation of what God is, we clearly and distinctly understand that existence belongs to his true and immutable nature. Hence we can now truly assert of God that he does exist.' Here at least the conclusion does follow from the premisses. But, what is more, the major premiss cannot be denied, because it has already been conceded that whatever we clearly and distinctly understand is true. Hence only the minor premiss remains, and here I confess that there is considerable difficulty. In the first place we are so accustomed to distinguishing existence from essence in the case of all other things that we fail to notice how closely existence belongs to essence in the case of God as compared with that of other things. Next, we do not distinguish what belongs to the true and immutable essence of a thing from what is attributed to it merely by a fiction of the intellect. So, even if we observe clearly enough that existence belongs to the essence of God, we do not draw the conclusion that God exists, because we do not know whether his essence is immutable and true, or merely invented by us.

But to remove the first part of the difficulty we must distinguish between possible and necessary existence. It must be noted that possible existence is contained in the concept or idea of everything that we clearly and distinctly understand; but in no case is necessary existence so contained, except in the case of the idea of God. Those who carefully attend to this difference between the idea of God and every other idea will undoubtedly perceive that even though our understanding of other 117 things always involves understanding them as if they were existing things, it does not follow that they do exist, but merely that they are capable of existing. For our understanding does not show us that it is necessary for actual existence to be conjoined with their other properties. But, from the fact that we understand that actual existence is necessarily and always conjoined with the other attributes of God, it certainly does follow that God exists.

To remove the second part of the difficulty, we must notice a point about ideas which do not contain true and immutable natures but merely ones which are invented and put together by the intellect. Such ideas can always be split up by the same intellect, not simply by an abstraction but by a clear and distinct intellectual operation, so that any ideas which the intellect cannot split up in this way were clearly not put together by the intellect. When, for example, I think of a winged horse or an actually existing lion, or a triangle inscribed in a square, I readily understand that I am also able to think of a horse without wings, or a lion which does not exist, or a triangle apart from a square, and so on; hence these things do not have true and immutable natures. But if I think of a triangle or a square (I will not now include the lion or the horse, since their natures are not transparently clear to us), then whatever I apprehend as being contained in the idea of a triangle – for example that its three angles are equal to two right angles – I can with truth assert of the triangle. And the same applies to the square with respect to whatever I apprehend as being contained in the idea of a square. For even if I can understand what a triangle is if I abstract the fact that its three angles are equal to two right angles, I cannot deny that this property applies to the

118 triangle by a clear and distinct intellectual operation – that is, while at the same time understanding what I mean by my denial. Moreover, if I consider a triangle inscribed in a square, with a view not to attributing to the square properties that belong only to the triangle, or attributing to the triangle properties that belong to the square, but with a view to examining only the properties which arise out of the conjunction of the two, then the nature of this composite will be just as true and immutable as the nature of the triangle alone or the square alone. And hence it will be quite in order to maintain that the square is not less than double the area of the triangle inscribed within it, and to affirm other similar properties that belong to the nature of this composite figure.

But if I were to think that the idea of a supremely perfect body contained existence, on the grounds that it is a greater perfection to exist both in reality and in the intellect than it is to exist in the intellect alone, I could not infer from this that the supremely perfect body exists, but only that it is capable of existing. For I can see quite well that this idea has been put together by my own intellect which has linked together all bodily perfections; and existence does not arise out of the other bodily perfections because it can equally well be affirmed or denied of them. Indeed, when I examine the idea of a body, I perceive that a body has no power to create itself or maintain itself in existence; and I rightly conclude that necessary existence – and it is only necessary existence that is at issue here – no more belongs to the nature of a body, however perfect, than it belongs to the nature of a mountain to be without a valley, or to the nature of a triangle to have angles whose sum is greater than two right angles. But instead of a body, let us now take a thing –

119 whatever this thing turns out to be – which possesses all the perfections which can exist together. If we ask whether existence should be included

among these perfections, we will admittedly be in some doubt at first. For our mind, which is finite, normally thinks of these perfections only separately, and hence may not immediately notice the necessity of their being joined together. Yet if we attentively examine whether existence belongs to a supremely powerful being, and what sort of existence it is, we shall be able to perceive clearly and distinctly the following facts. First, possible existence, at the very least, belongs to such a being, just as it belongs to all the other things of which we have a distinct idea, even to those which are put together through a fiction of the intellect. Next, when we attend to the immense power of this being, we shall be unable to think of its existence as possible without also recognizing that it can exist by its own power; and we shall infer from this that this being does really exist and has existed from eternity, since it is quite evident by the natural light that what can exist by its own power always exists. So we shall come to understand that necessary existence is contained in the idea of a supremely powerful being, not by any fiction of the intellect, but because it belongs to the true and immutable nature of such a being that it exists. And we shall also easily perceive that this supremely powerful being cannot but possess within it all the other perfections that are contained in the idea of God; and hence these perfections exist in God and are joined together not by any fiction of the intellect but by their very nature.

All this is manifest if we give the matter our careful attention; and it 120 does not differ from anything I have written before, except for the method of explanation adopted. This I have deliberately altered so as to appeal to a variety of different minds. But as I readily admit, it is the kind of argument which may easily be regarded as a sophism by those who do not keep in mind all the elements which make up the proof. For this reason I did have considerable doubts to begin with about whether I should use it; for I feared it might induce those who did not grasp it to have doubts about the rest of my reasoning. But there are only two ways of proving the existence of God, one by means of his effects, and the other by means of his nature or essence; and since I expounded the first method to the best of my ability in the Third Meditation, I thought that I should include the second method later on.

As to the 'formal' distinction which the learned theologian introduces on the authority of Scotus,[1] let me say briefly that this kind of distinction does not differ from a modal distinction;[2] moreover, it applies only to incomplete entities, which I have carefully distinguished from complete entities. It is sufficient for this kind of distinction that one thing be

1 Above p. 72.
2 For a more precise account of the types of distinction discussed here see *Principles*, Part I, art. 60–2: vol. I, pp. 213ff.

conceived distinctly and separately from another by an abstraction of the intellect which conceives the thing inadequately. It is not necessary to have such a distinct and separate conception of each thing that we can understand it as an entity in its own right, different from everything else; for this to be the case the distinction involved must be a real one. For example, the distinction between the motion and shape of a given body is a formal distinction. I can very well understand the motion apart from the shape, and vice versa, and I can understand either in abstraction from the body. But I cannot have a complete understanding of the motion apart from the thing in which motion occurs, or of the shape apart from the thing which has the shape; and I cannot imagine there to be motion in something which is incapable of possessing shape, or shape in something which is incapable of motion. In the same way, I cannot understand justice apart from the person who is just, or mercy apart from the person who is merciful; and I am not at liberty to imagine that the same person who is just is incapable of mercy. By contrast, I have a complete understanding of what a body is when I think that it is merely something having extension, shape and motion, and I deny that it has anything which belongs to the nature of a mind. Conversely, I understand the mind to be a complete thing, which doubts, understands, wills, and so on, even though I deny that it has any of the attributes which are contained in the idea of a body. This would be quite impossible if there were not a real distinction between the mind and the body.

These, gentlemen, are the points which I thought needed to be made in reply to your friend's very kind and extremely intelligent comments. If what I have said is inadequate, I ask your friend to let me know of any omissions or mistakes; and if you can prevail on him to do this for me, I shall regard it as a great service.

SECOND SET OF OBJECTIONS[1]

Sir,

The task of defending the Author of all things against a new race of giants,[2] and of demonstrating his existence, is one which you have undertaken with such great success that from now on men of good will can hope that no one who carefully reads your *Meditations* will fail to acknowledge the existence of an eternal power on whom every single thing depends. We therefore wanted to draw your attention to various passages, which are indicated below, and ask you to clarify them, so that, as far as possible, there may be nothing left in your work which is not clearly demonstrated. You have trained your mind by continual meditations for several years, so that what seems doubtful and very obscure to others is quite clear to you; indeed, you may have a clear mental intuition of these matters and perceive them as the primary and principal objects of the natural light. We are simply pointing out the issues on which it seems worthwhile to burden you with the task of providing a clearer and more extended explanation and demonstration. You have embarked on your arguments for the greater glory of God and the immense benefit of mankind and, once you have done what we ask, there will scarcely be anyone left who can deny that they do indeed have the force of demonstrations.

First, then, may we remind you that your vigorous rejection of the images of all bodies as delusive was not something you actually and really carried through, but was merely a fiction of the mind, enabling you to draw the conclusion that you were exclusively a thinking thing. We point this out in case you should perhaps suppose that it is possible to go on to draw the conclusion that you are in fact nothing more than a mind, or thought, or a thinking thing. And we make the point solely in connection with the first two Meditations, in which you clearly show that, if nothing else, it is certain that you, who are thinking, exist. But let us pause a little here. The position so far is that you recognize that you are a thinking thing, but you do not know what this

---

1 Compiled by Mersenne. See Translator's preface, above p. 64.
2 In Greek mythology the Giants rebelled against the Gods.

thinking thing is. What if it turned out to be a body which, by its various motions and encounters, produces what we call thought? Although you think you have ruled out every kind of body, you could have been mistaken here, since you did not exclude yourself, and you may be a
123 body. How do you demonstrate that a body is incapable of thinking, or that corporeal motions are not in fact thought? The whole system of your body, which you think you have excluded, or else some of its parts – for example those which make up the brain – may combine to produce the motions which we call thoughts. You say 'I am a thinking thing'; but how do you know that you are not corporeal motion, or a body which is in motion?

Secondly, from the idea of a supreme being, which you maintain is quite incapable of originating from you, you venture to infer that there must necessarily exist a supreme being who alone can be the origin of this idea which appears in your mind.[1] However, we can find simply within ourselves a sufficient basis for our ability to form the said idea, even supposing that the supreme being did not exist, or that we did not know that he exists and never thought about his existing. For surely I can see that, in so far as I think, I have some degree of perfection, and hence that others besides myself have a similar degree of perfection. And this gives me the basis for thinking of an indefinite number of degrees and thus positing higher and higher degrees of perfection up to infinity. Even if there were just one degree of heat or light, I could always imagine further degrees and continue the process of addition up to infinity. In the same way, I can surely take a given degree of being, which I perceive within myself, and add on a further degree, and thus construct the idea of a perfect being from all the degrees which are capable of being added on. You say, however, that an effect cannot possess any degree of reality or perfection that was not previously present in the cause. But we see that flies and other animals, and also plants, are produced from sun and rain and earth, which lack life. Now life is something nobler than any merely corporeal grade of being; and hence it does happen that an effect may derive from its cause some reality which is nevertheless not present in the
124 cause. But leaving this aside, the idea of a perfect being is nothing more than a conceptual entity, which has no more nobility than your own mind which is thinking. Moreover, if you had not grown up among educated people, but had spent your entire life alone in some deserted spot, how do you know that the idea would have come to you? You derived this idea from earlier preconceptions, or from books or from discussion with friends and so on, and not simply from your mind or from an existing supreme being. So a clearer proof needs to be provided

1 Cf. Med. III, above pp. 28–31.

that this idea could not be present within you if a supreme being did not exist; and when you have provided it, we shall all surrender. However, the fact that the natives of Canada, the Hurons and other primitive peoples, have no awareness of any idea of this sort seems to establish that the idea does come from previously held notions. It is even possible for you to form the idea from a previous examination of corporeal things, so that your idea would refer to nothing but this corporeal world, which includes every kind of perfection that can be thought of by you. In that case you could not infer the existence of anything beyond an utterly perfect corporeal being, unless you were to add something further which lifts us up to an incorporeal or spiritual plane. We may add that you can form the idea of an angel just as you can form the idea of a supremely perfect being; but this idea is not produced in you by an angel, although the angel is more perfect than you. But in fact you do not have the idea of God, just as you do not have the idea of an infinite number or an infinite line (even if you may have the idea, the number is still impossible). Moreover, the idea of the unity and simplicity of one perfection that includes all others arises merely from an operation of the reasoning intellect, in the same way as those universal unities which do not exist in reality but merely in the intellect (as can be seen in the case of generic unity, transcendental unity, and so on).

Thirdly, you are not yet certain of the existence of God, and you say that you are not certain of anything, and cannot know anything clearly and distinctly until you have achieved clear and certain knowledge of the existence of God.[1] It follows from this that you do not yet clearly and distinctly know that you are a thinking thing, since, on your own admission, that knowledge depends on the clear knowledge of an existing God; and this you have not yet proved in the passage where you draw the conclusion that you clearly know what you are.

Moreover, an atheist is clearly and distinctly aware that the three angles of a triangle are equal to two right angles; but so far is he from supposing the existence of God that he completely denies it. According to the atheist, if God existed there would be a supreme being and a supreme good; that is to say, the infinite would exist. But the infinite in every category of perfection excludes everything else whatsoever – every kind of being and goodness, as well as every kind of non-being and evil. Yet in fact there are many kinds of being and goodness, and many kinds of non-being and evil. We think you should deal with this objection, so that the impious have no arguments left to put forward.

Fourthly, you say that God cannot lie or deceive. Yet there are some

1 Cf. Med. III, above p. 25; Med. v, above p. 48.

schoolmen who say he can. Gabriel, for example, and Ariminensis,[1] among others, think that in the absolute sense God does lie, that is, communicate to men things which are opposed to his intentions and decrees. Thus he unconditionally said to the people of Nineveh, through the prophet, 'Yet forty days and Nineveh shall be destroyed.' And he said many other things which certainly did not occur, because he did not mean his words to correspond to his intentions or decrees. Now if God hardened Pharaoh's heart and blinded his eyes, and if he sent upon his prophets the spirit of untruthfulness, how do you conclude that we cannot be deceived by him? Cannot God treat men as a doctor treats the sick, or a father his children? In both these cases there is frequent deception though it is always employed beneficially and with wisdom. For if God were to show us the pure truth, what eye, what mental vision, could endure it?

It is not, however, necessary to suppose that God is a deceiver in order to explain your being deceived about matters which you think you clearly and distinctly know. The cause of this deception could lie in you, though you are wholly unaware of it. Why should it not be in your nature to be subject to constant – or at least very frequent – deception? How can you establish with certainty that you are not deceived, or capable of being deceived, in matters which you think you know clearly and distinctly? Have we not often seen people turn out to have been deceived in matters where they thought their knowledge was as clear as the sunlight? Your principle of clear and distinct knowledge thus requires a clear and distinct explanation, in such a way as to rule out the possibility that anyone of sound mind may be deceived on matters which he thinks he knows clearly and distinctly. Failing this, we do not see that any degree of certainty can possibly be within your reach or that of mankind in general.

Fifthly, if the will never goes astray or falls into sin so long as it is guided by the mind's clear and distinct knowledge, and if it exposes itself to danger by following a conception of the intellect which is wholly lacking in clarity and distinctness, then note what follows from this. A Turk, or any other unbeliever, not only does not sin in refusing to embrace the Christian religion, but what is more, he sins if he does embrace it, since he does not possess clear and distinct knowledge of its truth. Indeed, if this rule of yours is true, then there is almost nothing that the will is going to be allowed to embrace, since there is almost nothing that we know with the clarity and distinctness which you require for that kind of certainty which is beyond any doubt. So you see how, in your

1 Gabriel Biel, fifteenth-century philosopher; Gregory of Rimini, fourteenth-century theologian.

desire to champion the truth, you may end up proving too much, and thus overturn the truth rather than build it up.

Sixthly, in your reply to the First Set of Objections, you appear to go astray in one of your arguments, which you put as follows: 'That which we clearly and distinctly understand to belong to the true and immutable nature . . . of a thing can be truly asserted of that thing. But once we have made a sufficiently careful investigation of what God is, we clearly and distinctly understand that existence belongs to his nature.'[1] The conclusion should have been: 'hence, once we have made a sufficiently careful investigation of what God is, we can with truth affirm that existence belongs to the nature of God'. Now it does not follow from this that God in fact exists, but merely that he would have to exist if his nature is possible, or non-contradictory. In other words, the nature or essence of God cannot be conceived apart from existence; hence, granted the essence, God really exists. This comes down to an argument which others have stated as follows: 'If there is no contradiction in God's existing, it is certain that he exists; but there is no contradiction in his existing.' The difficulty here is with the minor premiss 'but there is no contradiction in his existing': those who attack the argument either claim to doubt the truth of this premiss, or deny it outright. Moreover, the phrase in your argument 'once we have made a sufficiently clear investigation of what God is' presupposes as true something which not everyone yet accepts; indeed you yourself admit that you apprehend infinite being only in an inadequate way. And clearly the same must be said of every single attribute of God. Whatever is in God is utterly infinite; so who can for a moment apprehend any aspect of God except in what may be called an utterly inadequate manner? How then can you have 'made a sufficiently clear and distinct investigation of what God is'?

Seventhly, you say not one word about the immortality of the human mind. Yet this is something you should have taken special care to prove 128 and demonstrate, to counter those people, themselves unworthy of immortality, who utterly deny and even perhaps despise it. What is more, you do not yet appear to have provided an adequate proof of the fact that the mind is distinct from every kind of body, as we mentioned under point one. We now make the additional point that it does not seem to follow from the fact that the mind is distinct from the body that it is incorruptible or immortal. What if its nature were limited by the duration of the life of the body, and God had endowed it with just so much strength and existence as to ensure that it came to an end with the death of the body?

These, Sir, are the points which we wanted you to clarify, so as to

1 Above p. 83.

enable everyone to derive the utmost benefit from reading your *Medita-tions*, which are argued with great subtlety and are also, in our opinion, true. And after giving your solutions to these difficulties it would be worthwhile if you set out the entire argument in geometrical fashion, starting from a number of definitions, postulates and axioms. You are highly experienced in employing this method, and it would enable you to fill the mind of each reader so that he could see everything as it were at a single glance, and be permeated with awareness of the divine power.

AUTHOR'S REPLIES TO THE SECOND SET OF OBJECTIONS

Gentlemen,

I read with great pleasure the comments which you made on my little book dealing with First Philosophy. They make me appreciate both your goodwill towards me and your piety towards God and zeal to further his glory. And I cannot but be very happy, not only because you have thought my arguments worthy of examination, but also because I think I can give you a reasonably adequate reply to all the criticisms that you make.

First, you warn me to remember that my rejection of the images of bodies as delusive was not something I actually and really carried through, but was merely a fiction of the mind, enabling me to draw the conclusion that I was a thinking thing; and I should not suppose that it followed from this that I was in fact nothing more than a mind.[1] But I already showed that I was quite well aware of this in the Second Meditation, where I said 'Yet may it not perhaps be the case that these very things which I am supposing to be nothing, because they are unknown to me, are in reality identical with the "I" of which I am aware? I do not know, and for the moment I shall not argue the point.'[2] Here I wanted to give the reader an express warning that at that stage I was not yet asking whether the mind is distinct from the body, but was merely examining those of its properties of which I can have certain and evident knowledge. And since I did become aware of many such properties, I cannot without qualification admit your subsequent point that 'I do not yet know what a thinking thing is.' I admit that I did not yet know whether this thinking thing is identical with the body or with something different from the body; but I do not admit that I had no knowledge of it. Surely, no one's knowledge of anything has ever reached the point where he knows that there is absolutely nothing further in the thing beyond what he is already aware of. The more attributes of a thing we perceive the better we are said to know it; thus we know people whom we have lived with for some time better than those whom we only know by sight, or have merely heard of – though even they are not said to be completely

1 Above p. 87.   2 Above p. 18.

93

unknown to us. In this sense I think I have demonstrated that the mind, considered apart from those attributes which are normally applied to the body, is better known than the body when it is considered apart from the mind. This was my sole purpose in the passage under discussion.

But I see the suggestion you are making. Given that I wrote only six Meditations on First Philosophy, you think my readers will be surprised that the only conclusion reached in the first two Meditations is the point just mentioned; and you think that as a result they will reckon that the Meditations are extremely thin and not worth publishing. My reply is simply that I am confident that anyone who judiciously reads the rest of what I wrote will have no occasion to suspect that I was short of material. And in the case of topics which required individual attention and needed to be considered on their own, it seemed quite reasonable to deal with them separately, Meditation by Meditation.

Now the best way of achieving a firm knowledge of reality is first to accustom ourselves to doubting all things, especially corporeal things. Although I had seen many ancient writings by the Academics and Sceptics on this subject, and was reluctant to reheat and serve this precooked material, I could not avoid devoting one whole Meditation to it. And I should like my readers not just to take the short time needed to go through it, but to devote several months, or at least weeks, to considering the topics dealt with, before going on to the rest of the book. If they do this they will undoubtedly be able to derive much greater benefit from what follows.

131   All our ideas of what belongs to the mind have up till now been very confused and mixed up with the ideas of things that can be perceived by the senses. This is the first and most important reason for our inability to understand with sufficient clarity the customary assertions about the soul and God. So I thought I would be doing something worthwhile if I explained how the properties or qualities of the mind are to be distinguished from the qualities of the body. Admittedly, many people had previously said that in order to understand metaphysical matters the mind must be drawn away from the senses; but no one, so far as I know, had shown how this could be done. The correct, and in my view unique, method of achieving this is contained in my Second Meditation. But the nature of the method is such that scrutinizing it just once is not enough. Protracted and repeated study is required to eradicate the lifelong habit of confusing things related to the intellect with corporeal things, and to replace it with the opposite habit of distinguishing the two; this will take at least a few days to acquire. I think that was the best justification for my devoting the whole of the Second Meditation to this topic alone.

You go on to ask how I demonstrate that a body is incapable of thinking.[1] You will forgive me if I reply that I have as yet provided no opportunity for this question to be raised. I first dealt with the matter in the Sixth Meditation where I said 'the fact that I can clearly and distinctly understand one thing apart from another is enough to make me certain that the two things are distinct', etc. And a little later on I said:

It is true that I have a body that is very closely joined to me. But nevertheless on the one hand I have a clear and distinct idea of myself, in so far as I am a thinking, non-extended thing; and on the other hand I have a distinct idea of body, in so far as this is an extended, non-thinking thing. And accordingly it is certain that I (that is, the mind) am really distinct from my body and can exist without it.[2]   132

From this we may easily go on to say 'whatever can think is a mind, or is called a mind; but since mind and body are in reality distinct, no body is a mind; therefore no body can think'.

I do not see what you can deny here. Do you claim that if we clearly understand one thing apart from another this is not sufficient for the recognition that the two things are really distinct? If so, you must provide a more reliable criterion for a real distinction – and I am confident that none can be provided. What will you suggest? Perhaps that there is a real distinction between two things if one can exist apart from the other? But now I will ask how you know that one thing can exist apart from another. You must be able to know this, if it is to serve as the criterion for a real distinction. You may say that you derive this knowledge from the senses, since you can see, or touch etc., the one thing when the other is not present. But the evidence of the senses is less reliable than that of the intellect: it can variously happen that one and the same thing appears under different forms or in several places or in several different ways, and so be taken for two things. And, after all, if you remember the remarks about the wax at the end of the Second Meditation you will realize that bodies are not strictly speaking perceived by the senses at all, but only by the intellect;[3] so having a sensory perception of one thing apart from another simply amounts to our having an idea of one thing and understanding that this idea is not the same as an idea of something else. The sole possible source of such understanding is that we perceive one   133 thing apart from another, and such understanding cannot be certain unless the idea of each thing is clear and distinct. So if the proposed criterion for a real distinction is to be reliable, it must reduce to the one which I put forward.

If there are those who claim that they do not have distinct ideas of mind and body, I can only ask them to pay careful attention to the contents of the Second Meditation. If, as may well be the case, they take

1 Above p. 88.   2 Above p. 54.   3 Above p. 22.

the view that the formation of thoughts is due to the combined activity of parts of the brain, they should realize that this view is not based on any positive argument, but has simply arisen from the fact that, in the first place, they have never had the experience of being without a body and that, in the second place, they have frequently been obstructed by the body in their operations. It is just as if someone had had his legs permanently shackled from infancy: he would think the shackles were part of his body and that he needed them for walking.

Secondly, when you say that we can find simply within ourselves a sufficient basis for forming the idea of God,[1] your claim in no way differs from my own view. I expressly said at the end of the Third Meditation that 'this idea is innate in me'[2] – in other words, that it comes to me from no other source than myself. I concede also that 'we could form this idea even supposing that we did not know that the supreme being exists'; but I do not agree that we could form the idea 'even supposing that the supreme being did not exist'.[3] On the contrary, I pointed out that the whole force of the argument lies in the fact that it would be impossible for me to have the power of forming this idea unless I were created by God.[4]

134   Your remarks about flies, plants etc.,[5] do not go to show that there can be a degree of perfection in the effect which was not previously present in the cause. For, since animals lack reason, it is certain that they have no perfection which is not also present in inanimate bodies; or, if they do have any such perfections, it is certain that they derive them from some other source, and that the sun, the rain and the earth are not adequate causes of animals. Suppose someone does not discern any cause cooperating in the production of a fly which possesses all the degrees of perfection possessed by the fly; suppose further that he is not sure whether there is any additional cause beyond those which he does discern: it would be quite irrational for him to take this as a basis for doubting something which, as I shall shortly explain at length, is manifest by the very light of nature.

I would add that the claim regarding flies is based on a consideration of material things, and so it could not occur to those who follow my Meditations and direct their thought away from the things which are perceivable by the senses with the aim of philosophizing in an orderly manner.

As for your calling the idea of God which is in us a 'conceptual entity',[6] this is not a compelling objection. If by 'conceptual entity' is meant something which does not exist, it is not true that the idea of God is a

1 Above p. 88.   2 Above p. 35.   3 Above p. 88.   4 Cf. above p. 35.
5 Above p. 88.   6 *Ibid.*

conceptual entity in this sense. It is true only in the sense in which every operation of the intellect is a conceptual entity, that is, an entity which has its origin in thought; and indeed this entire universe can be said to be an entity originating in God's thought, that is, an entity created by a single act of the divine mind. Moreover I have already insisted in various places that I am dealing merely with the objective perfection or reality of an idea; and this, no less than the objective intricacy in the idea of a machine of very ingenious design, requires a cause which contains in reality whatever is contained merely objectively in the idea. $\quad$ 135

I do not see what I can add to make it any clearer that the idea in question could not be present to my mind unless a supreme being existed. I can only say that it depends on the reader: if he attends carefully to what I have written he should be able to free himself from the preconceived opinions which may be eclipsing his natural light, and to accustom himself to believing in the primary notions, which are as evident and true as anything can be, in preference to opinions which are obscure and false, albeit fixed in the mind by long habit.

The fact that 'there is nothing in the effect which was not previously present in the cause, either in a similar or in a higher form' is a primary notion which is as clear as any that we have; it is just the same as the common notion 'Nothing comes from nothing.' For if we admit that there is something in the effect that was not previously present in the cause, we shall also have to admit that this something was produced by nothing. And the reason why nothing cannot be the cause of a thing is simply that such a cause would not contain the same features as are found in the effect.

It is also a primary notion that 'all the reality or perfection which is present in an idea merely objectively must be present in its cause either formally or eminently'.[1] This is the sole basis for all the beliefs we have ever had about the existence of things located outside our mind. For what could ever have led us to suspect that such things exist if not the simple fact that ideas of these things reach our mind by means of the senses?

Those who give the matter their careful attention and spend time meditating with me will clearly see that there is within us an idea of a supremely powerful and perfect being, and also that the objective reality of this idea cannot be found in us, either formally or eminently. I cannot force this truth on my readers if they are lazy, since it depends solely on their exercising their own powers of thought. $\quad$ 136

The very manifest conclusion from all this is that God exists. But there may be some whose natural light is so meagre that they do not see that it is a primary notion that every perfection that is present objectively in an

1 Cf. Med. III, above pp. 28ff, and footnote 2, p. 28.

idea must really exist in some cause of the idea. For their benefit I provided an even more straightforward demonstration of God's existence based on the fact that the mind which possesses the idea of God cannot derive its existence from itself.[1] So I do not see what more is required to make you surrender.

You suggest that I may have derived the idea which gives me my representation of God from preconceived notions of the mind, from books, conversations with friends etc., and not from my mind alone.[2] But there is no force in this suggestion. If I ask these other people (from whom I have allegedly got this idea) whether they derive it from themselves or from someone else, the argument proceeds in the same way as it does if I ask the same question of myself: my conclusion will always be that the original source of the idea is God.

Your further comment that the idea of God could have been formed from a previous examination of corporeal things seems to me just as implausible as saying that we have no faculty of hearing but acquire knowledge of sounds simply from seeing colours. Indeed, there seems to be a greater analogy or parity between colours and sounds than there is between corporeal things and God. When you ask me to 'add something further which lifts us up to an incorporeal or spiritual plane',[3] I cannot do better than refer you to my Second Meditation, in the hope that you will see that it is at least good for something. For what could I accomplish here in one or two sentences, if the lengthy account which I gave there – which was designed with this sole aim in mind, and to which I think I devoted as much effort as to anything I have ever written – failed to achieve anything at all?

The fact that I dealt only with the human mind in the Second Meditation is no drawback here. For I readily and freely confess that the idea which we have of the divine intellect, for example, does not differ from that which we have of our own intellect, except in so far as the idea of an infinite number differs from the idea of a number raised to the second or fourth power. And the same applies to the individual attributes of God of which we recognize some trace in ourselves.

But in addition to this, our understanding tells us that there is in God an absolute immensity, simplicity and unity which embraces all other attributes and has no copy in us, but is, as I have said before, 'like the mark of the craftsman stamped on his work'.[4] In virtue of this we recognize that, of all the individual attributes which, by a defect of our intellect, we assign to God in a piecemeal fashion, corresponding to the way in which we perceive them in ourselves, none belong to God and to ourselves in the same sense. Moreover, there are many indefinite

1 Med. III, above pp. 33ff.   2 Cf. above p. 88.   3 Above p. 89.   4 Med. III, above p. 35.

particulars of which we have an idea, such as indefinite (or infinite) knowledge and power, as well as number and length and so on, that are also infinite. Now we recognize that some of these (such as knowledge and power) are contained formally in the idea of God, whereas others (such as number and length) are contained in the idea merely eminently. And this would surely not be the case if the idea of God within us were merely a figment of our minds.

If the idea were a mere figment, it would not be consistently conceived by everyone in the same manner. It is very striking that metaphysicians unanimously agree in their descriptions of the attributes of God (at least in the case of those which can be known solely by human reason). You will find that there is much more disagreement among philosophers about the nature of anything which is physical or perceivable by the senses, however firm or concrete our idea of it may be.

No one can possibly go wrong when he tries to form a correct conception of the idea of God, provided he is willing to attend to the nature of a supremely perfect being. But some people muddle things up by including other attributes, which leads them to speak in a contradictory way: they construct an imaginary idea of God, and then – quite reasonably – go on to say that the God who is represented by this muddled idea does not exist. Thus, when you talk of an 'utterly perfect corporeal being',[1] and take the term 'utterly perfect' in its absolute sense, so that a corporeal being is taken to be a being in which all perfections are found, you are uttering a contradiction. The very nature of a body implies many imperfections, such as its divisibility into parts, the fact that each of its parts is different and so on; for it is self-evident that it is a greater perfection to be undivided than to be divided, and so on. If on the other hand by 'a perfect body' you simply mean that which is as perfect as a body can be, this will not be God.

As for your further point about the idea of an angel, namely that even though we are less perfect than an angel, there is no need for the idea to be produced in us by an angel,[2] I quite agree. I myself observed in the Third Meditation that the idea can be put together from the ideas which we have of God and of man.[3] So what you say does not in any way go against my position.

As for those who deny that they have the idea of God, but in its place form some image etc., although they reject the name, they concede the reality. I do not myself think that the idea is of the same kind as the images of material things which are pictured in the imagination; I maintain it is simply that which we perceive with the intellect, when the intellect apprehends, or judges, or reasons. Now in my thought or intellect I can somehow come upon a perfection that is above me; thus I

1 Above p. 89.   2 *Ibid.*   3 Above p. 29.

138

139

notice that, when I count, I cannot reach a largest number, and hence I recognize that there is something in the process of counting which exceeds my powers. And I contend that from this alone it necessarily follows, not that an infinite number exists, nor indeed that it is a contradictory notion, as you say, but that I have the power of conceiving that there is a thinkable number which is larger than any number that I can ever think of, and hence that this power is something which I have received not from myself but from some other being which is more perfect than I am.

It is irrelevant whether or not this concept of an indefinitely large number is called an 'idea'. But in order to understand what this being is which is more perfect than myself, and whether it is the infinite number itself, which really exists, or something else, we must consider not just the power of endowing me with the idea in question, but also all the other attributes which can exist in the being that is the source of the idea. And as a result we shall find that it can only be God.

140

Finally, when it is said that God 'cannot be thought of', this refers to the kind of thought that has an adequate grasp of God, not to the inadequate thought which we possess, and which is quite sufficient for knowledge of the existence of God. It is not important that the idea of the unity of all the perfections of God is said to be formed in the same way as the Porphyrian universals.[1] But there is a crucial difference, in that the idea in question denotes a certain positive perfection peculiar to God, whereas generic unity adds nothing real to the nature of the single individuals concerned.

Thirdly, when I said that we can know nothing for certain until we are aware that God exists,[2] I expressly declared that I was speaking only of knowledge of those conclusions which can be recalled when we are no longer attending to the arguments by means of which we deduced them.[3] Now awareness of first principles is not normally called 'knowledge' by dialectitians. And when we become aware that we are thinking things, this is a primary notion which is not derived by means of any syllogism. When someone says 'I am thinking, therefore I am, or I exist', he does not deduce existence from thought by means of a syllogism, but recognizes it as something self-evident by a simple intuition of the mind. This is clear from the fact that if he were deducing it by means of a syllogism, he would have to have had previous knowledge of the major premiss 'Everything which thinks is, or exists'; yet in fact he learns it from experiencing in his own case that it is impossible that he should think without existing. It is in the nature of our mind to construct general propositions on the basis of our knowledge of particular ones.

141

1 E.g. generic unity: cf. above p. 89 and note below, p. 410.
2 Above p. 89; cf. Med. III, above p. 25 and Med. v, above p. 48.
3 Cf. Med. v, above p. 48.

The fact that an atheist can be 'clearly aware that the three angles of a triangle are equal to two right angles'[1] is something I do not dispute. But I maintain that this awareness of his is not true knowledge, since no act of awareness that can be rendered doubtful seems fit to be called knowledge.[2] Now since we are supposing that this individual is an atheist, he cannot be certain that he is not being deceived on matters which seem to him to be very evident (as I fully explained). And although this doubt may not occur to him, it can still crop up if someone else raises the point or if he looks into the matter himself. So he will never be free of this doubt until he acknowledges that God exists.

It does not matter that the atheist may think he has demonstrations to prove that there is no God. For, since these proofs are quite unsound, it will always be possible to point out their flaws to him, and when this happens he will have to abandon his view.

It will be quite easy to make him do this if all he can produce by way of demonstration is the claim that you introduce at this point, namely that the infinite in every category of perfection excludes every other entity whatsoever, etc.[3] First, we may ask how he knows that this exclusion of all other entities belongs to the nature of the infinite. He will have no reasonable reply to make to this, since the term 'infinite' is not generally taken to mean something which excludes the existence of finite things. And, what is more, his knowledge of the nature of the infinite – since he regards it as a nonentity and hence as not having a real nature – must be restricted to what is contained in the mere verbal definition of the term   142 which he has learned from others. Secondly, what would the infinite power of this imaginary infinite amount to, if it could never create anything? Finally, the fact that we notice some power of thought within ourselves makes it easy for us to conceive that some other being may also have such a power, and that it is greater than our own. But even if we suppose that this power is increased to infinity, we do not on that account fear that our own power thereby diminishes. The same holds good for all the other attributes we ascribe to God, including power (provided we remember that any power that we possess is subject to the will of God). And hence God can be understood to be infinite without this in any way excluding the existence of created things.

Fourthly, in saying that God does not lie, and is not a deceiver,[4] I think

---

1 Above p. 89.
2 Descartes seems to distinguish here between an isolated cognition or act of awareness (*cognitio*) and systematic, properly grounded knowledge (*scientia*). Compare the remarks in *The Search for Truth* about the need to acquire 'a body of knowledge firm and certain enough to deserve the name "science"', below p. 408; see also p. 104 below, and *Rules*, vol. 1, pp. 10ff.
3 Above p. 89.
4 Above pp. 89f.

I am in agreement with all metaphysicians and theologians past and future. The points you make against this have no more force than if I had said that God is not subject to anger or other emotions, and you were to produce as counter-examples passages from Scripture where human feelings are attributed to God. As everyone knows, there are two quite distinct ways of speaking about God. The first is appropriate for ordinary understanding and does contain some truth, albeit truth which is relative to human beings; and it is this way of speaking that is generally employed in Holy Scripture. The second way of speaking comes closer to expressing the naked truth – truth which is not relative to human beings; it is this way of speaking that everyone ought to use when philosophizing, and that I had a special obligation to use in my *Meditations*, since my supposition there was that no other human beings were yet known to me, 143 and moreover I was considering myself not as consisting of mind and body but solely as a mind. It is very clear from this that my remarks in the *Meditations* were concerned not with the verbal expression of lies, but only with malice in the formal sense, the internal malice which is involved in deception.

However, the words of the prophet which you cite – 'Yet forty days and Nineveh shall be destroyed' – were not even a verbal lie but simply a threat, the fulfilment of which was conditional on a particular eventuality. And when God is said to have 'hardened the heart of Pharaoh', or words to that effect, this should not be taken to mean that he brought this about in a positive sense; he merely hardened Pharaoh's heart in a negative sense, by not bestowing on him the grace which would have brought about his change of heart. Nevertheless, I would not want to criticize those who allow that through the mouths of the prophets God can produce verbal untruths which, like the lies of doctors who deceive their patients in order to cure them, are free of any malicious intent to deceive.

Nevertheless – and this is a more important point – from time to time it does appear that we are really deceived by the natural instinct which God gave us, as in the case of the thirst felt by those who suffer from dropsy. These patients have a positive impulse to drink which derives from the nature God has bestowed on the body in order to preserve it; yet this nature does deceive them because on this occasion the drink will have a harmful effect. Nevertheless, this is not inconsistent with the goodness or veracity of God, and I have explained why in the Sixth Meditation.[1]

In the case of our clearest and most careful judgements, however, this 144 kind of explanation would not be possible, for if such judgements were

1 Above pp. 58–61.

false they could not be corrected by any clearer judgements or by means of any other natural faculty. In such cases I simply assert that it is impossible for us to be deceived. Since God is the supreme being, he must also be supremely good and true, and it would therefore be a contradiction that anything should be created by him which positively tends towards falsehood. Now everything real which is in us must have been bestowed on us by God (this was proved when his existence was proved); moreover, we have a real faculty for recognizing the truth and distinguishing it from falsehood, as is clear merely from the fact that we have within us ideas of truth and falsehood. Hence this faculty must tend towards the truth, at least when we use it correctly (that is, by assenting only to what we clearly and distinctly perceive, for no other correct method of employing this faculty can be imagined). For if it did not so tend then, since God gave it to us, he would rightly have to be regarded as a deceiver.

Hence you see that once we have become aware that God exists it is necessary for us to imagine that he is a deceiver if we wish to cast doubt on what we clearly and distinctly perceive. And since it is impossible to imagine that he is a deceiver, whatever we clearly and distinctly perceive must be completely accepted as true and certain.

But since I see that you are still stuck fast in the doubts which I put forward in the First Meditation, and which I thought I had very carefully removed in the succeeding Meditations, I shall now expound for a second time the basis on which it seems to me that all human certainty can be founded.

First of all, as soon as we think that we correctly perceive something, we are spontaneously convinced that it is true. Now if this conviction is so firm that it is impossible for us ever to have any reason for doubting what we are convinced of, then there are no further questions for us to ask: we have everything that we could reasonably want. What is it to us 145 that someone may make out that the perception whose truth we are so firmly convinced of may appear false to God or an angel, so that it is, absolutely speaking, false? Why should this alleged 'absolute falsity' bother us, since we neither believe in it nor have even the smallest suspicion of it? For the supposition which we are making here is of a conviction so firm that it is quite incapable of being destroyed; and such a conviction is clearly the same as the most perfect certainty.

But it may be doubted whether any such certainty, or firm and immutable conviction, is in fact to be had.

It is clear that we do not have this kind of certainty in cases where our perception is even the slightest bit obscure or confused; for such obscurity, whatever its degree, is quite sufficient to make us have doubts in such cases. Again, we do not have the required kind of certainty with regard to matters which we perceive solely by means of the senses, however clear such perception may be. For we have often noted that error can be detected in the senses, as when someone with dropsy feels thirsty or when someone with jaundice sees snow as yellow; for when he sees it as yellow he sees it just as clearly and distinctly as we do when we see it as white. Accordingly, if there is any certainty to be had, the only remaining alternative is that it occurs in the clear perceptions of the intellect and nowhere else.

Now some of these perceptions are so transparently clear and at the same time so simple that we cannot ever think of them without believing them to be true. The fact that I exist so long as I am thinking, or that what is done cannot be undone, are examples of truths in respect of which we manifestly possess this kind of certainty. For we cannot doubt 146 them unless we think of them; but we cannot think of them without at the same time believing they are true, as was supposed. Hence we cannot doubt them without at the same time believing they are true; that is, we can never doubt them.

It is no objection to this to say that we have often seen people 'turn out to have been deceived in matters where they thought their knowledge was as clear as the sunlight'.[1] For we have never seen, indeed no one could possibly see, this happening to those who have relied solely on the intellect in their quest for clarity in their perceptions; we have seen it happen only to those who tried to derive such clarity from the senses or from some false preconceived opinion.

It is also no objection for someone to make out that such truths might appear false to God or to an angel. For the evident clarity of our perceptions does not allow us to listen to anyone who makes up this kind of story.

There are other truths which are perceived very clearly by our intellect so long as we attend to the arguments on which our knowledge of them depends; and we are therefore incapable of doubting them during this time. But we may forget the arguments in question and later remember simply the conclusions which were deduced from them. The question will now arise as to whether we possess the same firm and immutable conviction concerning these conclusions, when we simply recollect that they were previously deduced from quite evident principles (our ability to call them 'conclusions' presupposes such a recollection). My reply is that the required certainty is indeed possessed by those whose knowledge of God enables them to understand that the intellectual faculty which he gave them cannot but tend towards the truth; but the required certainty

1 Above p. 90.

is not possessed by others. This point was explained so clearly at the end of the Fifth Meditation[1] that it does not seem necessary to add anything further here.

Fifthly, I am surprised at your denying that the will exposes itself to   147
danger by following a conception of the intellect which is wholly lacking in clarity and distinctness.[2] What can give the will certainty if it follows a perception which is not clear? Every philosopher and theologian – indeed everyone who uses his reason – agrees that the more clearly we understand something before giving our assent to it, the smaller is the risk we run of going wrong; and, by contrast, those who make a judgement when they are ignorant of the grounds on which it is based are the ones who go astray. Whenever we call a conception obscure or confused this is because it contains some element of which we are ignorant.

It follows that your objection concerning the faith which should be embraced[3] has no more force against me than it does against anyone who has ever developed the power of human reason – indeed, it has no force against anyone at all. For although it is said that our faith concerns matters which are obscure, the reasons for embracing the faith are not obscure but on the contrary are clearer than any natural light. We must distinguish between the subject-matter, or the thing itself which we assent to, and the formal reason which induces the will to give its assent: it is only in respect of the reason that transparent clarity is required. As for the subject-matter, no one has ever denied that it may be obscure – indeed obscurity itself. When I judge that obscurity must be removed from our conceptions to enable us to assent to them without any danger of going wrong, this very obscurity is the subject concerning which I form a clear judgement. It should also be noted that the clarity or transparency   148
which can induce our will to give its assent is of two kinds: the first comes from the natural light, while the second comes from divine grace. Now although it is commonly said that faith concerns matters which are obscure, this refers solely to the thing or subject-matter to which our faith relates; it does not imply that the formal reason which leads us to assent to matters of faith is obscure. On the contrary, this formal reason consists in a certain inner light which comes from God, and when we are supernaturally illumined by it we are confident that what is put forward for us to believe has been revealed by God himself. And it is quite impossible for him to lie; this is more certain than any natural light, and is often even more evident because of the light of grace.

The sin that Turks and other infidels commit by refusing to embrace the Christian religion does not arise from their unwillingness to assent to

1 Above pp. 48f.   2 Above p. 90.   3 *Ibid.*

obscure matters (for obscure they indeed are), but from their resistance to the impulses of divine grace within them, or from the fact that they make themselves unworthy of grace by their other sins. Let us take the case of an infidel who is destitute of all supernatural grace and has no knowledge of the doctrines which we Christians believe to have been revealed by God. If, despite the fact that these doctrines are obscure to him, he is induced to embrace them by fallacious arguments, I make bold to assert that he will not on that account be a true believer, but will instead be committing a sin by not using his reason correctly. And I think that all orthodox theologians have always taken a similar view on this matter. Furthermore, those who read my books will not be able to suppose that I did not recognize this supernatural light, since I expressly stated in the Fourth Meditation, where I was looking into the cause of falsity, that it produces in our inmost thought a disposition to will, without lessening our freedom.[1]

149

However, I should like you to remember here that, in matters which may be embraced by the will, I made a very careful distinction between the conduct of life and the contemplation of the truth. As far as the conduct of life is concerned, I am very far from thinking that we should assent only to what is clearly perceived. On the contrary, I do not think that we should always wait even for probable truths; from time to time we will have to choose one of many alternatives about which we have no knowledge, and once we have made our choice, so long as no reasons against it can be produced, we must stick to it as firmly as if it had been chosen for transparently clear reasons. I explained this on p. 26 of the *Discourse on the Method*.[2] But when we are dealing solely with the contemplation of the truth, surely no one has ever denied that we should refrain from giving assent to matters which we do not perceive with sufficient distinctness. Now in my *Meditations* I was dealing solely with the contemplation of the truth; the whole enterprise shows this to be the case, as well as my express declaration at the end of the First Meditation where I said that I could not possibly go too far in my distrustful attitude, since the task in hand involved not action but merely the acquisition of knowledge.[3]

Sixthly, in the passage where you criticize the conclusion of a syllogism which I produced,[4] it is you who seem to have made a mistake in the argument. In order to get the conclusion you want, you should have stated the major premiss as follows: 'That which we clearly understand to belong to the nature of something can be truly asserted to belong to its nature'; and if the premiss is put like this, it contains nothing but a useless tautology. But my major premiss was this: 'That which we clearly

150

1 Cf. above p. 40.   2 See *Discourse*, part 3: vol. 1, p. 123.   3 Above p. 15.
4 Above p. 91.

understand to belong to the nature of something can truly be affirmed of that thing.' Thus if being an animal belongs to the nature of man, it can be affirmed that man is an animal; and if having three angles equal to two right angles belongs to the nature of a triangle, it can be affirmed that a triangle has three angles equal to two right angles; and if existence belongs to the nature of God, it can be affirmed that God exists, and so on. Now the minor premiss of my argument was: 'yet it belongs to the nature of God that he exists'. And from these two premisses the evident conclusion to be drawn is the one which I drew: 'Therefore it can truly be affirmed of God that he exists.' The correct conclusion is not, as you want to argue: 'Therefore we can with truth affirm that existence belongs to the nature of God.'

Hence, to deploy the objection which you go on to make, you should have denied the major premiss and said instead 'What we clearly understand to belong to the nature of a thing cannot for that reason be affirmed of that thing unless its nature is possible, or non-contradictory.' But please notice how weak this qualification is. If by 'possible' you mean what everyone commonly means, namely 'whatever does not conflict with our human concepts', then it is manifest that the nature of God, as I have described it, is possible in this sense, since I supposed it to contain only what, according to our clear and distinct perceptions, must belong to it; and hence it cannot conflict with our concepts. Alternatively, you may well be imagining some other kind of possibility which relates to the object itself; but unless this matches the first sort of possibility it can never be known by the human intellect, and so it does not so much   151 support a denial of God's nature and existence as serve to undermine every other item of human knowledge. For as far as our concepts are concerned there is no impossibility in the nature of God; on the contrary, all the attributes which we include in the concept of the divine nature are so interconnected that it seems to us to be self-contradictory that any one of them should not belong to God. Hence, if we deny that the nature of God is possible, we may just as well deny that the angles of a triangle are equal to two right angles, or that he who is actually thinking exists; and if we do this it will be even more appropriate to deny that anything we acquire by means of the senses is true. The upshot will be that all human knowledge will be destroyed, though for no good reason.

I now turn to the argument which you compare with my own, *viz.* 'If there is no contradiction in God's existing it is certain that he exists; but there is no contradiction in his existing; therefore' etc.[1] Although materially true, this argument is formally a sophism. For in the major premiss the term 'contradiction' applies to the concept of the cause on

---

1 Above p. 91.

which the possibility of God's existence depends; in the minor premiss, however, it applies simply to the concept of the divine existence and nature itself. This is clear from the fact that if the major premiss is denied the proof will have to go as follows: 'If God does not yet exist, it is a contradiction that he should exist, since there can be no cause which is sufficient to bring him into existence; but (as was assumed), there is no contradiction in his existing; hence' etc. If on the other hand the minor premiss is denied, the proof will have to be stated thus: 'There is no contradiction in something if there is nothing in its formal concept which implies a contradiction; but there is nothing in the formal concept of the divine existence or nature which implies a contradiction; hence' etc.

152 These two proofs are very different. For it may be, with respect to a given thing, that we understand there to be nothing in the thing itself that precludes the possibility of its existence, while at the same time, from the causal point of view, we understand there to be something that prevents its being brought into existence.

But even if we conceive of God only in an inadequate or, if you like, 'utterly inadequate' way,[1] this does not prevent its being certain that his nature is possible, or not self-contradictory. Nor does it prevent our being able truly to assert that we have examined his nature with sufficient clarity (that is, with as much clarity as is necessary to know that his nature is possible and also to know that necessary existence belongs to this same divine nature). All self-contradictoriness or impossibility resides solely in our thought, when we make the mistake of joining together mutually inconsistent ideas; it cannot occur in anything which is outside the intellect. For the very fact that something exists outside the intellect manifestly shows that it is not self-contradictory but possible. Self-contradictoriness in our concepts arises merely from their obscurity and confusion: there can be none in the case of clear and distinct concepts. Hence, in the case of the few attributes of God which we do perceive, it is enough that we understand them clearly and distinctly, even though our understanding is in no way adequate. And the fact that, amongst other things, we notice that necessary existence is contained in our concept of God (however inadequate that concept may be) is enough to enable us to assert both that we have examined his nature with sufficient clarity, and that his nature is not self-contradictory.

153 *Seventhly*, as to why I wrote nothing concerning the immortality of the soul, I did already explain this in the Synopsis of my *Meditations*.[2] And, as I have shown above, I did provide an adequate proof of the fact that the soul is distinct from every body. However, you go on to say that it does not follow from the fact that the soul is distinct from the body that it

1 Above p. 91.   2 Above pp. 9f.

is immortal, since it could still be claimed that God gave it such a nature that its duration comes to an end simultaneously with the end of the body's life.[1] Here I admit that I cannot refute what you say. For I do not take it upon myself to try to use the power of human reason to settle any of those matters which depend on the free will of God. Our natural knowledge tells us that the mind is distinct from the body, and that it is a substance. But in the case of the human body, the difference between it and other bodies consists merely in the arrangement of the limbs and other accidents of this sort;[2] and the final death of the body depends solely on a division or change of shape. Now we have no convincing evidence or precedent to suggest that the death or annihilation of a substance like the mind must result from such a trivial cause as a change in shape, for this is simply a mode, and what is more not a mode of the mind, but a mode of the body which is really distinct from the mind. Indeed, we do not even have any convincing evidence or precedent to suggest that any substance can perish. And this entitles us to conclude that the mind, in so far as it can be known by natural philosophy, is   154 immortal.

But if your question concerns the absolute power of God, and you are asking whether he may have decreed that human souls cease to exist precisely when the bodies which he joined to them are destroyed, then it is for God alone to give the answer. And since God himself has revealed to us that this will not occur, there remains not even the slightest room for doubt on this point.

It remains for me to thank you for the helpful and frank way in which you have been kind enough to bring to my notice not only the points which have struck you, but also those which might be raised by atheists and other hostile critics. As far as I can see, all the objections which you raise are ones which I have already answered or ruled out in advance in the *Meditations*. As to the points about the flies generated by the sun, the natives of Canada, the inhabitants of Nineveh, the Turks and so on,[3] the objections you raise cannot occur to those who follow the road which I have indicated and who lay aside for a time whatever they have acquired from the senses, so as to attend to dictates of pure and uncorrupted reason. Hence I thought that I had already adequately ruled out such objections in advance. But despite this, I take the view that these objections of yours will greatly assist my enterprise. For I expect that hardly any of my readers will be prepared to give such careful attention to everything I have written that they will remember all the contents by the time they come to the end. Those who do not remember everything may easily fall prey to certain doubts; and they will subsequently see that   155

1 Cf. above p. 91.   2 Cf. Synopsis, above p. 10.   3 Above pp. 88–90.

their doubts have been dealt with in these replies of mine, or failing that, these replies will at least give them the opportunity to examine the truth more deeply.

I now turn to your proposal that I should set out my arguments in geometrical fashion to enable the reader to perceive them 'as it were at a single glance'.[1] It is worth explaining here how far I have already followed this method, and how far I think it should be followed in future. I make a distinction between two things which are involved in the geometrical manner of writing, namely, the order, and the method of demonstration.

The order consists simply in this. The items which are put forward first must be known entirely without the aid of what comes later; and the remaining items must be arranged in such a way that their demonstration depends solely on what has gone before. I did try to follow this order very carefully in my *Meditations*, and my adherence to it was the reason for my dealing with the distinction between the mind and the body only at the end, in the Sixth Meditation, rather than in the Second. It also explains why I deliberately and knowingly omitted many matters which would have required an explanation of an even larger number of things.

As for the method of demonstration, this divides into two varieties: the first proceeds by analysis and the second by synthesis.

Analysis shows the true way by means of which the thing in question was discovered methodically and as it were *a priori*,[2] so that if the reader is willing to follow it and give sufficient attention to all points, he will make the thing his own and understand it just as perfectly as if he had discovered it for himself. But this method contains nothing to compel

156   belief in an argumentative or inattentive reader; for if he fails to attend even to the smallest point, he will not see the necessity of the conclusion. Moreover there are many truths which – although it is vital to be aware of them – this method often scarcely mentions, since they are transparently clear to anyone who gives them his attention.

Synthesis, by contrast, employs a directly opposite method where the search is, as it were, *a posteriori* (though the proof itself is often more *a*

---

1 Above p. 92.

2 Descartes' use of the term *a priori* here seems to correspond neither with the modern, post-Leibnizian sense (where *a priori* truths are those which are known independently of experience), nor with the medieval, Thomist sense (where *a priori* reasoning is that which proceeds from cause to effect). What Descartes may mean when he says that analysis proceeds 'as it were *a priori*' (*tanquam a priori*) is that it starts from what is epistemically prior, i.e. from what is prior in the 'order of discovery' followed by the meditator. Cf. note 2, above p. 25.

priori than it is in the analytic method).[1] It demonstrates the conclusion clearly and employs a long series of definitions, postulates, axioms, theorems and problems, so that if anyone denies one of the conclusions it can be shown at once that it is contained in what has gone before, and hence the reader, however argumentative or stubborn he may be, is compelled to give his assent. However, this method is not as satisfying as the method of analysis, nor does it engage the minds of those who are eager to learn, since it does not show how the thing in question was discovered.

It was synthesis alone that the ancient geometers usually employed in their writings. But in my view this was not because they were utterly ignorant of analysis, but because they had such a high regard for it that they kept it to themselves like a sacred mystery.

Now it is analysis which is the best and truest method of instruction, and it was this method alone which I employed in my *Meditations*. As for synthesis, which is undoubtedly what you are asking me to use here, it is a method which it may be very suitable to deploy in geometry as a follow-up to analysis, but it cannot so conveniently be applied to these metaphysical subjects.

The difference is that the primary notions which are presupposed for the demonstration of geometrical truths are readily accepted by anyone, since they accord with the use of our senses. Hence there is no difficulty there, except in the proper deduction of the consequences, which can be done even by the less attentive, provided they remember what has gone before. Moreover, the breaking down of propositions to their smallest elements is specifically designed to enable them to be recited with ease so that the student recalls them whether he wants to or not. 157

In metaphysics by contrast there is nothing which causes so much effort as making our perception of the primary notions clear and distinct. Admittedly, they are by their nature as evident as, or even more evident than, the primary notions which the geometers study; but they conflict with many preconceived opinions derived from the senses which we have got into the habit of holding from our earliest years, and so only those who really concentrate and meditate and withdraw their minds from corporeal things, so far as is possible, will achieve perfect knowledge of them. Indeed, if they were put forward in isolation, they could easily be denied by those who like to contradict just for the sake of it.

1 Descartes may mean that though the proofs involved are *a priori* (*viz.*, in the traditional, Thomist sense), the method of synthesis starts from premises which are epistemically posterior – i.e. which are arrived at later in the order of discovery. (See previous footnote.)

This is why I wrote 'Meditations' rather than 'Disputations', as the philosophers have done, or 'Theorems and Problems', as the geometers would have done. In so doing I wanted to make it clear that I would have nothing to do with anyone who was not willing to join me in meditating and giving the subject attentive consideration. For the very fact that someone braces himself to attack the truth makes him less suited to perceive it, since he will be withdrawing his consideration from the convincing arguments which support the truth in order to find counter-arguments against it.

158   But at this point someone may raise the following objection: 'When we know that the proposition before us is true, we certainly should not look for arguments to contradict it; but so long as we remain in doubt about its truth it is right to deploy all the arguments on either side in order to find out which are the stronger. Nor does it seem that I am making a fair demand if I expect my arguments to be accepted as correct before they have been scrutinized, while at the same time prohibiting consideration of any counter-arguments.'

This is not a just criticism. For the arguments in respect of which I ask my readers to be attentive and not argumentative are not of a kind which could possibly divert their attention from any other arguments which have even the slightest chance of containing more truth than is to be found in mine. Now my exposition includes the highest level of doubt about everything, and I cannot recommend too strongly that each item should be scrutinized with the utmost care, so that absolutely nothing is accepted unless it has been so clearly and distinctly perceived that we cannot but assent to it. By contrast, the only opinions I want to steer my readers' minds away from are those which they have never properly examined – opinions which they have acquired not on the basis of any firm reasoning but from the senses alone. So in my view no one who restricts his consideration to my propositions can possibly think he runs a greater risk of error than he would incur by turning his mind away and directing it to other propositions which are in a sense opposed to mine and which reveal only darkness (i.e. the preconceived opinions of the senses).

I am therefore right to require particularly careful attention from my readers; and the style of writing that I selected was one which I thought would be most capable of generating such attention. I am convinced that

159   my readers will derive more benefit from this than they will themselves realize; for when the synthetic method of writing is used, people generally think that they have learned more than is in fact the case. In addition, I think it is fair for me to reject out of hand, and despise as worthless, the verdict given on my work by those who refuse to meditate with me and who stick to their preconceived opinions.

But I know that even those who do concentrate, and earnestly pursue the truth, will find it very difficult to take in the entire structure of my *Meditations*, while at the same time having a distinct grasp of the individual parts that make it up. Yet I reckon that both the overall and the detailed scrutiny is necessary if the reader is to derive the full benefit from my work. I shall therefore append here a short exposition in the synthetic style, which will, I hope, assist my readers a little. But they must please realize that I do not intend to include as much material as I put in the *Meditations*, for if I did so I should have to go on much longer than I did there. And even the items that I do include will not be given a fully precise explanation. This is partly to achieve brevity and partly to prevent anyone supposing that what follows is adequate on its own. Anyone who thinks this may give less careful attention to the *Meditations* themselves; yet I am convinced that it is the *Meditations* which will yield by far the greater benefit.

Arguments   160
*proving the existence of God and the distinction
between the soul and the body
arranged in geometrical fashion*

DEFINITIONS

I. *Thought*. I use this term to include everything that is within us in such a way that we are immediately aware of it. Thus all the operations of the will, the intellect, the imagination and the senses are thoughts. I say 'immediately' so as to exclude the consequences of thoughts; a voluntary movement, for example, originates in a thought but is not itself a thought.

II. *Idea*. I understand this term to mean the form of any given thought, immediate perception of which makes me aware of the thought. Hence, whenever I express something in words, and understand what I am saying, this very fact makes it certain that there is within me an idea of what is signified by the words in question. Thus it is not only the images depicted in the imagination which I call 'ideas'. Indeed, in so far as these images are in the corporeal imagination, that is, are depicted in some part 161 of the brain, I do not call them 'ideas' at all; I call them 'ideas' only in so far as they give form to the mind itself, when it is directed towards that part of the brain.

III. *Objective reality of an idea*. By this I mean the being of the thing which is represented by an idea, in so far as this exists in the idea. In the same way we can talk of 'objective perfection', 'objective intricacy' and so on. For whatever we perceive as being in the objects of our ideas exists objectively in the ideas themselves.

IV. Whatever exists in the objects of our ideas in a way which exactly corresponds to our perception of it is said to exist *formally* in those objects. Something is said to exist *eminently* in an object when, although it does not exactly correspond to our perception of it, its greatness is such that it can fill the role of that which does so correspond.[1]

V. *Substance.* This term applies to every thing in which whatever we perceive immediately resides, as in a subject, or to every thing by means of which whatever we perceive exists. By 'whatever we perceive' is meant any property, quality or attribute of which we have a real idea. The only idea we have of a substance itself, in the strict sense, is that it is the thing in which whatever we perceive (or whatever has objective being in one of our ideas) exists, either formally or eminently. For we know by the natural light that a real attribute cannot belong to nothing.

VI. The substance in which thought immediately resides is called *mind.* I use the term 'mind' rather than 'soul' since the word 'soul' is ambiguous and is often applied to something corporeal.[2]

VII. The substance which is the immediate subject of local extension and of the accidents which presuppose extension, such as shape, position, local motion and so on, is called *body*. Whether what we call mind and body are one and the same substance, or two different substances, is a question which will have to be dealt with later on.

VIII. The substance which we understand to be supremely perfect, and in which we conceive absolutely nothing that implies any defect or limitation in that perfection, is called *God*.

IX. When we say that something is *contained in the nature or concept* of a thing, this is the same as saying that it is true of that thing, or that it can be asserted of that thing.

X. Two substances are said to be *really distinct* when each of them can exist apart from the other.

POSTULATES[3]

The *first* request I make of my readers is that they should realize how feeble are the reasons that have led them to trust their senses up till now,

---

1 Cf. Med. III, above p. 28.
2 E.g. a tenuous wind permeating the body. Cf. Med. II, above p. 17.
3 Lat. *Postulata*. Descartes is here playing on words, since what follows is not a set of postulates in the Euclidian sense, but a number of informal requests.

and how uncertain are all the judgements that they have built up on the basis of the senses. I ask them to reflect long and often on this point, till they eventually acquire the habit of no longer placing too much trust in the senses. In my view this is a prerequisite for perceiving the certainty that belongs to metaphysical things.

Secondly, I ask them to reflect on their own mind, and all its attributes. They will find that they cannot be in doubt about these, even though they suppose that everything they have ever acquired from their senses is false. They should continue with this reflection until they have got into the habit of perceiving the mind clearly and of believing that it can be known more easily than any corporeal thing.

Thirdly, I ask them to ponder on those self-evident propositions that they will find within themselves, such as 'The same thing cannot both be and not be at the same time', and 'Nothingness cannot be the efficient cause   163 of anything', and so on. In this way they will be exercising the intellectual vision which nature gave them, in the pure form which it attains when freed from the senses; for sensory appearances generally interfere with it and darken it to a very great extent. And by this means the truth of the following axioms will easily become apparent to them.

Fourthly, I ask them to examine the ideas of those natures which contain a combination of many attributes, such as the nature of a triangle, or of a square, or of any other figure, as well as the nature of mind, the nature of body, and above all the nature of God, or the supremely perfect being. And they should notice that whatever we perceive to be contained in these natures can be truly affirmed of them. For example, the fact that its three angles are equal to two right angles is contained in the nature of a triangle; and divisibility is contained in the nature of body, or of an extended thing (for we cannot conceive of any extended thing which is so small that we cannot divide it, at least in our thought). And because of these facts it can be truly asserted that the three angles of every triangle are equal to two right angles and that every body is divisible.

Fifthly, I ask my readers to spend a great deal of time and effort on contemplating the nature of the supremely perfect being. Above all they should reflect on the fact that the ideas of all other natures contain possible existence, whereas the idea of God contains not only possible but wholly necessary existence. This alone, without a formal argument, will make them realize that God exists; and this will eventually be just as self-evident to them as the fact that the number two is even or that three   164 is odd, and so on. For there are certain truths which some people find self-evident, while others come to understand them only by means of a formal argument.

Sixthly, I ask my readers to ponder on all the examples that I went through in my *Meditations*, both of clear and distinct perception, and of obscure and confused perception, and thereby accustom themselves to distinguishing what is clearly known from what is obscure. This is something that it is easier to learn by examples than by rules, and I think that in the *Meditations* I explained, or at least touched on, all the relevant examples.

Seventhly, and lastly, when they notice that they have never detected any falsity in their clear perceptions, while by contrast they have never, except by accident, found any truth in matters which they grasp only obscurely, I ask them to conclude that it is quite irrational to cast doubt on the clear and distinct perceptions of the pure intellect merely because of preconceived opinions based on the senses, or because of mere hypotheses which contain an element of the unknown. And as a result they will readily accept the following axioms as true and free of doubt. Nevertheless, many of these axioms could have been better explained, and indeed they should have been introduced as theorems rather than as axioms, had I wished to be more precise.

AXIOMS OR COMMON NOTIONS

I. Concerning every existing thing it is possible to ask what is the cause of its existence. This question may even be asked concerning God, not because he needs any cause in order to exist, but because the immensity of his nature is the cause or reason why he needs no cause in order to exist.

II. There is no relation of dependence between the present time and the immediately preceding time, and hence no less a cause is required to preserve something than is required to create it in the first place.[1]

III. It is impossible that *nothing*, a non-existing thing, should be the cause of the existence of anything, or of any actual perfection in anything.

IV. Whatever reality or perfection there is in a thing is present either formally or eminently in its first and adequate cause.

V. It follows from this that the objective reality of our ideas needs a cause which contains this reality not merely objectively but formally or eminently. It should be noted that this axiom is one which we must necessarily accept, since on it depends our knowledge of all things, whether they are perceivable through the senses or not. How do we know, for example, that the sky exists? Because we see it? But this 'seeing' does not affect the mind except in so far as it is an idea – I mean

1 'Preserve', here and below, has the technical sense of 'to maintain in existence'.

an idea which resides in the mind itself, not an image depicted in the corporeal imagination. Now the only reason why we can use this idea as a basis for the judgement that the sky exists is that every idea must have a really existing cause of its objective reality; and in this case we judge that the cause is the sky itself. And we make similar judgements in other cases.

VI. There are various degrees of reality or being: a substance has more reality than an accident or a mode; an infinite substance has more reality than a finite substance. Hence there is more objective reality in the idea of a substance than in the idea of an accident; and there is more objective reality in the idea of an infinite substance than in the idea of a finite 166 substance.

VII. The will of a thinking thing is drawn voluntarily and freely (for this is the essence of will), but nevertheless inevitably, towards a clearly known good. Hence, if it knows of perfections which it lacks, it will straightaway give itself these perfections, if they are in its power.

VIII. Whatever can bring about a greater or more difficult thing can also bring about a lesser thing.

IX. It is a greater thing to create or preserve a substance than to create or preserve the attributes or properties of that substance. However, it is not a greater thing to create something than to preserve it, as has already been said.

X. Existence is contained in the idea or concept of every single thing, since we cannot conceive of anything except as existing. Possible or contingent existence is contained in the concept of a limited thing, whereas necessary and perfect existence is contained in the concept of a supremely perfect being.

PROPOSITION I

*The existence of God can be known
merely by considering his nature*

Demonstration

To say that something is contained in the nature or concept of a thing is the same as saying that it is true of that thing (Def. IX). But necessary existence is contained in the concept of God (Axiom X). Therefore it may 167 be truly affirmed of God that necessary existence belongs to him, or that he exists.

This is the syllogism which I employed above in replying to the sixth point in your Objections.[1] And its conclusion can be grasped as

1 Above pp. 106f.

self-evident by those who are free of preconceived opinions, as I said above, in the Fifth Postulate. But since it is not easy to arrive at such clear mental vision, we shall now endeavour to establish the same result by other methods.

PROPOSITION II

The existence of God can be demonstrated
a posteriori *merely from the fact that we*
have an idea of God within us

Demonstration

The objective reality of any of our ideas requires a cause which contains the very same reality not merely objectively but formally or eminently (Axiom v). But we have an idea of God (Def. II and VIII), and the objective reality of this idea is not contained in us either formally or eminently (Axiom VI); moreover it cannot be contained in any other being except God himself (Def. VIII). Therefore this idea of God, which is in us, must have God as its cause; and hence God exists (Axiom III).

168   PROPOSITION III

God's existence can also be demonstrated from the
fact that we, who possess the idea of God, exist

Demonstration

If I had the power of preserving myself, how much more would I have the power of giving myself the perfections which I lack (Axioms VIII and IX); for these perfections are merely attributes of a substance, whereas I am a substance. But I do not have the power of giving myself these perfections; if I did, I should already have them (Axiom VII). Therefore I do not have the power of preserving myself.

Now I could not exist unless I was preserved throughout my existence either by myself, if I have that power, or by some other being who has it (Axioms I and II). But I do exist, and yet, as has just been proved, I do not have the power of preserving myself. Therefore I am preserved by some other being.

Moreover, he who preserves me has within himself, either formally or eminently, whatever is in me (Axiom IV). But I have within me the perception of many of the perfections which I lack, as well as an idea of

God (Defs. II and VIII). Therefore he who preserves me has a perception of the same perfections.

Finally, this being cannot have the perception of any perfections which he lacks, or which he does not have within himself either formally or eminently (Axiom VII). For since he has the power of preserving me, as I have already said, how much more would he have the power of giving himself those perfections if he lacked them (Axioms VIII and IX). But he has the perception of all the perfections which I know I lack and which I conceive to be capable of existing only in God, as has just been proved. Therefore he has the perfections within himself either formally or eminently, and hence he is God.

169

COROLLARY

God created the heavens and the earth and everything in them. Moreover he can bring about everything which we clearly perceive in a way exactly corresponding to our perception of it

Demonstration
All this clearly follows from the preceding proposition. For in that proposition we proved that God exists from the fact that there must exist someone who possesses either formally or eminently all the perfections of which we have any idea. But we have the idea of a power so great that the possessor of this power, and he alone, created the heavens and the earth and is capable of producing everything that I understand to be possible. Therefore in proving God's existence we have also proved these other facts about him.

PROPOSITION IV

There is a real distinction between the mind and the body

Demonstration
God can bring about whatever we clearly perceive in a way exactly corresponding to our perception of it (preceding Corollary). But we clearly perceive the mind, that is, a thinking substance, apart from the body, that is, apart from an extended substance (Second Postulate). And conversely we can clearly perceive the body apart from the mind (as everyone readily admits). Therefore the mind can, at least through the power of God, exist without the body; and similarly the body can exist apart from the mind.

170

Now if one substance can exist apart from another the two are really distinct (Def. x). But the mind and the body are substances (Defs. v, vi and vii) which can exist apart from each other (as has just been proved). Therefore there is a real distinction between the mind and the body.

Notice that I introduce the power of God as a means to separate mind and body not because any extraordinary power is needed to bring about such a separation but because the preceding arguments have dealt solely with God, and hence there was nothing else I could use to make the separation. Our knowledge that two things are really distinct is not affected by the nature of the power that separates them.

On the First Meditation ('What can be called into doubt')

FIRST OBJECTION

From what is said in this Meditation it is clear enough that there is no
criterion enabling us to distinguish our dreams from the waking state and
from veridical sensations. And hence the images we have when we are
awake and having sensations are not accidents that inhere in external
objects, and are no proof that any such external object exists at all. So if
we follow our senses, without exercising our reason in any way, we shall
be justified in doubting whether anything exists. I acknowledge the
correctness of this Meditation. But since Plato and other ancient philosophers discussed this uncertainty in the objects of the senses, and since
the difficulty of distinguishing the waking state from dreams is commonly
pointed out, I am sorry that the author, who is so outstanding in the field
of original speculations, should be publishing this ancient material.

Reply
The arguments for doubting, which the philosopher here accepts as valid,
are ones that I was presenting as merely plausible. I was not trying to sell
them as novelties, but had a threefold aim in mind when I used them.
Partly I wanted to prepare my readers' minds for the study of the things   172
which are related to the intellect, and help them to distinguish these
things from corporeal things; and such arguments seem to be wholly
necessary for this purpose. Partly I introduced the arguments so that I
could reply to them in the subsequent Meditations. And partly I wanted
to show the firmness of the truths which I propound later on, in the light
of the fact that they cannot be shaken by these metaphysical doubts.
Thus I was not looking for praise when I set out these arguments; but I
think I could not have left them out, any more than a medical writer can
leave out the description of a disease when he wants to explain how it can
be cured.

---

1 By Hobbes; see Translator's preface, p. 64 above.

On the Second Meditation ('The nature of the human mind')

SECOND OBJECTION

I am a thinking thing.

Correct. For from the fact that I think, or have an image (whether I am awake or dreaming), it can be inferred that I am thinking; for 'I think' and 'I am thinking' mean the same thing. And from the fact that I am thinking it follows that I exist, since that which thinks is not nothing. But when the author adds 'that is, I am a mind, or intelligence, or intellect or reason',[1] a doubt arises. It does not seem to be a valid argument to say 'I am thinking, therefore I am thought' or 'I am using my intellect, hence I am an intellect.' I might just as well say 'I am walking, therefore I am a walk.' M. Descartes is identifying the thing which understands with intellection, which is an act of that which understands. Or at least he is identifying the thing which understands with the intellect, which is a power of that which understands. Yet all philosophers make a distinction between a subject and its faculties and acts, i.e. between a subject and its properties and its essences: an entity is one thing, its essence is another. Hence it may be that the thing that thinks is the subject to which mind, reason or intellect belong; and this subject may thus be something corporeal. The contrary is assumed, not proved. Yet this inference is the basis of the conclusion which M. Descartes seems to want to establish.

In the same passage we find the following: 'I know I exist; the question is, what is this "I" that I know. If the "I" is understood strictly as we have been taking it, then it is quite certain that knowledge of it does not depend on things of whose existence I am as yet unaware.'[2]

It is quite certain that the knowledge of the proposition 'I exist' depends on the proposition 'I am thinking' as the author himself has explained to us. But how do we know the proposition 'I am thinking'? It can only be from our inability to conceive an act without its subject. We cannot conceive of jumping without a jumper, of knowing without a knower, or of thinking without a thinker.

It seems to follow from this that a thinking thing is something corporeal. For it seems that the subject of any act can be understood only in terms of something corporeal or in terms of matter, as the author himself shows later on his example of the wax:[3] the wax, despite the changes in its colour, hardness, shape and other acts, is still understood to be the same thing, that is, the same matter that is the subject of all these changes. Moreover, I do not infer that I am thinking by means of another thought. For although someone may think that he *was* thinking (for this thought is simply an act of remembering), it is quite impossible

1 Above p. 18.   2 *Ibid.*   3 Above pp. 20ff.

for him to think that he *is* thinking, or to know that he is knowing. For then an infinite chain of questions would arise: 'How do you know that you know that you know . . . ?'

The knowledge of the proposition 'I exist' thus depends on the knowledge of the proposition 'I am thinking'; and knowledge of the latter proposition depends on our inability to separate thought from the matter that is thinking. So it seems that the correct inference is that the   174 thinking thing is material rather than immaterial.

Reply

When I said 'that is, I am a mind, or intelligence, or intellect or reason', what I meant by these terms was not mere faculties, but things endowed with the faculty of thought. This is what the first two terms are commonly taken to mean by everyone; and the second two are often understood in this sense. I stated this point so explicitly, and in so many places, that it seems to me there was no room for doubt.

There is no comparison here between 'a walk' and 'thought'. 'A walk' is usually taken to refer simply to the act of walking, whereas 'thought' is sometimes taken to refer to the act, sometimes to the faculty, and sometimes to the thing which possesses the faculty.

I do not say that the thing which understands is the same as intellection. Nor, indeed, do I identify the thing which understands with the intellect, if 'the intellect' is taken to refer to a faculty; they are identical only if 'the intellect' is taken to refer to the thing which understands. Now I freely admit that I used the most abstract terms I could in order to refer to the thing or substance in question, because I wanted to strip away from it everything that did not belong to it. This philosopher, by contrast, uses absolutely concrete words, namely 'subject', 'matter' and 'body', to refer to this thinking thing, because he wants to prevent its being separated from the body.

But I am not afraid that anyone will think my opponent's method is better suited to the discovery of the truth than my own; for his method lumps together a large number of different items, whereas I aim to distinguish each individual item as far as I can. But let us stop talking about terminology and discuss the issue itself.

'It may be', he says, 'that the thing that thinks is something corporeal.   175 The contrary is assumed, not proved.' But I certainly did not assume the contrary, nor did I use it as the 'basis' of my argument. I left it quite undecided until the Sixth Meditation, where it is proved.

He is quite right in saying that 'we cannot conceive of an act without its subject'. We cannot conceive of thought without a thinking thing, since that which thinks is not nothing. But he then goes on to say, quite without any reason, and in violation of all usage and all logic: 'It seems to follow from this that a thinking thing is something corporeal.' It may be that the subject of any act can be understood only in terms of a substance (or even, if he insists, in terms of 'matter', i.e. metaphysical matter); but it does not follow that it must be understood in terms of a body.

Logicians, and people in general, normally say that some substances are spiritual and some are corporeal. All that I proved with the example of the wax was that colour, hardness and shape do not belong to the formal concept of the wax itself. I was not dealing in that passage with the formal concept of the mind or even with that of the body.

It is irrelevant for the philosopher to say that one thought cannot be the subject of another thought. For who, apart from him, ever supposed that it could be? If I may briefly explain the point at issue: it is certain that a thought cannot exist without a thing that is thinking; and in general no act or accident can exist without a substance for it to belong to. But we do not come to know a substance immediately, through being aware of the substance itself; we come to know it only through its being the subject of certain acts. Hence it is perfectly reasonable, and indeed sanctioned by usage, for us to use different names for substances which we recognize as being the subjects of quite different acts or accidents. And it is reasonable for us to leave until later the examination of whether these different names signify different things or one and the same thing. Now there are certain acts that we call 'corporeal', such as size, shape, motion and all others that cannot be thought of apart from local extension; and we use the term 'body' to refer to the substance in which they inhere. It cannot be supposed that one substance is the subject of shape, and another substance is the subject of local motion etc., since all these acts fall under the common concept of extension. There are other acts which we call 'acts of thought', such as understanding, willing, imagining, having sensory perceptions, and so on: these all fall under the common concept of thought or perception or consciousness, and we call the substance in which they inhere a 'thinking thing' or a 'mind'. We can use any other term you like, provided we do not confuse this substance with corporeal substance. For acts of thought have nothing in common with corporeal acts, and thought, which is the common concept under which they fall, is different in kind from extension, which is the common concept of corporeal acts. Once we have formed two distinct concepts of these two substances, it is easy, on the basis of what is said in the Sixth Meditation, to establish whether they are one and the same or different.

Which of all these activities is distinct from my thinking? Which of them can be said to be separate from myself?[1]

Perhaps someone will answer this question as follows: I who am thinking am distinct from my thought; but my thought, though not separate from me, is distinct from me in the same way in which (as I have said above) jumping is distinct from the jumper. If M. Descartes is suggesting that he who understands is the same as the understanding, we shall be going back to the scholastic way of talking: the understanding understands, the sight sees, the will wills, and, by a very close analogy, the walking (or at least the faculty of walking) walks. All these expressions are obscure, improper, and quite unworthy of M. Descartes' usual clarity.

Reply

I do not deny that I, who am thinking, am distinct from my thought, in the way in which a thing is distinct from a mode. But when I ask 'Which of all these activities is distinct from my thinking?', I mean this to refer to the various modes of thinking which I have just listed, not to myself as a substance. And when I add, 'Which of them can be said to be separate from myself?', I simply mean that all these modes of thinking inhere in me. I do not see how one can pretend that there is any doubt or obscurity here.

FOURTH OBJECTION

I must therefore admit that the nature of this piece of wax is in no way revealed by my imagination, but is conceived by the mind alone.[2]

There is a great difference between imagining, that is, having an idea, 178 and conceiving in the mind, that is, using a process of reasoning to infer that something is, or exists. But M. Descartes has not explained how they differ. Even the Peripatetics of classical times taught clearly enough that a substance is not perceived by the senses but is inferred by reasoning.

Now, what shall we say if it turns out that reasoning is simply the joining together and linking of names or labels by means of the verb 'is'? It would follow that the inferences in our reasoning tell us nothing at all about the nature of things, but merely tell us about the labels applied to them; that is, all we can infer is whether or not we are combining the names of things in accordance with the arbitrary conventions which we

1 Above p. 19.
2 Above p. 21. Hobbes misquotes the text; in the original, Descartes uses the verb 'to perceive' (*percipere*) not 'to conceive' (*concipere*).

have laid down in respect of their meaning. If this is so, as may well be the case, reasoning will depend on names, names will depend on the imagination, and imagination will depend (as I believe it does) merely on the motions of our bodily organs; and so the mind will be nothing more than motion occurring in various parts of an organic body.

Reply

I did explain the difference between imagination and a purely mental conception in this very example, where I listed the features of the wax which we imagine and those which we conceive by using the mind alone. And I also explained elsewhere how one and the same thing, say a pentagon, is understood in one way and imagined in another.[1] As for the linking together that occurs when we reason, this is not a linking of names but of the things that are signified by the names, and I am surprised that the opposite view should occur to anyone. Who doubts

179 that a Frenchman and a German can reason about the same things, despite the fact that the words that they think of are completely different? And surely the philosopher refutes his own position when he talks of the arbitrary conventions that we have laid down concerning the meaning of words. For if he admits that the words signify something, why will he not allow that our reasoning deals with this something which is signified, rather than merely with the words? And surely on his account, when he concludes that the mind is a motion he might just as well conclude that the earth is the sky, or anything else he likes.

On the Third Meditation ('The existence of God')

FIFTH OBJECTION

Some of these [*viz.* human thoughts] are, as it were, the images of things, and it is only in these cases that the term "idea" is strictly appropriate – for example, when I think of a man, or a chimera, or the sky, or an angel, or God.[2]

When I think of a man, I am aware of an idea or image made up of a certain shape and colour; and I can doubt whether this image is the likeness of a man or not. And the same applies when I think of the sky. When I think of a chimera, I am aware of an idea or an image; and I can be in doubt as to whether it is the likeness of a non-existent animal which is capable of existing, or one which may or may not have existed at some previous time.

But when I think of an angel, what comes to mind is an image, now of a flame, now of a beautiful child with wings; I feel sure that this image

1 Med. VI, above pp. 50f.   2 Above p. 25.

has no likeness to an angel, and hence that it is not the idea of an angel. But I believe that there are invisible and immaterial creatures who serve 180 God; and we give the name 'angel' to this thing which we believe in, or suppose to exist. But the idea by means of which I imagine an angel is composed of the ideas of visible things.

In the same way we have no idea or image corresponding to the sacred name of God. And this is why we are forbidden to worship God in the form of an image; for otherwise we might think that we were conceiving of him who is incapable of being conceived.

It seems, then, that there is no idea of God in us. A man born blind, who has often approached fire and felt hot, recognizes that there is something which makes him hot; and when he hears that this is called 'fire' he concludes that fire exists. But he does not know what shape or colour fire has, and has absolutely no idea or image of fire that comes before his mind. The same applies to a man who recognizes that there must be some cause of his images or ideas, and that this cause must have a prior cause, and so on; he is finally led to the supposition of some eternal cause which never began to exist and hence cannot have a cause prior to itself, and he concludes that something eternal must necessarily exist. But he has no idea which he can say is the idea of that eternal being; he merely gives the name or label 'God' to the thing that he believes in, or acknowledges to exist.

Now from the premiss that we have an idea of God in our soul, M. Descartes proceeds to prove the theorem that God (that is, the supremely wise and powerful creator of the world) exists. But he ought to have given a better explanation of this 'idea' of God, and he should have gone on to deduce not only the existence of God but also the creation of the world.

Reply　　　　181

Here my critic wants the term 'idea' to be taken to refer simply to the images of material things which are depicted in the corporeal imagination; and if this is granted, it is easy for him to prove that there can be no proper idea of an angel or of God. But I make it quite clear in several places throughout the book, and in this passage in particular, that I am taking the word 'idea' to refer to whatever is immediately perceived by the mind. For example, when I want something, or am afraid of something, I simultaneously perceive that I want, or am afraid; and this is why I count volition and fear among my ideas. I used the word 'idea' because it was the standard philosophical term used to refer to the forms of perception belonging to the divine mind, even though we recognize that God does not possess any corporeal imagination. And besides, there was not any more appropriate term at my disposal. I think I did give a full enough explanation of the idea of God to satisfy those who are prepared to attend to my meaning; I cannot possibly satisfy those who prefer to attribute a different sense to my words than the one I intended. As for the comment at the end regarding the creation of the world, this is quite irrelevant.

SIXTH OBJECTION

Other thoughts have various additional forms: thus when I will or am afraid, or affirm, or deny, there is always a particular thing which I take as the object of my thought, but my thought includes something more than the likeness of that thing. Some thoughts in this category are called volitions or emotions, while others are called judgements.[1]

182   When someone wills, or is afraid, he has an image of the thing that he fears or the action that he wills; but what more does his thought include beyond this? This is not explained. Even if we grant that fear is a thought, it can only, as far as I can see, be the thought of the thing we are afraid of. For what is fear of a charging lion if not the idea of a charging lion plus the effect which this idea produces in the heart, which in turn induces in the frightened man that animal motion which we call 'flight'? Now this motion of flight is not a thought; so the upshot is that fear does not involve any thought, apart from the thought that consists in the likeness of the thing feared. And the same applies to willing.

As for affirmation and denial, these cannot be separated from language and names; thus brute beasts cannot affirm or deny, even in thought; and hence they cannot make judgements. Nevertheless the thought may be similar in man and beast. For when we assert that a man is running, our thought is no different from the thought that a dog has when he sees his master running. Hence affirmation and denial add nothing to simple thoughts except perhaps the thought that the names involved in the assertion denote the very things which the person making the assertion takes them to denote. But this is not a case of a thought's including more than a likeness of a thing; it is a case of its including the same likeness twice.

Reply
It is self-evident that seeing a lion and at the same time being afraid of it is different from simply seeing it. And seeing a man run is different from
183   silently affirming to oneself that one sees him. I see nothing here that needs answering.

1 Above pp. 25f.

SEVENTH OBJECTION

It only remains for me to examine how I received this idea from God. For I did not acquire it from the senses; it has never come to me unexpectedly, as usually happens with the ideas of things that are perceivable by the senses, when these things present themselves to the external sense organs – or seem to do so. And it was not invented by me either; for I am plainly unable either to take away anything from it or to add anything to it. The only remaining alternative is that it is innate in me, just as the idea of myself is innate in me.[1]

If, as seems to be the case, we do not have an idea of God (and it is not proved that we do), then the whole of this argument collapses. As for the idea of myself, this arises from sight, if we are thinking of 'myself' as my body; and if we are thinking of my soul, then the soul is something of which we have no idea at all. We rationally infer that there is something within the human body which gives it the animal motion by means of which it has sensations and moves; and we call this 'something' a soul, without having an idea of it.

Reply

If we do have an idea of God – and it is manifest that we do – then this whole objection collapses. As for the further point that we do not have an idea of the soul, but rationally infer its existence, this amounts to saying that although there is no image of the soul depicted in the corporeal imagination, we nevertheless do have what I call an idea of it.

EIGHTH OBJECTION   184

The other idea of the sun is based on astronomical reasoning, that is, it is derived from certain notions which are innate in me.[2]

It seems that there is only one idea of the sun at any one time, irrespective of whether we are looking at it with our eyes, or our reasoning gives us to understand that it is many times larger than it appears. The 'other' idea is not an idea of the sun, but is a rational inference that the idea of the sun would be many times larger if one looked at it from a much closer distance.

Certainly there can be different ideas of the sun at different times, e.g. if one looks at the sun with the naked eye and then later looks at it with a telescope. But astronomical arguments do not make the idea of the sun larger or smaller; they simply show that the idea that is acquired from the senses is deceptive.

1 Above p. 35.   2 Above p. 27.

Reply
Here again, what the objector says is not an idea of the sun, but which he
nevertheless describes, is precisely what I call an idea.

NINTH OBJECTION

Undoubtedly the ideas which represent substances to me amount to something
more and, so to speak, contain within themselves more objective reality than the
ideas which merely represent modes or accidents. Again, the idea that gives me
my understanding of a supreme God, eternal, infinite, omniscient, omnipotent
and the creator of all things that exist apart from him, certainly has in it more
185 objective reality than the ideas that represent finite substances.[1]

I have already frequently pointed out that we do not have an idea of
God, or of the soul. I will now add that we do not have an idea of
substance. For substance, in so far as it is the matter which is the subject
of accidental properties and of changes, is something that is established
solely by reasoning; it is not something that is conceived, or that presents
any idea to us. If this is true, how can one say that the ideas which represent
substances to me amount to something more or contain more objective
reality than those which represent accidents? Moreover, M. Descartes
should consider afresh what 'more reality' means. Does reality admit of
more and less? Or does he think one thing can be more of a thing than
another? If so, he should consider how this can be explained to us with
that degree of clarity that every demonstration calls for, and which he
himself has employed elsewhere.

Reply
I have frequently pointed out that I use the term 'idea' to apply to what is
established by reasoning as well as anything else that is perceived in any
manner whatsoever. I have also made it quite clear how reality admits of
more and less. A substance is more of a thing than a mode; if there are
real qualities or incomplete substances, they are things to a greater extent
than modes, but to a lesser extent than complete substances; and, finally,
if there is an infinite and independent substance, it is more of a thing than
a finite and dependent substance. All this is completely self-evident.

186   TENTH OBJECTION

So there remains only the idea of God; and I must consider whether there is anything in the idea which could not have originated in myself. By the word 'God'

1 Above p. 28.

I understand a substance that is infinite, independent, supremely intelligent, supremely powerful, and which created both myself and everything else (if anything else there be) that exists. All these attributes are such that the more carefully I concentrate on them, the less possible it seems that they could have originated from me alone. So from what has been said it must be concluded that God necessarily exists.[1]

When I consider the attributes of God in order to get an idea of God and to see whether there is anything in the idea that could not have been derived from ourselves, what I find, if I am not mistaken, is this. What we think of in connection with the name 'God' does not, I agree, originate in ourselves; but it need not be derived from any source other than external objects. By the term 'God' I understand a *substance*; that is, I understand that God exists (though my understanding does not come from an idea but from reasoning). This substance, moreover, is *infinite* (that is, it is impossible for me to conceive or imagine any supposed limits or extremities without being able to imagine further limits beyond them). And it follows from this that what arises in connection with the term 'infinite' is not the idea of the infinity of God but the idea of my own boundaries or limits. In addition, the substance is *independent*; that is, I do not conceive of a cause which produced God. From this it is clear that the idea which I have in connection with the term 'independent' is simply the memory of my own ideas, which began at different times and hence are dependent.

Hence to say that God is *independent* is simply to say that God belongs 187 to the class of things such that I cannot imagine their origin. Similarly, to say that God is *infinite* is the same as saying that he belongs to the class of things such that we do not conceive of them as having bounds. It follows that any idea of God is ruled out. For what sort of idea is it which has no origin and no limits?

God is *supremely intelligent*. What, may I ask, is the idea which enables M. Descartes to understand the operation of God's understanding?

Supremely powerful. Again, what idea enables us to understand power, which relates to future things, that is, things which do not yet exist. My own understanding of power comes from an image or memory of past actions, and I arrive at it as follows: 'if something acted, it was able to act; so if it continues to exist it will be able to act again, that is, it has the power of acting.' But these are all ideas which are capable of having arisen from external objects.

The creator of all that exists. I can construct for myself a sort of image of creation from what I have seen, e.g. a man being born or growing as it

1 Above p. 31.

were from a single point to the size and shape which he now has. This is the only sort of idea which anyone has in connection with the term 'creator'. But our ability to imagine the world to have been created is not a sufficient proof of the creation. Hence, even if the existence of something infinite, independent, supremely powerful etc. had been demonstrated, it still would not follow that a creator exists. Unless anyone thinks that the following inference is correct: 'There exists a being whom we *believe* to have created all things; therefore, the world was *in fact* created by him at some stage'.

188 Moreover, when M. Descartes says that the ideas of God and of our souls are innate in us, I should like to know if the souls of people who are in a deep, dreamless sleep are thinking. If they are not, they do not have any ideas at the time. It follows that no idea is innate; for what is innate is always present.

Reply

Nothing that we attribute to God can have been derived from external objects as a copy is derived from its original, since nothing in God resembles what is to be found in external, that is corporeal, things. Now any elements in our thought which do not resemble external objects manifestly cannot have originated in external objects, but must have come from the cause which produced this diversity in our thought.

And how, may I ask, does the philosopher derive his notion of God's understanding simply from external things? I can exactly explain the idea I have of God's understanding; for by an 'idea' I mean whatever is the form of a given perception. Now everyone surely perceives that there are things he understands. Hence everyone has the form or idea of understanding; and by indefinitely extending this he can form the idea of God's understanding. And a similar procedure applies to the other attributes of God.

In order to prove the existence of God, we made use of the idea of God which is in us. And such immense power is contained in this idea that we understand that, if God exists, it is a contradiction that anything else should exist which was not created by him. In view of this it clearly follows that in demonstrating the existence of God we have also demonstrated that God created the entire world, or all things which exist apart from him.

189 Lastly, when we say that an idea is innate in us, we do not mean that it is always there before us. This would mean that no idea was innate. We simply mean that we have within ourselves the faculty of summoning up the idea.

ELEVENTH OBJECTION

The whole force of the argument lies in this: I recognize that it would be impossible for me to exist with the kind of nature I have – that is, having within me the idea of God – were it not the case that God really existed. By 'God' I mean the very being the idea of whom is within me.[1]

Since it has not been demonstrated that we have the idea of God, and since the Christian religion obliges us to believe that God cannot be conceived of (which means, in my view, that we have no idea of him), it follows that no demonstration has been given of the existence of God, let alone the creation.

Reply

When they say that God 'cannot be conceived of', this refers to conceiving in such a way as to have a fully adequate grasp of him.[2] As for how we can have an idea of God, I have gone over this *ad nauseam*. There is absolutely nothing in this objection to invalidate my demonstrations.

On the Fourth Meditation ('Truth and falsity')   190

TWELFTH OBJECTION

I understand, then, that error as such is not something real but is merely a defect. Hence my going wrong does not require me to have a faculty specially bestowed on me by God.[3]

It is certain that ignorance is merely a defect, so we do not need any positive faculty in order to be ignorant. But the point is not so obvious in the case of error. It seems that stones and inanimate objects are incapable of making mistakes simply because they lack the power of reasoning and imagining. So the obvious inference is that in order to go wrong one needs the power of reasoning, or at least the power of imagining, and these are both positive faculties which have been given to all those, and only to those, who go wrong.

What is more, M. Descartes says 'I notice that my errors depend on two concurrent causes, namely on the faculty of knowledge which is in me, and on the faculty of choice or freedom of the will.'[4] This seems to contradict the earlier passage. And it should also be noted that the freedom of the will is assumed without proof, and in opposition to the view of the Calvinists.

1 Above p. 35.   2 See above footnote 1, p. 32.   3 Above p. 38.
4 Above p. 39.

Reply

It is true that in order to go wrong we need the faculty of reasoning, or rather of judging (that is, affirming and denying), since error is a defect in this faculty. But it does not follow that this defect is something real, any more than blindness is something real, although the mere fact that stones are incapable of vision does not make us call them blind. I am surprised that I have so far found not one valid argument in these objections. On the question of our freedom, I made no assumptions beyond what we all experience within ourselves. Our freedom is very evident by the natural light. Nor do I understand why this passage is said to contradict the earlier one.

There may indeed be many people who, when they consider the fact that God pre-ordains all things, cannot grasp how this is consistent with our freedom. But if we simply consider ourselves, we will all realize in the light of our own experience that voluntariness and freedom are one and the same thing. This is no place for examining the opinion of other people on this subject.

THIRTEENTH OBJECTION

For example, during these past few days I have been asking whether anything in the world exists, and I have realized that from the very fact of my raising this question it follows quite evidently that I exist. I could not but judge that something which I understood so clearly was true; but this was not because I was compelled so to judge by any external force, but because a great light in the intellect was followed by a great inclination in the will, and thus the spontaneity and freedom of my belief was all the greater in proportion to my lack of indifference.[1]

The phrase 'a great light in the intellect' is metaphorical, and so has no force in the argument. Moreover, anyone who is free from doubt claims he has such 'great light' and has no less strong a propensity of the will to affirm what he has no doubt about than someone who possesses real knowledge. Hence this 'light' can explain why someone obstinately defends or holds on to a given opinion, but it cannot explain his knowledge of its truth.

Further, it is not only knowing something to be true that is independent of the will, but also believing it or giving assent to it. If something is proved by valid arguments, or is reported as credible, we believe it whether we want to or not. It is true that affirmation and denial, defending and refuting propositions, are acts of will; but it does not follow that our inner assent depends on the will.

1 Above p. 41.

There is thus no valid demonstration of the subsequent conclusion, *viz.* 'In this incorrect use of free will may be found the privation which constitutes the essence of error'.[1]

Reply

It is quite irrelevant whether the phrase 'a great light' has force in the argument or not; what matters is whether it helps to explain matters – and it does. As everyone knows, a 'light in the intellect' means transparent clarity of cognition; and while perhaps not everyone who thinks he possesses this does in fact possess it, this does not prevent its being quite different from a stubborn opinion which is formed in the absence of any evident perception.

As for the claim that we assent to things which we clearly perceive, whether we want to or not, this is like saying that we seek a clearly known good whether we want to or not. The qualification 'or not' is inappropriate in such contexts, since it implies that we both will and do not will the same thing.

On the Fifth Meditation ('The essence of material things')   193

FOURTEENTH OBJECTION

When, for example, I imagine a triangle, even if perhaps no such figure exists, or has ever existed, anywhere outside my thought, there is still a determinate nature, or essence, or form of the triangle which is immutable and eternal, and not invented by me or dependent on my mind. This is clear from the fact that various properties can be demonstrated of the triangle.[2]

If the triangle does not exist anywhere, I do not understand how it has a nature. For what is nowhere is not anything, and so does not have any being or nature. A triangle in the mind arises from a triangle we have seen, or else it is constructed out of things we have seen. But once we use the label 'triangle' to apply to the thing which we think gave rise to the idea of a triangle, then the name remains even if the triangle itself is destroyed. Similarly, once we have conceived in our thought that all the angles of a triangle add up to two right angles, and we bestow on the triangle this second label 'having its angles equal to two right angles', then the label would remain even if no angles existed in the world. And thus eternal truth will belong to the proposition 'a triangle is that which has its three angles equal to two right angles'. But the nature of a triangle will not be eternal, for it might be that every single triangle ceased to exist.

1 *Ibid.*   2 Above pp. 44f.

Similarly, the proposition 'Man is an animal' will be eternally true because the names are eternal; but when the human race ceases to be, there will be no human nature any more.

194   It is clear from this that essence, in so far as it is distinct from existence, is nothing more than a linking of terms by means of the verb 'is'. And hence essence without existence is a mental fiction. It seems that essence is to existence as the mental image of a man is to a man; or the essence of Socrates is to the existence of Socrates as the proposition 'Socrates is a man' is to the proposition 'Socrates is, or exists'. Now when Socrates does not exist, the proposition 'Socrates is a man' signifies merely a linking of terms; and 'is' or 'to be' carries the image of the unity of a thing to which two terms are applied.

Reply

The distinction between essence and existence is known to everyone. And this talk about eternal names, as opposed to concepts or ideas of eternal truths, has already been amply refuted.

On the Sixth Meditation ('The existence of material things')

FIFTEENTH OBJECTION

For God has given me no faculty at all for recognizing this [*viz.* whether ideas are emitted by bodies or not]; on the contrary, he has given me a great propensity to believe that they are produced by corporeal things. So I do not see how God could be understood to be anything but a deceiver if the ideas were transmitted from a source other than corporeal things. It follows that corporeal things exist.[1]

195   The standard view is that doctors are not at fault if they deceive their patients for their health's sake, and that fathers are not at fault if they deceive their children for their own good. For the crime of deception consists not in the falsity of what is said but in the harm done by the deceiver. M. Descartes should thus consider the proposition 'God can in no case deceive us' and see whether it is universally true. For if it is not universally true, the conclusion 'Therefore corporeal things exist' does not follow.

Reply

My conclusion does not require that we can in no case be deceived (indeed, I have readily admitted that we are often deceived). All that I require is that we are not deceived in cases where our going wrong would suggest an intention to deceive on the part of God; for it is self-

1 Above p. 55.

contradictory that God should have such an intention. Once more my opponent's reasoning is invalid.

FINAL OBJECTION

For I now notice that there is a vast difference between the two [*viz.* between the waking state and dreams], in that dreams are never linked by memory with all the other actions of life.[1]

Consider someone who dreams that he is in doubt as to whether he is dreaming or not. My question is whether such a man could not dream that his dream fits in with his ideas of a long series of past events. If this is possible, then what appear to the dreamer to be actions belonging to his past life could be judged to be true occurrences, just as if he were awake. Moreover, as the author himself asserts, the certainty and truth of all knowledge depends solely on our knowledge of the true God. But in that case an atheist cannot infer that he is awake on the basis of memory of his past life. The alternative is that someone *can* know he is awake without knowledge of the true God.

196

Reply
A dreamer cannot really connect his dreams with the ideas of past events, though he may dream that he does. For everyone admits that a man may be deceived in his sleep. But afterwards, when he wakes up, he will easily recognize his mistake.

An atheist can infer that he is awake on the basis of memory of his past life. But he cannot know that this criterion is sufficient to give him the certainty that he is not mistaken, if he does not know that he was created by a non-deceiving God.

1 Above p. 61.

FOURTH SET OF OBJECTIONS[1]

Letter to a distinguished gentleman

Sir,

Though you have done me a kindness, you certainly want your reward. Indeed, you are exacting a heavy price for the great favour you have done me, in that you have allowed me to see this brilliant work only on condition that I should make public my opinion of it. This is certainly a hard condition, which only my eagerness to see this superb piece of work 197 has driven me to accept; and I would gladly try to get out of it if, instead of the traditional Praetor's dispensation applying to contracts entered into 'through force or fear', I could claim a new excusing condition applying to those 'made under the influence of pleasure'.

What exactly do you want? You can hardly be after my opinion of the author, since you already know how highly I rate his outstanding intelligence and exceptional learning. Moreover, you know of all the tedious commitments that keep me busy, and if you have an unsuitably high opinion of my powers, that certainly does not make me any less aware of my own inadequacy. Yet the work you are giving me to scrutinize requires both an uncommon intellect and, above all, a calm mind, which can be free from the hurly-burly of all external things and have the leisure to consider itself – something which, as you are well aware, can happen only if the mind meditates attentively and keeps its gaze fixed upon itself. Nevertheless, since you command, I must obey; and if I go astray it will be your fault, since it is you who are compelling me to write. Now it could be claimed that the work under discussion belongs entirely to philosophy; yet since the author has, with great decorum, submitted himself to the tribunal of the theologians, I propose to play a dual role here. Firstly I shall put forward what seem to me to be the possible philosophical objections regarding the major issues of the nature of our mind and of God; and then I shall set out the problems which a theologian might come up against in the work as a whole.

---

1 By Arnauld (see above p. 64). The Objections are addressed to Mersenne, who acted as intermediary between Arnauld and Descartes.

THE NATURE OF THE HUMAN MIND

The first thing that I find remarkable is that our distinguished author has laid down as the basis for his entire philosophy exactly the same principle as that laid down by St Augustine – a man of the sharpest intellect and a remarkable thinker, not only on theological topics but also on philosophical ones. In Book II chapter 3 of *De Libero Arbitrio*,[1] Alipius, when he is disputing with Euodius and is about to prove the existence of God, says the following: 'First, if we are to take as our starting point what is most evident, I ask you to tell me whether you yourself exist. Or are you perhaps afraid of making a mistake in your answer, given that, if you did not exist, it would be quite impossible for you to make a mistake?' This is like what M. Descartes says: 'But there is a deceiver of supreme power and cunning who is deliberately and constantly deceiving me. In that case I too undoubtedly exist, if he is deceiving me.'[2] But let us go on from here and, more to the point, see how this principle can be used to derive the result that our mind is separate from our body. 198

I can doubt whether I have a body, and even whether there are any bodies at all in the world. Yet for all that, I may not doubt that I am or exist, so long as I am doubting or thinking.

Therefore I who am doubting and thinking am not a body. For, in that case, in having doubts about my body I should be having doubts about myself.

Indeed, even if I obstinately maintain that there are no bodies whatsoever, the proposition still stands, namely that I am something, and hence I am not a body.

This is certainly very acute. But someone is going to bring up the objection which the author raises against himself: the fact that I have doubts about the body, or deny that it exists, does not bring it about that no body exists. 'Yet may it not perhaps be the case that these very things which I am supposing to be nothing, because they are unknown to me, are in reality identical with the "I" of which I am aware? I do not know,' he says 'and for the moment I shall not argue the point. I know that I exist; the question is, what is this "I" that I know? If the "I" is understood strictly as we have been taking it, then it is quite certain that knowledge of it does not depend on things of whose existence I am as yet unaware.'[3]

But the author admits that in the argument set out in the *Discourse on the Method* the proof excluding anything corporeal from the nature of 199

---

1 *On Free Will.* Augustine's views were a major source of inspiration for the Jansenist school of theology, of which Arnauld was a prominent supporter.
2 Med. II, above p. 17.
3 Above p. 18.

the mind was not put forward 'in an order corresponding to the actual truth of the matter' but merely in an order corresponding to his 'own perception'. So the sense of the passage was that he was aware of nothing at all which he knew belonged to his essence except that he was a thinking thing.[1] From this answer it is clear that the objection still stands in precisely the same form as it did before, and that the question he promised to answer still remains outstanding: How does it follow, from the fact that he is aware of nothing else belonging to his essence, that nothing else does in fact belong to it?[2] I must confess that I am somewhat slow, but I have been unable to find anywhere in the Second Meditation an answer to this question. As far as I can gather, however, the author does attempt a proof of this claim in the Sixth Meditation, since he takes it to depend on his having clear knowledge of God, which he had not yet arrived at in the Second Meditation. This is how the proof goes:

I know that everything which I clearly and distinctly understand is capable of being created by God so as to correspond exactly with my understanding of it. Hence the fact that I can clearly and distinctly understand one thing apart from another is enough to make me certain that the two things are distinct, since they are capable of being separated, at least by God. The question of what kind of power is required to bring about such a separation does not affect the judgement that the two things are distinct ... Now on the one hand I have a clear and distinct idea of myself, in so far as I am simply a thinking, non-extended thing; and on the other hand I have a distinct idea of body, in so far as this is simply an extended, non-thinking thing. And accordingly, it is certain that I am really distinct from my body, and can exist without it.[3]

We must pause a little here, for it seems to me that in these few words lies the crux of the whole difficulty.

First of all, if the major premiss of this syllogism is to be true, it must be taken to apply not to any kind of knowledge of a thing, nor even to clear and distinct knowledge; it must apply solely to knowledge which is adequate. For our distinguished author admits in his reply to the theologian, that if one thing can be conceived distinctly and separately from another 'by an abstraction of the intellect which conceives the thing inadequately', then this is sufficient for there to be a formal distinction between the two, but it does not require that there be a real distinction.[4] And in the same passage he draws the following conclusion:

By contrast, I have a complete understanding of what a body is when I think that it is merely something having extension, shape and motion, and I deny that it has

---

1 The argument in question comes in the *Discourse*, part 4: vol. 1, p. 127. Descartes' qualifying comments, quoted by Arnauld, are from the Preface to the *Meditations*; see above, p. 7.
2 See Preface, above p. 7.   3 Above p. 54.   4 Cf. First Replies, above pp. 85f.

anything which belongs to the nature of a mind. Conversely, I understand the mind to be a complete thing, which doubts, understands, wills, and so on, even though I deny that it has any of the attributes which are contained in the idea of a body. Hence there is a real distinction between the body and the mind.[1]

But someone may call this minor premiss into doubt and maintain that the conception you have of yourself when you conceive of yourself as a thinking, non-extended thing is an inadequate one; and the same may be true of your conception of yourself[2] as an extended, non-thinking thing. Hence we must look at how this is proved in the earlier part of the argument. For I do not think that this matter is so clear that it should be assumed without proof as a first principle that is not susceptible of demonstration.

As to the first part of your claim, namely that you have a complete understanding of what a body is when you think that it is merely something having extension, shape, motion etc., and you deny that it has anything which belongs to the nature of a mind, this proves little. For those who maintain that our mind is corporeal do not on that account suppose that every body is a mind. On their view, body would be related to mind as a genus is related to a species. Now a genus can be understood apart from a species, even if we deny of the genus what is proper and peculiar to the species – hence the common maxim of logicians, 'The negation of the species does not negate the genus.' Thus I can understand the genus 'figure' apart from my understanding of any of the properties which are peculiar to a circle. It therefore remains to be proved that the mind can be completely and adequately understood apart from the body.

201

I cannot see anywhere in the entire work an argument which could serve to prove this claim, apart from what is suggested at the beginning: 'I can deny that any body exists, or that there is any extended thing at all, yet it remains certain to me that I exist, so long as I am making this denial or thinking it. Hence I am a thinking thing, not a body, and the body does not belong to the knowledge I have of myself.'[3]

But so far as I can see, the only result that follows from this is that I can obtain some knowledge of myself without knowledge of the body. But it is not yet transparently clear to me that this knowledge is complete and adequate, so as to enable me to be certain that I am not mistaken in excluding body from my essence. I shall explain the point by means of an example.

Suppose someone knows for certain that the angle in a semi-circle is a right angle, and hence that the triangle formed by this angle and the diameter of the circle is right-angled. In spite of this, he may doubt, or

1 Above p. 86.   2 '. . . i.e. your body' (supplied in French version).
3 Not an exact quotation. Cf. Med. II, above pp. 17–19.

not yet have grasped for certain, that the square on the hypotenuse is equal to the squares on the other two sides; indeed he may even deny this if he is misled by some fallacy. But now, if he uses the same argument as that proposed by our illustrious author, he may appear to have confirmation of his false belief, as follows: 'I clearly and distinctly perceive', he may say, 'that the triangle is right-angled; but I doubt that the square on the hypotenuse is equal to the squares on the other two sides; therefore it does not belong to the essence of the triangle that the square on its hypotenuse is equal to the squares on the other sides.'

Again, even if I deny that the square on the hypotenuse is equal to the square on the other two sides, I still remain sure that the triangle is right-angled, and my mind retains the clear and distinct knowledge that one of its angles is a right angle. And given that this is so, not even God could bring it about that the triangle is not right-angled.

I might argue from this that the property which I doubt, or which can be removed while leaving my idea intact, does not belong to the essence of the triangle.

Moreover, 'I know', says M. Descartes, 'that everything which I clearly and distinctly understand is capable of being created by God so as to correspond exactly with my understanding of it. And hence the fact that I can clearly and distinctly understand one thing apart from another is enough to make me certain that the two things are distinct, since they are capable of being separated by God.'[1] Yet I clearly and distinctly understand that this triangle is right-angled, without understanding that the square on the hypotenuse is equal to the squares on the other sides. It follows on this reasoning that God, at least, could create a right-angled triangle with the square on its hypotenuse not equal to the squares on the other sides.

I do not see any possible reply here, except that the person in this example does not clearly and distinctly perceive that the triangle is right-angled. But how is my perception of the nature of my mind any clearer than his perception of the nature of the triangle? He is just as certain that the triangle in the semi-circle has one right angle (which is the criterion of a right-angled triangle) as I am certain that I exist because I am thinking.

Now although the man in the example clearly and distinctly knows that the triangle is right-angled, he is wrong in thinking that the aforesaid relationship between the squares on the sides does not belong to the nature of the triangle. Similarly, although I clearly and distinctly know my nature to be something that thinks, may I, too, not perhaps be wrong in thinking that nothing else belongs to my nature apart from the fact

1 Med. VI, above p. 54.

that I am a thinking thing? Perhaps the fact that I am an extended thing may also belong to my nature.

Someone may also make the point that since I infer my existence from the fact that I am thinking, it is certainly no surprise if the idea that I form by thinking of myself in this way represents to my mind nothing other than myself as a thinking thing. For the idea was derived entirely from my thought. Hence it seems that this idea cannot provide any evidence that nothing belongs to my essence beyond what is contained in the idea.

It seems, moreover, that the argument proves too much, and takes us back to the Platonic view (which M. Descartes nonetheless rejects) that nothing corporeal belongs to our essence, so that man is merely a rational soul and the body merely a vehicle for the soul – a view which gives rise to the definition of man as 'a soul which makes use of a body'.

If you reply that body is not straightforwardly excluded from my essence, but is ruled out only and precisely in so far as I am a thinking thing, it seems that there is a danger that someone will suspect that my knowledge of myself as a thinking thing does not qualify as knowledge of a being of which I have a complete and adequate conception; it seems instead that I conceive of it only inadequately, and by a certain intellectual abstraction.

Geometers conceive of a line as a length without breadth, and they conceive of a surface as length and breadth without depth, despite the fact that no length exists without breadth and no breadth without depth. In the same way, someone may perhaps suspect that every thinking thing 204 is also an extended thing – an extended thing which, besides the attributes it has in common with other extended things, such as shape, motion, etc., also possesses the peculiar power of thought. This would mean that although, simply in virtue of this power, it can by an intellectual abstraction be apprehended as a thinking thing, in reality bodily attributes may belong to this thinking thing. In the same way, although quantity can be conceived in terms of length alone, in reality breadth and depth belong to every quantity, along with length.

The difficulty is increased by the fact that the power of thought appears to be attached to bodily organs, since it can be regarded as dormant in infants and extinguished in the case of madmen. And this is an objection strongly pressed by those impious people who try to do away with the soul.

So far I have dealt with the real distinction between our mind and the body. But since our distinguished author has undertaken to demonstrate the immortality of the soul, it may rightly be asked whether this evidently follows from the fact that the soul is distinct from the body. According to the principles of commonly accepted philosophy this by no means follows, since people ordinarily take it that the souls of brute animals are distinct from their bodies, but nevertheless perish along with them.

I had got as far as this in my comments, and was intending to show how the author's principles, which I thought I had managed to gather from his method of philosophizing, would enable the immortality of the soul to be inferred very easily from the real distinction between the mind and the body. But at this point, a little study composed by our illustrious author was sent to me,[1] which apart from shedding much light on the work as a whole, puts forward the same solution to the point at issue which I was on the point of proposing.

As far as the souls of the brutes are concerned, M. Descartes elsewhere 205 suggests clearly enough that they have none. All they have is a body which is constructed in a particular manner, made up of various organs in such a way that all the operations which we observe can be produced in it and by means of it.[2]

But I fear that this view will not succeed in finding acceptance in people's minds unless it is supported by very solid arguments. For at first sight it seems incredible that it can come about, without the assistance of any soul, that the light reflected from the body of a wolf onto the eyes of a sheep should move the minute fibres of the optic nerves, and that on reaching the brain this motion should spread the animal spirits throughout the nerves in the manner necessary to precipitate the sheep's flight.

One point which I will add here is that I wholly agree with the distinguished author's doctrines concerning the distinction between the imagination and the intellect or thought, and the greater certainty which attaches to what we grasp by means of reason as against what we observe by means of the bodily senses. I long ago learned from Augustine, in Chapter 15 of *De Animae Quantitate*, that we must completely dismiss those who believe that what we see with the intellect is less certain than what we see with these bodily eyes, which have to contend with a perpetual discharge of phlegm.[3] This leads Augustine to say in the *Soliloquies*, Book 1, Chapter 4, that when doing geometry he found the senses to be like a ship. He goes on:

For when they had brought me to the place I was aiming for, I sent them away, and, now that I had set foot on the shore, began to examine these matters using my thought alone. But for a long time my footsteps remained unsteady. Hence I think that a man can sooner sail on dry land than he can perceive geometrical matters through the senses, even though the senses do appear to give us some small assistance when we begin to learn.

1 The Synopsis (see above pp. 9f).   2 Cf. *Discourse*, part 5: vol. 1, pp. 139ff.
3 One of the four 'humours' of medieval physiology.

The first proof of the existence of God, which our author sets out in the Third Meditation, falls into two parts. The first part is that God exists if there is an idea of God in me; the second is that given that I possess such an idea, the only possible source of my existence is God.

In the first part, the only thing I would criticize is this. The author first asserts that 'falsity in the strict sense can occur only in judgements'; but a little later he admits that ideas can be false – not 'formally false' but 'materially false',[1] and this seems to me to be inconsistent with the author's own principles.

I am afraid that on a topic as obscure as this I may not be able to explain what I want to say with sufficient lucidity; but an example will clarify the issue. The author says that 'if cold is merely the absence of heat, the idea of cold which represents it to me as a positive thing will be materially false'.[2]

But if cold is merely an absence, then there cannot be an idea of cold which represents it to me as a positive thing, and so our author is here confusing a judgement with an idea.

What is the idea of cold? It is coldness itself in so far as it exists objectively in the intellect. But if cold is an absence, it cannot exist objectively in the intellect by means of an idea whose objective existence is a positive entity. Therefore, if cold is merely an absence, there cannot ever be a positive idea of it, and hence there cannot be an idea which is materially false.

This is confirmed by the very argument that the author uses to prove that the idea of an infinite being cannot but be a true idea, since, though I can pretend that such a being does not exist, I cannot pretend that the idea of such a being does not represent anything real to me. 207

The same can plainly be said of any positive idea. For although it can be imagined that cold, which I suppose to be represented by a positive idea, is not something positive, it cannot be imagined that the positive idea does not represent anything real and positive to me. For an idea is called 'positive' not in virtue of the existence it has as a mode of thinking (for in that sense all ideas would be positive), but in virtue of the objective existence which it contains and which it represents to our mind. Hence the idea in question may perhaps not be the idea of cold, but it cannot be a false idea.

But, you may reply, it is false precisely because it is not the idea of cold. No: it is your judgement that is false, if you judge that it is the idea of cold. The idea itself, within you, is completely true. In the same way, the

1 Above p. 30. 2 *Ibid.* (not an exact quotation).

idea of God should never be called false – not even 'materially false', even though someone may transfer it to something which is not God, as idolaters have done.

Lastly, what does the idea of cold, which you say is materially false, represent to your mind? An absence? But in that case it is true. A positive entity? But in that case it is not the idea of cold. Again, what is the cause of the positive objective being which according to you is responsible for the idea's being materially false? 'The cause is myself', you may answer, 'in so far as I come from nothing.' But in that case, the positive objective being of an idea can come from nothing, which violates the author's most important principles.

But let us go on to the second half of the proof, where the author asks 'whether I who have the idea of an infinite being could derive my existence from any other source than an infinite being, and, in particular, whether I could derive my existence from myself'.[1] The author maintains 208 that I could not derive my existence from myself since 'if I had bestowed existence on myself I should also have given myself all the perfections of which I find I have an idea'.[2] But his theological critic has an acute reply to this: the phrase 'to derive one's existence from oneself' should be taken not positively but negatively, so that it simply means 'not deriving one's existence from another'. 'But now', the critic continues, 'if something derives its existence from itself in the sense of "not from another", how can we prove that this being embraces all things and is infinite? This time I shall not listen if you say "If it derives its existence from itself, it could have given itself all things." For it does not derive its existence from itself as a cause, nor did it exist prior to itself so that it could choose in advance what it should subsequently be.'[3]

To refute this argument, M. Descartes maintains that the phrase 'deriving one's existence from oneself' should be taken not negatively but positively, even when it refers to God, so that God 'in a sense stands in the same relation to himself as an efficient cause does to its effect'.[4] This seems to me to be a hard saying, and indeed to be false.

Thus I partly agree with M. Descartes and partly disagree with him. I agree that I could only derive my existence from myself if I did so in the positive sense, but I do not agree that the same should be said of God. On the contrary, I think it is a manifest contradiction that anything should derive its existence positively and as it were causally from itself. Hence I propose to establish the same result as our author, but by a completely different route, as follows.

In order to derive my existence from myself, I should have to derive my

1 Cf. above pp. 32–4.   2 Above p. 33.   3 First Objections, above pp. 68t.
4 First Replies, above p. 80.

existence from myself positively and, as it were, causally. Therefore it is 209 impossible that I derive my existence from myself.

The major premiss of this syllogism is proved by the author's own arguments based on the fact that, since the moments of time can be mutually separated, 'it does not follow from the fact that I exist now that I shall continue to exist unless there is some cause which as it were creates me afresh at each moment'.[1]

As for the minor premiss,[2] I think it is so clear by the natural light that it is scarcely susceptible of any proof, apart from the trivial kind of proof that establishes a well-known result by means of premisses that are less well-known. What is more, the author seems to have recognized its truth, since he has not ventured to deny it openly. Consider, for example, what he says in replying to his theological critic:

I did not say that it was impossible for something to be the efficient cause of itself. This is obviously the case when the term 'efficient' is taken to apply only to causes which are prior in time to their effects, or different from them. But such a restriction does not seem appropriate in the present context . . . for the natural light does not establish that the concept of an efficient cause requires that it be prior in time to its effect.[3]

This is quite true, so far as the first disjunct goes, but why has he omitted the second one? Why did he not add that the natural light does not establish that the concept of an efficient cause requires that it be different from its effect? Was it because the light of nature did not permit him to make this assertion?

Since every effect depends on a cause and receives its existence from a cause, surely it is clear that one and the same thing cannot depend on 210 itself or receive its existence from itself.

Again, every cause is the cause of an effect, and every effect is the effect of a cause. Hence there is a mutual relation between cause and effect. But a relation must involve two terms.

What is more, it is absurd to conceive of a thing's receiving existence yet at the same time possessing that existence prior to the time when we conceive that it received it. Yet this is just what would happen if we were to apply the notion of cause and effect to the same thing in respect of itself. For what is the notion of a cause? The bestowing of existence. And what is the notion of an effect? Receiving existence. The notion of a cause is essentially prior to the notion of an effect.

Now we cannot conceive of something under the concept of a cause as bestowing existence unless we conceive of it as possessing existence; for

1 Cf. above p. 33.
2 That I cannot derive my existence from myself positively and causally.
3 First Replies, above p. 78.

no one can give what he does not have. Hence we should be conceiving of a thing as having existence before conceiving it as having received existence; yet in the case of any receiver, the receiving precedes the possessing.

The argument can also be put as follows. No one gives what he does not have. Hence no one can give himself existence unless he already has it. But if he already has it, why should he give it to himself?

Finally, the author asserts that 'it is evident by the natural light that the distinction between creation and preservation is only a conceptual one'.[1] But it is evident by the same natural light that nothing can create itself. Therefore nothing can preserve itself.

But if we may come down from the general thesis to the particular case of God, it will now in my view be even clearer that God cannot derive his existence from himself in the positive sense, but can do so only in the negative sense of not deriving it from anything else.

211   This is clear first of all from the argument that the author himself uses to prove that if a body derives existence from itself it must do so in the positive sense. He says: 'The separate divisions of time do not depend on each other; hence the fact that the body in question is supposed to have existed up till now "from itself", that is, without a cause, is not sufficient to make it continue to exist in future, unless there is some power in it which, as it were, recreates it continuously.'[2]

But so far from this argument being applicable in the case of a supremely perfect or infinite being, we can actually infer the opposite result, and for opposite reasons. Contained within the idea of an infinite being, is the fact that the duration of this being is infinite, i.e. not restricted by any limits; and it follows from this that it is indivisible, permanent, and existing all at once, so that the concepts of 'before' and 'after' cannot be applied, except through an error and imperfection of our intellect.

It manifestly follows from this that an infinite being cannot be conceived of as existing even for a moment unless it is also conceived of as having always existed and as being bound to continue to exist for eternity (the author himself establishes this elsewhere). And hence it is pointless to ask why this being should continue in existence.

Augustine, whose remarks on the subject of God are as worthwhile and sublime as any that have appeared since the time of the sacred authors, frequently explains that in God there is no past or future but only eternally present existence. This makes it even clearer that the question of why God should continue in existence cannot be asked without absurdity, since the question manifestly involves the notions of

1 Above p. 33.   2 First Replies, above p. 79.

'before' and 'after', past and future, which should be excluded from the concept of an infinite being.

Moreover, God cannot be thought of as deriving his existence 'from himself' in the positive sense, as if he had created himself in the beginning. For then he would have existed before he existed. God is thought of as deriving existence 'from himself' only (as our author frequently declares) because he does in reality keep himself in existence.

But self-preservation does not apply to an infinite being any more than an original self-creation. For what, may I ask, is preservation if not a continual re-creation of something. Thus all preservation presupposes original creation. What is more, the very terms 'continuation' and 'preservation' imply some potentiality, whereas an infinite being is pure actuality, without any potentiality.

We should therefore conclude that God cannot be conceived of as deriving existence from himself in the positive sense, except through an imperfection of our intellect, which conceives of God after the fashion of created things. A further argument will make this even clearer.

We look for the efficient cause of something only in respect of its existence, not in respect of its essence. For example, if I see a triangle, I may look for the efficient cause that is responsible for the existence of this triangle; but I cannot without absurdity inquire into the efficient cause of this triangle's having three angles equal to two right angles. If anyone makes such an inquiry, the correct response would be not to give an efficient cause, but to explain that this is the nature of a triangle. This is why mathematicians, who do not deal with the existence of the objects they study, never give demonstrations involving efficient or final causes. But it belongs to the essence of an infinite being that it exists, or, if you will, that it continues in existence, no less than it belongs to the essence of a triangle to have its three angles equal to two right angles. Now if anyone asks why a triangle has its three angles equal to two right angles, we should not answer in terms of an efficient cause, but should simply say that this is the eternal and immutable nature of a triangle. And similarly, if anyone asks why God exists, or continues in existence, we should not try to find either in God or outside him any efficient cause, or quasi-efficient cause (I am arguing about the reality, not the name); instead, we should confine our answer to saying that the reason lies in the nature of a supremely perfect being.

The author says that the light of nature establishes that if anything exists we may always ask why it exists – that is, we may inquire into its efficient cause, or if it does not have one, we may demand why it does not have one.[1] To this I answer that if someone asks why God exists, we

---
1 First Replies, above p. 78.

should not answer in terms of an efficient cause, but should explain that he exists simply because he is God, or an infinite being. And if someone asks for an efficient cause of God, we should reply that he does not need an efficient cause. And if the questioner goes on to ask why he does not need an efficient cause, we should answer that this is because he is an infinite being, whose existence is his essence. For the only things that require an efficient cause are those in which actual existence may be distinguished from essence.

This disposes of the argument which follows the passage just quoted: 'Hence', says the author, 'if I thought that nothing could possibly have the same relation to itself as an efficient cause has to its effect, I should certainly not conclude that there was a first cause. On the contrary, I should go on to ask for the cause of the so-called "first" cause, and thus I would never reach anything which was the first cause of everything else.'[1]

Not at all. If I thought we ought to look for the efficient cause, or quasi-efficient cause, of any given thing, then what I would be looking for would be a cause distinct from the thing in question, since it is completely evident to me that nothing can possibly stand in the same relation to itself as that in which an efficient cause stands to its effect.

I think the author's attention should be drawn to this point, so that he can give the matter his careful and attentive consideration. For I am sure that it will scarcely be possible to find a single theologian who will not object to the proposition that God derives his existence from himself in the positive sense, and as it were causally.

I have one further worry, namely how the author avoids reasoning in a circle when he says that we are sure that what we clearly and distinctly perceive is true only because God exists.[2]

But we can be sure that God exists only because we clearly and distinctly perceive this. Hence, before we can be sure that God exists, we ought to be able to be sure that whatever we perceive clearly and evidently is true.

Let me add something which I forgot to include earlier. The author lays it down as certain that there can be nothing in him, in so far as he is a thinking thing, of which he is not aware,[3] but it seems to me that this is false. For by 'himself, in so far as he is a thinking thing', he means simply his mind, in so far as it is distinct from the body. But all of us can surely see that there may be many things in our mind of which the mind is not aware. The mind of an infant in its mother's womb has the power of thought, but is not aware of it. And there are countless similar examples, which I will pass over.

1 Above p. 78.   2 Cf. Med. v, above p. 48.   3 Cf. Med. iii, above p. 33.

POINTS WHICH MAY CAUSE DIFFICULTY TO THEOLOGIANS

In order to bring to an end a discussion that is growing tiresomely long, I would now like to aim for brevity, and simply indicate the issues rather than argue them out in detail.

First, I am afraid that the author's somewhat free style of philoso-phizing, which calls everything into doubt, may cause offence to some people. He himself admits in the *Discourse on the Method* that this approach is dangerous for those of only moderate intelligence; but I agree that the risk of offence is somewhat reduced in the Synopsis.[1]

Nevertheless, I rather think that the First Meditation should be furnished with a brief preface which explains that there is no serious doubt cast on these matters but that the purpose is to isolate temporarily those matters which leave room for even the 'slightest' and most 'exaggerated' doubt (as the author himself puts it elsewhere);[2] it should be explained that this is to facilitate the discovery of something so firm and stable that not even the most perverse sceptic will have even the slightest scope for doubt. Following on from this point, where we find the clause 'since I did not know the author of my being', I would suggest a substitution of the clause 'since I was pretending that I did not know . . .'[3]

In the case of the Fourth Meditation ('Truth and Falsity'), I am extremely anxious, for many reasons which would take too long to list, that the author should make two things clear, either in the Meditation itself or in the Synopsis.

The first is that when the author is inquiring into the cause of error, he is dealing above all with the mistakes we commit in distinguishing between the true and the false, and not those that occur in our pursuit of good and evil.

The discussion of the first kind of error is all that is needed for the author's plan and aim, and the comments he makes there on the cause of error would give rise to the most serious objections if they were stretched out of context to cover the pursuit of good and evil. Hence it seems to me that prudence requires, and the order of exposition to which our author is so devoted demands, that anything which is not relevant and which could give rise to controversy should be omitted. For otherwise the reader may be drawn into pointless quarrels over irrelevancies and be hindered in his perception of what is essential.

The second point I should like our author to stress is that, where he

215

216

---

1 *Discourse*, part 2, (see vol. 1, p. 118); Synopsis, above pp. 9, 11.
2 Cf. Med. II, above p. 16; Med. VI, above p. 61.
3 Med. VI, above p. 53. Descartes adopted Arnauld's advice and inserted a qualifying phrase in brackets.

asserts that we should assent only to what we clearly and distinctly know, he is dealing solely with matters concerned with the sciences and intellectual contemplation, and not with matters belonging to faith and the conduct of life, and hence that his strictures apply only to rashly adopted views of the opinionated, and not to the prudent beliefs of the faithful.[1]

As St Augustine wisely points out in *De Utilitate Credendi*,[2] Chapter 15,

There are three things in the soul of man which it is very important to distinguish, even though they are closely related: understanding, belief and opinion.

A person *understands* if he grasps something by means of a reliable reason. He *believes* if he is influenced by weighty authority to accept a truth even though he does not grasp it by means of a reliable reason. And he is guilty of being *opinionated* if he thinks he knows something of which he is ignorant.

To be opinionated is a very grave fault, for two reasons. Firstly, if someone is convinced that he knows the answer already, he will be unable to learn, even when there is something to be learnt. And secondly, hastiness is in itself a mark of a disordered soul.

If we understand something, then we owe it to reason; if we believe something, we owe it to authority; and if we are opinionated about something, this is based on error. This distinction will help us to understand that we are not guilty of being hasty and opinionated when we hold on to our faith in matters which we do not yet grasp.

217   Those who say that we should believe nothing but what we know are obsessed with avoiding the charge of being opinionated, which it must be admitted is a disgraceful and wretched fault. But we should carefully reflect on the fact that there is a very great difference between, on the one hand, reckoning one knows something and, on the other hand, understanding that one is ignorant about it yet believing it under the influence of some authority. If we reflect on this we will surely avoid the charges of error on the one hand, and inhumanity and arrogance on the other.

A little later, in Chapter 12 Augustine adds 'I could produce many arguments to show that absolutely nothing in human society will be safe if we decide to believe only what we can regard as having been clearly perceived.' These, then, are the views of St Augustine.

M. Descartes, prudent man that he is, will readily judge how important it is to make the distinctions just outlined. For otherwise those many people who in our age are prone to impiety may distort his words in order to subvert the faith.

But what I see as likely to give the greatest offence to theologians is that according to the author's doctrines it seems that the Church's

---

1 See footnote to Synopsis, above p. 11.   2 'On the Benefits of Faith'.

teaching concerning the sacred mysteries of the Eucharist cannot remain completely intact.

We believe on faith that the substance of the bread is taken away from the bread of the Eucharist and only the accidents remain. These are extension, shape, colour, smell, taste and other qualities perceived by the senses.

But the author thinks there are no sensible qualities, but merely various motions in the bodies that surround us which enable us to perceive the various impressions which we subsequently call 'colour', 'taste' and 'smell'. Hence only shape, extension and mobility remain. Yet the author denies that these powers are intelligible apart from some substance for them to inhere in, and hence he holds that they cannot exist without such 218 a substance. He repeats this in his reply to his theological critic.[1]

Further, he recognizes no distinction between the states of a substance and the substance itself except for a formal one; yet this kind of distinction seems insufficient to allow for the states to be separated from the substance even by God.

I am sure that the great piety of our illustrious author will lead him to ponder on this matter attentively and diligently, and that he will take the view that he is obliged to devote his most strenuous efforts to the problem. For otherwise, even though his intention was to defend the cause of God against the impious, he may appear to have endangered the very faith, founded by divine authority, which he hopes will enable him to obtain that eternal life of which he has undertaken to convince mankind.

1 First Replies, above p. 86.

AUTHOR'S REPLIES TO THE FOURTH SET OF OBJECTIONS

I could not possibly wish for a more perceptive or more courteous critic of my book than the gentleman whose comments you have sent me.[1] He has dealt with me so considerately that I can easily perceive his goodwill towards myself and the cause that I defend. At the same time, where he has attacked me he has looked into the issues so deeply, and examined all the related topics so carefully, that I am sure that there are no outstanding difficulties elsewhere that have escaped his watchful attention. What is more, where he thinks my views are not acceptable, he has pressed his criticisms so acutely that I am not afraid of anyone's supposing that he has kept back any objections for the sake of the cause. In view of this, I am not so much disturbed by his criticisms as happy that he has not found more to attack.

219

REPLY TO PART ONE, DEALING WITH THE NATURE OF THE HUMAN MIND

I shall not waste time here by thanking my distinguished critic for bringing in the authority of St Augustine to support me, and for setting out my arguments so vigorously that he seems to fear that their strength may not be sufficiently apparent to anyone else.

But I will begin by pointing out where it was that I embarked on proving 'how, from the fact that I am aware of nothing else belonging to my essence (that is, the essence of the mind alone) apart from the fact that I am a thinking thing, it follows that nothing else does in fact belong to it'.[2] The relevant passage is the one where I proved that God exists – a God who can bring about everything that I clearly and distinctly recognize as possible.[3]

Now it may be that there is much within me of which I am not yet aware (for example, in this passage I was in fact supposing that I was not

---

1 Descartes addresses Mersenne, who acted as intermediary between him and Arnauld, author of the Fourth Set of Objections; see Translator's preface, above p. 64.
2 See above p. 140.   3 Cf. above Med. v, pp. 48f, and Med. vi, p. 54.

yet aware that the mind possessed the power of moving the body, or that it was substantially united to it). Yet since that of which I am aware is sufficient to enable me to subsist with it and it alone, I am certain that I could have been created by God without having these other attributes of which I am unaware, and hence that these other attributes do not belong to the essence of the mind.

For if something can exist without some attribute, then it seems to me that that attribute is not included in its essence. And although mind is part of the essence of man, being united to a human body is not strictly speaking part of the essence of mind.

I must also explain what I meant by saying that 'a real distinction   220 cannot be inferred from the fact that one thing is conceived apart from another by an abstraction of the intellect which conceives the thing inadequately. It can be inferred only if we understand one thing apart from another completely, or as a complete thing.'[1]

I do not, as M. Arnauld assumes,[2] think that adequate knowledge of a thing is required here. Indeed, the difference between complete and adequate knowledge is that if a piece of knowledge is to be *adequate* it must contain absolutely all the properties which are in the thing which is the object of knowledge. Hence only God can know that he has adequate knowledge of all things.

A created intellect, by contrast, though perhaps it may in fact possess adequate knowledge of many things, can never know it has such knowledge unless God grants it a special revelation of the fact. In order to have adequate knowledge of a thing all that is required is that the power of knowing possessed by the intellect is adequate for the thing in question, and this can easily occur. But in order for the intellect to know it has such knowledge, or that God put nothing in the thing beyond what it is aware of, its power of knowing would have to equal the infinite power of God, and this plainly could not happen on pain of contradiction.

Now in order for us to recognize a real distinction between two things it cannot be required that our knowledge of them be adequate if it is impossible for us to know that it is adequate. And since, as has just been explained, we can never know this, it follows that it is not necessary for our knowledge to be adequate.

Hence when I said that 'it does not suffice for a real distinction that one thing is understood apart from another by an abstraction of the intellect   221 which conceives the thing inadequately', I did not think this would be

1 Cf. above p. 140, and First Replies, above pp. 85f.
2 The name is supplied here and elsewhere for the reader's convenience; in the original Descartes refers to his critic simply as 'the distinguished gentleman'.

taken to imply that *adequate* knowledge was required to establish a real distinction. All I meant was that we need the sort of knowledge that we have not ourselves made *inadequate* by an abstraction of the intellect.

There is a great difference between, on the one hand, some item of knowledge being wholly adequate, which we can never know with certainty to be the case unless it is revealed by God, and, on the other hand, its being adequate enough to enable us to perceive that we have not rendered it inadequate by an abstraction of the intellect.

In the same way, when I said that a thing must be understood *completely*, I did not mean that my understanding must be adequate, but merely that I must understand the thing well enough to know that my understanding is *complete*.

I thought I had made this clear from what I had said just before and just after the passage in question. For a little earlier I had distinguished between 'incomplete' and 'complete' entities, and I had said that for there to be a real distinction between a number of things, each of them must be understood as 'an entity in its own right which is different from everything else'.[1]

And later on, after saying that I had 'a complete understanding of what a body is', I immediately added that I also 'understood the mind to be a complete thing'. The meaning of these two phrases was identical; that is, I took 'a complete understanding of something' and 'understanding something to be a complete thing' as having one and the same meaning.

But here you may justly ask what I mean by a 'complete thing', and how I prove that for establishing a real distinction it is sufficient that two things can be understood as 'complete' and that each one can be understood apart from the other.

222   My answer to the first question is that by a 'complete thing' I simply mean a substance endowed with the forms or attributes which enable me to recognize that it is a substance.

We do not have immediate knowledge of substances, as I have noted elsewhere. We know them only by perceiving certain forms or attributes which must inhere in something if they are to exist; and we call the thing in which they inhere a 'substance'.

But if we subsequently wanted to strip the substance of the attributes through which we know it, we would be destroying our entire knowledge of it. We might be able to apply various words to it, but we could not have a clear and distinct perception of what we meant by these words.

I am aware that certain substances are commonly called 'incomplete'. But if the reason for calling them incomplete is that they are unable to exist on their own, then I confess I find it self-contradictory that they

1 First Replies, above p. 86.

should be substances, that is, things which subsist on their own, and at the same time incomplete, that is, not possessing the power to subsist on their own. It is also possible to call a substance incomplete in the sense that, although it has nothing incomplete about it *qua* substance, it is incomplete in so far as it is referred to some other substance in conjunction with which it forms something which is a unity in its own right.

Thus a hand is an incomplete substance when it is referred to the whole body of which it is a part; but it is a complete substance when it is considered on its own. And in just the same way the mind and the body are incomplete substances when they are referred to a human being which together they make up. But if they are considered on their own, they are complete.

For just as being extended and divisible and having shape etc. are 223 forms or attributes by which I recognize the substance called *body*, so understanding, willing, doubting etc. are forms by which I recognize the substance which is called *mind*. And I understand a thinking substance to be just as much a complete thing as an extended substance.

It is quite impossible to assert, as my distinguished critic maintains, that 'body may be related to mind as a genus is related to a species'.[1] For although a genus can be understood without this or that specific differentia, there is no way in which a species can be thought of without its genus.

For example, we can easily understand the genus 'figure' without thinking of a circle (though our understanding will not be distinct unless it is referred to some specific figure and it will not involve a complete thing unless it also comprises the nature of body). But we cannot understand any specific differentia of the 'circle' without at the same time thinking of the genus 'figure'.

Now the mind can be perceived distinctly and completely (that is, sufficiently for it to be considered as a complete thing) without any of the forms or attributes by which we recognize that body is a substance, as I think I showed quite adequately in the Second Meditation. And similarly a body can be understood distinctly and as a complete thing, without any of the attributes which belong to the mind.

But here my critic argues that although I can obtain some knowledge of myself without knowledge of the body, it does not follow that this knowledge is complete and adequate, so as to enable me to be certain that I am not mistaken in excluding body from my essence.[2] He explains 224 the point by using the example of a triangle inscribed in a semi-circle, which we can clearly and distinctly understand to be right-angled

1 Above p. 141. 2 *Ibid.*

although we do not know, or may even deny, that the square on the hypotenuse is equal to the squares on the other sides. But we cannot infer from this that there could be a right-angled triangle such that the square on the hypotenuse is not equal to the squares on the other sides.

But this example differs in many respects from the case under discussion.

First of all, though a triangle can perhaps be taken concretely as a substance having a triangular shape, it is certain that the property of having the square on the hypotenuse equal to the squares on the other sides is not a substance. So neither the triangle nor the property can be understood as a complete thing in the way in which mind and body can be so understood; nor can either item be called a 'thing' in the sense in which I said 'it is enough that I can understand one thing (that is, a complete thing) apart from another' etc.[1] This is clear from the passage which comes next: 'Besides I find in myself faculties' etc. I did not say that these faculties were *things*, but carefully distinguished them from things or substances.

Secondly, although we can clearly and distinctly understand that a triangle in a semi-circle is right-angled without being aware that the square on the hypotenuse is equal to the squares on the other two sides, we cannot have a clear understanding of a triangle having the square on its hypotenuse equal to the squares on the other sides without at the same time being aware that it is right-angled. And yet we can clearly and distinctly perceive the mind without the body and the body without the mind.

Thirdly, although it is possible to have a concept of a triangle inscribed in a semi-circle which does not include the fact that the square on the hypotenuse is equal to the squares on the other sides, it is not possible to have a concept of the triangle such that no ratio at all is understood to hold between the square on the hypotenuse and the squares on the other sides. Hence, though we may be unaware of what that ratio is, we cannot say that any given ratio does not hold unless we clearly understand that it does not belong to the triangle; and where the ratio is one of equality, this can never be understood. Yet the concept of body includes nothing at all which belongs to the mind, and the concept of mind includes nothing at all which belongs to the body.

So although I said 'it is enough that I can clearly and distinctly understand one thing apart from another' etc., one cannot go on to argue 'yet I clearly and distinctly understand that this triangle is right-angled without understanding that the square on the hypotenuse' etc.[2] There are three reasons for this. First, the ratio between the square on the

1 Med. VI, above p. 54.   2 Above p. 142.

hypotenuse and the squares on the other sides is not a complete thing. Secondly, we do not clearly understand the ratio to be equal except in the case of a right-angled triangle. And thirdly, there is no way in which the triangle can be distinctly understood if the ratio which obtains between the square on the hypotenuse and the squares on the other sides is said not to hold.

But now I must explain how the mere fact that I can clearly and   226 distinctly understand one substance apart from another is enough to make me certain that one excludes the other.[1]

The answer is that the notion of a *substance* is just this – that it can exist by itself, that is without the aid of any other substance. And there is no one who has ever perceived two substances by means of two different concepts without judging that they are really distinct.

Hence, had I not been looking for greater than ordinary certainty, I should have been content to have shown in the Second Meditation that the mind can be understood as a subsisting thing despite the fact that nothing belonging to the body is attributed to it, and that, conversely, the body can be understood as a subsisting thing despite the fact that nothing belonging to the mind is attributed to it. I should have added nothing more in order to demonstrate that there is a real distinction between the mind and the body, since we commonly judge that the order in which things are mutually related in our perception of them corresponds to the order in which they are related in actual reality. But one of the exaggerated doubts which I put forward in the First Meditation went so far as to make it impossible for me to be certain of this very point (namely whether things do in reality correspond to our perception of them), so long as I was supposing myself to be ignorant of the author of my being. And this is why everything I wrote on the subject of God and truth in the Third, Fourth and Fifth Meditations contributes to the conclusion that there is a real distinction between the mind and the body, which I finally established in the Sixth Meditation.

And yet, says M. Arnauld, 'I have a clear understanding of a triangle   227 inscribed in a semi-circle without knowing that the square on the hypotenuse is equal to the squares on the other sides.'[2] It is true that the triangle is intelligible even though we do not think of the ratio which obtains between the square on the hypotenuse and the squares on the other sides; but it is not intelligible that this ratio should be denied of the triangle. In the case of the mind, by contrast, not only do we understand it to exist without the body, but, what is more, all the attributes which belong to a body can be denied of it. For it is of the nature of substances that they should mutually exclude one another.

1 Cf. Med. VI, above p. 54.   2 Cf. above p. 142.

M. Arnauld goes on to say: 'Since I infer my existence from the fact that I am thinking, it is certainly no surprise if the idea that I form in this way represents me simply as a thinking thing.'[1] But this is no objection to my argument. For it is equally true that when I examine the nature of the body, I find nothing at all in it which savours of thought. And we can have no better evidence for a distinction between two things than the fact that if we examine either of them, whatever we find in one is different from what we find in the other.

Nor do I see why this argument 'proves too much'.[2] For the fact that one thing can be separated from another by the power of God is the very least that can be asserted in order to establish that there is a real distinction between the two. Also, I thought I was very careful to guard against anyone inferring from this that man was simply 'a soul which makes use of a body'. For in the Sixth Meditation, where I dealt with the distinction between the mind and the body, I also proved at the same time that the mind is substantially united with the body.[3] And the arguments which I used to prove this are as strong as any I can remember ever having read. Now someone who says that a man's arm is a substance that is really distinct from the rest of his body does not thereby deny that the arm belongs to the nature of the whole man. And saying that the arm belongs to the nature of the whole man does not give rise to the suspicion that it cannot subsist in its own right. In the same way, I do not think I proved too much in showing that the mind can exist apart from the body. Nor do I think I proved too little in saying that the mind is substantially united with the body, since that substantial union does not prevent our having a clear and distinct concept of the mind on its own, as a complete thing. The concept is thus very different from that of a surface or a line, which cannot be understood as complete things unless we attribute to them not just length and breadth but also depth.

Finally the fact that 'the power of thought is dormant in infants and extinguished in madmen'[4] (I should say not 'extinguished' but 'disturbed'), does not show that we should regard it as so attached to bodily organs that it cannot exist without them. The fact that thought is often impeded by bodily organs, as we know from our own frequent experience, does not at all entail that it is produced by those organs. This latter view is one for which not even the slightest proof can be adduced.

I must admit, however, that the fact that the mind is closely conjoined with the body, which we experience constantly through our senses, does result in our not being aware of the real distinction between mind and body unless we attentively meditate on the subject. But I think that those who repeatedly ponder on what I wrote in the Second Meditation will be

228

229

1 Cf. above p. 143.   2 *Ibid.*   3 Above pp. 56ff.   4 Above p. 143.

easily convinced that the mind is distinct from the body, and distinct not just by a fiction or abstraction of the intellect: it can be known as a distinct thing because it is in reality distinct.

I will not answer my critic's further observations regarding the immortality of the soul, because they do not conflict with my views. As far as the souls of the brutes are concerned, this is not the place to examine the subject, and, short of giving an account of the whole of physics, I cannot add to the explanatory remarks I made in Part 5 of the *Discourse on the Method*.[1] But to avoid passing over the topic in silence, I will say that I think the most important point is that, both in our bodies and those of the brutes, no movements can occur without the presence of all the organs or instruments which would enable the same movements to be produced in a machine. So even in our own case the mind does not directly move the external limbs, but simply controls the animal spirits which flow from the heart via the brain into the muscles, and sets up certain motions in them; for the spirits are by their nature adapted with equal facility to a great variety of actions. Now a very large number of the motions occurring inside us do not depend in any way on the mind. These include heartbeat, digestion, nutrition, respiration when we are asleep, and also such waking actions as walking, singing and the like, when these occur without the mind attending to them. When people take a fall, and stick out their hands so as to protect their head, it is not reason that instructs them to do this; it is simply that the sight of the impending fall reaches the brain and sends the animal spirits into the nerves in the manner necessary to produce this movement even without any mental volition, just as it would be produced in a machine. And since our own experience reliably informs us that this is so, why should we be so amazed that the 'light reflected from the body of a wolf onto the eyes of a sheep'[2] should equally be capable of arousing the movements of flight in the sheep?

But if we wish to determine by the use of reason whether any of the movements of the brutes are similar to those which are performed in us with the help of the mind, or whether they resemble those which depend merely on the flow of the animal spirits and the disposition of the organs, then we should consider the differences that can be found between men and beasts. I mean the differences which I set out in Part 5 of the *Discourse on the Method*, for I think these are the only differences to be found. If we do this, it will readily be apparent that all the actions of the brutes resemble only those which occur in us without any assistance from the mind. And we shall be forced to conclude from this that we know of absolutely no principle of movement in animals apart from the

230

1 See above p. 144 and vol. 1, pp. 139ff.   2 Above p. 144.

disposition of their organs and the continual flow of the spirits which are produced by the heat of the heart as it rarefies the blood. We shall also see that there was no excuse for our imagining that any other principle of motion was to be found in the brutes. We made this mistake because we failed to distinguish the two principles of motion just described; and on seeing that the principle depending solely on the animal spirits and organs exists in the brutes just as it does in us, we jumped to the conclusion that the other principle, which consists in mind or thought, also exists in them. Things which we have become convinced of since our earliest years, even though they have subsequently been shown by rational arguments to be false, cannot easily be eradicated from our beliefs unless we give the relevant arguments our long and frequent attention.

231

REPLY TO PART TWO, CONCERNING GOD

Up till now I have attempted to refute my critic's arguments and to stand up to his attack. But from now I will follow the example of those who are matched with opponents who are superior in strength: instead of meeting him head on I will dodge his blows.

Only three criticisms are raised by M. Arnauld in this section, and they can all be accepted if they are taken in the sense which he intends. But when I wrote what I did, I meant it in another sense, which seems to me to be equally correct.

The first point is that certain ideas are materially false.[1] As I interpret this claim, it means that the ideas are such as to provide subject-matter for error. But M. Arnauld concentrates on ideas taken in the formal sense, and maintains that there is no falsity in them.

The second point is that God derives his existence from himself 'positively and as it were causally'.[2] By this I simply meant that the reason why God does not need any efficient cause in order to exist depends on a positive thing, that is, the very immensity of God, which is as positive as anything can be. M. Arnauld, however, shows that God is not self-created or self-preserved by any positive influence of an efficient cause; and this I quite agree with.

232

The third and last point is that 'there can be nothing in our mind of which we are not aware'.[3] I meant this to refer to the operations of the mind; but M. Arnauld takes it to apply to the mind's powers, and so denies it.

But let us deal with the points more carefully one at a time. When M. Arnauld says 'if cold is merely an absence, there cannot be an idea of cold which represents it as a positive thing',[4] it is clear that he is dealing solely

1 Above p. 145.   2 Above pp. 146ff.   3 Above p. 150.   4 Above p. 145.

with an idea taken in the *formal* sense. Since ideas are forms of a kind, and are not composed of any matter, when we think of them as representing something we are taking them not *materially* but *formally*. If, however, we were considering them not as representing this or that but simply as operations of the intellect, then it could be said that we were taking them materially, but in that case they would have no reference to the truth or falsity of their objects. So I think that the only sense in which an idea can be said to be 'materially false' is the one which I explained. Thus, whether cold is a positive thing or an absence does not affect the idea I have of it, which remains the same as it always was. It is this idea which, I claim, can provide subject-matter for error if it is in fact true that cold is an absence and does not have as much reality as heat; for if I consider the ideas of cold and heat just as I received them from my senses, I am unable to tell that one idea represents more reality to me than the other. 233

I certainly did not 'confuse a judgement with an idea'.[1] For I said that the falsity to be found in an idea is *material* falsity, while the falsity involved in a judgement can only be *formal*.

When my critic says that the idea of cold 'is coldness itself in so far as it exists objectively in the intellect',[2] I think we need to make a distinction. For it often happens in the case of obscure and confused ideas – and the ideas of heat and cold fall into this category – that an idea is referred to something other than that of which it is in fact the idea. Thus if cold is simply an absence, the idea of cold is not coldness itself as it exists objectively in the intellect, but something else, which I erroneously mistake for this absence, namely a sensation which in fact has no existence outside the intellect.

The same point does not apply to the idea of God, or at least to the idea of God which is clear and distinct, since it cannot be said to refer to something with which it does not correspond. But as for the confused ideas of gods which are concocted by idolaters, I see no reason why they too cannot be called materially false, in so far as they provide the idolaters with subject-matter for false judgements. Yet ideas which give the judgement little or no scope for error do not seem as much entitled to be called materially false as those which give great scope for error. It is easy to show by means of examples that some ideas provide much greater scope for error than others. Confused ideas which are made up at will by 234 the mind, such as the ideas of false gods, do not provide as much scope for error as the confused ideas arriving from the senses, such as the ideas of colour and cold (if it is true, as I have said, that these ideas do not represent anything real). The greatest scope for error is provided by the

1 *Ibid.*   2 *Ibid.*

ideas which arise from the sensations of appetite. Thus the idea of thirst which the patient with dropsy has does indeed give him subject-matter for error, since it can lead him to judge that a drink will do him good, when in fact it will do him harm.

But my critic asks what the idea of cold, which I described as materially false, represents to me. If it represents an absence, he says, it is true; and if it represents a positive entity, it is not the idea of cold.[1] This is right; but my only reason for calling the idea 'materially false' is that, owing to the fact that it is obscure and confused, I am unable to judge whether or not what it represents to me is something positive which exists outside of my sensation. And hence I may be led to judge that it is something positive though in fact it may merely be an absence.

Hence in asking what is the cause of the positive objective being which, in my view, is responsible for the idea being materially false, my critic has raised an improper question. For I do not claim that an idea's material falsity results from some positive entity; it arises solely from the obscurity of the idea – although this does have something positive as its underlying subject, namely the actual sensation involved.

Now this positive entity exists in me, in so far as I am something real. But the obscurity of the idea is the only thing that leads me to judge that the idea of the sensation of cold represents some object called 'cold' which is located outside me; and this obscurity in the idea does not have a real cause but arises simply from the fact that my nature is not perfect in all respects.

This does not in any way violate my fundamental principles. One fear that I might have had, however, is that since I have never spent very much time reading philosophical texts, my calling ideas which I take to provide subject-matter for error 'materially false' might have involved too great a departure from standard philosophical usage. This might, I say, have worried me, had I not found the word 'materially' used in an identical sense to my own in the first philosophical author I came across, namely Suarez, in the *Metaphysical Disputations*, Part IX, Section 2, Number 4.[2]

But let me now turn to my critic's principal complaint – though it is one which seems to me to be the least well-taken of all his objections. This concerns the passage where I said that 'we are entitled to think that in a sense God stands in the same relation to himself as an efficient cause to its effect'.[3] M. Arnauld says that it is 'a hard saying, and indeed false' to suggest that God is the efficient cause of himself; but I actually denied that suggestion in the passage just quoted. For in saying that God 'in a sense' stands in the same relation as an efficient cause, I made it clear that

235

1 Above p. 146.   2 See note above p. 69.
3 First Replies, above p. 80; Arnauld's comments, above p. 146.

I did not suppose he was the same as an efficient cause; and in using the phrase 'we are quite entitled to think' I meant that I was explaining the matter in these terms merely on account of the imperfection of the human intellect. Indeed, throughout the rest of the passage I confirmed this. Right at the beginning, having said 'if anything exists we may always inquire into its efficient cause', I immediately went on 'or, if it does not have one, we may demand why it does not need one'.[1] These words make it quite clear that I did believe in the existence of something that does not need an efficient cause. And what could that be, but God? A little later on I said that 'there is in God such great and inexhaustible power that he never required the assistance of anything in order to exist, and does not now require any assistance for his preservation, so that he is in a sense his own cause'. Here the phrase 'his own cause' cannot possibly be taken to mean an efficient cause; it simply means that the inexhaustible power of God is the cause or reason for his not needing a cause. And since that inexhaustible power or immensity of the divine essence is as *positive* as can be, I said that the the reason or cause why God needs no cause is a *positive* reason or cause. Now this cannot be said of any finite thing, even though it is quite perfect of its kind. If a finite thing is said to derive its existence 'from itself', this can only be understood in a *negative* sense, meaning that no reason can be derived from its positive nature which could enable us to understand that it does not require an efficient cause.

 Similarly, in every passage where I made a comparison between the formal cause (or reason derived from God's essence, in virtue of which he needs no cause in order to exist or to be preserved) and the efficient cause (without which finite things cannot exist), I always took care to make it explicitly clear that the two kinds of cause are different. And I never said that God preserves himself by some positive force, in the way in which created things are preserved by him; I simply said that the immensity of his power or essence, in virtue of which he does not need a preserver, is a *positive* thing.

 Hence I can readily admit everything my critic puts forward to prove that God is not the efficient cause of himself and that he does not preserve himself by any positive power or by continuously re-creating himself; and this is the sole result established by M. Arnauld's arguments. But I hope that even M. Arnauld will not deny that the immensity of the power in virtue of which God needs no cause in order to exist is a *positive* thing in God, and that nothing which is similarly *positive* can be understood to exist in any other thing in such a way that it does not need an efficient cause in order to exist. That is all I meant when I said that, with the sole exception of God, the only sense in which anything can be said to derive

1 Above p. 78.

its existence 'from itself' is a *negative* one. And I had no need to make any further assumptions in order to resolve the difficulty which had been raised.

But since M. Arnauld has given me such a sombre warning, that 'it will scarcely be possible to find a single theologian who will not object to the proposition that God derives his existence from himself in a positive sense and as it were causally',[1] I will explain a little more carefully why this way of talking is extremely useful and even necessary when dealing with the topic under discussion. Indeed, as I shall show, it seems to me to be wholly innocent of any suspicion of being likely to cause offence.

I am aware that theologians writing in Latin do not use the word *causa* ['cause'] in matters of divinity when they are dealing with the procession of Persons in the Holy Trinity. Whereas the Greek writers use αἴτιος and ἀρχή interchangeably, they prefer to use only the word *principium* ['principle'] taken in its most general sense, to avoid giving anyone an excuse to infer that the Son is less important than the Father. But where there is no such risk of error, and we are dealing with God not as a Trinity but simply as a unity, I do not see why the word 'cause' is to be avoided at all costs, especially when we come to a context where it seems extremely useful and almost necessary to use the term.

Now if the term 'cause' serves to demonstrate the existence of God, it can hardly be more useful; and if it is impossible to achieve complete clarity in the proof without it, the term can hardly be more necessary.

But I think it is clear to everyone that a consideration of efficient causes is the primary and principal way, if not the only way, that we have of proving the existence of God. We cannot develop this proof with precision unless we grant our minds the freedom to inquire into the efficient causes of all things, even God himself. For what right do we have to make God an exception, if we have not yet proved that he exists? In every case, then, we must ask whether a thing derives its existence *from itself* or *from something else*; and by this means the existence of God can be inferred, even though we have not given an explicit account of what it means to say that something derives its existence 'from itself'. Those who follow the sole guidance of the natural light will in this context spontaneously form a concept of cause that is common to both an efficient and a formal cause: that is to say, what derives its existence 'from another' will be taken to derive its existence from that thing as an efficient cause, while what derives its existence 'from itself' will be taken to derive its existence from itself as a formal cause – that is, because it has the kind of essence which entails that it does not require an efficient

1 Above p. 150.

cause. Accordingly, I did not explain this point in my *Meditations*, but 239
left it out, assuming it was self-evident.

Now some people are accustomed to judge that nothing can be the
efficient cause of itself, and they carefully distinguish an efficient cause
from a formal cause. Hence, when they see the question raised as to
whether anything derives its existence from itself, it can easily happen
that they think only of an efficient cause in the strict sense, and thus they
suppose that the phrase 'from itself' must be taken not as meaning 'from
a cause', but only in the negative sense, as meaning 'without a cause'
(that is, as implying something such that we must not inquire why it
exists). If we accept this interpretation of the phrase 'from itself', then it
will not be possible to produce any argument for the existence of God
based on his effects, as was correctly shown by the author of the First Set
of Objections;[1] and hence this interpretation must be totally rejected.

To give a proper reply to this, I think it is necessary to show that, in
between 'efficient cause' in the strict sense and 'no cause at all', there is a
third possibility, namely 'the positive essence of a thing', to which the
concept of an efficient cause can be extended. In the same way in
geometry the concept of the arc of an indefinitely large circle is
customarily extended to the concept of a straight line; or the concept of a
rectilinear polygon with an indefinite number of sides is extended to that
of a circle. I thought I explained this in the best way available to me when
I said that in this context the meaning of 'efficient cause' must not be
restricted to causes which are prior in time to their effects or different 240
from them. For, first, this would make the question trivial, since everyone
knows that something cannot be prior to, or distinct from, itself; and
secondly, the restriction 'prior in time' can be deleted from the concept
while leaving the notion of an efficient cause intact.[2]

The fact that a cause need not be prior in time is clear from the fact
that the notion of a cause is applicable only during the time when it is
producing its effect, as I have said.

The fact that the second restriction cannot also be deleted implies
merely that a cause which is not distinct from its effects is not an efficient
cause in the strict sense, and this I admit. It does not, however, follow
that such a cause is in no sense a positive cause that can be regarded as
analogous to an efficient cause; and this is all that my argument requires.
The same natural light that enables me to perceive that I would have
given myself all the perfections of which I have an idea, if I had given
myself existence, also enables me to perceive that nothing can give itself
existence in the restricted sense usually implied by the proper meaning of

1 Above pp. 68f.
2 Descartes here rephrases his earlier argument, First Replies, above p. 78.

the term 'efficient cause'. For in this sense, what gives itself existence would have to be different from itself in so far as it receives existence; yet to be both the same thing and not the same thing – that is, something different – is a contradiction.

Hence, when we ask whether something can give itself existence, this must be taken to be the same as asking whether the nature or essence of something is such that it does not need an efficient cause in order to exist.

The further proposition that if there is such a being he will give himself all the perfections of which he possesses an idea, if indeed he does not yet
241　have them,[1] means that this being cannot but possess in actuality all the perfections of which he is aware. This is because we perceive by the natural light that a being whose essence is so immense that he does not need an efficient cause in order to exist, equally does not need an efficient cause in order to possess all the perfections of which he is aware: his own essence is the eminent source which bestows on him whatever we can think of as being capable of being bestowed on anything by an efficient cause.

The words 'he will give himself all the perfections, if indeed he does not yet have them' are merely explanatory. For the same natural light enables us to perceive that it is impossible for such a being to have the power and will to give itself something new; rather, his essence is such that he possesses from eternity everything which we can now suppose he would bestow on himself if he did not yet possess it.

Nonetheless, all the above ways of talking, which are derived by analogy with the notion of efficient causation, are very necessary for guiding the natural light in such a way as to enable us to have a clear awareness of these matters. It is exactly the same sort of comparison between a sphere (or other curvilinear figure) and a rectilinear figure that enabled Archimedes to demonstrate various properties of the sphere which could scarcely be understood otherwise. And just as no one criticizes these proofs, although they involve regarding a sphere as similar to a polyhedron, so it seems to me that I am not open to criticism in this context for using the analogy of an efficient cause to explain features which in fact belong to a formal cause, that is, to the very essence of God.

There is no possible risk of error involved in using this analogy, since
242　the one feature peculiar to an efficient cause, and not transferable to a formal cause, involves an evident contradiction which could not be accepted by anyone, namely that something could be different from itself, or the same thing and not the same thing at one time.

It should also be noted that I have attributed to God the dignity of being a cause in such a way as not to imply that he has any of the

1 Cf. Med. III, above pp. 33f, discussed by Arnauld, above p. 146.

indignity of being an effect. Just as theologians in saying that the Father is the 'originating principle' of the Son do not thereby admit that the Son is something 'originated', so, in admitting that God can in a sense be called 'the cause of himself', I have nowhere implied that he can in the same way be called 'the effect of himself'. For an effect is normally referred principally to its efficient cause and is regarded as being inferior to it, although it is often superior to other causes.

In taking the whole essence of a thing to be its formal cause in this context, I am simply following the footsteps of Aristotle. For in the *Posterior Analytics*, Book 2, Chapter 11, Aristotle passes over the material cause, and calls the first kind of $\alpha\grave{\iota}\tau\acute{\iota}\alpha$, or cause, $\tau\grave{o}\ \tau\acute{\iota}\ \hat{\eta}\nu\ \epsilon\hat{\iota}\nu\alpha\iota$,[1] or the 'formal' cause, as it is normally rendered in philosophical Latin. He then extends this notion to all the essences of all things, since at this point he is not dealing with the causes of a physical compound (any more than I am in this context), but is dealing generally with the causes from which any kind of knowledge can be derived.

It was, however, scarcely possible for me to deal with this topic without attributing the term 'cause' to God. This can be shown from the fact that in trying to achieve the same result as I did by another route my critic has completely failed to achieve his objective, at least in my view. First of all he explains at length that God is not the efficient cause of   243 himself, since the notion of an efficient cause requires that it be distinct from its effect. Next he shows that God does not derive his existence from himself in the 'positive' sense, where 'positive' is taken to imply the positive power of a cause. And then he shows that God does not really preserve himself, if 'preservation' is taken to mean the continuous creation of a thing. All this I gladly admit. But then he again tries to show that God cannot be called the efficient cause of himself on the grounds that 'we look for the efficient cause of something only in respect of its existence, not in respect of its essence'. He goes on,

But it belongs to the essence of an infinite being that it exists no less than it belongs to the essence of a triangle to have its three angles equal to two right angles. And hence if someone asks whether God exists, we should no more give an answer in terms of an efficient cause than we should do so if someone asks why the three angles of a triangle are equal to two right angles.[2]

This syllogism can easily be turned against M. Arnauld, as follows: although we do not ask for an efficient cause with respect to something's essence, we can nevertheless ask for an efficient cause with respect to something's existence; but in the case of God, essence is not distinct from existence; hence we can ask for the efficient cause in the case of God.

1 Literally, 'what it is to be something'.   2 Cf. above p. 149.

But to reconcile our two positions, the answer to the question why God exists should be given not in terms of an efficient cause in the strict sense, but simply in terms of the essence or formal cause of the thing. And precisely because in the case of God there is no distinction between existence and essence, the formal cause will be strongly analogous to an efficient cause, and hence can be called something close to an efficient cause.

Finally, M. Arnauld adds:

244   If someone asks for an efficient cause of God, we should reply that he does not need an efficient cause. And if the questioner goes on to ask why he does not need an efficient cause, we should answer that this is because he is an infinite being, whose existence is his essence. For the only things that require an efficient cause are those in which actual existence may be distinguished from essence.[1]

This, he says, disposes of my argument, that 'if I thought that nothing could possibly have the same relation to itself as an efficient cause has to its effect, then in the course of my inquiry into the causes of things I should never reach anything which was the first cause of everything else'.[2] But it seems to me that this point neither disposes of my argument nor in any way shakes it or weakens it. On the contrary, the principal force of my proof depends on it, and the same is true of absolutely all the proofs that can possibly be constructed to demonstrate the existence of God from his effects. Moreover, almost all theologians maintain that an argument based on God's effects is the only kind of argument that can be adduced to prove his existence.

Thus, in refusing to allow us to say that God stands toward himself in a relation analogous to that of an efficient cause, M. Arnauld not only fails to clarify the proof of God's existence, but actually prevents the reader from understanding it. This is especially true at the end when he concludes that 'if we thought we ought to look for the efficient cause, or quasi-efficient cause, of any given thing, then what we would be looking for would be a cause distinct from the thing in question'.[3] How would those who do not yet know that God exists be able to inquire into the efficient cause of other things, with the aim of eventually arriving at knowledge of God, unless they thought it possible to inquire into the efficient cause of anything whatsoever? And how could they reach the
245   end of their inquiries by arriving at God as the first cause if they thought that for any given thing we must always look for a cause which is distinct from it?

Let us suppose that Archimedes, in speaking of the properties which he demonstrated of a sphere by taking it as analogous to a rectilinear figure

1 Above p. 150.   2 First Replies, above p. 78.   3 Above p. 150.

inscribed in a square, had said this: 'If I thought that a sphere could not be taken to be a rectilinear or quasi-rectilinear figure with an infinite number of sides, I should attach no force to my proof, since the proof does not strictly apply to a sphere as a curvilinear figure but applies to it only as a rectilinear figure with infinitely many sides.' And let us also suppose that M. Arnauld objected to taking the sphere in this way, but nevertheless wanted to retain Archimedes' proof. It seems to me that the move M. Arnauld has made regarding God is just the same as if he were to say: 'If I thought that Archimedes' conclusion was supposed to hold of a rectilinear figure with infinitely many sides, I should not accept that it applied to a sphere, since I am quite sure and certain that a sphere is in no sense a rectilinear figure.' In saying this he would not only be failing to establish Archimedes' result, but would be preventing himself and others from properly understanding the proof.

I have pursued this issue at somewhat greater length than perhaps the subject required, in order to show that I am extremely anxious to prevent anything at all being found in my writings which could justifiably give offence to the theologians.

Lastly, as to the fact that I was not guilty of circularity[1] when I said that the only reason we have for being sure that what we clearly and distinctly perceive is true is the fact that God exists, but that we are sure that God exists only because we perceive this clearly: I have already given an adequate explanation of this point in my reply to the Second Objections, under the headings *Thirdly* and *Fourthly*, where I made a distinction between what we in fact perceive clearly and what we remember having perceived clearly on a previous occasion.[2] To begin with, we are sure that God exists because we attend to the arguments which prove this; but subsequently it is enough for us to remember that we perceived something clearly in order for us to be certain that it is true. This would not be sufficient if we did not know that God exists and is not a deceiver.

As to the fact that there can be nothing in the mind, in so far as it is a thinking thing, of which it is not aware,[3] this seems to me to be self-evident. For there is nothing that we can understand to be in the mind, regarded in this way, that is not a thought or dependent on a thought. If it were not a thought or dependent on a thought it would not belong to the mind *qua* thinking thing; and we cannot have any thought of which we are not aware at the very moment when it is in us. In view of this I do not doubt that the mind begins to think as soon as it is implanted in the body of an infant, and that it is immediately aware of its thoughts,

246

---

1 *Ibid.*   2 Above pp. 100f, pp. 103f.   3 Above pp. 33, 150.

even though it does not remember this afterwards because the impressions of these thoughts do not remain in the memory.

But it must be noted that, although we are always actually aware of the acts or operations of our minds, we are not always aware of the mind's faculties or powers, except potentially. By this I mean that when we concentrate on employing one of our faculties, then immediately, if the faculty in question resides in our mind, we become actually aware of it, and hence we may deny that it is in the mind if we are not capable of becoming aware of it.

REPLY TO THE POINTS WHICH MAY CAUSE DIFFICULTY TO THEOLOGIANS

I have countered M. Arnauld's first group of arguments and I have side-stepped the second group. The arguments in the final section I completely agree with, except for the last one, and here I hope I can persuade him, without difficulty, to come round to my view.

I completely concede, then, that the contents of the First Meditation, and indeed the others, are not suitable to be grasped by every mind. I have stated this whenever the opportunity arose, and I shall continue to do so. This was the sole reason why I did not deal with these matters in the *Discourse on the Method*, which was written in French, but reserved them instead for the *Meditations*, which I warned should be studied only by very intelligent and well-educated readers. No one should object that I would have done better to avoid writing on matters which a large number of people ought to avoid reading about; for I regard these matters as so crucial that I am convinced that without them no firm or stable results can ever be established in philosophy. Although fire and knives cannot safely be handled by careless people or children, no one thinks that this is a reason for doing without them altogether, since they are so useful for human life.

The next point concerns the fact that in the Fourth Meditation I dealt only 'with the mistakes we commit in distinguishing between the true and the false and not those that occur in our pursuit of good and evil', and that when I asserted that 'we should assent only to what we clearly know' this was always subject to the exception of 'matters which belong to faith and the conduct of life'.[1] Now this is something that the entire context of my book makes clear; moreover I have explained the point quite explicitly in my reply to the Second Objections, under the heading *Fifthly*, and I have also given advance warning of it in the Synopsis.[2] I say this in order to show how much I respect M. Arnauld's judgement and how much I welcome his advice.

1 Above pp. 15 1f.   2 Above pp. 11, 106.

There remains the sacrament of the Eucharist, with which M. Arnauld believes my views are in conflict. He says: 'We believe on faith that the substance of the bread is taken away from the bread of the Eucharist and only the accidents remain'; and he thinks that I do not admit that there are any real accidents but recognize only modes which are unintelligible apart from some substance for them to inhere in, and hence that they cannot exist without such a substance.[1]

I think I can easily get round this objection if I say that I have never denied that there are real accidents. It is true that in the *Optics* and the *Meteorology* I did not make use of such qualities in order to explain the matters which I was dealing with, but in the *Meteorology*, p. 164, I expressly said that I was not denying their existence.[2] And in the *Meditations*, although I was supposing that I did not yet have any knowledge of them, I did not thereby suppose that none existed. The analytic style of writing that I adopted there allows us from time to time to make certain assumptions that have not yet been thoroughly examined; and this comes out in the First Meditation where I made many assumptions which I proceeded to refute in the subsequent Meditations. Further, it was certainly not my intention at that point to establish any definite results concerning the nature of accidents; I simply set down what appeared to be true of them on a preliminary survey. Lastly, my saying that modes are not intelligible apart from some substance for them to inhere in should not be taken to imply any denial that they can be separated from a substance by the power of God; for I firmly insist and believe that many things can be brought about by God which we are incapable of understanding.

But if I may express myself rather more freely, I will not hide the fact that I am convinced that what affects our senses is simply and solely the surface that constitutes the limit of the dimensions of the body which is perceived by the senses. For contact with an object takes place only at the surface, and nothing can have an effect on any of our senses except through contact, as not just I but all philosophers, including even

---

1 Above p. 153.

2 Descartes' page reference is to the 1637 edition of the *Meteorology*. The relevant passage runs as follows:

To make you accept all these suppositions more easily, bear in mind that I do not conceive of these particles of terrestrial matter as atoms or indivisible particles. I regard them as all being composed of one single kind of matter, and believe that each of them could be divided repeatedly in infinitely many ways, and that there is no more difference between them than there is between stones of various different shapes cut from the same rock. Bear in mind too, that to avoid a breach with the philosophers, I have no wish to deny any further items which they may imagine in bodies over and above what I have described, such as 'substantial forms', their 'real qualities', and so on. It simply seems to me that my arguments must be all the more acceptable in so far as I can make them depend on fewer things. (AT VI, 239)

Aristotle, maintain. So bread or wine, for example, are perceived by the senses only in so far as the surface of the bread or wine is in contact with our sense organs, either immediately, or via the air or other bodies, as I maintain, or, as many philosophers hold, by the intervention of 'intentional forms'.[1]

But we must note that our conception of the surface should not be based merely on the external shape of a body that is felt by our fingers; we should also consider all the tiny gaps that are found in betweeen the particles of flour that make up the bread, and the tiny gaps between the particles of alcohol, water, vinegar and lees or tartar that are mixed together to form wine; and the same applies to the particles of other bodies. For, since these particles have various shapes and motions, they can never be joined together, however tightly, without many spaces being left between them – spaces which are not empty but full of air or other matter. Thus in the case of bread, we can see with the naked eye relatively large gaps which can be filled not just with air but with water or wine or other liquids. And since bread does not lose its identity despite the fact that the air or other matter contained in its pores is replaced, it is clear that this matter does not belong to the substance of the bread. Hence the surface of the bread is not the area most closely marked out by the outline of an entire piece of bread, but is the surface immediately surrounding its individual particles.

We must also note that not only does this surface move in its entirety when a whole piece of bread is moved from one place to another, but there is also partial movement when some particles of the bread are agitated by air or other bodies which enter its pores. Hence if there are any bodies whose nature is such that some or all of their parts are in continual motion (which I think is true of most of the particles of bread and all those of wine), then the surfaces of these bodies must be understood to be in some sort of continual motion.

Finally we must note that the surface of the bread or wine or any other body should not in this context be taken to be a part of the substance or the quantity of the body in question, nor should it be taken to be a part of the surrounding bodies. It should be taken to be simply the boundary that is conceived to be common to the individual particles and the bodies that surround them; and this boundary has absolutely no reality except a modal one.

Given that contact occurs only at this boundary, and that we have sensory awareness of something only by contact, we may now consider

250

251

---

1 According to the scholastic theory referred to here, what is directly perceived via the senses is not the object itself but a 'form' or 'semblance' (Lat. *species*) transmitted from object to observer.

the statement that the substances of the bread and wine are changed into the substance of something else in such a way that this new substance is contained within the same boundaries as those occupied by the previous substances, or exists in precisely the same place where the bread and wine were – or rather (since their boundaries are in continual motion) in the same place where they would be if they were still present. Clearly, from this statement alone, it necessarily follows that the new substance must affect all our senses in exactly the same way as that in which the bread and wine would be affecting them if no transubstantiation had occurred.

Now the teaching of the Church in the Council of Trent session 13, canons 2 and 4 is that 'the whole substance of the bread is changed into the substance of the body of Our Lord Christ while the form[1] of the bread remains unaltered'. Here I do not see what can be meant by the 'form' of the bread if not the surface that is common to the individual particles of the bread and the bodies which surround them.

As I have already said, it is at this surface alone that contact occurs. And Aristotle himself admits, in the *De Anima*, Book 3, Chapter 13, that not just the sense that is specifically called the sense of touch but 'all the other senses, too, perceive by means of touching': 'καὶ τὰ ἄλλα αἰσθητήρια ἀφῇ αἰσθάνεται'.

Everyone agrees that 'form' here means precisely what is required 252 in order to act on the senses. And everyone who believes that the bread is changed into the body of Christ also supposes that this body of Christ is precisely contained within the same surface that would contain the bread were it present. Christ's body, however, is not supposed to be present in a place strictly speaking, but to be present 'sacramentally and with that form of existence which we cannot express in words but nonetheless, when our thought is illumined by faith, can understand to be possible with God, and in which we should most steadfastly believe'.[2] All these matters are so neatly and correctly explained by means of my principles that I have no reason to fear that anything here will give the slightest offence to orthodox theologians; on the contrary I am confident that I will receive their hearty thanks for putting forward opinions in physics which are far more in accord with theology than those commonly accepted. For as far as I know, the Church has never taught that the 'forms' of the bread, and wine that remain in the sacrament of the Eucharist are real accidents, which miraculously subsist on their own

---

1 Lat. *species*; see preceding footnote.
2 A further quotation from session 13 of the Council of Trent; see preceding paragraph but one. The decrees of the Council (1545–63) were and are a recognized authority on matters of Roman Catholic doctrine.

when the substance in which they used to inhere has been removed.[1]

It may be, however, that the theologians who first attempted to give a
253 philosophical account of this topic were so firmly convinced that the
accidents which stimulate our senses were something real and distinct
from a substance that it did not even cross their minds that there could
ever be any doubt on this matter. And hence, without any scrutiny or
valid argument, they supposed that the 'forms' of the bread were real
accidents of this sort; and they then became wholly occupied with
explaining how these accidents could exist without a subject. But, as it
turned out, they found that this task presented so many difficulties that
this alone should have told them that they had strayed from the true
path, like travellers who come upon rough ground and impassable
terrain.

First of all, they seem to run into a contradiction – at least those who
concede that all sense-perception occurs by means of contact – in
supposing that objects, in order to stimulate the senses, require anything
more than the various configurations of their surfaces; for it is self-
evident that a surface is on its own sufficient to produce contact. If,
however, they do not concede that sense-perception occurs through
contact, then nothing they can contribute to the topic will have any
semblance of truth.

Next, the human mind cannot think of the accidents of the bread as
real, and yet existing apart from its substance, without conceiving of
them by employing the notion of a substance. So it seems to be a
contradiction, given that the whole substance of the bread changes, as the
Church believes, to suppose that something real which was previously in
the bread nonetheless remains. For if something real is understood to
remain it must be thought of as something which subsists; and though
the word 'accident' may be used to describe it, it must nonetheless be
conceived of as a substance. Hence the supposition that real accidents
remain is in fact just like saying that the whole substance of the bread
254 changes but nevertheless a part of that substance called a 'real accident'
remains. And though this may not be a verbal contradiction, it certainly
involves a conceptual contradiction.

This seems to be the chief reason why some people have taken issue
with the Church of Rome on this matter. But surely everyone agrees that
when we are free, and there is no theological or indeed philosophical
reason to compel us to adopt an alternative view, we should prefer
opinions that cannot give others any opportunity or pretext for turning

---

1 The seven paragraphs that follow were not included in the first edition of the
Meditations with Objections and Replies, which simply prints a short concluding
sentence at this point.

away from the true faith. Yet the supposition of real accidents is inconsistent with theological arguments, as I think I have just shown clearly enough; and it is also completely opposed to philosophical principles, as I hope I shall clearly demonstrate in the comprehensive philosophical treatise on which I am now working.[1] I shall show there how colour, taste, heaviness, and all other qualities which stimulate the senses, depend simply on the exterior surface of bodies.

Lastly, we cannot suppose that there are real accidents without gratuitously adding something new and indeed incomprehensible to the miracle of the transubstantiation (which can be inferred simply from the words of the consecration). The gratuitous addition would involve the alleged real accidents existing apart from the substance of the bread in such a way that they do not thereby themselves become substances. This is not only contrary to human reason but also violates the theological axiom that the words of the consecration bring about nothing more than what they signify; moreover theologians prefer not to attribute to miracles what can be explained by natural reason. All these difficulties are completely removed if my explanation of this matter is adopted. For my account not only makes it unnecessary to posit a miracle in order to explain the preservation of the accidents once the substance has been removed, but it goes so far as to make it impossible for them to be removed without a fresh miracle (e.g. one which would alter the relevant dimensions). Tradition has it that this has sometimes occurred when in place of the consecrated bread some flesh, or a tiny child, has appeared in the hands of the priest. But it has never been believed that these happenings were due to the cessation of a miracle; they have always been ascribed to a new miracle.

255

Moreover, there is nothing incomprehensible or difficult in the supposition that God, the creator of all things, is able to change one substance into another, or in the supposition that the latter substance remains within the same surface that contained the former one. Nor can anything be more in accordance with reason or more widely accepted among philosophers than the general statement that not just all sense-perception but, in general, all action between bodies occurs through contact, and that this contact can take place only at the surface. It clearly follows from this that any given surface must always act and react in the same way, even though the substance which is beneath it is changed.

So if I may speak the truth here without fear of causing offence, I venture to hope that a time will come when the theory of real accidents will be rejected by theologians as irrational, incomprehensible and hazardous for the faith, while my theory will be accepted in its place as

1 Descartes refers to the *Principles of Philosophy*; see esp. Part 4, arts. 198ff: vol. I, p. 284.

certain and indubitable. I thought it right to state this openly here, in order to forestall, as far as I could, the slanders of those who want to seem more learned than others and are thus never more annoyed than when some new proposal is made in the sciences which they cannot pretend they knew about already. The truer and more important such people believe a doctrine is, the more fiercely, in many cases, they will attack it; and when they are unable to refute it by rational argument, they will claim without any justification that it is inconsistent with holy scripture and revealed truth. To try to use the authority of the Church in order to subvert the truth in this way is surely the height of impiety. But I appeal against the verdict of such people to the higher court of pious and orthodox theologians to whose judgement and correction I most willingly submit myself.

FIFTH SET OF OBJECTIONS

From P. Gassendi to that distinguished gentleman René Descartes

Sir,

Mersenne did me a great favour in allowing me to see your splendid book, the *Meditations on First Philosophy*. I am most impressed by your excellent arguments, your intellectual acumen and your brilliant style. And I am happy to congratulate you on the highly intelligent and successful way in which you have attempted to extend the boundaries of the sciences and explain matters which have remained highly obscure in all previous ages. Mersenne asked me, as a friend of his, to write to you if I had any unresolved doubts about your book, but it has been hard for me to comply with his request. I foresaw that I should simply be displaying my lack of intelligence if I did not accept your arguments, or rather my rashness if I ventured to utter a word of opposition which would make me seem to be attacking you. Nonetheless, I have yielded to my friend, thinking that you would be sure to accept and approve of a plan that is more his than mine; and I am sure that your good nature will make you see that my intention was simply to uncover the reasons which gave rise to my doubts. I assure you that I shall be more than satisfied if you have the patience to read through my comments; and if they lead you to have even the slightest doubts about your own arguments, or to spend time in replying to them that was destined for more important projects, then I am certainly not responsible for that. Indeed, I am almost embarrassed to come before you with my doubts, since I am quite certain that there is not one of them which has not frequently occurred to you in the course of your meditations only to be rejected as worthless or else deliberately passed over. The comments which I shall make, then, I intend merely as suggestions; and they are suggestions which do not concern the actual results which you have undertaken to prove, but merely the method and validity of the proof. I acknowledge, of course, the existence of almighty God and the immortality of our souls; my hesitation simply relates to the force of the arguments that you employ to prove these and other related metaphysical matters.

On the First Meditation: 'What can be called into doubt'

In the case of the First Meditation, there is very little for me to pause over, for I approve of your project for freeing your mind from all preconceived opinions. There is just one point I am not clear about, namely why you did not make a simple and brief statement to the effect that you were regarding your previous knowledge as uncertain so that you could later single out what you found to be true. Why instead did

258 you consider everything as false, which seems more like adopting a new prejudice than relinquishing an old one? This strategy made it necessary for you to convince yourself by imagining a deceiving God or some evil demon who tricks us, whereas it would surely have been sufficient to cite the darkness of the human mind or the weakness of our nature. Furthermore, in order to call everything into doubt you pretend that you are asleep and consider that everything which occurs is an illusion. But can you thereby compel yourself to believe you are not awake, and to consider as false and uncertain whatever is going on around you? Whatever you say, no one will believe that you have really convinced yourself that not one thing you formerly knew is true, or that your senses, or God, or an evil demon, have managed to deceive you all the time. Would it not have been more in accord with philosophical honesty and the love of truth simply to state the facts candidly and straightforwardly, rather than, as some critics might put it, to resort to artifice, sleight of hand and circumlocution? But since you have decided to take this route, I do not wish to press the point any further.

On the Second Meditation: 'The nature of the human mind, and how it is better known than the body'

1. Turning to the Second Meditation, I see that you still persist with your elaborate pretence of deception, but you go on to recognize at least that you, who are the subject of this deception, exist. And thus you conclude that this proposition, *I am, I exist*, is true whenever it is put forward by

259 you or conceived in your mind.[1] But I do not see that you needed all this apparatus, when on other grounds you were certain, and it was true, that you existed. You could have made the same inference from any one of your other actions, since it is known by the natural light that whatever acts exists.

You add that you do not yet have a sufficient understanding of what you are. Here I agree with you in earnest and readily accept what you say; this is the point at which all the hard work begins. But it seems that

1 Above p. 17.

you could have raised this question without all the circumlocutions and elaborate suppositions.

You next decide to meditate on what you formerly believed yourself to be, so that when the doubtful elements are removed only what is 'certain and unshakeable' may remain.[1] Here your procedure will meet with universal approval. You now get to grips with the problem. You formerly believed you were a man; and now you ask 'What is a man?' You deliberately dismiss the common definitions and concentrate on 'the first thought that came to mind', namely that you had a face and hands and the other limbs making up what you called the body. The next thought was that you were nourished, that you moved about, and that you engaged in sense-perception and thinking – actions which you attributed to the soul. Fair enough – provided we are careful to remember your distinction between the soul and the body. You say that you did not know what the soul was, but imagined it to be merely 'something like a wind or fire or ether' which permeated the more solid parts of your body. That is worth remembering. As for the body, you had no doubt that its nature consists in its being 'capable of taking on shape and having boundaries and filling a space so as to exclude any other body from it, and in its being perceived by touch, sight, hearing, smell and taste and being moved in various ways'.[2] But you can continue to attribute these things to bodies even now, provided you do not attribute all of them to every single body (thus wind is a body, and yet it is not perceived by sight). But you cannot exclude the other attributes you go on to mention, since wind and fire are capable of moving many things. When you go on to say that you previously denied that a body has the 'power of self-movement', it is not clear how you can still maintain this. For it would imply that every body must by its nature be immobile, and that all its movements come from some incorporeal principle, and that we cannot suppose that water flows or an animal moves without some incorporeal power of movement.

2. You go on to ask whether, now that you are supposing you are being deceived, you can still affirm that you possess any of the attributes which you believed to belong to the nature of body. And after a very careful examination you say that you can find in yourself no attributes of this kind.[3] But in this passage you are already regarding yourself not as a whole man but as an inner or hidden component – the kind of component which you had previously considered the soul to be. I ask you then, Soul, or whatever name you want me to address you by, have you by this time corrected the thought which previously led you to imagine that you were something like a wind diffused through the parts of the body? Certainly not. So why is it not possible that you are a wind, or

1 Cf. above p. 17.   2 *Ibid.*   3 Above p. 18.

rather a very thin vapour, given off when the heart heats up the purest type of blood, or produced by some other source, which is diffused through the parts of the body and gives them life? May it not be this vapour which sees with the eyes and hears with the ears and thinks with the brain and performs all the other functions which are commonly ascribed to you? If this is so, why should you not have the same shape as your whole body has, just as the air takes on the same shape as the vessel that contains it? Why should you not suppose that you are enclosed within the body's skin, or in the same medium as that which surrounds the body? Why should you not occupy space, or the parts of a space which the solid body or its parts do not fill? I mean that the solid body has pores through which you may be diffused, in such a way that your own parts and the parts of the body are not to be found in the same areas, just as in a mixture of wine and water the parts of the wine are not to be found where the parts of the water are, although our sight is unable to separate out the two. Again, why should you not be able to exclude any other body from the space which you occupy, given that the spaces which you occupy cannot be occupied at the same time by the parts of the more solid body? Why should you not be in motion in many different ways? For, given that you move many of your limbs, how could you accomplish this unless you were in motion yourself? You certainly cannot be immobile, since exertion is required when you move the limbs, nor can you be at rest if you are to produce movement in the body. If all this is so, then why do you say that you have within you 'none of the attributes which belong to the nature of the body'?

3. You go on to say that, of the attributes ascribed to the soul, neither nutrition nor movement are to be found in you.[1] But, in the first place, something may be a body without receiving nutrition. Next, if you are the kind of body which we have described as a vapour, then given that the limbs, being more solid, are nourished by a more solid substance, why should you, being more rarefied, not also be nourished by a more rarefied substance? Moreover, when the body to which these limbs belong is growing, are not you growing also? And when the body is weak, are not you weak too? As far as movement is concerned, since it is you who cause your limbs to move, and they never assume any position unless you make them do so, how can this occur without movement on your part? You say 'since now I do not have a body, these are mere fabrications'. But if you are fooling with us or being fooled yourself, there is nothing to delay us here. If, however, you are speaking seriously, then you have to prove that you do not have a body which you inform,[2]

---

1 Above p. 18.
2 In scholastic terminology the soul is said to 'inform' (*informare*) the body.

and also that your nature is not such that you are nourished and move in conjunction with the body.

You go on to say that you do not have sense-perception. But surely it is you who see colours, hear sounds etc. 'This', you say, 'does not occur without a body.' I agree. But in the first place you have a body, and you yourself are present within the eye, which obviously does not see without you. And secondly, you could be a rarefied body operating by means of the sense organs. You say 'in my dreams I have appeared to perceive through the senses many things which I afterwards realized I did not perceive through the senses at all'. Admittedly, you may be deceived when, although the eye is not in use, you seem to have sense-perception of something that cannot in fact be perceived without the eye. But this kind of falsity is not something you have experienced all the time; and indeed you have normally used your eyes in order to see and to take in the images which you may now have without the eyes being in use.

Finally, you reach the conclusion that *thinking* belongs to you.[1] This must be accepted, but it remains for you to prove that the power of thought is something so far beyond the nature of a body that neither a vapour nor any other mobile, pure and rarefied body can be organized in such a way as would make it capable of thought. You will have to prove at the same time that the souls of the brutes are incorporeal, given that they think or are aware of something internal over and above the functions of the external senses, not only when they are awake but also when dreaming. You will also have to prove that this solid body of yours contributes nothing whatever to your thought (for you have never been without it, and have so far never had any thoughts when separated from it). You will thus have to prove that you think independently of the body 263 in such a way that you can never be hampered by it or disturbed by the foul and dense vapours or fumes which from time to time have such a bad effect on the brain.

4. You conclude: 'I am, then, in the strict sense a thing that thinks; that is, I am a mind, or intelligence, or intellect, or reason.'[2] Here I must admit that I had been labouring under a misapprehension. I thought that I was addressing a human soul, or the internal principle by which a man lives, has sensations, moves around and understands. Instead I find I was addressing a mind alone, which has divested itself not just of the body but also of the very soul. Are you, Sir, following the example of the ancients who, although believing that the soul was diffused through the whole body, nonetheless thought that the principal part – the ἡγεμονικὸν or 'controlling element' – had its seat in a specific part of the body, such as the brain or the heart? They did of course believe that

1 Above p. 18.   2 *Ibid.*

the soul was also to be found in this part, but they thought that the mind was, as it were, added to and united with the soul that existed there, thus informing this part along with the soul. I ought to have remembered this from the discussion in your *Discourse on the Method*, where you seemed to want to say that all the functions which are attributed to the vegetative and sensitive soul do not depend on the rational soul but can be exercised before the rational soul arrives in the body, as is the case with the brutes who, on your view, possess no reason.[1] How I forgot this I do not know, unless it was because I was still in doubt about whether you preferred not to use the word 'soul' to apply to the principle responsible for the vegetative and sensory functions in both us and the brutes, but wanted instead to say that the soul in the strict sense was our mind. But since it is the vegetative and sensitive principle that is properly speaking said to 'animate' us, the only function performed by the mind is to enable us to think – and this you do in fact assert. Since this is so, let us use the term 'mind', and let it be strictly a 'thinking thing'.

264

You add that thought alone cannot be separated from you.[2] Certainly there is no reason not to grant you this, particularly if you are simply a mind, and you are not prepared to allow that your substance is distinct from the substance of the soul except conceptually. Nonetheless I want to stop here and ask whether, in saying that thought cannot be separated from you, you mean that you continue to think indefinitely, so long as you exist. This would accord with the claims of those noted philosophers who, to prove that we are immortal, assume that we are in perpetual motion or, as I interpret it, that we are perpetually thinking. But it will hardly convince those who do not see how you are able to think during deep sleep or indeed in the womb. And here I pause again and ask whether you think that you were infused into the body, or one of its parts, while still in the womb or at birth. But I do not want to press the point too insistently and ask whether you remember what you thought about in the womb or in the first few days or months or even years after you were born; nor, if you answer that you have forgotten, shall I ask why this is so. I do suggest, however, that you should bear in mind how obscure, meagre and virtually non-existent your thought must have been during those early periods of your life.

You go on to say that you are not 'that structure of limbs which is called a human body'. We must accept this, since you are considering yourself solely as a thinking thing and as a part of the whole composite that is a human being – a part that is distinct from the external and more solid part. 'I am not', you say, 'some thin vapour which permeates the limbs – a wind, fire, air, breath, or whatever I depict in my

1 Cf. *Discourse*, part 5: vol. 1, p. 139.   2 Cf. above p. 18.

imagination; for these are things which I have supposed to be nothing. Let this supposition stand.'[1] But stop here, O Mind, and let those 'suppositions', or rather fictions, finally depart. You say 'I am not a vapour or anything of this kind.' But if the entire soul is something of this kind, why should you, who may be thought of as the noblest part of the soul, not be regarded as being, so to speak, the flower, or the most refined and pure and active part of it? You say: 'It may be that these very things which I am supposing to be nothing are something real, and that they are not distinct from the "I" of which I am aware. I do not know, and for the moment I shall not argue the point.' But if you do not know, if you are not arguing the point, why do you assume that you are none of these things? You say: 'I know I exist; and knowledge of this thing taken strictly cannot depend on that of which I am unaware.' Fair enough; but remember that you have not yet made certain that you are not air or a vapour or something else of this sort.

5. You next take what you call the imagination and proceed to describe what it is. You say that 'imagining is simply the contemplation of the shape or image of a corporeal thing',[2] and you say this so that you can go on to infer that it is some form of thought other than imagination that enables you to know your nature. But since you are allowed to define imagination as you like, then if you are corporeal – and you have not yet proved the contrary – why, may I ask, cannot your contemplation of yourself involve some corporeal form or image? And when you do contemplate yourself in this way, I ask you whether you find that anything comes to mind apart from some pure, transparent, rarefied substance like a wind, which pervades the whole body or at least the brain or some other part, and which animates you and performs all your functions. 'I realize', you say, 'that none of the things that the imagination enables me to grasp is at all relevant to this knowledge of myself which I possess.' But you do not say how you recognize this. And since you had decided a little earlier that you did not yet know whether these things belonged to you, how, may I ask, do you now arrive at the conclusion just quoted?

6. You say next that 'the mind must be most carefully diverted from such things if it is to perceive its own nature as distinctly as possible'.[3] Good advice. But after you have most carefully diverted yourself from these things, tell me, please, how distinctly you have managed to perceive your nature? In saying that you are simply 'a thing that thinks' you mention an operation of which all of us were already well aware; but you tell us nothing of the substance which performs this operation – what kind of substance it is, and what it consists of, how it organizes itself to

1 *Ibid.* 2 Above p. 19. 3 *Ibid.*

perform so many different functions in so many different ways, and other matters of this kind, of which we have been ignorant up till now.

You say that we can perceive by the intellect what we cannot perceive by the imagination (and you identify the imagination with the 'common' sense).[1] But, my good Mind, can you establish that there are several internal faculties and not one simple and universal one, which enables us to know whatever we know? When I see the sun with open eyes, sensory perception obviously occurs. And when I then think about the sun with my eyes closed, internal cognition obviously occurs. But how, ultimately, can I tell that I am perceiving the sun with the 'common' sense or faculty of imagination, as opposed to the mind or intellect, which implies that I can at will apprehend the sun now by means of the intellect, which is distinct from the imagination, and now by means of the imagination, which is distinct from the intellect? If, after brain damage or some injury to the imaginative faculty, the intellect remained as before, performing its proper functions all unimpaired, then we could say that the intellect was as distinct from the imagination as the imagination is distinct from the external senses. But since things do not happen this way, there is surely no ready way of establishing the distinction.

To say, as you do, that imagination occurs when we contemplate the image of some corporeal thing, surely implies that since there is no other way in which we may contemplate bodies, our knowledge of them must be derived from the imagination alone – or at any rate that no other faculty of knowing can be recognized.

You say that you cannot stop thinking that the corporeal things of which you form images in your thought, and which the senses investigate, are known with much more distinctness than this puzzling 'you' which cannot be pictured in the imagination; and thus it is surprising that you should have a more distinct knowledge and grasp of things which are doubtful and foreign to you.[2] First of all, you are quite right in using the phrase 'this puzzling "you"'. For you really do not know what you are or what your nature is, and hence you cannot be any more confident that your nature is such as to be incapable of falling under the imagination. Next, all our knowledge appears to have its source in our senses, and although you deny the maxim 'Whatever is in the intellect must previously have existed in the senses',[3] it seems that it is nevertheless true. For unless our knowledge enters in a single rush – κατὰ περίπτωσιν or 'at a stroke' as they say – it is slowly established by analogy, composition, division, extrapolation and restriction, and in other similar ways

---

1 See above pp. 21f and footnote p. 59.   2 Above p. 20.
3 A standard slogan of empiricist philosophers; it is attributed by Aquinas to Aristotle. For Descartes' implicit denial of the maxim, cf. Med. II, pp. 21f, and Med. V, pp. 44f.

which I need not list here. So it is no surprise if the things which rush in of their own accord and strike the senses should make a more vivid impression on the mind than things which the mind itself, when the occasion arises, constructs and compounds for itself out of the material which impinges on the senses. Moreover, you call corporeal things doubtful but, if you are prepared to admit the truth, you are just as certain of the existence of the body which you inhabit and of all the objects which surround you as you are of your own existence. And if it is solely the operation called 'thought' which makes you manifest to yourself, what happens with regard to the way in which other things are manifested? They are made manifest not just by various operations but also by many very evident attributes, such as size, shape, solidity, colour, taste, etc.; and thus, although they exist outside you, it is no surprise that your knowledge and grasp of them should be more distinct than your knowledge and grasp of yourself. But as to how it is possible for you to understand something that is foreign to you better than you understand yourself, I answer that the same thing happens in the case of the eye, which sees other things but does not see itself.

7. 'But what then am I?' you ask. 'A thing that thinks. What is that? A thing that doubts, understands, affirms, denies, is willing, is unwilling, and also imagines and has sensory perceptions.'[1] This is a long list, but I will not query each individual item. The only point I would question is your statement that you are a thing which has sensory perceptions. This is surprising, since you had previously maintained the opposite. Or did you perhaps mean that in addition to yourself there is a bodily faculty which resides in the eyes, ears and other organs? Is it perhaps this faculty that receives the forms of sensible things and thus initiates the act of sense-perception which you then complete, it being you who really sees and hears and has the other sensory perceptions? This, I think, is what makes you class both sense-perception and imagination as kinds of thought. Fair enough; but in that case you must consider whether the sense-perception which the brutes have does not also deserve to be called 'thought', since it is not dissimilar to your own. This would mean that the brutes, too, have a mind which is not unlike yours.

You may say that you occupy the citadel in your brain and there receive whatever messages are transmitted by the animal spirits which move through the nerves, and sense-perception thus occurs there, where you dwell, despite the fact that it is said to occur throughout the body. Let us accept this; but the brutes have nerves, animal spirits and a brain, and in the brain there is a principle of cognition that receives the

1 Above p. 19.

messages from the spirits in an exactly similar fashion and thus completes the act of sense-perception. You may say that this principle in the brains of animals is simply the corporeal imagination or faculty of forming images. But in that case you must show that you who reside in the brain are something different from the corporeal imagination or the human faculty of forming images. I asked you a little while ago for a criterion which would prove that you are something different, but I do not think you will be able to supply one. You may cite operations which far surpass those performed by animals. But although man is the foremost of the animals, he still belongs to the class of animals; and similarly, though you prove yourself to be the most outstanding of imaginative faculties, you still count as one of these faculties. You may attach the special label 'mind' to yourself, but although the name may be more impressive, this does not mean that your nature is therefore different. To prove that your nature is different (that is, incorporeal, as you maintain), you ought to produce some operation which is of a quite different kind from those which the brutes perform — one which takes place outside the brain, or at least independently of the brain; and this you do not do. On the contrary, when the brain is disturbed, you are disturbed, and when the brain is overwhelmed you are overwhelmed, and if the images of things leave the brain you do not retain any trace of them. You may say that everything which occurs in animals happens by means of a blind impulse of the
270 animal spirits and the other organs, in just the same way as motion is produced in a clock or other machine. This may be true in the case of functions like nutrition or the pulsing of the arteries, which occur in exactly similar fashion in the case of man. But can you cite any sensory acts or so-called 'passions of the soul' which are produced by a blind impulse in the case of the brutes but not in our case? A scrap of food transmits its image into the eye of a dog, and the image is then transferred to the brain and as it were hooks on to the soul, so that the soul and the entire body joined to it is drawn towards the morsel as if by the most tiny and delicate chains. And if someone aims a stone, the stone transmits its image and, like a lever, pushes the soul away and simultaneously drives off the body or forces it to flee. But does not all this occur in the case of man? Perhaps you have in mind some quite different way in which this occurs in man, in which case I should be much obliged if you would explain it.

You may say that you are free and the soul has the power of preventing a man from both fleeing and advancing. But the principle of cognition does just this in the case of an animal: a dog, despite his fear of threats and blows may rush forward to grab a morsel it has seen — and a man often does just the same sort of thing! You may say that a dog barks simply from impulse and not, as happens when a man speaks, from choice. But in the case of man, too, there are causes at work which may lead us to judge that he speaks from some impulse. What you attribute to choice occurs as a result of a stronger impulse, and indeed the brute, too, exercises choice, when one impulse is greater than another. Indeed, I have seen a dog matching his barks to the sound of a trumpet, so as to imitate all the changes in the notes, whether sharp or flat, or slow or fast. And it managed to do this even when the tempo of the notes was arbitrarily and unexpectedly speeded up, or when the notes were unexpectedly drawn out. You say that the brutes lack reason. Well, of course they lack human reason, but they do not lack their own kind of reason. So it does not seem appropriate to call them ἄλογα ['irrational'] except by comparison with us or with our kind of reason; and in any case λόγος or reason seems to be a general term, which can be attributed to them no less than the cognitive faculty or internal sense. You may say that animals do not employ rational argument. But although they do not reason so perfectly or about as many subjects as man, they still reason, and the difference seems to be merely one of degree. You may say they do not speak. But although they do not produce human speech (since of course they are not human beings), they still produce their own form of speech, which they employ just as we do ours. You may say that even a delirious man can still string words together to express his meaning, which even the wisest of the brutes cannot do. But surely you are not being fair if you expect the brutes to employ human language and are not prepared to consider their own kind of language. But to go into this would need a much longer discussion.

8. Next you introduce the example of the wax, and you spend some time explaining that the so-called accidents of the wax are one thing, and the wax itself, or substance of the wax, is another. You say that in order to have a distinct perception of the wax itself or its substance we need only the mind or intellect, and not sensation or imagination.[1] But the first point is just what everyone commonly asserts, *viz.* that the concept of the wax or its substance can be abstracted from the concepts of its accidents. But does this really imply that the substance or nature of the wax is itself distinctly conceived? Besides the colour, the shape, the fact that it can melt, etc. we conceive that there is something which is the subject of the accidents and changes we observe; but what this subject is, or what its nature is, we do not know. This always eludes us; and it is only a kind of conjecture that leads us to think that there must be something underneath the accidents. So I am amazed at how you can say that once the forms have been stripped off like clothes, you perceive more perfectly and

1 Cf. above pp. 20–2.

evidently what the wax is. Admittedly, you perceive that the wax or its substance must be something over and above such forms; but what this something is you do not perceive, unless you are misleading us. For this 'something' is not revealed to you in the way in which a man can be revealed when, after first of all seeing just his hat and garments, we then remove the clothes so as to find out who and what he is. Moreover, when you think you somehow perceive this underlying 'something', how, may I ask, do you do so? Do you not perceive it as something spread out and extended? For you do not conceive of it as a point, although it is the kind of thing whose extension expands and contracts. And since this kind of extension is not infinite but has limits, do you not conceive of the thing as having some kind of shape? And when you seem as it were to see it, do you not attach to it some sort of colour, albeit not a distinct one? You certainly take it to be something more solid, and so more visible, than a mere void. Hence even your 'understanding' turns out to be some sort of imagination. If you say you conceive of the wax apart from any extension, shape or colour, then you must in all honesty tell us what sort of conception you do have of it.

What you have to say about 'men whom we see, or perceive with the mind, when we make out only their hats or cloaks'[1] does not show that it is the mind rather than the imagination that makes judgements. A dog, which you will not allow to possess a mind like yours, certainly makes a similar kind of judgement when it sees not its master but simply his hat or clothes. Indeed, even if the master is standing or sitting or lying down or reclining or crouching down or stretched out, the dog still always recognizes the master who can exist under all these forms, even though like the wax, he does not keep the same proportions or always appear under one form rather than another. And when a dog chases a hare that is running away, and sees it first intact, then dead, and afterwards skinned and chopped up, do you suppose that he does not think it is the same hare? When you go on to say that the perception of colour and hardness and so on is 'not vision or touch but is purely mental scrutiny',[2] I accept this, provided the mind is not taken to be really distinct from the imaginative faculty. You add that this scrutiny 'can be imperfect and confused or perfect and distinct depending on how carefully we concentrate on what the wax consists in'. But this does not show that the scrutiny made by the mind, when it examines this mysterious something that exists over and above all the forms, constitutes clear and distinct knowledge of the wax; it shows, rather, that such knowledge is constituted by the scrutiny made by the senses of all the possible accidents and changes which the wax is capable of taking on. From these we shall

1 Cf. p. 21.   2 *Ibid.*

certainly be able to arrive at a conception and explanation of what we mean by the term 'wax'; but the alleged naked, or rather hidden, substance is something that we can neither ourselves conceive nor explain to others.

9. You now go on as follows:

What am I to say about this mind, or about myself? (So far, remember, I am not admitting that there is anything else in me except a mind.) What, I ask, is this 'I' which seems to perceive the wax so distinctly? Surely my awareness of my own self is not merely much truer and more certain than my awareness of the wax, but also much more distinct and evident. For if I judge that the wax esists from the fact that I see it, how much more does this prove that I exist? It is possible that what I see is not really the wax; it is possible that I do not even have eyes with which to see anything. But when I see, or think I see (I am not here distinguishing 274
the two), it is simply not possible that I who am now thinking am not something. By the same token, if I judge that the wax exists from the fact that I touch it, the same result follows, namely that I exist. If I judge that it exists from the fact that I imagine it, or for any other reason, exactly the same thing follows. And the result that I have grasped in the case of the wax may be applied to everything else located outside me.[1]

I give this long quotation so that you may realize that it demonstrates that you do indeed distinctly know that you exist because of the fact that you distinctly see and know that the wax and its accidents exist. But it does not prove that you therefore know, either distinctly or indistinctly, what you are or what your nature is. Such a proof would have been well worthwhile, since your existence is not in doubt. Note, however, that I do not propose to press this point, any more than I insisted on a point that arose earlier. This was that although you are not here admitting that you have anything apart from a mind, and hence you are excluding eyes, hands and the other bodily organs, you nevertheless speak of the wax and its accidents which you see and touch, etc. Yet to see these things without eyes or touch them without hands (or, as you put it, think that you see and touch them) is obviously impossible.

You proceed as follows.

If my perception of the wax seemed more distinct after it was established not just by sight or touch but by many other considerations, it must be admitted that I know myself even more distinctly. This is because every consideration whatsoever which contributes to my perception of the wax, or of any other body, cannot 275
but establish even more effectively the nature of my own mind.[2]

But just as your conclusions about the wax merely establish your perception of the existence of your mind and not its nature, so all your

---

1 Cf. above p. 22.   2 *Ibid.*

other considerations will fail to establish any result beyond this. If you aim to deduce anything further from your perception of the substance of the wax or other things, your only valid conclusion will be that since our conception of this substance is merely a confused perception of something unknown, the same applies to our conception of the mind. Hence you may well repeat your earlier phrase 'this puzzling "I"'.[1]

Now for your conclusion.

I see that without any effort I have now finally got back to where I wanted. I now know that even bodies are not strictly perceived by the senses or the faculty of imagination but by the intellect alone, and that this perception derives not from their being touched or seen; and hence I know plainly that I can achieve an easier and more evident perception of my own mind than of anything else.[2]

This is what you claim; but I do not see how you can deduce or 'know plainly' that anything more can be perceived concerning your mind beyond the fact that it exists. So what you promised in the title of this Meditation, namely that it would establish that the human mind is better known than the body, has not, so far as I can see, been achieved. Your aim was not to prove that the human mind exists, or that its existence is better known than the existence of the body, since its existence, at all events, is something which no one questions. Your intention was surely to establish that its nature is better known than the nature of the body, and this you have not managed to do. As regards the nature of the body, you have, O Mind, listed all the things we know: extension, shape, occupation of space, and so on. But what, after all your efforts, have you told us about yourself? You are not a bodily structure, you are not air, not a wind, not a thing which walks or senses, you are not this and not that. Even if we grant these results (though some of them you did in fact reject), they are not what we are waiting for. They are simply negative results; but the question is not what you are not, but what you are. And so you refer us to your principal result, that you are a thing that thinks – i.e. a thing that doubts, affirms etc. But to say first of all that you are a 'thing' is not to give any information. This is a general, imprecise and vague word which applies no more to you than it does to anything in the entire world that is not simply a nothing. You are a 'thing'; that is, you are not nothing, or, what comes to the same thing, you are something. But a stone is something and not nothing, and so is a fly, and so is everything else. When you go on to say that you are a *thinking* thing, then we know what you are saying; but we knew it already, and it was not what we were asking you to tell us. Who doubts that you are thinking? What we are unclear about, what we are looking for, is that

276

<hr>

1 Above p. 20. 2 Above pp. 22f.

inner substance of yours whose property is to think. Your conclusion should be related to this inquiry, and should tell us not that you are a thinking thing, but what sort of thing this 'you' who thinks really is. If we are asking about wine, and looking for the kind of knowledge which is superior to common knowledge, it will hardly be enough for you to say 'wine is a liquid thing, which is compressed from grapes, white or red, sweet, intoxicating' and so on. You will have to attempt to investigate and somehow explain its internal substance, showing how it can be seen to be manufactured from spirits, tartar, the distillate, and other ingredients mixed together in such and such quantities and proportions. Similarly, given that you are looking for knowledge of yourself which is superior to common knowledge (that is, the kind of knowledge we have had up till now), you must see that it is certainly not enough for you to announce that you are a thing that thinks and doubts and understands etc. You should carefully scrutinize yourself and conduct a kind of chemical investigation of yourself, if you are to succeed in uncovering and explaining to us your internal substance. If you provide such an explanation, we shall ourselves doubtless be able to investigate whether or not you are better known than the body whose nature we know so much about through anatomy, chemistry, so many other sciences, so many senses and so many experiments.

On the Third Meditation: 'The existence of God'

1. In the Third Meditation you recognize that your clear and distinct knowledge of the proposition 'I am a thing that thinks' is responsible for the certainty which you have regarding it; and you conclude from this that you can lay down the general rule 'Everything which I perceive very clearly and distinctly is true.'[1] Admittedly this may be the best rule that it was possible to find when everything was shrouded in so much darkness. But when we see that many great thinkers, who ought surely to have perceived very many things clearly and distinctly, have judged that the truth of things is hidden either in God or in a deep well, is it not reasonable to suspect that this rule may lead us astray? Moreover, given the arguments of the sceptics, of which you are aware, it seems that the only thing that we can consider as clearly and distinctly perceived and therefore infer to be true is that if something appears to anyone to be the case then it appears to be the case. I clearly and distinctly perceive the pleasant taste of a melon, and hence it is true that the taste of a melon appears to me to be of this kind. But how can I convince myself that it is therefore true that a flavour of this kind really exists in the melon? When

1 Above p. 24.

I was a boy and in good health I took a different view and clearly and distinctly perceived quite a different taste in the melon. And I see that many people also take a different view, as do many animals that have a strong sense of taste and are in the best of health. Is one truth then inconsistent with another? Or is it not rather as follows: if something is clearly and distinctly perceived this does not mean that it is true in itself; all that is true is that it is clearly and distinctly perceived to be such and such? And the same sort of account must be given of matters concerning the mind. At one time I could have sworn that for a given quantity, we cannot go from a smaller quantity to a larger quantity without passing through a quantity equal to the original; again, I could have sworn that it is impossible that two lines should not eventually meet if they are produced to infinity. I thought I perceived these things so clearly and distinctly that I counted them among the truest and most indubitable axioms. Nevertheless, afterwards I came across arguments which convinced me that the opposite was the case and that I perceived it even more clearly and distinctly. Yet now, when I consider the nature of mathematical propositions, I am in doubt again. So it may be said to be true that I recognize that such and such propositions concerning quantities, lines and so on, are indeed just as I conceive or suppose them to be; but it cannot safely be asserted that they are therefore true in themselves. But whatever may be the case regarding mathematical matters, when it comes to the other questions which we are now dealing with, why, may I ask, do people have so many different opinions about them? Everyone thinks that he clearly and distinctly perceives the truth which he champions. In case you should say that the majority are either hesitant or insincere in their beliefs, consider that there are those who face even death for their opinions, even though they see others suffering the same fate for the opposite cause. You can hardly think that their dying words are not utterly sincere. Admittedly you yourself mention the difficulty that 'you previously accepted as wholly certain many things which you afterwards realized were doubtful'.[1] But in this passage you neither resolve the difficulty nor confirm your rule. You merely take the opportunity to discuss the ideas which may deceive you into thinking that they represent things external to yourself, when in fact they may never have existed outside you. You also talk once again of the deceiving God who can mislead you about the propositions 'Two and three are five' and 'A square has no more than four sides'; and the implication here is that we must not expect confirmation of your rule until you have shown that there is a God who cannot be a deceiver. But if I may make a suggestion, what you ought to be working on is not so much establishing this rule,

1 Above p. 24.

which makes it so easy for us to accept falsehoods as true, but putting forward a method to guide us and show us when we are mistaken and when not, on those occasions when we think we clearly and distinctly perceive something.

2. You next distinguish ideas (by which you mean thoughts in so far as they are like images) into three classes: innate, adventitious and made up. In the first class you put 'your understanding of what a thing is, what truth is and what thought is'. In the second class you put 'your hearing a noise, seeing the sun and feeling a fire'. And in the third class you put 'your invented idea of sirens and hippogriffs'. You add that all your ideas may perhaps be adventitious or they may all be innate or all made up, since you have not as yet clearly perceived their origin.[1] But in case some fallacy should creep in before you have managed to perceive the origin of your ideas, I should like to go further and note that all ideas seem to be adventitious – to proceed from things which exist outside the mind and come under one of our senses. The mind has the faculty (or rather is itself the faculty) of perceiving adventitious ideas – those which it receives through the senses and which are transmitted by things; these ideas, I say, are quite unadorned and distinct, and are received just exactly as they are. But in addition to this, the mind has the faculty of putting these ideas together and separating them in various ways, of enlarging them and diminishing them, of comparing them, and so on.

Hence the third class of ideas, at any rate, is not distinct from the second. For the idea of a chimera is simply the idea of the head of a lion, the body of a goat and the tail of a serpent, out of which the mind puts together one idea, although the individual elements are adventitious. Similarly the idea of a giant, or a man supposed to be as big as a mountain or the whole world, is merely adventitious. It is the idea of a man of ordinary size which the mind enlarges at will, although the more the idea is enlarged the more confused the conception becomes. Again the idea of a pyramid, or of a town, or of something else which we have not so far seen, is simply the adventious idea of a pyramid or town or something else which we have seen, with the form somewhat modified so that the idea is repeated and rearranged in a fairly confused way.

As for the forms which you say are innate, there do not seem to be any: whatever ideas are said to belong to this category also appear to have an external origin. You say 'I derive from my own nature my understanding of what a thing is.'[2] I do not think you here mean the actual power of understanding, which we undoubtedly have and which is not in question; you are talking about the idea of a *thing*. Moreover you are not talking of the idea of some particular thing; for the sun, this stone, and all

1 Above p. 26.   2 *Ibid.*

individual items are things, and yet you do not say that our ideas of them are innate. So you must be talking of the idea of a thing considered in general, which is virtually synonymous with 'entity', and has a similarly wide extension. But how, I ask you, can this idea be in the mind unless all the individual things exist, together with all the kinds of things from which the mind abstracts so as to form the concept which is not peculiar to any individual item but nonetheless fits them all? For surely if the idea of a thing is innate, the idea of an animal, or a plant, or a stone, or of any universal will also be innate. We shall not need to bother separating out all the particulars which lead us, after setting aside the various distinguishing characteristics, to arrive at the one element which seems common to all, or in other words the idea of a general class.

You also say that you derive from your own nature 'your understanding of what truth is',[1] by which I take it you mean your idea of truth. But if truth is simply the conformity of a judgement with the thing which is the subject of the judgement, then truth is some sort of relation, and hence is not anything distinct from the thing and the idea which are so related. Or, which amounts to the same thing, truth is nothing distinct from the idea of the thing, in so far as the idea represents both itself and the thing as being of such and such a kind. Thus the idea of truth is simply the idea of a thing in so far as it conforms to that thing, or in so far as it represents the thing as it is; and it follows that if the idea of the thing in question is not innate but adventitious, then the idea of truth will itself also be adventitious and not innate. And since this applies to any particular truth, it can also apply to truth in general, the notion or idea of which is derived from the notions or ideas of particular things (in the way just explained with regard to the idea of a thing).

Again, you say that you derive from your own nature 'your understanding of what thought is' (by which, again, I take you to mean your idea of thought). But just as the mind can, from the idea of one town, construct the idea of another, so from the idea of one action such as seeing or tasting, it can construct the idea of another action such as thought. For there is a recognized analogy between the various cognitive faculties, so that knowledge of one easily leads to knowledge of the other. However, there is no need to labour over the idea of thought; we should reserve our attention for the idea of the mind itself, and hence the soul. For if we grant that this idea is innate, there will be no harm in admitting that the idea of thought is also innate. So we must wait until you have proved innateness in the case of the mind or the soul.

3. You seem next to call into doubt not only whether any ideas proceed from external things, but even whether there are any external things at all.[2] Your reasoning appears to be as follows. Although you have

---

1 Above p. 26.   2 Above p. 27.

within you ideas of things which are called 'external', the ideas do not establish that the things exist, since the ideas do not necessarily arise from the things, but could come from yourself or from some other unknown source. This, I think, is why you said earlier that you had not previously perceived the earth, the sky and the stars, but only the ideas of the earth, the sky and the stars, which might give rise to a delusion. Now if you do not yet believe that the earth, sky, stars and so on exist, why, may I ask, do you walk on the earth and move your body to look at the sun? Why do you approach the fire to feel the warmth? Why do you go to the table for a meal to satisfy your hunger? Why do you move your tongue to speak or your hand to write down these Meditations for us? Certainly your doubts can be uttered – they can be devised with great subtlety – but they do not further your enterprise. And since you are really in no doubt that the things outside you exist, let us be serious and straightforward and talk of things as they are. If, granting the existence of external objects, you think it cannot be satisfactorily demonstrated that the ideas which we have are derived from them, you will have to dispose not only of the objections raised by your arguments, but of further difficulties that can be raised.

You admit that we accept that our ideas come from external things, since 'nature has apparently taught us this and we know by experience that they do not depend on us, or on our will'.[1] But if I may pass over these arguments and their solution, you should also have raised and answered, amongst other things, the question of why a man born blind has no idea of colour, or a man born deaf has no idea of sound. Surely this is because external objects have not been able to transmit any images of themselves to the minds of such unfortunates, because the doors have been closed since birth and there have always been barriers in place which have prevented these images from entering.

Later on you press the example of the sun, of which you have two ideas: one is derived from the senses, and this makes the sun appear small; the other is based on astronomical reasoning and gives us a conception of the sun as huge. The latter idea, you say, is truer and more closely resembles the sun, and it is not drawn from the senses but derived from innate notions or produced in some other way.[2] But both these ideas of the sun resemble the sun and are true, or conform to the sun, though one does so more than the other. In just the same way, if we have two ideas of the same man, one transmitted from ten feet away and the other from a hundred or a thousand feet, both ideas resemble the man and are true, or conform to him, but the former idea does so more than the latter. The idea which comes from nearby is not so weakened as the

283

---

1 Above p. 26. 2 Above p. 27.

one which comes from farther away. Were you not to grasp this point fully I could explain it quite briefly if you allowed me to.

Although the second, vast idea of the sun is perceived by the mind alone, it does not follow that the idea is derived from some innate notion. Since experience establishes, and reasoning based on experience confirms, that objects when distant appear smaller than they do when they are near us, the idea of the sun which comes to us through sense-perception is so amplified by the mind's own power as to correspond exactly with the agreed distance of the sun from us, so that its diameter equals so many radii of the earth.

If you want to grasp the fact that no part of this idea has been implanted in us by nature, you should inquire about the idea which a man born blind has. You will find first of all that the idea in his mind has no colour or luminosity. Next you will find that it is not even round, unless someone has told him the sun is round and he has previously held a round object in his hands. And lastly you will find that the idea is not nearly so large, unless he has amplified his previously accepted idea as a result of reasoning or the influence of some authority.

But may I interpose a question here? Do we, who have looked at the sun so often, and have so often seen its apparent diameter and reasoned about its true diameter, do we, I ask you, have any other than the ordinary image of the sun? Reasoning tells us that the sun is more than a hundred and sixty times bigger than the earth, but do we therefore have an idea of such a vast body? We certainly amplify the idea derived from the senses as much as possible, and exert our mind as much as we can. But despite this, all we succeed in constructing for ourselves is darkness and obscurity. If we wish to have a distinct idea of the sun, then our mind must always return to the image which it has received via the eye. It is enough if the mind accepts that the sun is in reality bigger, and that it would have a larger idea if the eye could move closer to the sun; but in the meantime the idea that the mind attends to is nevertheless no larger than the one it actually takes in.

4. Next, you recognize the inequality and diversity to be found among our ideas. You say:

Undoubtedly, the ideas which represent substances to me amount to something more and, so to speak, contain within themselves more objective reality than the ideas which merely represent modes or accidents. Again, the idea that gives me my understanding of a supreme God, eternal, infinite, omnipotent and the creator of all things that exist apart from him, certainly has in it more objective reality than the ideas that represent finite substances.[1]

1 Above p. 28.

Here you move on at a great pace, and we must stop you for a while. I am not bothered by what you call 'objective reality'. It is commonly said that external things exist 'subjectively' or 'formally' in themselves, but exist 'objectively' or 'ideally' in the intellect; and it is enough that you appear to follow this usage and mean simply that an idea must conform to the thing of which it is an idea. Thus an idea contains representatively nothing which is not in fact in the thing itself, and the more reality the thing represented has in itself, the more representative reality the idea possesses. You do in fact immediately afterwards distinguish between objective and formal reality, where 'formal reality', as I understand it, applies to the idea itself not as it represents something but as an entity in its own right. But we agree that the idea, or its objective reality, is not to be measured by the total formal reality of the thing (i.e. the reality which the thing has in itself) but merely by that part of the thing of which the intellect has acquired knowledge (i.e. by the knowledge that the intellect has of the thing). Thus you will be said to have a perfect idea of a man if you have looked at him carefully and often from all sides; but your idea will be imperfect if you have merely seen him in passing and on one occasion and from one side. But if you have not seen the man himself, but only a mask covering his face and a set of clothes which completely cover his body, then we must say either that you do not have an idea of him at all or, if you do have one, that it is very imperfect and utterly confused.

In the light of this I claim that we do have a distinct and genuine idea of accidents, but that our idea of the unseen substance beneath them is confused and utterly fictitious. So when you say that there is more objective reality in the idea of a substance than in the idea of its accidents, first of all it has to be denied that we have a true idea or representation of a substance, and hence that this idea possesses any objective reality. And next, even if we grant that it has some objective reality, we must still deny that this is greater than the reality to be found in the idea of the accidents, since whatever reality of this sort it possesses it gets from the ideas of the accidents under which, or in the guise of which, we conceive of the substance (as I said above when I stated that a substance cannot be conceived except as something extended and having shape and colour).

As for what you add about the idea of God, since you are not yet sure whether God exists, how, may I ask, do you know that God is represented by the idea you have of him as 'supreme, eternal, infinite, omnipotent and the creator of all things'? Do you not take this from your previously conceived knowledge of God, that is, from having heard these attributes ascribed to him? If you had not previously heard anything of this sort, would you still describe God in this way? You will reply that you have introduced this just as an example, without meaning to lay

286

down any definition at this stage. Fair enough; but watch out that you do not later take it as already established.

You claim that there is in the idea of an infinite God more objective reality than in the idea of a finite thing.[1] But first of all, the human intellect is not capable of conceiving of infinity, and hence it neither has nor can contemplate any idea representing an infinite thing. Hence if someone calls something 'infinite' he attributes to a thing which he does not grasp a label which he does not understand. For just as the thing extends beyond any grasp of it he can have, so the negation of a limit which he attributes to its extension is not understood by him, since his intelligence is always confined within some limit.

287   Next, although every supreme perfection is normally attributed to God, it seems that such perfections are all taken from things which we commonly admire in ourselves, such as longevity, power, knowledge, goodness, blessedness and so on. By amplifying these things as much as we can, we assert that God is eternal, omnipotent, omniscient, supremely good, supremely blessed and so on. Hence the idea representing all these things does not contain more objective reality than the finite things taken together; the idea in question is compounded and augmented from the ideas of these finite things in the manner just described. For if someone calls something 'eternal' he does not thereby embrace in his mind the entire extent of its duration – the duration which had no beginning and will never have an end. Similarly, someone who uses the term 'omnipotent' does not embrace the whole multitude of possible effects; and so on in the case of the remaining attributes.

Lastly, can anyone claim that he has a genuine idea of God, an idea which represents God as he is? What an insignificant thing God would be if he were nothing more, and had no other attributes, than what is contained in our puny idea! Surely we must believe that there is less of a comparison between the perfections of God and man than there is between those of an elephant and a tick on its skin. If anyone, after observing the perfections of the tick, formed within himself an idea which he called 'the idea of an elephant' and said that it was an authentic idea, would he not be regarded as utterly foolish? So can we really congratulate ourselves if, after seeing the perfections of a man, we form an idea which we maintain is the idea of God and is genuinely representative of him? How, may I ask, are we to detect in God the presence of those puny perfections which we find in ourselves? And when we do recognize them, what sort of divine essence will that allow us to imagine? God is infinitely beyond anything we can grasp, and when our 288   mind addresses itself to contemplate him, it is not only in darkness but is

1 Above p. 28.

reduced to nothing. Hence we have no basis for claiming that we have any authentic idea which represents God; and it is more than enough if, on the analogy of our human attributes, we can derive and construct an idea of some sort for our own use – an idea which does not transcend our human grasp and which contains no reality except what we perceive in other things or as a result of encountering other things.

5. You next assume that it is 'manifest by the natural light that there must be at least as much in the efficient and total cause as there is in the effect'.[1] This enables you to infer that there must be at least as much formal reality in the cause of an idea as there is objective reality in the idea. But this is a very big step to take, and we must stop you here for a while.

First, it seems that the common maxim 'There is nothing in the effect which is not in the cause' should be taken to refer to material rather than efficient causes. An efficient cause is something external to the effect and often of a quite different nature. Although an effect is said to get its reality from its efficient cause, it does not follow that the efficient cause necessarily has this reality in itself; it may have borrowed it from elsewhere. This is transparently clear if we consider effects produced by some skill. Although a house gets all its reality from the builder, the builder does not have this reality in himself – he simply takes it from some other source and passes it on to the house. The sun does the same when it transforms inferior matter in various ways so as to produce various animals. Even a parent, who admittedly passes some sort of matter on to his offspring, derives it not from an efficient but from a material principle. Your objection that the effect must be contained in the cause 'either formally or eminently' proves nothing more than that an 289 effect sometimes has a form which resembles the form of its cause, while sometimes it has a dissimilar and imperfect form, so that the form of its cause is eminently superior. But it does not follow that even an eminent cause bestows on the effect some of its essence (that is, that which it contains formally), or that it shares its form with the effect. This may seem to happen in the case of the begetting of living creatures from the seed, but I hardly think you will say that a father, in begetting his son, chops off a part of his rational soul and gives it to him. In a word, an efficient cause does not contain its effect except in the sense that it may shape it and produce it out of a given material.

To discuss what you say about objective reality, I will introduce the example of my own image, which I can look at either in a mirror which I hold up to my face, or in a painting. Now I myself am the cause of the image in the mirror in so far as I transmit my semblance[2] on to the

1 *Ibid.*   2 Lat. *species*: see footnote, above p. 174.

mirror, while the painter is the cause of the image displayed on the canvas. And in just the same way, if the idea or image of me is in you or in any other intellect, one may ask whether I myself am its cause – in so far as I transmit my semblance onto the eye and via the eye through to the intellect – or whether there is some other cause which traces the image out in the intellect as if with a pen or pencil. It seems, however, that no cause other than myself is required; for although your intellect may subsequently amplify or reduce the idea of me, or may combine it with something else, or deal with it in some other way, I myself am the primary cause of all the reality which the idea contains within itself. And if this applies to me it must also be taken to apply to any external object.

290

Now the reality belonging to this idea is, according to your distinction, of two kinds. Its *formal* reality cannot be any other than that fine and subtle substance which flows from me, and is then received by the intellect and fashioned into an idea. (If you will not allow that the semblance proceeding from an object is a substantial effluence, then make it whatever you like, but you will only diminish its reality.) The *objective* reality, on the other hand, can be nothing but the representation or likeness of me which the idea carries, or at any rate the pattern according to which the parts of the idea are fitted together so as to represent me. Whichever way you take it, it seems to be nothing real, since it is merely a relation between the various parts and between the parts and myself; in other words, it is merely a mode of the idea's formal reality, in virtue of which it has taken on this particular form. But never mind; let us call it 'objective reality', since this is what you want.

If the example is set up in this way, it seems that you ought to compare the formal reality of the idea with my formal reality or my substance, and you should compare the objective reality of the idea with the proportion obtaining between my various parts or my external form and outline. But what you want to do is to compare the objective reality of the idea with my formal reality.

But however we analyse the axiom referred to above, it is clear not only that there is in me as much formal reality as there is objective reality in the idea of me, but also that the formal reality of the idea is virtually nothing by comparison with my formal reality or my entire substance. Hence we must grant you that 'there must be at least as much formal reality in the cause of an idea as there is objective reality in the idea';[1] for the entire contents of the idea are virtually nothing in comparison with its cause.

291

6. Your next step is as follows. If the objective reality of any one of your ideas turns out to be so great that you do not contain it within you

1 Cf. above pp. 28f.

either eminently or formally, and hence cannot yourself be its cause, it follows necessarily that something besides you exists in the world. For if this were not so, you would have no argument to convince yourself of the existence of anything else.[1] Certainly, from what you have already said, you are not the cause of the reality of your ideas; the cause is, rather, the things themselves which are represented through the ideas, and which send images of themselves to you as if to a mirror (though you may sometimes take these images as the basis for constructing pictures of chimeras). But whether or not you yourself are the cause, does that make you uncertain about whether anything besides you exists in the world? Please give a straight answer; for whatever turns out to be the case regarding ideas, we hardly need to look for arguments to prove that other things exist.

You then make a survey of the ideas which are in you, and besides the idea of yourself you list the ideas of God, corporeal and inanimate things, angels, animals and men. Since you say there is no problem about the idea of yourself, you are then able to infer that the ideas of men, animals and angels can be put together from the ideas which you have of yourself, of God and of corporeal things; you also infer that the ideas of corporeal things could have come from yourself.[2] What I find strange here is how you can claim that there is no problem about the idea you are said to have of yourself (an idea which is so fertile that it enables you to derive so many other ideas from it). For in fact you either have no idea of yourself 292 at all, or you have one which is very confused and imperfect, as we have noted when commenting on the previous Meditation. The inference which you yourself drew in that Meditation was that there was nothing which you could perceive more easily or evidently than yourself. But since you neither have nor are capable of having any idea of yourself, should we not rather say that you can perceive anything at all more easily and more evidently than yourself?

When I think about why it is that sight does not see itself and the intellect does not understand itself, it occurs to me that nothing acts on itself. Thus the hand (or the tip of the finger) does not strike itself and the foot does not kick itself. Now if we are to become aware of something, it is necessary for the thing to act on the cognitive faculty by transmitting its semblance[3] to the faculty or by informing the faculty with its semblance. Hence it seems clear that the faculty itself, not being outside itself, cannot transmit a semblance of itself to itself, and hence cannot produce any awareness of itself or, in other words, cannot perceive itself. Why do you think that the eye can see itself in a mirror although it cannot see itself in itself? It is because there is a space between the eye and

1 Cf. above p. 29.   2 Cf. above pp. 29f.   3 See footnote, above p. 174.

the mirror, and the eye acts on the mirror, transmitting a semblance of itself onto it, so that the mirror in turn acts on the eye by sending its own semblance back to it. Show me a mirror that you yourself can act on in this way, and I promise that, when it reflects your semblance back to you, you will finally manage to perceive yourself – though not by direct but by a reflexive kind of cognition. But since you cannot provide such a mirror, there is no hope of your knowing yourself.

I could also be awkward and ask how you are supposed to have an idea of God – unless it is the kind of idea we have been talking about and is acquired in the way just discussed. And how can you have an idea of the angels, since I take it you would never have thought of them if you had not been told about them? What about animals and other things? If they had not impinged on your senses I am practically certain you would never have had any ideas of them, just as you have no idea of countless things which you have never seen or heard of. But setting all this aside, I do admit that the ideas which we have in our minds of various things can be compounded together to give rise to many more forms of other things. But the ideas which you list do not seem adequate to account for such a great diversity of forms, or even for the distinct and determinate ideas we have of each specific thing.

However, I will pause only at the ideas of corporeal things. There is a considerable difficulty about how you can derive these from yourself or simply from the idea of yourself,[1] when you claim to be incorporeal and consider yourself as such. For if you have knowledge only of an incorporeal substance, how can it be that you also have some grasp of corporeal substance? Is there any analogy between the latter and the former? You may say they have it in common that they are capable of existing, but this point of agreement cannot be understood unless we have some prior understanding of each of the two things which have this in common. Before we can form the common notion you make use of here, we must understand the particular items to which it applies. If the intellect can form the idea of corporeal substance from its understanding of an incorporeal substance, then there is surely no reason to doubt that a blind man, or one who has been confined in utter darkness since birth, can form in his mind the idea of light and colours. You say that you can go on to acquire the idea of extension, shape and motion and other properties common to the things which can be perceived by the senses, which is easy enough for you to say; but what surprises me is why you do not find it just as easy to derive light and colours and so on. But we must not spend too much time on these matters.

7. You then draw the following conclusion:

_____
1 Cf. above pp. 30f.

So there remains only the idea of God; and I must consider whether there is anything in the idea which could not have originated in myself. By the word 'God' I understand a substance that is infinite, independent, supremely intelligent, supremely powerful, and which created both myself and everything else (if anything else there be) that exists. All these attributes are such that, the more carefully I concentrate on them, the less possible it seems that they could have originated from me alone. So from what has been said it must be concluded that God necessarily exists.[1]

This, of course, is the result you were aiming for. But although I accept the conclusion, I do not see how it follows from your reasoning. You say that the attributes which you understand to be in God are of such a kind that they could not have originated from you alone, and you hope to show from this that they must have originated from God. First of all, it is absolutely true that they did not originate from you alone, and that you did not acquire your understanding of them from yourself or through your own efforts. But this is because they in fact originated and were derived from things, parents, teachers, professors and from the human society in which you have moved. 'But I am merely a mind', you may say; 'I am not admitting anything outside of me – not even ears to hear with or men to talk to.' You may say this, but would you be saying it if you did not hear with your ears or if there was no one to tell you anything? Let us discuss this seriously: tell me in good faith whether you do not in fact derive all the language which you use of God from the human society in 295 which you live. And if this is true of the words, is it not also true of the underlying notions which these words express? Hence although these ideas do not come from you alone, it seems that they do not therefore come from God, but that they come from another source. Furthermore, in the case of all these ideas, once you have obtained them by encountering things, can you not afterwards get them from yourself? Do you really therefore comprehend something which is beyond our human grasp? Granted, if you understood the nature of God, there would be reason to think that you had learnt this from God; but all the characteristics you attribute to God are nothing other than various perfections which you have noticed in people and other things, and which the human mind has the power to understand, put together and amplify, as I have already explained several times.

You say that the idea of a substance may come from yourself, since you are a substance, but that the idea of an infinite substance could not come from you, because you are not infinite.[2] But you do not possess the idea of an infinite substance except verbally, and in the sense in which people are said to 'grasp the infinite' (which is really not grasping it at all).

1 Above p. 31.   2 *Ibid.*

Hence it is not necessary that this idea should originate from an infinite substance: it can be constructed by the process of composition and amplification which has already been explained. The early philosophers, by taking in this visible space and this single world and a few principles of this kind, got their ideas of these things; and they then took these ideas and amplified them to form ideas of an infinite universe, an infinite number of worlds and infinite principles. Do you then propose to say that they did not form such ideas by their own mental powers, but that it was an infinite universe, infinite worlds and infinite principles that made these ideas come into their minds? You insist that your perception of the infinite is arrived at by means of 'a true idea'.[1] But if it were a true idea, it would represent the infinite as it is, and you would hence perceive its principal feature – the one we are dealing with here – namely its infinity. But in fact your thought always stops at something finite, and you call it 'infinite' only because you do not perceive what is beyond the reach of your perception; hence it is quite right to say that you perceive the infinite by a negation of the finite. It will not do to say that you 'perceive more reality in an infinite substance than in a finite one'.[2] To do this you would have to perceive an infinite reality, which you do not in fact do. Indeed, you do not really 'perceive more' at all: all you do is to amplify the finite and then imagine that what is enlarged has more reality than it does when it remains small. Or do you want to say that those early philosophers perceived more reality – a reality that really existed – when they conceived of several worlds than when they simply thought of one world? This leads me, incidentally, to point out that the reason why our mind is so much more confused when it amplifies a semblance or image is probably that it pulls this semblance away from its proper setting, destroys the distinctness of its parts, and thus so weakens the whole idea that it finally vanishes altogether. I should mention, however, that the mind is sometimes confused for precisely the opposite reason, namely when it reduces an idea too much.

You say that it does not matter that you do not grasp the infinite or everything that is in it, but that it is enough that you should understand a few of its attributes for it to be said that you have a true and completely clear and distinct idea of it.[3] But if you do not grasp the infinite, but merely the finite, you do not have a true idea of the infinite, but only of the finite. You can at most be said to know part of the infinite; but this does not mean you know the infinite itself. A man who has never left an underground cave may be said to know part of the world, but that does not mean that he knows the world itself; he would turn out to be a fool if he thought that his idea of this tiny portion of the world was a true and

1 Above p. 31.　2 *Ibid.*　3 Cf. p. 32.

authentic idea of the entire world. You say, however, that it is in the nature of the infinite not to be grasped by a finite creature like yourself.[1] I accept this; but it is not in the nature of a true idea of an infinite thing to represent such a tiny part of it, or rather what is no part at all, since it is no fraction of the whole. You say that it is enough that you understand the few attributes which you do perceive clearly. Does this mean that if you want to have an authentic idea of a man it is enough to see the tip of one of his hairs? Would it not be a fine likeness of me if a painter merely painted one of my hairs, or only its tip? But the gap between the tip of one of my hairs and the whole of me is not just much smaller or very much smaller, but infinitely smaller than the gap between everything we know of the infinite, or God, and God himself in his entirety. In a word, the attributes that we do know prove nothing about God which they do not also prove of the infinite set of worlds mentioned in the above example. Indeed, these infinite worlds can be understood from our clear perception of this one world very much more clearly than God, or an infinite being, can be understood from your perception of your substance, whose nature you have not yet established.

8. In another passage you argue as follows: 'How could I understand that I doubted or desired – that is, lacked something – and that I was not wholly perfect, unless there were in me some idea of a more perfect being which enabled me to recognize my own defects by comparison?'[2] But it is   298 hardly surprising that you should be in doubt about something, or desire something or recognize that you lack something, given that you do not know everything, are not everything, and do not possess everything. Is this what makes you recognize that you are not wholly perfect? That is indeed perfectly true and can be said without any malice. But do you therefore understand that there is something more perfect than you? Surely when you desire something it is not always in some sense more perfect than you. When you desire some bread, the bread is not in any sense more perfect than you or your body; it is merely more perfect than the emptiness of your stomach. How, then, do you infer that there is something more perfect than you? Surely it is because you see the totality, which includes you and the bread and everything else; since individual parts of the whole have some perfection, and some subserve others and can come to their aid, it is easy to understand that there is more perfection in the whole than in the part; and since you are merely a part, you have to acknowledge that there is something more perfect than you. This, then, is how you may come to have the idea of a being more perfect than you, and then to recognize your defects by comparing yourself with it. I pass over the fact that various individual parts of the whole may also

1 *Ibid.*   2 Above p. 31.

be more perfect than you, and that you may desire what they have and thus recognize your defects by comparing yourself with them. Thus you might have known a man who was healthier, stronger, better looking, more learned, more restrained and hence more perfect than you; if so, it would not have been difficult for you to conceive an idea of this man and, by comparing yourself with it, to come to understand that you did not have the same degree of health, strength and the other perfections that were to be found in him.

A little later you raise a possible objection to your argument: 'But perhaps I am something greater than I myself understand, and all the perfections which I attribute to God are potentially in me, even though not yet actualized, as could happen if my knowledge were gradually increased to infinity.' But you reply: 'though it is true that there is a gradual increase in my knowledge, and that I can have many potentialities which are not yet actual, this is all quite irrelevant to the idea of God, which contains nothing that is potential; indeed, this gradual increase in knowledge is itself the surest sign of imperfection'.[1] But although the features which you perceive in the idea actually exist in the idea, it does not follow that they actually exist in the real thing corresponding to the idea. An architect makes up an idea of a house in his mind, and this idea actually consists of the specified walls, floors, roof, windows and so on; but the house itself and its components do not yet exist in actuality but only in potentiality. Similarly, the aforementioned idea of the ancient philosophers actually contains an infinity of worlds, but you will not therefore say that this infinity of worlds actually exists. Thus whether something is potentially in you or not, it is enough that your idea or knowledge can be gradually increased or amplified; but we must not infer from this that what is known or represented by the idea actually exists. The point you next recognize – that your knowledge will never become infinite – I readily accept; but you should also recognize that you will never have a true and genuine idea of God, since there always remains much more, infinitely more, to be discovered about him – infinitely more than remains to be discovered about a man when all you have seen is the tip of one of his hairs. Indeed, even if you have not seen the whole man, you have nevertheless seen other men, and this will enable you, by comparison, to make some conjecture about him. But we have never had an opportunity to know anything which resembles God and his immensity.

You say that you 'take God to be actually infinite, so that nothing can be added to his perfection'.[2] But you are here making a judgement about something of which you are ignorant. Your judgement is based simply on

1 Cf. above p. 32.   2 Ibid.

a presumption, like that of the philosophers who supposed there to be infinite worlds, infinite principles and an infinite universe so immense that nothing could be added to it. Your further comment that 'the objective being of an idea cannot come from potential being but only from actual being' can hardly be true, given what we have said about the ideas belonging to the architect and the ancient philosophers, especially when you remember that ideas of this sort are constructed from other ideas, which the intellect originally derived from actually existing causes.

9. You next ask whether, given that you possess an idea of a being more perfect than you, you could exist if no such being existed. And you say in reply, 'From whom, in that case, would I derive my existence? From myself, presumably, or from my parents, or from some other beings less perfect than God.'[1] And you go on to prove that you do not derive your existence from yourself. But this is quite unnecessary. You then provide a reason why you have not always existed. But this too is redundant, except in so far as you want at the same time to infer that you have a cause which not only creates you but preserves you. Thus, from the fact that your lifetime has many parts, you infer that since each part is independent of the others you must be created anew in each individual part. But you should see that there is another way this problem can be understood. There are admittedly some effects that need the efficient cause which first produced them to be continuously present if they are to keep going and not give out at any given moment. The light of the sun is such an effect (though in cases of this kind it is not so much one and the same effect that continues as 'an equivalent effect', as they say in the case of the flow of water in a river). But there are other effects which we see 301 continuing not only when the acknowledged cause is no longer active, but even, if you like, when it is destroyed and reduced to nothing. Such effects include those produced by procreation and manufacture, which are so numerous that it would be tedious to list them; it suffices for my point that you are one of them, whatever your cause may eventually turn out to be. But you say that the parts of your lifetime are 'independent of each other'. Here I am tempted to ask if we can think of anything whose parts are more inseparable from one another than your duration. Can we think of anything whose parts are more inviolably linked and connected? Is there anything whose later parts are more inevitable, or more closely tied to the earlier parts, or more dependent on them? But not to press the point, what difference does this dependence or independence of the parts of your duration make to your creation or preservation? Surely these parts are merely external – they follow on without playing any active role. They make no more difference to your creation and preservation

1 Above p. 33.

than the flow or passage of the particles of water in a river makes to the creation and preservation of some rock past which it flows. You say that from the fact that you existed a little while ago it does not follow that you must exist now.[1] I agree; but this is not because a cause is needed to create you anew, but because there is no guarantee that there is not some cause present which might destroy you, or that you may not have some weakness within you which may now finally bring about your demise.

You say that 'it is therefore evident by the natural light that the distinction between creation and preservation is only a conceptual one'.[2] But how is this 'evident', if not in the case of light itself and similar effects? You add that you have no power to bring it about that you will continue to exist a short time from now, since you are not conscious of such a power, and yet you are a thinking thing. But you do have a power in virtue of which you can suppose that you will exist a short time from now, although not necessarily or indubitably, since this power or natural constitution of yours, whatever it is, does not go so far as to guard against every external or internal cause that may destroy you. So you will indeed continue to exist, not because you have some power which creates you anew, but because you have a power sufficient to ensure that you will continue unless some destructive cause intervenes. Your conclusion, that you depend on some being distinct from yourself, is in fact correct, not in the sense that you are created anew by this being, but rather in the sense that you were once created by it. You go on to say that this being is not your parents or any other such cause. But why should it not be your parents, since it seems so evident that it was they who produced you, along with your body? This is not to mention the sun and other concurrent causes. 'But', you say, 'I am a thinking thing, and I have the idea of God in me.' But were not your parents and their minds also thinking things possessing the idea of God? Hence you should not here insist on the dictum you mentioned earlier, *viz.* 'There must be at least as much in the cause as in the effect.' You say that if the cause is something other than God we may ask whether it derives its existence from itself or from some other cause: if from itself, it will be God; if from some other cause we may repeat the question until we reach a cause which derives its existence from itself, and is God, since an infinite regress is not permissible.[3] But if your parents were the cause of your existence, then that cause may have derived its existence not from itself but from another cause; and the same may be true of that prior cause, and so on *ad infinitum*. You cannot prove that such an infinite regress is absurd unless you also prove that the world began at some time, and hence that there must have been a first parent who had no parent. An infinite regress

302

---

1 Above p. 33.   2 *Ibid.*   3 Cf. above p. 34.

seems to be absurd only in the case of causes which are so linked and subordinated to each other that a cause which is lower in the chain cannot act without the motive power of one which is higher. This occurs when something is pushed by a stone, the stone by a stick, and the stick by a hand, or when the first link of a chain lifts a weight, and that link is pulled by the previous link and so on. In such cases we must eventually reach one link in the chain which is the first to move. But an infinite series does not seem to be absurd when we have causes which are arranged in such a way that if the earlier cause is destroyed the subsequent cause depending on it survives and can still act. Hence when you say 'It is clear enough that an infinite regress is impossible here', you must ask whether this was equally evident to Aristotle, who was strongly convinced that there was never any first parent. You go on as follows: nor can several partial causes have contributed to your creation, so that you received from them the ideas of the various perfections you attribute to God; for these perfections can be found only in one single God whose unity and simplicity is one of his most important perfections.[1] But whether you had one cause or several, it is not necessary that it was these causes which implanted in you the ideas of their perfections, which you have managed to unite. And in any case you allow us to raise the question of why, given that you do not have several causes, it should not have been possible for several things to have existed such that you first admired their perfections and then went on to derive the notion of that blessed thing in whom they are all supposed to exist together. You know how the poets describe Pandora. Surely you might have admired various people's outstanding knowledge, wisdom, justice, steadfastness, power, health, beauty, felicity, longevity and so on, and then put all these things together and considered how admirable it would be if one person had all these perfections at once. Why should you not then have augmented all these perfections in various degrees, until it seemed that this person would be all the more admirable if his knowledge, power, duration and so on were unlimited, so that he was omniscient, omnipotent, eternal and so on? And when you saw that such perfections could not belong to human nature, why should you not have supposed that if they were all combined in one nature, that would be a blessed nature indeed? And why should you not then think it worth investigating whether or not such a being existed? Why should not certain arguments then be produced to make it seem more reasonable that he should exist rather than not exist? And why should you not accordingly remove all bodily attributes and other limitations which imply some imperfection? Very many people certainly seem to have proceeded in this way; but since there are various modes

1 *Ibid.*

and degrees of reasoning, some have allowed God to remain corporeal, some have said he has human limbs, some have said he is not one but many, and others have produced other all too common accounts. As for the perfection of unity which you speak of, there is certainly no contradiction in conceiving of all the perfections which we attribute to God as being intimately connected and inseparable. But for all that, the idea which you have of these perfections was not placed in you by God but was derived by you from the things you have seen, and was then amplified in the way already explained. Thus Pandora is depicted as a goddess endowed with all gifts and perfections; and this is not the only example, since people have also conceived of the perfect republic, the perfect orator and so on. Finally, from the fact that you exist and have the idea of a perfect being within you, you conclude that you have a most evident demonstration of the existence of God. But although the conclusion that God exists is true, it is not clear from what you have said that you have provided a most evident demonstration of it.

10. 'It only remains', you say, 'for me to examine how I received this idea from God. For I did not acquire it from the senses, and it was not invented by me either (for I am plainly unable either to take anything

305   away from it or to add anything to it). The only remaining alternative is that it is innate in me, just as the idea of myself is innate in me.'[1] But I have already said several times that you could have partly derived it from the senses and partly made it up. When you say that you cannot add anything to it or take anything away, remember that when you first acquired it, it was not as perfect as it is now. Consider that there may be men or angels or other natures more learned than you from which you may in the future receive some information about God which you have not hitherto known. Consider also that God, at any rate, could give you such information and instruct you so clearly either in this life or the next that you would have to consider your previous knowledge of him as worthless. Whatever sort of knowledge you may finally arrive at, consider that we can ascend from the perfection of created things to knowledge of the perfections of God in such a way that we can uncover more and more perfections every day; and hence we cannot at any one moment possess a perfect idea of God, but only one that becomes more and more perfect each day. You go on as follows:

And indeed it is no surprise that God, in creating me, should have placed this idea in me to be, as it were, the mark of the craftsman stamped on his work. The mark need not be anything distinct from the work itself. But the mere fact that God created me is a very strong basis for believing that I am somehow made in his image and likeness, and that I perceive that likeness, which includes the idea of

---

1 Above p. 35.

God, by the same faculty which enables me to perceive myself. That is, in understanding myself I understand that I am a thing which is incomplete and dependent on another and which aspires without limit to ever greater and better things; but I also understand at the same time that he on whom I depend has within him all those greater things, not just indefinitely and potentially but actually and infinitely, and hence that he is God.[1]   306

All your assertions here are quite plausible, and I do not deny their truth; but how, may I ask, do you prove them? Setting aside my previous points, let me ask you this. If the idea of God is in you like the mark of a craftsman stamped on his work, how is this stamping carried out? What is the form of this 'mark' you talk of? How do you recognize it? If it is 'not distinct' from the work or the thing itself, are you yourself, then, an idea? Are you nothing else but a mode of thought? Are you both the mark which is stamped and the subject on which it is stamped? You say that it is reasonable to believe that you are made in the image and likeness of God. This is certainly believable given religious faith, but how may it be understood by natural reason, unless you are putting forward an anthropomorphic picture of God? Moreover, what can that likeness consist in? Since you are dust and ashes, can you presume that you resemble that eternal, incorporeal, immense, most perfect, most glorious and above all most invisible and incomprehensible nature? Have you known that nature face to face, that you compare yourself with it and can assert that you resemble it? The fact that he created you, you say, makes it reasonable to believe you resemble him. On the contrary, this fact makes such a resemblance utterly unlikely, since the work is not similar to the workman except when he engenders it by communicating his nature to it. But you are not begotten of God in this way: you are not his offspring, or a participator in his nature, but are merely created by him, that is, produced by him in accordance with an idea. Hence you cannot say that you resemble him any more than a house resembles a bricklayer. This objection stands even if we grant what you have not yet proved, namely that you were created by God. You say that you perceive the likeness when you understand that you are a thing which is incomplete and dependent and aspires to greater and better things. But is this not   307 rather an argument for a dissimilarity between you and God, since God is, by contrast with you, utterly complete and independent and self-sufficient, being the greatest and best of all things? I pass over the fact that when you understand yourself to be dependent you are not immediately entitled to understand that the thing on which you depend is anything other than your parents; or if you do understand it to be something else, this does not explain why you should think you resemble

1 *Ibid.*

it. I also pass over the fact that it is surprising that everyone else, or every other mind, should not share your understanding, especially since there is no reason why God should not be thought to have imprinted the idea of himself on them as well as on you. This one fact surely shows that there is no idea imprinted on us by God; for if there were, if one and the same idea were always imprinted on everyone, then everyone would conceive of God in terms of a similar form and image, and would give him the same attributes and have exactly the same view of him, whereas, notoriously, the opposite is true. But I have already spent too much time on this topic.

On the Fourth Meditation: 'Truth and falsity'

1. In the Fourth Meditation you begin by going over the results which you consider you have demonstrated in the previous Meditations – results which, you presume, have opened the way for further progress. To avoid delay here, I shall not keep insisting that you should have provided a firmer demonstration of these results; I shall simply ask you to remember what has been conceded and what not, so that the discussion may avoid being dragged into the realm of preconceived opinion.

308   Next you reason that it is impossible that God should deceive you;[1] and in order to make excuses for the deceptive and error-prone faculty which God gave you, you suggest that the fault lies in nothingness, which you say you have some idea of, and which you say you participate in, since you take yourself to be something intermediate between nothingness and God. This is a splendid argument! I will pass over the impossibility of explaining how we have an idea of nothingness, and what kind of idea it is, and how we participate in nothingness, and so on. I will simply point out that this distinction does not obviate the fact that God could have given man a faculty of judgement that was immune from error. Without giving him a faculty of infinite scope, he could have given him the kind of faculty which would never lead him to assent to falsehood, so that he would clearly perceive anything he did know, and would avoid making any definite assertion on one side or the other in cases where he was ignorant.

When you discuss this objection you state that it is no cause for surprise if you do not understand the reason for some of God's actions.[2] This is correct, but it is still surprising that you should have a true idea which represents God as omniscient, omnipotent and wholly good, and yet that you should nonetheless observe that some of his works are not wholly perfect. For given that he could have made things more perfect

---

1 Above p. 37.   2 Above p. 38.

but did not do so, this seems to show that he must have lacked either the knowledge or the power or the will to do so. He was certainly imperfect if, despite having the knowledge and the power, he lacked the will and preferred imperfection to perfection.

Your rejection of the employment of final causes in physics[1] might have been correct in a different context, but since you are dealing with God, there is obviously a danger that you may be abandoning the principal argument for establishing by the natural light the wisdom, providence and power of God, and indeed his existence. Leaving aside the entire world, the heavens and its other main parts, how or where will you be able to get any better evidence for the existence of such a God than from the function of the various parts in plants, animals, man and yourself (or your body), seeing that you bear the likeness of God? We know that certain great thinkers have been led by a study of anatomy not just to achieve a knowledge of God but also to sing thankful hymns to him for having organized all the parts and harmonized their functions in such a way as to deserve the highest praise for his care and providence.

You will say that it is the physical causes of this organization and arrangement which we should investigate, and that it is foolish to have recourse to purposes rather than to active causes or materials. But no mortal can possibly understand or explain the active principle that produces the observed form and arrangement of the valves which serve as the openings to the vessels in the chambers of the heart. Nor can we understand the source from which this active principle acquires the material from which the valves are fashioned, or how it makes them operate, or what organic structure it employs, or how it makes use of them, or what it requires to ensure that they are of the correct hardness, consistency, fit, flexibility, size, shape and position. Since, I say, no physicist is able to discern and explain these and similar structures, why should he not at least admire their superb functioning and the ineffable Providence which has so appositely designed the valves for this function? Why should the physicist not be praised if he then sees that we must necessarily acknowledge some first cause which arranged these and all other things with such supreme wisdom and in such precise conformity with his purposes?

You say that it is rash to investigate the purposes of God.[2] But while this may be true if you are thinking of the purposes which God himself wished to remain hidden or ordered us not to investigate, it surely does not apply to the purposes which he left on public display, as it were, and which can be discovered without much effort – purposes which are in any

1 Above p. 39.   2 *Ibid.*

case of such a kind as to lead us to bestow great praise on God as their author.

You may say that the idea of God which is in each of us suffices to give us true and authentic knowledge of God and his purposes, without any reference to the purposes of things or anything else. But not everyone is in your happy position of having such a perfect idea from birth and seeing it before him with such clarity. And since there are some to whom God has not granted such clear vision, you should not begrudge their being able to come to know and glorify the craftsman by an inspection of his works. I need hardly stress that this does not prevent our being allowed to make use of the idea of God, since this too appears to be entirely derived from our knowledge of things in the world; indeed were you to admit the truth, you would say that you owed a considerable amount, if not everything, to this kind of knowledge. For I ask you, what progress do you think you would have made if, since being implanted in the body, you had remained within it with your eyes closed and your ears stopped and, in short, with no external senses to enable you to perceive this universe of objects or anything outside you? Would you not have been absorbed in private meditation, eternally turning thoughts over and over? Answer in all honesty and tell me what idea of God and yourself you think you would have acquired under such circumstances.

2. The solution which you go on to offer is that a created thing which appears imperfect should be considered not as a whole, but as a part of the universe, and from this point of view it will be perfect.[1] This is an admirable distinction; but here we are dealing with the imperfection of a part not as a part, or in comparison with the complete whole, but as something complete in itself which performs its special function. And even if you relate this to the universe, we are still faced with the problem of whether the universe would not really have been more perfect if all its parts had been perfect than it is now when many of its parts are imperfect. Thus a republic whose citizens are all good will be more perfect than one in which most or some of the citizens are bad.

So when you go on to say later on that the universe will be in some sense more perfect if some of its parts are subject to error than it would be if they were all alike,[2] this is like saying that a republic has, in a sense, more perfection if some of its citizens are bad than it would have if they were all good. Hence, just as it seems that a good ruler ought to prefer it if all his citizens are good, so it seems that the author of the universe ought to have ordained that all the parts of the universe should be created such as to be immune from error. You could say that the perfection of the parts which are immune from error appears greater by contrast with

1 Above p. 39.   2 Above pp. 42f.

those which are liable to error; but they are not intrinsically more perfect. In the same way, the virtue of good men does in a sense shine out more by contrast with those who are vicious, but it is not for that reason intrinsically more shining. Hence, just as we should not want some of the citizens to be bad merely so as to make the good citizens stand out more brightly, so it seems that it should never have been allowed that some 312 parts of the universe should be subject to error just so that those which were immune from error should shine more brightly.

You say that you have no right to complain that the role God wished you to undertake in the world is not the principal one or the most perfect of all.[1] But this does not eliminate the question of why God was not satisfied with giving you a role to play which was the least perfect of a set of perfect roles, without actually giving you an imperfect role. A ruler cannot be blamed for not appointing all the citizens to the highest offices but keeping some in lower, and others in the lowest, positions; but he would be criticized if he not only assigned some to the lowest offices but also assigned some to positively base roles.

You say that you cannot produce any reason to prove that God ought to have given you a greater faculty of knowledge than he did; and no matter how skilled you understand a craftsman to be, this does not make you think that he ought to have put into every one of his works all the perfections which he is able to put into some of them.[2] But the objection which I have just raised still stands. The difficulty, you see, is not so much why God did not give you a greater faculty of knowledge, but why he gave you a faculty subject to error. The question is not why the supreme craftsman did not want to bestow all the perfections on all his works, but why he wished to bestow imperfections on some of them.

You say that although you have no power to avoid error through having a clear perception of things, you can still avoid it by firmly resolving to adhere to the rule of not assenting to anything which you do not clearly perceive.[3] But although you can always keep this rule carefully 313 in mind, is it not still an imperfection not to perceive clearly matters which you need to decide upon, and hence to be perpetually liable to the risk of error?

You say that error resides in the mental operation itself in so far as it proceeds from you and is a kind of privation, but not in the faculty God gave you, nor in its operation in so far as it depends on him.[4] But although the error does not immediately reside in the faculty God gave you, it does indirectly attach to it, since it was created with the kind of imperfection which makes error possible. Admittedly, as you say, you have no cause for complaint against God who, despite owing you

1 Above p. 43. 2 Above p. 39. 3 Cf. above p. 43. 4 Cf. above p. 41.

nothing, bestowed on you the good gifts which you should thank him for. But there is still cause to wonder why he did not bestow more perfect gifts on you, given that he had the knowledge and the power and was not malevolent.

You go on to say that you have no cause to complain that God's concurrence is involved in your acts when you go wrong. For in so far as these acts depend on God, they are all true and good; and your ability to perform them means that there is, in a sense, more perfection in you than would be the case if you lacked this ability. You continue: 'As for the privation involved – which is all that the essential definition of falsity and wrong consists in – this does not in any way require the concurrence of God, since it is not a thing and should not be referred to him.'[1] But although this is a subtle distinction it is not quite enough to resolve the problem. For even if God does not concur in the privation in which the falsity and error of the act consists, he nonetheless concurs in the act itself; and if he did not concur in it, it would not be a privation. In any case, he is the author of that power in you which is subject to deception and error; and hence he is the author of a power which is, so to speak, ineffective. Thus the defect in the act should not, it seems, be referred so much to the power which is ineffective as to the author who made it ineffective and did not choose to make it effective, or more effective, though he was able to do so. It is certainly no fault in a workman if he does not trouble to make an enormous key to open a tiny box; but it is a fault if, in making the key small, he gives it a shape which makes it difficult or impossible to open the box. Similarly, God is admittedly not to be blamed for giving puny man a faculty of judging that is too small to cope with everything, or even with most things or the most important things; but this still leaves room to wonder why he gave man a faculty which is uncertain, confused and inadequate even for the few matters which he did want us to decide upon.

3. You next ask what is the cause of error or falsity in you.[2] First of all, I do not question your basis for saying the intellect is simply the faculty of being aware of ideas, or of apprehending things simply and without any affirmation or negation; nor do I dispute your calling the will or freedom of choice a faculty whose function is to affirm or deny, to give or withhold assent. My only question concerns why, on your account, our will or freedom of choice is not restricted by any limits, whereas the intellect is restricted. In fact it seems that these two faculties have an equally broad scope; certainly the scope of the intellect is at the very least no narrower than that of the will, since the will never aims at anything which the intellect has not already perceived.

1 Above p. 42. 2 Above pp. 40f.

I said that the scope of the intellect was 'at the very least no narrower'; in fact its scope seems to be even wider than that of the will. For the will or choice or judgement, and hence our selection or pursuit or avoidance of something, never occurs unless we have previously apprehended that thing, and unless the idea of that thing has been previously perceived and set before us by the intellect. What is more, there are many things which we understand only obscurely, so that no judgement or pursuit or   315 avoidance occurs in respect of them. Also, the faculty of judgement is often undecided, and if there are reasons of equal weight on either side, or no reasons at all, no judgement follows; but the intellect still continues to apprehend the matters on which no judgement has been passed.

You say that you can always understand the possibility of your faculties being increased more and more, including the intellectual faculty itself, of which you can form an infinite idea.[1] But this itself shows that the intellect is not any more limited than the will, since it can extend itself even to an infinite object. You say that you recognize your will to be equal to that of God – not, indeed, in respect of its extent, but essentially. But surely the same could be said of the intellect too, since you have defined the essential notion of the intellect in just the same way as you have defined that of the will. In short, will you please tell us if the will can extend to anything that escapes the intellect? It seems, then, that error does not arise, as you allege, from the fact that the scope of the will is wider than that of the intellect and the will extends itself to judge of matters which the intellect does not perceive. The scope of both faculties is equal, and error arises instead from the fact that the perception of the intellect is faulty and the judgement of the will is faulty.

Hence there is no basis for your extending the will beyond the bounds of the intellect, since the will never makes judgements about things which the intellect does not perceive, and it makes faulty judgements only because the intellect has faulty perceptions.

When you talk about the argument you constructed concerning the   316 existence of things, and compare the case of your own existence,[2] you proceed correctly as far as the judgement of your own existence is concerned, but your assumption appears to be incorrect in so far as it concerns other things. For what you claim, or rather pretend, is not something you are really in doubt about: you emphatically judge that something apart from you and distinct from you exists, for you already have a prior understanding of something apart from you and distinct from you. When you suppose that you have not yet come upon any persuasive reason in favour of one alternative rather than the other,[3] this is indeed a possible supposition. But you ought simultaneously to

1 Above pp. 39–40.   2 Cf. above p. 41.   3 *Ibid.*

suppose that in that case no judgement will follow, and that your will will always be indifferent and will not decide to make a definite judgement until the intellect comes upon some plausible argument which favours one side more than the other.

You go on to say that this indifference extends to cases where you do not have sufficiently clear knowledge; for although probable conjectures may pull you in one direction, the mere knowledge that they are conjectures may push your assent the other way.[1] But this seems quite untrue. For if your conjectures are pulling you in one direction, the knowledge that they are merely conjectures may indeed make your judgement come down on that side, albeit with some reluctance and hesitation; but it can never make your judgement come down on the other side unless other conjectures occur subsequently to you which are not just equally probable but more probable.

You add that your point is confirmed by your experience of the last few days, when you supposed that opinions you believed to be absolutely true were false. But remember that I have not allowed you to make this supposition. You cannot really have felt or been convinced that you had never seen the sun or the earth or men and so on, or that you had never heard sounds or walked or eaten or written or spoken or performed similar activities involving the use of your body and its organs.

Finally, the essence of error does not seem to consist in the incorrect use of free will, as you allege, so much as in the disparity between our judgement and the thing which is the object of our judgement. And it seems that error arises when our intellectual apprehension of the thing does not correspond with the way the thing really is. Hence the blame does not seem to lie with the will for not judging correctly, so much as with the intellect for not displaying the object correctly. The dependence of the will on the intellect seems to be as follows. If the intellect perceives something clearly, or seems to do so, the will in that case will make a judgement that is approved and settled, irrespective of whether it is in fact true, or merely thought to be true. But when the intellect's perception is obscure, then the will in this case will make a judgement that is doubtful and tentative, but which will, nonetheless, be regarded for the time being as truer than its opposite, irrespective of whether it really accords with the truth of the matter or not. This means that we do not have the power so much to guard against error as to guard against persisting in error; and if we want to use our judgement correctly, we should not so much restrain our will as apply our intellect to develop clearer awareness, which the judgement will always then follow.

4. You then conclude by exaggerating the beneficial results which you

1 Above p. 41.

can derive from this Meditation, and you lay down a rule for arriving at the truth. You say that you will reach the truth if only you give sufficient attention to all the things which you perfectly understand, and separate these from all the other cases where your apprehension is more confused and obscure.[1]

This is certainly true, but it is the kind of truth that could have been 318 understood without any reference to the foregoing Meditation; and hence the Meditation seems to have been wholly superfluous. But please note, distinguished Sir, that the difficulty does not seem to be about whether we must clearly and distinctly understand something if we are to avoid error, but about what possible skill or method will permit us to discover that our understanding is so clear and distinct as to be true and to make it impossible that we should be mistaken. As I objected at the beginning, we are often deceived even though we think we know something as clearly and distinctly as anything can possibly be known. You also raised this objection against yourself, but we are still waiting for the aforementioned skill or method, and it should be your principal task to work on this problem.

On the Fifth Meditation: 'The essence of material things, and the existence of God considered a second time'

1. In the Fifth Meditation you say first of all that you distinctly imagine quantity (that is, extension in length, breadth and depth) and also number, shape, position, motion and duration.[2] From among all these ideas, which you say you have, you select shape, and from all the shapes you select a triangle, which you discuss as follows:

Even if perhaps no such figure exists, or has ever existed, anywhere outside my thought, there is still a determinate nature which is not invented by me or dependent on my mind. This is clear from the fact that various properties can be 319 demonstrated of the triangle, for example that its three angles equal two right angles and that its greatest side subtends its greatest angle, and so on. And since these properties are ones which I now clearly recognize, whether I want to or not, even if I never thought of them at all when I first imagined the triangle, it follows that they cannot have been invented by me.[3]

This is all you have to say about the essence of material things, for the few comments you add next are part of the same argument. But I do not want to stop and raise objections here; I will only suggest that it seems very hard to propose that there is any 'immutable and eternal nature' apart from almighty God.

---

1 Above p. 43. 2 Above p. 44. 3 Above p. 45.

You will say that all that you are proposing is the scholastic point that the natures or essences of things are eternal, and that eternally true propositions can be asserted of them. But this is just as hard to accept; and in any case it is impossible to grasp how there can be a human nature if no human being exists, or how we can say a rose is a flower when not even one rose exists.

The schoolmen say that talking of the essence of things is one thing and talking of their existence is another, and that although things do not exist from eternity their essences are eternal. But in that case, since the most important element in things is their essence, does God do anything very impressive when he produces their existence? Is he doing any more than a tailor does when he tries a suit of clothes on someone? How can people defend the thesis that the essence of man, which is in Plato, say, is eternal and independent of God? Is this supposed to be because it is universal? But everything to be found in Plato is particular. It is true that after seeing the nature of Plato and of Socrates, and similar natures of other men, the intellect habitually abstracts from them some common concept in respect of which they all agree, and which can then be regarded as the universal nature or essence of man, in so far as it is understood to apply to every man. But it is surely inexplicable that there should have been a universal nature before Plato and the others existed, and before the intellect performed the abstraction.

You will say that the proposition 'Man is an animal' is true even if no man exists, and hence that it is eternally true. But it seems not to be true except in the sense that whenever a man exists he will be an animal. Admittedly there does seem to be a distinction between the two propositions 'Man is' and 'Man is an animal', in that existence is more expressly signified by the former and essence by the latter. But nevertheless the former does not rule out essence, nor does the latter rule out existence; on the contrary, when we say 'Man is' we mean *man the animal*, and when we say 'Man is an animal' we mean *man while he exists*. But what is more, since the proposition 'Man is an animal' has no greater necessity than the proposition 'Plato is a man', it follows that even the latter proposition will have eternal truth, and the individual essence of Plato will be just as independent of God as the universal essence of man; and the same follows in similar cases which it would be tiresome to pursue. I must add, however, that although man is said to be of such a nature that he cannot exist without being an animal, we should not therefore imagine that such a nature is something which exists anywhere outside the intellect. All that is meant is that if anything is a man, it must resemble other things to which we apply the same label, 'man', in virtue of their mutual similarity. This similarity, I maintain, belongs to the individual natures, and it is from this that the intellect takes its cue in forming the concept, or idea, or form of a common nature to which everything that will count as a man must conform.

Thus I maintain that the same thing applies to your triangle and its nature. The triangle is a kind of mental rule which you use to find out 321 whether something deserves to be called a triangle. But we should not therefore say that such a triangle is something real, or that it is a true nature distinct from the intellect. For it is the intellect alone which, after seeing material triangles, has formed this nature and made it a common nature, as we have explained in the case of the nature of man.

It follows that we should not suppose that the properties demonstrated of material triangles belong to them because they derive them from the ideal triangle. Rather, they themselves possess these properties in their own right, and it is the ideal triangle which does not possess them except in so far as the intellect, after inspecting the material triangles, has attributed such properties to it, only to give them back to the material triangles again in the course of the demonstration. In the same way, the properties of human nature are not in Plato and Socrates in the sense that Plato and Socrates have received them from the universal nature; rather, the universal nature has the properties only because the intellect gave them to it after observing them in Plato, Socrates and others; and it will give them back to those individuals again when it is called on to produce the appropriate arguments.

We know that the intellect, after seeing Plato and Socrates and others, all of whom are rational, constructed the universal proposition 'Every man is rational.' And subsequently, when it wishes to prove that Plato is rational, it uses the universal proposition as a premiss in a syllogism. And yet, O Mind, you claim that you have the idea of a triangle and would have had it even if you had never seen bodies with a triangular shape, just as you have the idea of many other figures which have never impinged on your senses.[1]

But as I was saying earlier, if you had up till now been deprived of all your sensory functions, so that you had never either seen or touched the 322 various surfaces or extremities of bodies, do you think you would have been able to acquire or form within yourself the idea of a triangle or other figure? You say that you have many ideas in you which never came into your mind via the senses.[2] But of course it is easy for you to have these ideas, since you fashioned them from ideas which did come to you via the senses, and you formed them into various other ideas, in the ways explained above.

I should also have said something here about the false nature of a

1 Cf. above p. 45.   2 *Ibid.*

triangle which is supposed to consist of lines which lack breadth, to contain an area which has no depth, and to terminate in three points which have no dimensions at all; but this would have taken me too far off the subject.

2. You next attempt to demonstrate the existence of God, and the thrust of your argument is contained in the following passage:

> When I concentrate, it is quite evident that existence can no more be separated from the essence of God than the fact that its three angles equal two right angles can be separated from the essence of a triangle, or than the idea of a mountain can be separated from the idea of a valley. Hence it is just as much of a contradiction to think of God (that is, a supremely perfect being) lacking existence (that is, lacking a perfection) as it is to think of a mountain without a valley.[1]

But we must note here that the kind of comparison you make is not wholly fair.

It is quite all right for you to compare essence with essence, but instead of going on to compare existence with existence or a property with a property, you compare existence with a property. It seems that you should have said that omnipotence can no more be separated from the essence of God than the fact that its angles equal two right angles can be separated from the essence of a triangle. Or, at any rate, you should have said that the existence of God can no more be separated from his essence than the existence of a triangle can be separated from its essence. If you had done this, both your comparisons would have been satisfactory, and I would have granted you not only the first one but the second one as well. But you would not for all that have established that God necessarily exists, since a triangle does not necessarily exist either, even though its essence and existence cannot in actual fact be separated. Real separation is impossible no matter how much the mind may separate them or think of them apart from each other – as indeed it can even in the case of God's essence and existence.

Next we must note that you place existence among the divine perfections, but do not place it among the perfections of a triangle or mountain, though it could be said that in its own way it is just as much a perfection of each of these things. In fact, however, existence is not a perfection either in God or in anything else; it is that without which no perfections can be present.

For surely, what does not exist has no perfections or imperfections, and what does exist and has several perfections does not have existence as one of its individual perfections; rather, its existence is that in virtue of

323

---

1 Above p. 46.

which both the thing itself and its perfections are existent, and that without which we cannot say that the thing possesses the perfections or that the perfections are possessed by it. Hence we do not say that existence 'exists in a thing' in the way perfections do; and if a thing lacks existence, we do not say it is imperfect, or deprived of a perfection, but say instead that it is nothing at all.

Thus, just as when you listed the perfections of the triangle you did not include existence or conclude that the triangle existed, so when you listed the perfections of God you should not have included existence among them so as to reach the conclusion that God exists, unless you wanted to beg the question.

You say that existence is distinct from essence in the case of all other things, but not in the case of God.[1] But how, may I ask, are we to distinguish the essence of Plato from his existence, except merely in our thought? Suppose that Plato no longer exists: where now is his essence? Surely in the case of God the distinction between essence and existence is of just this kind: the distinction occurs in our thought.

You then raise an objection against your argument: it does not follow from the fact that you think of a mountain with a valley, or a winged horse, that a mountain or a horse with wings exists; and similarly from the fact that you think of God as existing it does not follow that he exists. You argue that a sophism is concealed here.[2] But it can hardly have been very difficult to expose the sophism which you yourself constructed – especially since you did so by asserting that it is a manifest contradiction that an existing God should not exist, while omitting to point out that the same applies in the case of a man or a horse.

But if you had taken the mountain and its valley, or the horse and its wings, as comparable to God and his knowledge (or his power or other attributes), then the objection would still have stood, and you would have had to try to explain how it is possible for us to think of a sloping mountain or a winged horse without thinking of them as existing, yet impossible to think of a wise and powerful God without thinking of him as existing.

You say that you are not free to think of God without existence (that is, a supremely perfect being without a supreme perfection) as you are free to imagine a horse with or without wings.[3] The only comment to be added to this is as follows. You are free to think of a horse not having wings without thinking of the existence which would, according to you, be a perfection in the horse if it were present; but, in the same way, you are free to think of God as having knowledge and power and other perfections without thinking of him as having the existence which would

324

325

1 Cf. above p. 47. 2 Above p. 46. 3 *Ibid.*

complete his perfection, if he had it. Just as the horse which is thought of as having the perfection of wings is not therefore deemed to have the existence which is, according to you, a principal perfection, so the fact that God is thought of as having knowledge and other perfections does not therefore imply that he has existence. This remains to be proved. And although you say that both existence and all the other perfections are included in the idea of a supremely perfect being, here you simply assert what should be proved, and assume the conclusion as a premiss. Otherwise I could say that the idea of a perfect Pegasus contains not just the perfection of his having wings but also the perfection of existence. For just as God is thought of as perfect in every kind of perfection, so Pegasus is thought of as perfect in his own kind. It seems that there is no point that you can raise in this connection which, if we preserve the analogy, will not apply to Pegasus if it applies to God, and *vice versa*.

You say that in thinking of a triangle it is not necessary to think that it has three angles equal to two right angles, though this is nonetheless true, as appears afterwards when you give the matter your attention; and similarly, although it is possible to think of the other perfections of God without thinking of his existence, it is nonetheless true that he exists, as becomes clear when you attend to the fact that existence is a perfection.[1] You surely see the point that can be made here: just as we afterwards recognize that the triangle has this property because it is proved by a demonstration, so, if we are to recognize that existence belongs to God, this must be proved by a demonstration. Otherwise I shall easily be able to establish that anything has any property at all.

You say that your attributing all perfections to God is not like your thinking that all quadrilateral figures can be inscribed in a circle; for the latter assumption is mistaken, since you afterwards find that a rhombus cannot be inscribed in a circle, but the former supposition is not mistaken since you afterwards find that existence belongs to God.[2] Your two suppositions, however, seem exactly alike; or if not, you must show that whereas it is a contradiction for a rhombus to be inscribed in a circle, it is not a contradiction for God to exist. I will pass over your other assertions which are either unexplained or unproved or else established by arguments already discussed. These include the statements that, apart from God, there is nothing else of which you are capable of thinking such that existence belongs to its essence; that it is unintelligible that there should be two or more Gods of this kind; that such a God has existed from eternity and will abide for eternity; and, finally, that you perceive many other attributes in God, none of which can be removed or altered.[3] These assertions should be looked at more closely and investigated more

326 (in left margin)

1 Cf. above pp. 46f.   2 *Ibid.*   3 Above p. 47.

carefully if their truth is to be uncovered and they are to be regarded as certain, etc.

3. Finally, you say that the certainty and truth of all knowledge depends uniquely on your knowledge of the true God, so that without such knowledge no true certainty or knowledge is attainable.[1] You illustrate this point as follows:

> When I consider the nature of a triangle, it appears most evident to me, steeped as I am in the principles of geometry, that its three angles are equal to two right angles; and so long as I attend to the proof, I cannot but believe this to be true. But as soon as I turn my mind's eye away from the proof, then, in spite of remembering that I perceived it very clearly, I can easily fall into doubt about its truth, if I am without knowledge of God. For I could convince myself that I have a natural disposition to go wrong from time to time in matters which I think I perceive as evidently as can be. This will seem even more likely when I remember that there have been cases where I have regarded things as true and certain, but have later been led by other arguments to judge them to be false. Now, however, I have perceived that God exists, and at the same time I have understood that everything else depends on him and that he is no deceiver; and I have drawn the conclusion that everything which I clearly and distinctly perceive is of necessity true. Accordingly, even if I am no longer attending to the arguments which led me to judge that this is true, as long as I remember that I clearly and distinctly perceived it, there are no counter-arguments which can be adduced to make me doubt it, but on the contrary I have true and certain knowledge of it. And I have knowledge not just of this matter, but of all other matters which I remember ever having demonstrated, in geometry and so on.[2]

327

Here, Sir, I accept that you are speaking seriously; and there is nothing I can say except that I do not think you will find it easy to make anyone believe that before you established the above conclusion about God you were less certain of these geometrical proofs than you were afterwards. These proofs certainly seem to be so evident and certain that they compel our assent all by themselves, and once they have been perceived they do not allow the intellect to remain in further doubt. So, indeed, when faced with these proofs, the mind may very well tell the evil demon to go hang himself, just as you yourself emphatically asserted that you could not possibly be deceived about the proposition or inference 'I am thinking, hence I exist', even though you had not yet arrived at knowledge of God. Of course it is quite true – as true as anything can be – that God exists, is the author of all things, and is not a deceiver; but these truths seem less evident than the geometrical proofs, as is shown by the fact that many people dispute the existence of God, the creation of the world, and so on, whereas no one impugns the demonstrations of geometry.

328

1 Cf. above p. 49.   2 Above p. 48.

In view of this, is there anyone whom you will convince that the geometrical proofs depend for their evidence and certainty on the proofs
concerning God? Surely no one imagines that such atheists as
Diagoras or Theodorus[1] cannot be made completely certain of these
geometrical proofs. And how often do you find a believer who, if he is
asked why he is certain that the square on the hypotenuse of a
right-angled triangle is equal to the squares on the other sides, will
answer: 'Because I know that God exists and cannot deceive, and that he
is the source of this geometrical truth and of all other things'? Will he
not answer instead 'Because I know it and am convinced of it by an
indubitable demonstration'? And how much more likely is it that
Pythagoras, Plato, Archimedes and Euclid and the other mathematicians
will answer this way? For none of them seems to have thought about God
in order to make himself completely certain of his demonstrations! But
since you are assuring us only of your own views and not those of others,
and since your position is in any case a pious one, there is really no
reason why I should dispute what you say.

On the Sixth Meditation: 'The existence of material things and the real distinction between mind and body'

1. I have no objection to what you say at the beginning of the Sixth
Meditation, namely that material things 'are capable of existing in so far
as they are the subject-matter of pure mathematics'.[2] In fact, however,
material things are the subject-matter of applied, not pure, mathematics,
and the subject-matter of pure mathematics – including the point, the
line, the surface, and the indivisible figures which are composed of these
elements and yet remain indivisible – cannot exist in reality. The only
point that gave me pause is that here again you distinguish between
imagining and understanding. But surely, O Mind, these two appear to
be acts of one and the same faculty, as we have suggested above, and if
there is a distinction between them it seems to be no more than one of
degree. Notice that this can now be proved from what you say.

You said previously that 'imagining is simply contemplating the shape
or image of a corporeal thing'.[3] But in the present passage you do not
deny that understanding consists of contemplating triangles, pentagons,
chiliagons, myriagons and so on; and these are shapes of corporeal
things. You now set up your distinction. Imagination, you say, involves
the application of the cognitive faculty to a body, but understanding does
not require this kind of application or effort. And hence, when without

---

1 Diagoras of Melos and Theodorus of Cyrene, fourth cent. B.C.; both cited by Cicero as
   noted atheists (*De Natura Deorum* I, 2).
2 Above p. 50.   3 Above p. 19.

329

any effort you perceive a triangle as a figure consisting of three angles, you say that you 'understand' it; but when, not without some effort on your part, you make the figure become, as it were, present before you, contemplate and examine it, and discern the three angles distinctly and in detail, then you say you 'imagine' it. Thus you perceive without effort that a chiliagon is a figure with a thousand angles, but you cannot by any mental application or effort discern them or make them become, as it were, present before you, or see them all in detail. You are in a confused state, just as you are when dealing with a myriagon or any other figure of this sort; and hence you think that in the case of the chiliagon or myriagon you have understanding, not imagination.[1]

But for all that, there is nothing to prevent your extending your imagination, as well as your understanding, to the chiliagon, just as you do to the triangle. For you do make an effort to get some sort of picture of this figure with all its many angles, even though the number of angles is so large that you cannot grasp it distinctly. In any case, although you perceive that the word 'chiliagon' signifies a figure with a thousand angles, that is just the meaning of the term, and it does not follow that you *understand* the thousand angles of the figure any better than you *imagine* them.

Note, moreover, that the loss of distinctness and the onset of confusedness is gradual. You will perceive – imagine or understand – a quadrilateral more confusedly than a triangle but more distinctly than a pentagon; and you will perceive the pentagon more confusedly than a quadrilateral and more distinctly than a hexagon; and so on, until you reach the point where you have nothing you can explicitly visualize. And because you can no longer grasp the figure explicitly, you do not bother to make a supreme mental effort.

Hence if you want to say that you are simultaneously 'imagining and understanding' a figure when you are aware of it distinctly and with some discernible effort, whereas you are merely 'understanding' it when you see it only confusedly and with little or no effort, then I am prepared to allow this usage. But it will not follow that you have the basis for setting up more than one type of internal cognition, since it is purely a contingent matter, and a question of degree, whether you contemplate any given figure distinctly or confusedly, and with or without a concentrated effort. At any rate, when we wish to run through all the figures from a heptagon or octagon right up to a chiliagon, and attend all the time to the greater or lesser degree of distinctness or concentration involved, we shall surely not be able to say at what point, or with what figure, our imagination stops, leaving us with understanding alone. What

1 Cf. above pp. 50f.

we shall find, surely, is that there is a progressive scale of awareness such that the distinctness and effort involved continuously and imperceptibly decreases, while the confusion and slackening of effort increases. In any case, you must bear in mind that you are belittling the understanding while extolling the imagination. Do you not invite us to scorn the former and commend the latter when you attribute slackness and confusion to the one and diligence and clarity of vision to the other?

You assert later on that the power of imagining, in so far as it is distinct from the power of understanding, is not a necessary constituent of your essence.[1] But how can that be if they are one and the same power, and the difference in functioning is merely one of degree?

You add that when the mind imagines, it turns towards the body, but when it understands, it turns towards itself and to the ideas it has within it.[2] But what if the mind cannot turn to itself or to one of its ideas without simultaneously turning to something corporeal or something represented by a corporeal idea? For triangles, pentagons, chiliagons, myriagons, and the other figures, or their ideas, are wholly corporeal; and when it understands, the mind cannot attend to them except as corporeal or quasi-corporeal objects. As for the ideas of allegedly immaterial things, such as those of God and an angel and the human soul or mind, it is clear that even the ideas we have of these things are corporeal or quasi-corporeal, since (as previously mentioned) the ideas are derived from the human form and from other things which are very rarefied and simple and very hard to perceive with the senses, such as air or ether. When you say that your conjecture that some body exists is only probable, you cannot mean this seriously, and so it need not hold us up.

2. You next discuss the senses, and first of all you make a splendid survey of the things you had previously become aware of via the senses and believed to be true with nature alone as your judge and guide. You next relate the experiences which so shook the faith you had in the senses as to make you retreat to the position we saw you take up in the First Meditation.[3]

I have no intention of starting an argument here about the truthfulness of the senses. For although there is deception or falsity, it is not to be found in the senses; for the senses are quite passive and report only appearances, which must appear in the way they do owing to their causes. The error or falsity is in the judgement or the mind, which is not circumspect enough and does not notice that things at a distance will for one reason or another appear smaller and more blurred than when they are nearby, and so on. Nevertheless, when deception occurs, we must not deny that it exists; the only difficulty is whether it occurs all the time, thus

1 Cf. above p. 51.   2 *Ibid.*   3 Above pp. 51f.

making it impossible for us ever to be sure of the truth of anything which we perceive by the senses.

It is quite unnecessary to look for obvious examples here. With regard to the cases you mention, or rather put forward as presenting a problem, I will simply say that it seems to be quite uncontroversial that when we look at a tower from nearby, and touch it, we are sure that it is square, even though when we were further off we had occasion to judge it to be round, or at any rate to doubt whether it was square or round or some other shape.

Similarly the feeling of pain which still appears to occur in the foot or hand after these limbs have been amputated[1] may sometimes give rise to deception, because the spirits responsible for sensation have been accustomed to pass into the limbs and produce a sensation in them. But such deception occurs, of course, in people who have suffered amputation; those whose bodies are intact are so certain that they feel pain in the foot or hand when they see it is pricked, that they cannot be in doubt.

Again, since during our lives we are alternately awake or dreaming, a dream may give rise to deception because things may appear to be present when they are not in fact present. But we do not dream all the time, and for as long as we are really awake we cannot doubt whether we are awake or dreaming.

Thus, although we can think that our nature makes us liable to be deceived even in cases where the truth seems utterly certain, we can nonetheless think that we have a natural capacity for arriving at the truth. We are sometimes deceived when we do not detect a sophism or when a stick is partially immersed in water; but equally, we sometimes have an understanding of the truth, as in the case of a geometrical demonstration or when the stick is taken out of the water, and in neither of these cases can there be any doubt at all about the truth. And even in the other cases where doubt is permissible, at least we may not doubt that things appear to us in such and such a way: it cannot but be wholly true that they appear as they do.

Reason may indeed persuade us not to accept much of what nature impels us to believe, but at least it cannot take away the truth of the appearances or the 'phenomena'. There is no need, however, to discuss here the question of whether the opposition between reason and sensory impulses is simply analogous to the right hand's holding up the left when it is dropping from tiredness, or whether some other analogy is appropriate.

3. You next come to the task you have set yourself, but in a way which looks like petty skirmishing. You say: 'But now, when I am beginning to

1 Cf. above p. 53.

achieve a better knowledge of myself and the author of my being, although I do not think I should heedlessly accept everything I seem to have acquired from the senses, neither do I think that everything should be called into doubt.'[1] This is quite right, though undoubtedly you must have thought this before.

The next passage is as follows:

First, I know that everything that I clearly and distinctly understand is capable of being created by God so as to correspond exactly with my understanding of it. Hence the fact that I can clearly and distinctly understand one thing apart from another is enough to make me certain that the two things are distinct, since they are capable of being separated, at least by God. The question of what kind of power is required to bring about such a separation does not affect the judgement that the two things are distinct.[2]

The point that must be made about this is that you are using something which is obscure to prove something which is clear (though I do not suggest that the inference itself contains any obscurity). I will not complain that you should previously have proved the existence of God and the extent of his power in order to show that he is capable of bringing about whatever you are capable of understanding. I should like to ask only about the property of the triangle – that its longest side subtends the greatest angle: do you understand this property of the triangle separately from its other property of having its three angles equal to two right angles? And do you therefore admit that God could separate the former property from the latter and isolate it, enabling the triangle to have one property and not the other, or enabling the property to exist apart from the triangle?

But I shall not detain you any further on this point, since the separation in question is of little relevance. You go on as follows: 'Thus, simply by knowing I exist and seeing at the same time that absolutely nothing else belongs to my nature or essence except that I am a thinking thing, I can infer correctly that my essence consists solely in the fact that I am a thinking thing.'[3] Here I ought to detain you, but it is enough to repeat what I said in connection with the Second Meditation. Alternatively, let us wait and see what inference you intend to draw.

Here it is:

It is true that I may have (or, to anticipate, that I certainly have) a body that is very closely joined to me. But, nevertheless, on the one hand, I have a clear and distinct idea of myself, in so far as I am simply a thinking, non-extended thing, and, on the other hand, I have a distinct idea of body, in so far as it is simply an extended, non-thinking thing. And accordingly, it is certain that I am really distinct from my body and can exist without it.[4]

1 Above p. 54.   2 *Ibid.*   3 *Ibid.*   4 *Ibid.*

This, then, was the result you were aiming for. And therefore, since the crux of the problem lies here, we must stop for a while to see how you manage to establish this conclusion. The principal point concerns the distinction between you and *body*. What body do you mean? Obviously this solid body composed of limbs which you undoubtedly refer to when you say 'I have a body which is joined to me' and 'It is certain that I am distinct from my body' etc.

And yet, O Mind, there is no difficulty about this body. There would be a problem if I were to follow the majority of philosophers and object that you are an *entelechy*,[1] perfection, actuality, form, appearance, or, in common speech, 'mode', of the body. Such philosophers do not acknowledge that you are any more distinct or separable from this body than a shape or other mode is separable from it; and this point holds whether you are the entire soul or else some additional νοῦς δυνάμει (the so-called 'potential intellect') or νοῦς παθητικός (the 'passive intellect'). But I would like to be more generous and consider you as the νοῦς ποιητικός or 'active intellect', and indeed to regard you as χωριστός or 'separable', albeit in another sense than the usual one.

The philosophers I have just referred to regarded the active intellect as common to all men (if not to all things) and as enabling the passive intellect to understand in exactly the same way – and with exactly the same necessity – as that in which light enables the eye to see (hence they frequently compared it with the light from the sun and regarded it as coming from outside). But I shall consider you instead (and you will be quite happy with this) as a specific sort of intellect exercising control in the body.

Now the difficulty, to repeat, is not about whether or not you are separable from this body (and this is why I suggested above that you had no need to have recourse to God's power in order to establish that things which you understand apart from each other are separate). Rather, the difficulty concerns the body which you yourself are – for you may be a rarefied body infused into this solid one or occupying some part of it. At all events you have not yet convinced us that you are something wholly incorporeal. And although in the Second Meditation you declared that you are not a wind, fire, air or breath, I did warn you that you had asserted this without any proof.[2]

You said there that you were not arguing about these things at that stage; but you never went on to discuss them, and you never gave any sort of proof that you are not a body of this sort. I had hoped that you

336

337

1 A reference to Aristotle's definition of the soul; for this and what follows in this paragraph, cf. *De Anima* III, 4 and 5.
2 Med. II, above p. 18; cf. above p. 185.

would now offer one; but what discussion and proof you do offer simply
establishes that you are not this solid body, and, as I have just said, there
is no difficulty about this.

4. 'But', you say, 'on the one hand I have a clear and distinct idea of
myself, in so far as I am simply a thinking, non-extended thing; and on
the other hand I have a distinct idea of body, in so far as it is simply an
extended, non-thinking thing.'[1] Now as far as the idea of body is
concerned, it does not seem that it ought to cause us too much trouble. If
you are talking of the idea of body in the general sense, then we must
repeat our objection that you still have to prove that being capable of
thought is inconsistent with the nature of body. For you would be
begging the question, if you set up the inquiry as to whether you are a
rarefied body in such a way as to presuppose that thought and body are
incompatible.

But your claim undoubtedly concerns merely this solid body from
which you maintain you are distinct and separable. And thus I do not so
much dispute that you have an idea of this body as insist that you could
not have such an idea if you were really an unextended thing. For how,
may I ask, do you think that you, an unextended subject, could receive
the semblance[2] or idea of a body that is extended? If such a semblance
comes from a body then it is undoubtedly corporeal, and has a number of
338 parts or layers, and so is extended. If it is imprinted in you from some
other source, since it must still represent an extended body, it must still
have parts and hence be extended. For if it lacks parts, how will it
manage to represent parts? If it lacks extension, how will it represent an
extended thing? If it lacks shape, how will it represent a thing that has a
shape? If it has no position, how will it represent a thing which has upper
and lower parts, parts on the right and parts on the left, and parts in the
middle? If it lacks all variation, how will it represent various colours and
so on? It seems, then, that the idea does not wholly lack extension. Yet if
it is extended, how can you, if you are unextended, have become its
subject? How will you adapt it to yourself or make use of it? And how
will you gradually experience its fading and disappearing?

As far as your idea of yourself is concerned, there is nothing to add to
what I have already said, especially regarding the Second Meditation. For
what emerges there is that, far from having a clear and distinct idea of
yourself you have no idea of yourself at all. This is because although you
recognize that you are thinking, you still do not know what kind of thing
you, who are thinking, are. And since it is only this operation that you
are aware of, the most important element is still hidden from you, namely
the substance which performs this operation. This leads me to suggest

1 Above p. 54.   2 See footnote above p. 174.

that you may be compared to a blind man who, on feeling heat and being told that it comes from the sun, thinks he has a clear and distinct idea of the sun in that, if anyone asks him what the sun is, he can reply: 'It is a heating thing.'

But I should add that you say not only that you are a thinking thing but also that you are a thing which is unextended. I shall ignore the fact that this is asserted without proof, even though it is still in question, and simply ask you first of all: do you therefore have a clear and distinct idea of yourself? You say that you are not extended; that is, you say what you are not, not what you are. In order to have a clear and distinct, or, what is the same thing, a true and authentic idea of something, is it not necessary to know the thing positively and, so to speak, affirmatively? Or is it enough to know that it is not some other thing? Would someone have a clear and distinct idea of Bucephalus if he simply knew that he was not a fly?[1]

But I will not press this point, but ask you this instead. You say you are a thing which is not extended; but are you not diffused throughout the body? I have no idea what reply you will give, for although from the start I gathered that you were in the brain, this was something I arrived at by conjecture rather than by simply following your views. The source of my conjecture was a later passage, where you say that you are 'not affected by all parts of the body but only by the brain, or only by one small part of it'.[2] But I was not at all certain whether this meant that you were in fact present only in the brain (or a part of it); for you might be present throughout the body but affected only in one part of it – just as we commonly say that the soul is diffused throughout the whole body but sees only in the eye.

A similar doubt was raised by the phrase 'although the whole mind seems to be united to the whole body'.[3] For in this passage you do not actually assert that you are united to the whole body, but neither do you deny it. Whatever your view is, let me, if I may, assume to begin with that you are diffused throughout the entire body. Now whether you are identical with one soul or something different from it, my question is this: are you really unextended, given that you stretch from head to foot, are coextensive with the body and have parts corresponding to all its parts? Will you reply that you are unextended because you are wholly in the whole body and wholly in every part of it? But if this is your view, what, may I ask, do you mean by it? Can one thing exist simultaneously and in its entirety in several places? Our faith tells us this is true in the case of the sacred mystery of the Eucharist. But the discussion here concerns you,

339

340

---

1 Bucephalus was Alexander the Great's horse.
2 Above p. 59.   3 *Ibid.*

as a natural object, and is being conducted in accordance with the natural light. Is it really permissible to understand there to be several different places simultaneously occupied by no more than one object? And is not a hundred more than one? Again, if a thing is wholly in one place, can it also be in other places unless it is itself outside itself just as one place is outside another? Whatever you say, it will remain obscure and uncertain whether you are entirely present in any given part, or else present in each part by means of your various parts. What is much clearer is that nothing can exist simultaneously and in its entirety in several places; and hence it will turn out to be even more evident that you are not wholly in all the individual parts but wholly in the whole body. This means that you are diffused throughout the body by means of your parts, and thus have extension.

Let us now assume instead that you are in the brain alone, or simply in a small part of it. You will see that the same awkwardness arises. For however small the part in question is, it is still extended, and since you are coextensive with it, you too are therefore extended and have particular parts corresponding to its parts. Will you say that you take the relevant part of the brain to be a point? This is surely incredible; but let it be a point. If it is a physical point, the difficulty still stands, since such a point is extended and does not wholly lack parts. If it is a mathematical point, then such a point, as you are aware, is purely imaginary. But let us grant this imaginary point, or rather let us pretend that there is in the brain a mathematical point to which you are joined and in which you exist. Look what a useless fiction this will turn out to be. For if we adopt it, we shall have to imagine that you exist at the conjunction of the nerves by means of which all the regions informed[1] by the soul transmit to the brain the ideas or images of the things perceived by the senses. But, first, all the nerves do not meet at one point: for one thing the brain joins up with the spinal column, and many nerves from all over the back terminate there; and, for another thing, the nerves which do go into the middle of the head are not found to terminate in the same part of the brain. But even if we grant that all the nerves do meet, they cannot meet at a mathematical point, since they are corporeal things, not mathematical lines, and so cannot come together at a mathematical point. And even if we grant that they do come together, the spirits which pass through the nerves cannot enter or leave the nerves since they are bodies and a body cannot exist in a non-place or pass through a non-place (which is what a mathematical point is). And even if we grant that they can exist in and pass through a non-place, if you exist in a point which has no right-hand or left-hand or upper or lower regions etc., you

1 See note 2, above p. 182.

cannot possibly judge where the spirits come from or what messages they bring.

The same problem, I maintain, arises concerning the spirits which you must transmit in order to communicate feelings or instructions, or to initiate movement. I will pass over the fact that we cannot grasp how, if you exist in a point, you can set up motions in the spirits without being a body or having a body that would allow you to be in contact with them and make them move. If you say they move by themselves and you merely direct their movements, remember that you elsewhere denied that a body can move by itself,[1] which implies that you are the cause of the movement. Then you must explain to us how this 'directing' of movement can occur without some effort — and therefore motion — on your part. How can there be effort directed against anything, or motion set up in it, unless there is mutual contact between what moves and what is moved? And how can there be contact without a body when, as is transparently clear by the natural light, 'naught apart from body, can touch or yet be touched'.[2]

But why should I spend any more time on this when the onus is on you to prove that you are an unextended and hence incorporeal thing? You will hardly, I think, support your claim by pointing out that man is commonly said to consist of a body and a rational soul — as if it followed from the fact that one part is said to be a body that we must not call the other part a body. If you did take this line, you would give us the chance to make a distinction and say that man consists of two kinds of body, a solid one and a rarefied one, the common name 'body' being retained by the former, while the latter is called the 'soul'. I will pass over the fact that the same could then be said of the other animals to whom you are not prepared to grant a mind like your own; they would then be lucky indeed, since on your account they would at least have a soul! So when you conclude that it is certain that you are really distinct from your body,[3] you see that I will grant you this conclusion, but will not therefore grant that you are incorporeal, as opposed to being a kind of very rarefied body distinct from your more solid body.

You add that hence you 'can exist apart from the body'.[4] But once we have granted you that you can exist without your solid body — just as the vapour with its distinctive smell can exist when it passes out of the apple and is dispersed into the atmosphere — what will you have gained? Well, you will certainly have established more than is intended by those philosophers we mentioned who consider that you will wholly perish when you die; for on their view you are like a shape which, if the surface

342

---

1 Cf. Med. II, above pp. 17f.   2 A reference to Lucretius, *De Rerum Natura* I, 305.
3 Above p. 54.   4 *Ibid.*

is altered, disappears in such a way as to become nothing at all.[1] Indeed, supposing you are some corporeal or tenuous substance, you would not be said to vanish wholly at your death or to pass into nothingness; you would be said to subsist by means of your dispersed parts. We would, however, have to say that, because of this dispersal, you would not continue to think, or be a thinking thing, a mind or a soul. In raising all these objections I am, as always, not casting doubt on the conclusion you are trying to prove; I am simply unhappy about the force of the argument you have presented.

5. In the course of your discussion you go on to mention several points relevant to your thesis, and I will not stop to deal with all of them. One passage that strikes me is this:

Nature teaches me by these sensations of pain, hunger, thirst and so on, that I am not merely present in my body as a sailor is present in a ship, but that I am very closely joined and, as it were, intermingled with it, so that I and the body form a unit. If this were not so, I, who am nothing but a thinking thing, would not feel pain when the body was hurt, but would perceive the damage purely by the intellect, just as a sailor perceives by sight if anything in his ship is broken. Similarly, when the body needed food or drink, I should have an explicit understanding of the fact, instead of having confused sensations of hunger and thirst. For these sensations of hunger, thirst, pain and so on are nothing but confused modes of thinking which arise from the union and, as it were, intermingling of the mind with the body.[2]

All this is quite right, but you still have to explain how that 'joining and, as it were, intermingling' or 'confusion' can apply to you if you are incorporeal, unextended and indivisible. If you are no larger than a point, how are you joined to the entire body, which is so large? How can you be joined even to the brain, or a tiny part of it, since (as noted above) no matter how small it is, it still has size or extension? If you wholly lack parts, how are you intermingled or 'as it were intermingled', with the particles of this region? For there can be no intermingling between things unless the parts of each of them can be intermingled. And if you are something separate, how are you compounded with matter so as to make up a unity? Moreover, since all compounding, conjunction or union takes place between the component parts, must there not be some relationship between these parts? Yet what relationship can possibly be understood to exist between corporeal and incorporeal parts? Can we grasp how stone and air are compressed together, e.g. in a pumice stone, so as to make a genuine compound? Yet there is a much closer relationship between a stone and air, which is also a body, than there is between the body and a soul, or wholly incorporeal mind. Again, must

1 Above p. 233.   2 Above p. 56.

not every union occur by means of close contact? And, as I asked before, how can contact occur without a body? How can something corporeal take hold of something incorporeal so as to keep it joined to itself? And how can the incorporeal grasp the corporeal to keep it reciprocally bound to itself, if it has nothing at all to enable it to grasp or be grasped?

Hence, since you admit that you feel pain, how, may I ask, do you think you are capable of having this sensation if you are incorporeal and unextended? Pain involves being acted upon and cannot be understood as occurring except as a result of something pushing in and separating the components and thus interfering with their continuity. The state of pain is an unnatural state, but if something is by its nature homogeneous, simple, indivisible and immutable, how can it get into an unnatural state or be acted upon unnaturally? Again, since pain either is an alteration, or involves an alteration, how can something be altered if it has no more parts than a point, and hence cannot change or alter its nature without being reduced to nothing? I may add that pain comes from the foot and the arm and other regions at the same time, and hence surely you would have to have various parts enabling you to receive pain in various ways if you are not to have a confused sensation which seems to come from only one part. In a word, the general difficulty still remains of how the corporeal can communicate with the incorporeal and of what· relationship may be established between the two.

6. I will pass over the remainder of your long and elegant discussion where you set about showing that something exists besides yourself and God. You deduce that your body and bodily faculties exist, and that there are other bodies which transmit semblances of themselves to your senses and to yourself, and produce the feelings of pleasure and pain which give rise to your desires and aversions.

From this you finally derive your crowning result. 'In matters regarding the well-being of the body', you say, 'all the senses report the truth much more frequently than not.' And you infer from this that you should 'not have any further fears about the falsity of what the senses tell you every day'. Similarly, you go on to say regarding dreams that they are 'never linked by memory with all the other actions of life as waking experiences are'; and you thus establish that you are encountering real objects and are 'not asleep but awake'. You then say that 'from the fact that God is not a deceiver it follows that in cases like these you are completely free from error'. This is a very pious statement, and your final conclusion that human life is subject to error and we must 'acknowledge the weakness of our nature' is certainly an excellent one.[1]

These, distinguished Sir, are the points which it occurred to me to raise

1 Above pp. 61f.

in connection with your *Meditations*. I repeat that you have no reason to worry about them since my powers of judgement are so meagre that you should not regard my views as of any value at all. When some dish pleases my palate but I see others do not like it, I do not defend my taste as being more perfect than anyone else's; and similarly, when an opinion appeals to me but is unwelcome to others, I am very far from supposing I have managed to come closer to the truth. I think it is more correct to say that everyone is satisfied with his own views, and that wanting everyone to have the same view is as unfair as wanting everyone's tastes to coincide. I say this to assure you that so far as I am concerned you should think yourself free to regard all these comments of mine as wholly worthless and to ignore them altogether. I shall be happy if you recognize my strong affection for you, and appreciate how much respect I have for your powers. I may have couched some of my comments in a somewhat blunt fashion, as is bound to happen when one is expressing disagreement; if this has happened I wholly retract them, and beg you to blot them out. Please consider that my chief aim has been to do you some service and to keep my friendship with you safe and in good repair. And so I take my leave. Written in Paris on 16 May in the Year of Grace 1641.

Distinguished Sir,

In criticizing my *Meditations* you have produced a very elegant and careful essay which I think will be of great benefit in shedding light on their truth. So I consider that I am greatly indebted both to you, for writing down your objections, and to the Reverend Father Mersenne for encouraging you to do so. That gentleman is extremely anxious to inquire into all things, and is an indefatigable supporter of everything that furthers the glory of God; he very well knows that the best way of discovering whether my arguments deserve to be regarded as true demonstrations is to subject them to the examination and vigorous attack of a number of critics of outstanding learning and intelligence, so as to test whether I can give a satisfactory reply to all their objections. With this in mind he has challenged as many people as possible to attempt such a critique; and some, including, I am delighted to say, yourself, have agreed to his request. In fact you have not so much used philosophical arguments to refute my opinions as employed various debating skills to get round them; but this itself is a source of pleasure to me, since it leads me to suppose that it will not be easy to produce any further arguments against me, apart from those contained in the preced- 348 ing objections of my other critics, which you have read. For if there had been any such arguments, your diligence and acumen would certainly have discovered them. I think your purpose has rather been to bring to my attention the devices which might be used to get round my arguments by those whose minds are so immersed in the senses that they shrink from all metaphysical thoughts, and thus to give me the opportunity to deal with them. In replying to you I shall therefore address you not as a discerning philosopher but rather as one of those men of the flesh whose ideas you have presented.

Objections raised against the First Meditation[1]

You say that you approve of my project for freeing my mind from preconceived opinions; and indeed no one can pretend that such a project

1 Above p. 180.

should not be approved of. But you would have preferred me to have carried it out by making a 'simple and brief statement' – that is, only in a perfunctory fashion. Is it really so easy to free ourselves from all the errors which we have soaked up since our infancy? Can we really be too careful in carrying out a project which everyone agrees should be performed? But no doubt you wanted to point out that most people, although verbally admitting that we should escape from preconceived opinions, never do so in fact, because they do not spend any care or effort on the task and they reckon that nothing they have once accepted as true should be regarded as a preconceived opinion. You act the part of such people here, and do it very well, omitting none of the points they might raise. But none of the points you bring forward seems reminiscent of what a philosopher might say. For when you say that there is no need to imagine that God is a deceiver or that we are dreaming and so on, a philosopher would have supposed that he had to supply a reason why these matters should not be called into doubt; or if he had no such reason – and in fact none exists – then he would not have made the remark. Nor would a philosopher have added that in this context 'it would be sufficient to cite the darkness of the human mind or the weakness of our nature'. It is no help in correcting our errors to say that we make mistakes because our mind is in darkness or our nature is weak; this is just like saying that we make mistakes because we are prone to error. It is more helpful to pay attention, as I did, to all the circumstances where we may happen to go wrong, to prevent our heedlessly giving assent in such cases. Again, a philosopher would not have said that 'considering everything as false is more like adopting a new prejudice than relinquishing an old one'; or at least he would have first tried to prove that such a supposition might give rise to the risk of some deception. But you, on the contrary, assert a little later that I cannot 'compel myself to regard what I supposed to be false as being in fact uncertain and false' – i.e. to adopt the new prejudice which you feared I might adopt. A philosopher would be no more surprised at such suppositions of falsity than he would be if, in order to straighten out a curved stick, we bent it round in the opposite direction. The philosopher knows that it is often useful to assume falsehoods instead of truths in this way in order to shed light on the truth, e.g. when astronomers imagine the equator, the zodiac, or other circles in the sky, or when geometers add new lines to given figures. Philosophers frequently do the same. If someone calls this 'having recourse to artifice, sleight of hand and circumlocution' and says it is unworthy of 'philosophical honesty and the love of truth' then he certainly shows that he himself, so far from being philosophically honest or being prepared to employ any argument at all, simply wants to indulge in rhetorical display.

Objections raised against the Second Meditation[1]

1. Here you continue to employ rhetorical tricks instead of reasoning. You pretend that I am playing a game when I am serious, and you take me to be making serious statements and genuine assertions when I am merely raising questions and putting forward commonly held views in order to inquire into them further. When I said that the entire testimony of the senses should be regarded as uncertain and even as false,[2] I was quite serious; indeed this point is so necessary for an understanding of my *Meditations* that if anyone is unwilling or unable to accept it, he will be incapable of producing any objection that deserves a reply. However, we must note the distinction which I have insisted on in several passages, between the actions of life and the investigation of the truth.[3] For when it is a question of organizing our life, it would, of course, be foolish not to trust the senses, and the sceptics who neglected human affairs to the point where friends had to stop them falling off precipices deserved to be laughed at. Hence I pointed out in one passage that no sane person ever seriously doubts such things.[4] But when our inquiry concerns what can be known with complete certainty by the human intellect, it is quite unreasonable to refuse to reject these things in all seriousness as doubtful and even as false; the purpose here is to come to recognize that certain other things which cannot be rejected in this way are thereby more certain and in reality better known to us.

My statement that I did not yet have a sufficient understanding of what this 'I' who thinks is[5] is one that you do not accept as having been made seriously and in good faith; but I did provide a full explanation of the statement. You also question my statements that I had no doubts about what the nature of the body consisted in, and that I attributed to it no power of self-movement, and that I imagined the soul to be like a wind or fire, and so on; but these were simply commonly held views which I was rehearsing so as to show in the appropriate place that they were false.

It is hardly honest to say that I refer nutrition, motion, sensation, etc. to the soul and then immediately to add 'Fair enough, provided we are careful to remember your distinction between the soul and the body.'[6] For shortly afterwards I expressly referred nutrition to the body alone; and as for movement and sensation, I refer them to the body for the most part, and attribute nothing belonging to them to the soul, apart from the element of thought alone.

Again, what reason have you for saying that I 'did not need all this apparatus' to prove I existed?[7] These very words of yours surely show

351

352

1 Above pp. 18off.   2 Cf. above p. 16.   3 Cf. above pp. 15 and 172.
4 Cf. Synopsis, p. 11.   5 Above p. 17.   6 Above p. 181.   7 Above p. 180.

that I have the best reason to think that I have not used enough apparatus, since I have not yet managed to make you understand the matter correctly. When you say that I 'could have made the same inference from any one of my other actions' you are far from the truth, since I am not wholly certain of any of my actions, with the sole exception of thought (in using the word 'certain' I am referring to metaphysical certainty, which is the sole issue at this point). I may not, for example, make the inference 'I am walking, therefore I exist', except in so far as the awareness of walking is a thought. The inference is certain only if applied to this awareness, and not to the movement of the body which sometimes – in the case of dreams – is not occurring at all, despite the fact that I seem to myself to be walking. Hence from the fact that I think I am walking I can very well infer the existence of a mind which has this thought, but not the existence of a body that walks. And the same applies in other cases.

2. You then adopt a droll figure of speech and pretend to interrogate me as if I were present; and you address me no longer as a whole man but as a disembodied soul.[1] I think that you are indicating here that these objections of yours did not originate in the mind of a subtle philosopher but came from flesh alone. I ask you then, O Flesh, or whatever name you want me to address you by, have you so little to do with the mind that you were unable to notice when I corrected the common view whereby that which thinks is supposed to be like a wind or similar body? I of course corrected this view when I showed that it can be supposed that there is no wind or any other body in the world, yet nonetheless everything which enables me to recognize myself as a thinking thing still remains.[2] Hence all your subsequent questions as to whether I might not still be a wind or occupy space or be in motion in several ways, and so on,[3] are so fatuous as to need no reply.

3. There is no more force in your next question as to why, if I am a rarefied body, I cannot be nourished, and so on.[4] For I deny that I am a body. Let me clear up one point once and for all. You almost always use the same style, not attacking my arguments but ignoring them as if they did not exist, or quoting them in an imperfect or truncated form; and you string together various difficulties of the sort commonly raised by philosophical novices against my conclusions or against others like them – or even unlike them. These difficulties are irrelevant, or else I have discussed and resolved them in the appropriate place. In view of this it is not worth my while to answer all your questions individually; if I did so, I should have to repeat a hundred times what I have already written. I shall simply deal briefly with the points which might possibly cause

1 Above p. 181.   2 Above pp. 18f.   3 Above pp. 182f.   4 *Ibid.*

difficulty to readers who are not utterly stupid. As for readers who are impressed by the number of words employed rather than the force of the arguments, I do not value their approval so highly that I am prepared to become more verbose in order to merit it.

First of all then, let me point out that I do not accept your statement that the mind grows and becomes weak along with the body.[1] You do not prove this by any argument. It is true that the mind does not work so perfectly when it is in the body of an infant as it does when in an adult's body, and that its actions can often be slowed down by wine and other corporeal things. But all that follows from this is that the mind, so long as it is joined to the body, uses it like an instrument to perform the operations which take up most of its time. It does not follow that it is made more or less perfect by the body. Your inference here is no more valid than if you were to infer from the fact that a craftsman works badly whenever he uses a faulty tool that the good condition of his tools is the source of his knowledge of his craft.

It should also be noted, O Flesh, that you seem to misunderstand completely what the use of rational argument involves. To prove that I should not suspect the trustworthiness of the senses you say that even if, when the eye is not in use, I have seemed to have sense-perception of things that cannot in fact be perceived without the eye, this kind of falsity is not something I have experienced all the time.[2] This makes it seem as if the fact that we have discovered error on some occasions is not a sufficient reason for doubt. You also talk as if it were possible for us, whenever we make a mistake, to notice that we are mistaken; but on the contrary the error consists precisely in the fact that we do not recognize it as a case of error.

Finally, O Flesh, since you often demand arguments from me when you have none yourself and the onus of proof is on you, you should realize that in order to philosophize correctly there is no need for us to prove the falsity of everything which we do not admit because we do not know whether or not it is true. We simply have to take great care not to admit anything as true when we cannot prove it to be so. Hence, when I discover that I am a thinking substance, and form a clear and distinct concept of this thinking substance that contains none of the things that belong to the concept of corporeal substance, this is quite sufficient to enable me to assert that I, in so far as I know myself, am nothing other than a thinking thing. This is all that I asserted in the Second Meditation, which is what we are dealing with here. I did not have to admit that this thinking substance was some mobile, pure and rarefied body, since I had no convincing reason for believing this. If you have such a reason, it is

354

355

1 *Ibid.*   2 Above p. 183.

your job to explain it; you should not demand that I prove the falsity of something which I refused to accept precisely because I had no knowledge of it. It is as if, when I said that I now live in Holland, you were to say that this must not be accepted unless I can prove that I am not also in China or in any other part of the world, on the grounds that it is perhaps possible, through the power of God, that the same body should exist in two different places. When you add that I will also have to prove that 'the souls of the brutes are incorporeal' and that 'this solid body contributes nothing to my thought',[1] you show that you are ignorant both of where the onus of proof lies and of what must be proved by each party. For I do not think that the souls of the brutes are incorporeal, or that this solid body contributes nothing to our thought; it is simply that this is not at all the place to consider these topics.

4. The next question you raise concerns the obscurity arising from the ambiguity in the word 'soul'.[2] But I took such care to eliminate this ambiguity when it arose that it is tiresome to repeat myself here. I shall

356   say only that it is generally the ignorant who have given things their names, and so the names do not always fit the things with sufficient accuracy. Our job, however, is not to change the names after they have been adopted into ordinary usage; we may merely emend their meanings when we notice that they are misunderstood by others. Thus, primitive man probably did not distinguish between, on the one hand, the principle by which we are nourished and grow and accomplish without any thought all the other operations which we have in common with the brutes, and, on the other hand, the principle in virtue of which we think. He therefore used the single term 'soul' to apply to both; and when he subsequently noticed that thought was distinct from nutrition, he called the element which thinks 'mind', and believed it to be the principal part of the soul. I, by contrast, realizing that the principle by which we are nourished is wholly different – different in kind – from that in virtue of which we think, have said that the term 'soul', when it is used to refer to both these principles, is ambiguous. If we are to take 'soul' in its special sense, as meaning the 'first actuality' or 'principal form of man',[3] then the term must be understood to apply only to the principle in virtue of which we think; and to avoid ambiguity I have as far as possible used the term 'mind' for this. For I consider the mind not as a part of the soul but as the thinking soul in its entirety.

You say you want to stop and ask whether I think the soul always thinks.[4] But why should it not always think, since it is a thinking

1 Above p. 183.   2 *Ibid.*
3 Standard scholastic definitions of the soul derived from Aristotle; cf. *De Anima* II, 2.
4 Above p. 184.

substance? It is no surprise that we do not remember the thoughts that the soul had when in the womb or in a deep sleep, since there are many other thoughts that we equally do not remember, although we know we had them when grown up, healthy and wide-awake. So long as the mind is joined to the body, then in order for it to remember thoughts which it had in the past, it is necessary for some traces of them to be imprinted on the brain; it is by turning to these, or applying itself to them, that the mind remembers. So is it really surprising if the brain of an infant, or a man in a deep sleep, is unsuited to receive these traces?[1]

357

Lastly, there is the passage where I said that it may perhaps be that that of which I do not yet have knowledge (namely my body) is not distinct from the 'I' of which I am aware (namely my mind); 'I do not know', I said, 'and I shall not argue the point.'[2] Here you object: 'If you do not know, if you are not arguing the point, why do you assume that you are none of these things?'[3] But it is false that I assumed anything I did not know. On the contrary, since I did not know whether the body was identical with the mind or not, I did not make any assumptions on this matter, but considered only the mind; it was only afterwards, in the Sixth Meditation, that I said there was a real distinction between the mind and the body, and here I did not assume it but demonstrated it. But you, O Flesh, are utterly at fault here, because, despite having little or no rational basis for proving that the mind is not distinct from the body, you nonetheless assume this.

5. What I wrote about the imagination will be clear enough to those who study it closely, but it is not surprising if those who do not meditate on it find it very obscure. But I should point out to such people that there is no inconsistency between my assertion that certain things do not belong to the knowledge I have of myself and my previous statement that I did not know whether certain things belong to me or not.[4] For 'belonging to me' is clearly quite different from 'belonging to the knowledge which I have of myself'.

6. The things you say here,[5] O best of Flesh, seem to me to amount to grumblings more than objections, and so they require no answer.

7. Here again you produce a lot of grumblings, but they do not require a reply any more than the previous lot. Your questions about the brutes[6] are not appropriate in this context since the mind, when engaged in private meditation, can experience its own thinking but cannot have any

358

---

1 For a detailed account of the brain traces referred to here, see *Treatise on Man*: vol. 1, pp. 105ff.
2 Above p. 18.   3 Above p. 185.   4 Above p. 185; cf. Med. II, above pp. 18f.
5 Above pp. 185-7.   6 Above pp. 187-9.

experience to establish whether the brutes think or not; it must tackle this question later on, by an *a posteriori* investigation of their behaviour. I will not pause to disown the foolish claims which you then put into my mouth; I am content to have pointed out once that you do not report everything I say accurately. In fact I did frequently provide a criterion to establish that the mind is different from the body, namely that the whole nature of the mind consists in the fact that it thinks, while the whole nature of the body consists in its being an extended thing; and there is absolutely nothing in common between thought and extension. I also distinctly showed on many occasions that the mind can operate independently of the brain; for the brain cannot in any way be employed in pure understanding, but only in imagining or perceiving by the senses. Admittedly, when imagination or sensation is strongly active (as occurs when the brain is in a disturbed state), it is not easy for the mind to have leisure for understanding other things. But when the imagination is less intense, we often have the experience of understanding something quite apart from the imagination. When, for example, we are asleep and are

359 aware that we are dreaming, we need imagination in order to dream, but to be aware that we are dreaming we need only the intellect.

8. Here, as frequently elsewhere, you merely show that you do not have an adequate understanding of what you are trying to criticize. I did not abstract the concept of the wax from the concept of its accidents.[1] Rather, I wanted to show how the substance of the wax is revealed by means of its accidents, and how a reflective and distinct perception of it (the sort of perception which you, O Flesh, seem never to have had) differs from the ordinary confused perception. I do not see what argument you are relying on when you lay it down as certain that a dog makes discriminating judgements in the same way as we do.[2] Seeing that a dog is made of flesh you perhaps think that everything which is in you also exists in the dog. But I observe no mind at all in the dog, and hence believe there is nothing to be found in a dog that resembles the things I recognize in a mind.

9. I am surprised that you should say here that all my considerations about the wax demonstrate that I distinctly know that I exist, but not that I know what I am or what my nature is;[3] for one thing cannot be demonstrated without the other. Nor do I see what more you expect here, unless it is to be told what colour or smell or taste the human mind has, or the proportions of salt, sulphur and mercury from which it is compounded. You want us, you say, to conduct 'a kind of chemical investigation' of the mind, as we would of wine.[4] This is indeed worthy of

360 you, O Flesh, and of all those who have only a very confused conception

1 Cf. p. 189.   2 Above p. 190.   3 Above p. 191.   4 Above p. 193.

of everything, and so do not know the proper questions to ask about each thing. But as for me, I have never thought that anything more is required to reveal a substance than its various attributes; thus the more attributes of a given substance we know, the more perfectly we understand its nature. Now we can distinguish many different attributes in the wax: one, that it is white; two, that it is hard; three, that it can be melted; and so on. And there are correspondingly many attributes in the mind: one, that it has the power of knowing the whiteness of the wax; two, that it has the power of knowing its hardness; three, that it has the power of knowing that it can lose its hardness (i.e. melt), and so on. (Someone can have knowledge of the hardness without thereby having knowledge of the whiteness, e.g. a man born blind; and so on in other cases.) The clear inference from this is that we know more attributes in the case of our mind than we do in the case of anything else. For no matter how many attributes we recognize in any given thing, we can always list a corresponding number of attributes in the mind which it has in virtue of knowing the attributes of the thing; and hence the nature of the mind is the one we know best of all. Finally, in this section, you make an incidental criticism as follows: although I have not admitted that I have anything apart from a mind, I nevertheless speak of the wax which I see and touch, and yet this is impossible without eyes and hands.[1] But you should have noticed that I had carefully pointed out that I was not here dealing with sight and touch, which occur by means of bodily organs, but was concerned solely with the thought of seeing and touching, which, as we experience every day in our dreams, does not require these organs. Of course you cannot have failed to notice this – your purpose was simply to show us what absurd and unjust quibbles can be thought up by those   361
who are more anxious to attack a position than to understand it.

Objections raised against the Third Meditation

1. Bravo! Here at last you produce an argument against me – something which, as far as I can see, you have at no point done up till now. You wish to prove that the rule 'Whatever we clearly and distinctly perceive is true' is not a reliable one, and you say that great thinkers, who ought surely to have perceived many things clearly and distinctly, have nevertheless judged that the truth of things is hidden in God or in a deep well.[2] Your argument from authority is, I admit, sound enough; but, O Flesh, you certainly should not have presented it to a mind so withdrawn from corporeal things that it does not even know whether any people existed before it, and hence is not influenced by their authority. Your next point,

1 Above p. 191.   2 Above p. 193.

taken from the sceptics, is a standard move, and not a bad one, but it proves nothing. Nor is anything proved by the fact that some people face death to defend opinions that are in fact false; for it can never be proved that they clearly and distinctly perceive what they so stubbornly affirm. You say at the end of this section that what we should be working on is not so much a rule to establish the truth as a method for determining whether or not we are deceived when we think we perceive something clearly.[1] This I do not dispute; but I maintain that I carefully provided such a method in the appropriate place, where I first eliminated all preconceived opinions and afterwards listed all my principal ideas, distinguishing those which were clear from those which were obscure or confused.

2. I am amazed at the line of argument by which you try to prove that all our ideas are adventitious and that none of them are constructed by us. You say that the mind has the faculty not just of perceiving adventitious ideas but also 'of putting them together and separating them in various ways, of enlarging them and diminishing them, of comparing them and so on'.[2] Hence you conclude that the ideas of chimeras, which the mind makes up by the process of putting together and separating etc., are not constructed by the mind but are adventitious. By this argument you could prove that Praxiteles never made any statues on the grounds that he did not get from within himself the marble from which he sculpted them; or you could prove that you did not produce these objections on the grounds that you composed them out of words which you acquired from others rather than inventing them yourself. But in fact the form of a chimera does not consist in the parts of the goat or lion, nor does the form of your objections consist in the individual words you have used; they both consist simply in the fact that the elements are put together in a certain way.

It is also surprising that you maintain that the idea of a thing cannot be in the mind unless the ideas of an animal, a plant, a stone, and all the universals are there.[3] This is like saying that if I am to recognize myself to be a thinking thing, I must also recognize animals and plants, since I must recognize a *thing* or the nature of a thing. Your comments on the idea of truth are equally false. And at the end of the section you confine your attack to matters about which I made no assertions at all, and so you are simply beating the air.

3. Here, aiming to destroy the arguments which led me to judge that the existence of material things should be doubted, you ask why, in that case, I walk on the earth, etc.[4] This obviously begs the question. For you

362

363

---

1 Above pp. 194f.   2 Above p. 195.   3 Above p. 196.   4 Above p. 197.

assume what had to be proved, namely that it is so certain that I walk on the earth that there can be no doubt of it.

In addition to the arguments which I put forward against myself and refuted, you suggest the following: why is there no idea of colour in a man born blind, and no idea of sound in a man born deaf?[1] Here you show plainly that you have no telling arguments to produce. How do you know that there is no idea of colour in a man born blind? From time to time we find in our own case that even though we close our eyes, sensations of light and colour are nevertheless aroused. And even if we grant what you say, those who deny the existence of material things may just as well attribute the absence of ideas of colour in the man born blind to the fact that his mind lacks the faculty for forming them; this is just as reasonable as your claim that he does not have the ideas because he is deprived of sight.

Your next point about the two ideas of the sun[2] proves nothing. Your taking the two ideas as one on the grounds that they are referred to only one sun is like saying that a true statement does not differ from a false one because it is asserted of the same subject. In saying that the idea we arrive at by astronomical reasoning is not in fact an idea, you are restricting the term 'idea' to images depicted in the corporeal imagination; but this goes against my explicit assumption. 364

4. You repeat your mistake when you deny that we have a true idea of a substance on the grounds that a substance is perceived not by the imagination but by the intellect alone.[3] And yet, O Flesh, I have already made it clear that I will have nothing to do with those who are prepared to use only their imagination and not their intellect.

You next say that 'whatever reality the idea of a substance possesses, it gets from the ideas of the accidents under which, or in the guise of which, we conceive of the substance'.[4] Here you prove that in fact you have no distinct idea of a substance. For a substance can never be conceived in the guise of its accidents, nor can it derive its reality from them. (On the contrary, philosophers commonly conceive of accidents in the guise of substances, since they often say that they are 'real'.) In fact no reality, i.e. no being apart from a purely modal one, can be attributed to accidents unless it is taken from the idea of a substance.

You go on to say that we have the idea of God merely as a result of having heard certain attributes being ascribed to him.[5] Would you please explain where the first men who originally told us of these attributes got this self same idea of God? If they got it from themselves, why cannot we

1 *Ibid.*   2 Above pp. 197f.   3 Cf. above p. 199.   4 *Ibid.*   5 *Ibid.*

also derive it from ourselves? If they got it by divine revelation, then God exists.

You add: 'If someone calls something "infinite", he attributes to a thing which he does not grasp a label which he does not understand.'[1] 365 Here you fail to distinguish between, on the one hand, an understanding which is suited to the scale of our intellect (and each of us knows by his own experience quite well that he has this sort of understanding of the infinite) and, on the other hand, a fully adequate conception of things (and no one has this sort of conception either of the infinite or of anything else, however small it may be). Moreover, it is false that the infinite is understood through the negation of a boundary or limit; on the contrary, all limitation implies a negation of the infinite.

It is also false that the idea representing all the perfections which we attribute to God 'does not contain more objective reality than do the finite things'.[2] You yourself admit that these perfections must be amplified by our intellect if they are to be attributed to God. So do you think that the perfections which are amplified in this way are not, as a result, greater than they would be if they were not amplified? And how could we have a faculty for amplifying all created perfections (i.e. conceiving of something greater or more ample than they are) were it not for the fact that there is in us an idea of something greater, namely God? Finally, it is again false that God would be 'a puny thing if he were no greater than our understanding of him'. For we understand God to be infinite, and there can be nothing greater than the infinite. You are confusing understanding with imagination, and are supposing that we imagine God to be like some enormous man, just us if someone who had never seen an elephant were to imagine it was like some enormous tick, which, I agree, would be extremely foolish.

366   5. You say a great deal here to give the appearance of contradicting me, but in fact you do not contradict me at all, since you reach exactly the same conclusion as I do. Nevertheless you include in your discussion many assertions with which I strongly disagree. You say that the axiom 'There is nothing in the effect which did not previously exist in the cause' should be taken to refer to material rather than efficient causes;[3] but it is unintelligible that perfection of form should ever pre-exist in a material cause; it can do so only in an efficient cause. Nor do I agree that the formal reality of an idea is a substance,[4] and so on.

6. If you had any argument to prove the existence of material things you would undoubtedly have produced it here. But all you do is to ask whether my mind is uncertain as to whether anything apart from itself

1 Above p. 200.   2 *Ibid.*   3 Above p. 201.   4 Above p. 202.

exists in the world;[1] and you pretend that there is no need to look for arguments to decide this, thus appealing simply to our preconceived opinions. Here you succeed in showing, much more clearly than if you had not said anything at all, that you cannot produce any argument to support your assertion.

None of your subsequent discussion concerning ideas needs to be answered, since you restrict the term 'idea' to images depicted in the imagination, whereas I extend it to cover any object of thought.

But I should like to ask in passing about the argument you use to prove that 'nothing acts on itself'.[2] It is unusual for you to use arguments, but here you prove your case with the example of the finger which does not strike itself and the eye which does not see itself in itself but in a mirror. It is, however, easy to answer this by saying that it is not the eye which sees the mirror rather than itself, but the mind alone which recognizes the mirror, the eye and itself. Other counter-examples can also be cited from the realm of corporeal things: when a top turns itself round in a circle, is not the turning an action which it performs on itself?

Finally it should be noted that I did not assert that the ideas of material things are derived from the mind, as you somewhat disingenuously make out.[3] Later on I explicitly showed that these ideas often come to us from bodies, and that it is this that enables us to prove the existence of bodies. In the passage under discussion I simply explained that we never find so much reality in these ideas as to oblige us to conclude (given the premiss that there is nothing in the effect which did not previously exist in the cause, either formally or eminently) that they could not have originated in the mind alone. And this claim you do not attack at all.

7. Everything you say here you have said before, and has already been disposed of by me. I shall make one point about the idea of the infinite. This, you say, cannot be a true idea unless I grasp the infinite; you say that I can be said, at most, to know part of the infinite, and a very small part at that, which does not correspond to the infinite any better than a picture of one tiny hair represents the whole person to whom it belongs.[4] My point is that, on the contrary, if I can grasp something, it would be a total contradiction for that which I grasp to be infinite. For the idea of the infinite, if it is to be a true idea, cannot be grasped at all, since the impossibility of being grasped is contained in the formal definition of the infinite. Nonetheless, it is evident that the idea which we have of the infinite does not merely represent one part of it, but really does represent the infinite in its entirety. The manner of representation, however, is the manner appropriate to a human idea; and undoubtedly God, or some other intelligent nature more perfect than a human mind, could have a

367

368

1 Above p. 203. 2 Above pp. 203f. 3 Above p. 204. 4 Above pp. 206f.

much more perfect, i.e. more accurate and distinct, idea. Similarly we do not doubt that a novice at geometry has an idea of a whole triangle when he understands that it is a figure bounded by three lines, even though geometers are capable of knowing and recognizing in this idea many more properties belonging to the same triangle, of which the novice is ignorant. Just as it suffices for the possession of an idea of the whole triangle to understand that it is a figure contained within three lines, so it suffices for the possession of a true and complete idea of the infinite in its entirety if we understand that it is a thing which is bounded by no limits.

8. You repeat the same mistake in this section when you deny that we have a true idea of God. For even though we do not know everything which is in God, nonetheless all the attributes that we do recognize to be in him are truly there. You also say that if someone desires some bread, 'the bread is not more perfect than him';[1] and that although a feature which I perceive in an idea actually exists in the idea, 'it does not follow that it actually exists in the thing corresponding to the idea';[2] and finally that I am 'making a judgement about something of which I am ignorant'.[3] But these and similar comments simply show that you, O Flesh, are anxious to rush in and attack many statements whose meaning you do not follow. The fact that someone desires some bread does not imply that the bread is more perfect than he is, but merely that someone who needs bread is in a more imperfect state than when he does not need it. Again, from the fact that something exists in an idea I do not infer that it exists in reality, except when we can produce no other cause for the idea but the actual existence of the thing which it represents. And this is true, as I demonstrated, only in the case of God, and not in the case of a plurality of worlds or anything else. Again, I am not 'making a judgement about something of which I am ignorant', for I produced reasons to back up my judgement − reasons which are so solid that you have not been able to mount the slightest attack against any of them.

9. When you deny that in order to be kept in existence we need the continual action of the original cause,[4] you are disputing something which all metaphysicians affirm as a manifest truth − although the uneducated often fail to think of it because they pay attention only to the causes of *coming into being* and not the causes of *being itself*. Thus an architect is the cause of a house and a father of his child only in the sense of being the causes of their coming into being; and hence, once the work is completed it can remain in existence quite apart from the 'cause' in this sense. But the sun is the cause of the light which it emits, and God is the cause of created things, not just in the sense that they are causes of the *coming* into being of these things, but also in the sense that they are

1 Above p. 207.   2 Above p. 208.   3 *Ibid.*   4 Above p. 209.

causes of their *being*; and hence they must always continue to act on the effect in the same way in order to keep it in existence.

This can be plainly demonstrated from my explanation of the independence of the divisions of time. You try in vain to evade my argument by talking of the necessary 'connection' which exists between the divisions of time considered in the abstract.[1] But this is not the issue: we are considering the time or duration of the thing which endures, and here you would not deny that the individual moments can be separated from those immediately preceding and succeeding them, which implies that the thing which endures may cease to be at any given moment.

You say that we have a power which is sufficient to ensure that we shall continue to exist unless some destructive cause intervenes.[2] But here you do not realize that you are attributing to a created thing the perfection of a creator, if the created thing is able to continue in existence independently of anything else. Similarly, you are attributing to the creator the imperfection of a created thing, since you imply that the creator would have to tend towards non-being by performing a positive action whenever he wished to bring our existence to an end.

Your further contention, that it is not absurd that there should be an infinite regress,[3] is undermined by what you yourself say later on. For you admit that an infinite regress is absurd 'in the case of causes which are so linked that a cause which is lower in the chain cannot act without one which is higher'.[4] But it is causes of this sort, and only of this sort, that are at issue here, since we are dealing with causes of being, not causes of coming into being, such as parents. Hence you cannot set the authority of Aristotle against me here; nor does your point about Pandora undermine my position. You agree that I can gradually augment, in varying degrees, all the perfections that I observe in people, until I see that they have become the kind of perfections that cannot possibly belong to human nature; and this is quite sufficient to enable me to demonstrate the existence of God. For it is this very power of amplifying all human perfections up to the point where they are recognized as more than human which, I maintain and insist, would not have been in us unless we had been created by God. But I am not at all surprised that you cannot see that I have given an utterly evident demonstration of this, because there is, so far as I can see, not one of my arguments which you have so far managed to perceive correctly.

10. When you attack my statement that nothing can be added to or taken away from the idea of God,[5] it seems that you have paid no attention to the common philosophical maxim that the essences of things

1 *Ibid.*   2 Above p. 210.   3 *Ibid.*   4 Above p. 211.   5 Above p. 212.

are indivisible. An idea represents the essence of a thing, and if anything is added to or taken away from the essence, then the idea automatically becomes the idea of something else. This is how the ideas of Pandora and of all false Gods are formed by those who do not have a correct conception of the true God. But once the idea of the true God has been conceived, although we may detect additional perfections in him which we had not yet noticed, this does not mean that we have augmented the idea of God; we have simply made it more distinct and explicit, since, so long as we suppose that our original idea was a true one, it must have contained all these perfections. Similarly, the idea of a triangle is not augmented when we notice various properties in the triangle of which we were previously ignorant. You must also realize that the idea of God is not gradually formed by us when we amplify the perfections of his creatures;[1] it is formed all at once and in its entirety as soon as our mind reaches an infinite being which is incapable of any amplification.

372   You ask how I prove that the idea of God is present in us like the mark of a craftsman stamped on his work. 'How is this stamping carried out', you ask, 'and what is the form of this "mark"?'[2] Suppose there is a painting in which I observe so much skill that I judge that it could only have been painted by Apelles, and I say that the inimitable technique is like a kind of mark which Apelles stamped on all his pictures to distinguish them from others. The question you raise is just like asking, in this case, 'What is the form of this mark, and how is the stamping carried out?' It certainly seems that if you asked such a question you would deserve to be laughed at rather than answered.

You go on as follows: 'If the mark is not distinct from the work, are you yourself, then, an idea? Are you nothing else but a mode of thought? Are you yourself both the mark which is stamped and the subject on which it is stamped?'[3] Here again you do not deserve an answer. Suppose I had said that the technique by which we can distinguish the paintings of Apelles from others is not anything distinct from the pictures themselves. The point you make seems just as silly as if you were to reply here that in that case the pictures are nothing but the technique, and do not consist of any material, and hence are simply a mode of painting.

You then deny that we are made in the image of God, and say that this would make God like a man; and you go on to list the ways in which human nature differs from the divine nature. Is this any cleverer than trying to deny that one of Apelles' pictures was made in the likeness of Alexander on the grounds that this would mean that Alexander was like a picture, and yet pictures are made of wood and paint, and not of flesh
373   and bones like Alexander? It is not in the nature of an image to be

1 Above p. 212.   2 Above p. 213.   3 *Ibid.*

identical in all respects with the thing of which it is an image, but merely to imitate it in some respects. And it is quite clear that the wholly perfect power of thought which we understand to be in God is represented by means of that less perfect faculty which we possess.

You prefer to compare the creation of God to the labour of a workman rather than to parental procreation, but you have no reason to do so. Even if the three modes of action involved here are completely different in kind, nevertheless the analogy between natural procreation and divine creation is closer than that between artificial production and divine creation. I did not say, however, that the resemblance between us and God is as close as that between children and parents. Again, it is not always true that there is no resemblance between the work of a craftsman and the craftsman himself, as is clear in the case of a sculptor who produces a statue resembling himself.

How unfairly you report my words when you pretend that I said I perceive my likeness to God in the fact that I am an incomplete and dependent thing.[1] On the contrary, I cited these facts as evidence of a dissimilarity, to prevent anyone thinking I wished to make men equal to God. What I said was this: I not only perceive that I am in this respect inferior to God in so far as I aspire to greater things, but also that these greater things are in God; and moreover, there is in me something resembling these greater qualities, since I venture to aspire to them.[2]

Finally, you say that it is surprising that everyone else should not share my understanding of God, since he imprinted the idea of himself on them just as he did on me.[3] This is just like your being surprised at the fact that although everyone is aware of the idea of a triangle not everyone notices equally many properties in it and some people may draw false conclusions about it.

374

Objections raised against the Fourth Meditation

1. I did explain quite adequately what sort of idea of nothingness we have, and how we participate in non-being:[4] the idea of nothingness I called a 'negative idea', and I said that 'participating in non-being' simply means that we are not the supreme being and that we lack very many things.[5] But you are always looking for flaws where none exist.

When you say that I 'observe that some of God's works are not wholly perfect',[6] you are plainly inventing something I neither wrote nor thought. I simply said that if certain things are considered not from the

1 *Ibid.* 2 Cf. p. 35. 3 Above p. 214. 4 *Ibid.*
5 Above p. 38. 6 Above p. 214.

point of view of the part they play in the world but as separate wholes, then they can appear to be imperfect.

The points you make to defend the notion of a final cause[1] should be applied to efficient causation. The function of the various parts of plants and animals etc. makes it appropriate to admire God as their efficient cause – to recognize and glorify the craftsman through examining his works; but we cannot guess from this what purpose God had in creating any given thing. In ethics, then, where we may often legitimately employ conjectures, it may admittedly be pious on occasion to try to guess what purpose God may have had in mind in his direction of the universe; but in physics, where everything must be backed up by the strongest arguments, such conjectures are futile. We cannot pretend that some of God's purposes are more out in the open than others; all are equally hidden in the inscrutable abyss of his wisdom. Nor should you pretend that none of us mortals is incapable of understanding other kinds of cause; they are all much easier to discover than God's purposes, and the kinds of cause which you put forward as typical of the difficulties involved are in fact ones that many people consider they do know about.

Finally you ask me what sort of idea my mind would have had of God and of itself if, ever since being implanted in the body, it had remained within it, with the eyes closed and with none of the senses functioning.[2] Since your question is asked in such an open and frank manner, I shall give you a straightforward and honest reply. I do not doubt that the mind – provided we suppose that in thinking it received not just no assistance from the body but also that it received no interference from it – would have had exactly the same ideas of God and itself that it now has, with the sole difference that they would have been much purer and clearer. The senses often impede the mind in many of its operations, and in no case do they help in the perception of ideas. The only thing that prevents all of us noticing equally well that we have these ideas is that we are too occupied with perceiving the images of corporeal things.

2. Throughout this section you assume incorrectly that our being liable to error is a positive imperfection, when in fact it is simply (especially with respect to God) the negation of greater perfection among created things. Moreover, your comparison between the citizens of a republic and the parts of the universe[3] is not quite accurate: the bad character of the citizens is, in relation to the republic, something positive, but this does not apply to man's liability to error, or his lack of all perfections, when this is taken in relation to the good of the universe. A better comparison to make might be the comparison between someone who wanted the whole of the human body to be covered with eyes so as

1 Above p. 215.   2 Above p. 216.   3 *Ibid.*

to look more beautiful (there being no part of the body more beautiful than the eye), and someone who thinks that there ought not to have been any creatures in the world who were liable to error (i.e. not wholly perfect).

Your supposition that God has assigned us base roles and has given us imperfections, and so on,[1] is plainly false. It is also quite false that God gave man a faculty which is 'uncertain, confused and inadequate even for the few matters which he did want us to decide upon'.[2]

3. You here ask me to say briefly whether the will can extend to anything that escapes the intellect.[3] The answer is that this occurs whenever we happen to go wrong. Thus when you judge that the mind is a kind of rarefied body, you can understand that the mind is itself, i.e. a thinking thing, and that a rarefied body is an extended thing; but the proposition that it is one and the same thing that thinks and is extended is one which you certainly do not understand. You simply want to believe it, because you have believed it before and do not want to change your view. It is the same when you judge that an apple, which may in fact be poisoned, is nutritious: you understand that its smell, colour and so on, are pleasant, but this does not mean that you understand that this particular apple will be beneficial to eat; you judge that it will because you want to believe it. So, while I do admit that when we direct our will towards something, we always have some sort of understanding of some aspect of it, I deny that our understanding and our will are of equal scope. In the case of any given object, there may be many things about it that we desire but very few things of which we have knowledge. And when we make a bad judgement, it is not that we exercise our will in a bad fashion, but that the object of our will is bad. Again, we never understand anything in a bad fashion; when we are said to 'understand in a bad fashion', all that happens is that we judge that our understanding is more extensive than it in fact is.

377

You next deny certain propositions about the indifference of the will.[4] But although these propositions are self-evident, I am not prepared to set about proving them here. These are the sorts of things that each of us ought to know by experience in his own case, rather than having to be convinced of them by rational argument; and you, O Flesh, do not seem to attend to the actions the mind performs within itself. You may be unfree, if you wish; but I am certainly very pleased with my freedom since I experience it within myself. What is more, you have produced no arguments to attack it but merely bald denials. I affirm what I have experienced and what anyone else can experience for himself, whereas your denial seems merely to be based on your own apparent failure to

1 Above p. 217.   2 Above p. 218.   3 Above p. 219.   4 Above pp. 219f.

have the appropriate experience; so my own view is probably entitled to receive more widespread acceptance.

378   Your own words, however, establish that you have in fact had the experience of freedom. You deny that we can guard against making mistakes because you refuse to allow that the will can be directed to anything which is not determined by the intellect; but you admit at the same time that we can guard against persisting in error.[1] Now this would be quite impossible unless the will had the freedom to direct itself, without the determination of the intellect, towards one side or the other; and this you have just denied. If the intellect has already determined the will to put forward some false judgement, then what is it, may I ask, that determines the will when first it begins to guard against persisting in error? If it is determined by itself, then it can after all be directed towards an object which the intellect does not impel it towards – which you denied, and which is the sole point in dispute. If on the other hand it is determined by the intellect, then it is not the will that is guarding against error; all that occurs is that, just as it was previously directed towards a falsehood set before it by the intellect, now it happens, purely by chance, to turn towards the truth, because the intellect presents the truth to it. I would also like to know what is your conception of the nature of falsity, and how you think it can be an object of the intellect. My own view is this. Since I understand falsity to be merely a privation of the truth, I am convinced that there would be a total contradiction involved in the intellect's apprehending falsity under the guise of truth; but this would have to be the case if the intellect were ever to determine the will to embrace what is false.

    4. As for the beneficial results to be derived from these *Meditations*,[2] I did clearly point out, in the short Preface which I think you have read,
379 that those who do not bother to grasp the proper order of my arguments and the connection between them, but merely try to quarrel with individual passages, will not get much benefit from the book.[3] As for the method enabling us to distinguish between the things that we really perceive clearly and those that we merely think we perceive clearly, I believe, as I have already said, that I have been reasonably careful to supply such a method; but I have little confidence that those who spend so little effort on getting rid of their preconceived opinions that they complain that I have not dealt with them in a 'simple and brief statement'[4] will arrive at a clear perception of it.

---

1 Above p. 220.   2 Above pp. 220f.   3 Cf. Preface to the reader, above p. 8.
4 Above p. 180.

Objections raised against the Fifth Meditation

1. Here, after quoting one or two of my comments, you say that this is 'all I have to say' about the topic under discussion.[1] This obliges me to point out that you have not paid sufficient attention to the way in which what I wrote all fits together. I think this interconnection is such that, for any given point, all the preceding remarks and most of those that follow contribute to the proof of what is asserted. Hence you cannot give a fair account of what I have to say on any topic unless you go into everything I wrote about all the other related issues.

You say that you think it is 'very hard' to propose that there is anything 380 immutable and eternal apart from God.[2] You would be right to think this if I was talking about existing things, or if I was proposing something as immutable in the sense that its immutability was independent of God. But just as the poets suppose that the Fates were originally established by Jupiter, but that after they were established he bound himself to abide by them, so I do not think that the essences of things, and the mathematical truths which we can know concerning them, are independent of God. Nevertheless I do think that they are immutable and eternal, since the will and decree of God willed and decreed that they should be so. Whether you think this is hard or easy to accept, it is enough for me that it is true.

The points you go on to make against the universals of the dialecticians[3] do not touch me, since my understanding of universals is not the same as theirs. But as for the essences we know clearly and distinctly, such as the essence of a triangle or of any other geometrical figure, I can easily make you admit that the ideas of them which we have are not taken from particular instances. For you say here that they are false,[4] presumably because they do not accord with your previously held view of the nature of things.

You say later on that the 'subject-matter of pure mathematics, including the point, the line, the surface, and the indivisible figures which are composed of these elements and yet remain indivisible, cannot exist in reality'.[5] It follows from this that no triangle, and not one of the properties which are understood to belong to its essence or to that of any other geometrical figure, has ever existed, and hence that these essences 381 have not been derived from any existing things. And yet you say, they are false. This is your view, and you presumably hold it because you suppose

---

1 Above p. 221.   2 *Ibid.*
3 Above p. 222. 'Dialectic' is Descartes' normal term for scholastic logic.
4 Above pp. 223f.   5 Above p. 228.

the nature of things to be such that these essences do not accord with it. But unless you are maintaining that the whole of geometry is also false, you cannot deny that many truths can be demonstrated of these essences; and since they are always the same, it is right to call them immutable and eternal. The fact that they may not accord with your suppositions about the nature of things, or with the atomic conception of reality invented by Democritus and Epicurus, is merely an extraneous feature which changes nothing; in spite of this they undoubtedly conform to the true nature of things established by God. Not that there are in the world substances which have length but no breadth, or breadth but no depth; it is rather that the geometrical figures are considered not as substances but as boundaries within which a substance is contained.

I do not, incidentally, concede that the ideas of these figures ever came into our mind via the senses,[1] as everyone commonly believes. For although the world could undoubtedly contain figures such as those the geometers study, I nonetheless maintain that there are no such figures in our environment except perhaps ones so small that they cannot in any way impinge on our senses. Geometrical figures are composed for the most part of straight lines; yet no part of a line that was really straight could ever affect our senses, since when we examine through a magnify-
382 ing glass those lines which appear most straight we find they are quite irregular and always form wavy curves. Hence, when in our childhood we first happened to see a triangular figure drawn on paper, it cannot have been this figure that showed us how we should conceive of the true triangle studied by geometers, since the true triangle is contained in the figure only in the way in which a statue of Mercury is contained in a rough block of wood. But since the idea of the true triangle was already in us, and could be conceived by our mind more easily than the more composite figure of the triangle drawn on paper, when we saw the composite figure we did not apprehend the figure we saw, but rather the true triangle. It is just the same as when we look at a piece of paper on which some lines have been drawn in ink to represent a man's face: the idea that this produces in us is not so much the idea of these lines as the idea of a man. Yet this would certainly not happen unless the human face were already known to us from some other source, and we were more accustomed to think of the face than the lines drawn in ink; indeed, we are often unable to distinguish the lines from one another when they are moved a short distance away from us. Thus we could not recognize the geometrical triangle from the diagram on the paper unless our mind already possessed the idea of it from some other source.

2. Here I do not see what sort of thing you want existence to be, nor

1 Above p. 223.

why it cannot be said to be a property just like omnipotence[1] – provided, of course, that we take the word 'property' to stand for any attribute, or for whatever can be predicated of a thing; and this is exactly how it should be taken in this context. Moreover, in the case of God necessary existence is in fact a property in the strictest sense of the term, since it applies to him alone and forms a part of his essence as it does of no other thing. Hence the existence of a triangle should not be compared with the existence of God, since the relation between existence and essence is manifestly quite different in the case of God from what it is in the case of the triangle.

To list existence among the properties which belong to the nature of God is no more 'begging the question'[2] than listing among the properties of a triangle the fact that its angles are equal to two right angles.

Again, it is not true to say that in the case of God, just as in the case of a triangle, existence and essence can be thought of apart from one another;[3] for God is his own existence, but this is not true of the triangle. I do not, however, deny that possible existence is a perfection in the idea of a triangle, just as necessary existence is a perfection in the idea of God; for this fact makes the idea of a triangle superior to the ideas of chimeras, which cannot possibly be supposed to have existence. Thus at no point have you weakened the force of my argument in the slightest, and you remain trapped by the sophism which you say I could have exposed so easily.[4]

The next points you raise are ones which I have already adequately answered elsewhere. And you are quite mistaken when you say that the demonstration of God's existence is not like the demonstration that the three angles of a triangle are equal to two right angles.[5] The reasoning is the same in both cases, except that the demonstration which establishes God's existence is much simpler and clearer than the corresponding demonstration about the triangle. I shall pass over your remaining points because, in saying that I explain nothing[6] you yourself explain and prove nothing – except that you are incapable of proving anything.

3. To set against the point you make here about Diagoras, Theodorus, Pythagoras and others,[7] I cite the case of the sceptics who did have doubts about these very geometrical demonstrations. And I insist that they could not have done so had they known the true nature of God. Moreover one thing is not proved to be better known than another just because a greater number of people think it is true; what shows it to be better known is simply that those who know the true nature of both

margin: 383

margin: 384

---

1 Above p. 224. 2 Above p. 225. 3 Above p. 224. 4 Above p. 225.
5 Above p. 226. 6 *Ibid.* 7 Above p. 228.

things see that it is prior in the order of knowledge and more evident and more certain.

Objections raised against the Sixth Meditation

1. I have already dealt with your denial of the statement that material things exist in so far as they are the subject-matter of pure mathematics.[1]

385   It is false that our understanding of a chiliagon is confused; for many properties can be very clearly and very distinctly demonstrated of it, which could certainly not happen if we perceived it only in a confused manner, or – as you claim – only in a verbal way.[2] In fact we have a clear understanding of the whole figure, even though we cannot imagine it in its entirety all at once. And it is clear from this that the powers of understanding and imagining do not differ merely in degree but are two quite different kinds of mental operation. For in understanding the mind employs only itself, while in imagination it contemplates a corporeal form. And although geometrical figures are wholly corporeal, this does not entail that the ideas by means of which we understand them should be thought of as corporeal (unless they fall under the imagination).

Lastly you say that the ideas of God, an angel and the human mind are 'corporeal or quasi-corporeal, since they are derived from the human form and from other things which are very rarefied and simple and hard to perceive with the senses, such as air or ether'.[3] This is a thought which is worthy of you alone, O Flesh. For if anyone thus represents God, or the mind, to himself he is attempting to imagine something which is not imaginable, and all he will succeed in forming is a corporeal idea to which he falsely assigns the name 'God' or 'the mind'. A true idea of the mind contains only thought and its attributes, none of which is corporeal.

2. Here you show quite clearly that you are relying entirely on a preconceived opinion which you have never got rid of. You maintain that we never suspect any falsity in situations where we have never detected it, and hence that when we look at a tower from nearby and touch it we are

386   sure that it is square, if it appears square. You also maintain that when we are really awake, we cannot doubt whether we are awake or asleep, and so on.[4] But you have no reason to think that you have previously noticed all the circumstances in which error can occur; moreover, it is easy to prove that you are from time to time mistaken in matters which you accept as certain. But when you come round to saying that 'at least we may not doubt that things appear as they do',[5] you are back on the

1 Above p. 228; cf. pp. 261f.   2 Above p. 229.   3 Above p. 230.
4 Above pp. 230f.   5 p. 231.

right road: I made this very assertion in the Second Meditation. But the point at issue in the present context concerned the truth about the things located outside us, and you have not managed to say anything true about this.

3. I shall not stop to deal with your tedious and repetitious assertions here, e.g. that I did not prove various truths when in fact I demonstrated them,[1] or that I discussed only this solid body,[2] when in fact I dealt with every kind of body – even the most rarefied kind. What counter, other than a flat denial, should one offer to assertions of this kind, which are not supported by any argument? But I should like to know in passing what evidence you have to establish that I dealt with this solid body rather than rarefied ones. Was it that I said 'I have a body which is joined to me', and 'it is certain that I am distinct from my body'?[3] I do not see why these words should not apply equally to a rarefied as to a solid body, and I do not think anyone but you will fail to see this. In any case, in the Second Meditation I did show that the mind can be understood as an existing substance even though we understand that nothing exists such as a wind or fire or vapour or breath or any other body, however thin and rarefied. But whether this substance was in actual fact distinct from any body whatsoever is something that I said I was not arguing about at that point; I discussed and demonstrated this claim in the Sixth Meditation. But you show that you have completely failed to understand any of this, since you confuse the question of what we may understand this substance to be with the question of what it really is.

4. Here you ask how I think that I, an unextended subject, could receive the semblance or idea of a body that is extended.[4] I answer that the mind does not receive any corporeal semblance; the pure understanding both of corporeal and incorporeal things occurs without any corporeal semblance. In the case of imagination, however, which can have only corporeal things as its object, we do indeed require a semblance which is a real body: the mind applies itself to this semblance but does not receive it.[5]

Your point about the idea of the sun, which a man born blind derives merely from its heat,[6] is easily refuted. The blind man can have a clear and distinct idea of the sun as a thing that gives heat, even though he does not have an idea of it as a thing that gives light. Your comparison

387

---

1 Above p. 232.   2 Above p. 233.   3 Above p. 54; cf. p. 232.   4 Above p. 234.
5 Descartes rejects the scholastic theory that sense-perception involves the transmission from object to observer of a 'form' or 'semblance' (Lat. *species*) of the object. He does, however, maintain that imagination and sense-perception involve the mind's 'applying itself to' or 'contemplating' corporeal images in the brain. See above Med. VI, p. 51.
6 Above p. 235.

between me and the blind man is incorrect. First, our knowledge of a thinking thing is much more extensive than the blind man's knowledge of a 'heating thing' – indeed it is much more extensive than our knowledge of anything else, as I showed in the appropriate place. Secondly, the only people who can prove that the idea of the sun formed by the blind man does not contain everything that can be perceived of the sun are those who are endowed with sight and detect in addition its light and shape. You, by contrast, so far from knowing more of the mind than I do, are 388   not even aware of the one thing that I do know; so in this respect you are more like the blind man, whereas I, and all the rest of the human race, can at least be said to have one good eye.

When I added that the mind is not extended, I did not intend to explain what the mind is, but merely to point out that those who think it is extended are in error. In the same way, if anyone asserted that Bucephalus was Music,[1] there would be every point in someone else saying that this was false. You go on to try to prove that the mind is extended on the grounds that it makes use of a body that is extended;[2] but here your argument seems no better than if you were to infer that Bucephalus is Music on the grounds that he neighs and whinnies, thus producing sounds which have some relation to music. Even though the mind is 389   united to the whole body, it does not follow that it is extended throughout the body, since it is not in its nature to be extended, but only to think. Nor does it understand extension by means of an extended semblance which is present within it (although it does *imagine* extension by turning to a corporeal semblance which is extended, as I have explained). Finally, it is not necessary for the mind itself to be a body, although it has the power of moving the body.

5. Your comments on the union of the mind with the body[3] are similar 390   to what you have said earlier. At no point do you produce objections to my arguments; you merely put forward doubts that you think follow from my conclusions, though in fact they merely arise from your desire to call in the imagination to examine matters which are not within its proper province. Thus when you try to compare the intermingling of mind and body with the intermingling of two bodies,[4] it is enough for me to reply that we should not set up any comparison between such things, because they are quite different in kind; and we should not imagine that the mind has parts on the grounds that it has an understanding of parts in the body. How do you arrive at the conclusion that everything the mind understands must be in the mind? If this were so, then, since the mind has an understanding of the magnitude of the terrestrial globe, it would

1 Above p. 235; Descartes apparently misreads Gassendi's *musca* ('fly') as *musica*.
2 Above pp. 235f.   3 Above pp. 238f.   4 Above p. 238.

surely have to possess this magnitude within itself, and hence not just be extended but have a greater extension than the earth.

6. Here[1] you do not contradict me on any point, although you still have a great deal to say. And this allows the reader to realize that he should not judge how many arguments you have from the number of words you produce.

In this long discussion between Mind and Flesh, Mind has disagreed with Flesh on many points, as was only to be expected. But now, as I come to an end, I recognize the true Gassendi, admire him as an outstanding philosopher, and embrace him as a man of intellectual honesty and moral integrity whose friendship I shall always try to deserve by any acts of kindness I can perform. I therefore beg him not to take it hard that I have used a philosopher's licence in refuting his objections, since everything he has had to say has given me great satisfaction. I have, amongst other things, been delighted that such a celebrated writer has, in 391 the whole course of his long and careful essay, not managed to produce a single reasoned objection to my arguments, or even my conclusions, which I have not been able to answer with great ease.

1 Above pp. 239f.

Appendix to the Fifth Set of Objections and Replies

AUTHOR'S NOTE CONCERNING THE FIFTH SET OF OBJECTIONS[1]

Before the publication of the first edition of these *Meditations*, I wanted them to be examined not only by the Doctors of the Sorbonne, but also by all other learned men who would take the trouble to scrutinize them. My aim was to have their objections and my replies published as a continuation of the *Meditations*, following the order in which they had been produced, and I hoped that this would serve to make the truth more evident. The Fifth Set of Objections which were sent to me did not seem to me to be the most important, and they were extremely long; but nonetheless I agreed to have them published in their appropriate place out of courtesy to their author. I even allowed him to see the proofs, to prevent anything being printed of which he did not approve.

199 But since that time he has produced a large volume containing his original objections together with several new 'counter-objections' or answers to my replies. In this book he complains of my publishing his objections, as if I had done so against his will, and says that he sent them to me only for my private instruction. Because of this, I am quite happy to oblige him now by removing his objections from the present volume, and this is why, when I learnt that M. Clerselier was taking the trouble to translate the other sets of objections, I asked him to omit the fifth set.[2]

---

1 This item (*Avertissement de l'auteur touchant les cinquièmes objections*) and the following item, the letter to Clerselier of 12 January 1646, both appeared in the first French edition of the *Meditations, Objections and Replies*, published in 1647.

    After reading Descartes' Replies to his Objections, Gassendi had gone on to compose a further set of criticisms which were published in a volume entitled *Disquisitio Metaphysica sive Dubitationes et Instantiae* (*Metaphysical Enquiry: Doubts and Counter-Objections*, Amsterdam, 1644). The *Doubts* were Gassendi's original objections of 1641; the *Counter-Objections* were his new criticisms. In his 'Author's Note', Descartes explains his reaction to these developments; in the letter to Clerselier he replies in more detail to some of Gassendi's *Counter-Objections*.

    Marginal references for both items are to the French text in AT IX, part 1.

2 In fact Clerselier did not abide by Descartes' request. In his French version of 1647, although he printed this 'Author's Note' (and the letter which follows) immediately after

But to prevent the reader having any cause to regret their omission, I should make it clear here that I have recently re-read these objections together with the new counter-arguments in the lengthy volume which contains them, with the purpose of extracting all the points I judged to require an answer. But I have not been able to discover a single objection which those who have some slight understanding of my *Meditations* will not, in my view, be able to answer quite easily without any help from me. As for those who judge a book by the size of the volume or by its title, I have no desire to cultivate their approval.

LETTER FROM M. DESCARTES TO M. CLERSELIER SERVING AS   202
A REPLY TO A SELECTION OF THE PRINCIPAL COUNTER-
OBJECTIONS PRODUCED BY M. GASSENDI AGAINST THE
PRECEDING REPLIES

Sir,

When you saw that I had failed to reply to the large volume of counter-objections which the author of the Fifth Objections produced in answer to my replies, you were kind enough to ask some of your friends to collect together the strongest arguments from the volume. I am greatly indebted to you for doing this and for sending me the selection which they produced. You have here shown that you are more concerned for my reputation than I am myself; for I assure you that it is a matter of   203
indifference to me whether I am respected or despised by people who are capable of being convinced by arguments of the sort which this book contains. The most intelligent of my friends who have read the book have assured me that they have found nothing in it to arrest their attention, and they are the only readers whom I desire to please. I know that most people take more notice of appearances than of truth, and that their judgements are more often incorrect than correct. And this is why I do not think their approval is worth my bothering to take all the steps that might help to secure it. But nonetheless I am very grateful for the selection of arguments which you have sent me, and I feel myself obliged to reply to them more in recognition of the work your friends have put in than through any need to defend myself. For I think that those who have taken the trouble to make the selection must now judge, as I do, that all the objections which the book in question contains are based simply on a misunderstanding of certain terms or else on various suppositions that are false. But although all the points which they have noted are of this

the Fourth Replies, he also included the Fifth Objections and Replies, though he relegated them to the end of the volume.

sort, they have in fact been so diligent as to add a number of observations which I have no recollection of having read in the book itself.[1]

They note three criticisms made against the First Meditation: (1) that I am asking for something impossible in wanting us to give up every kind of preconceived opinion; (2) that in thinking we have given up our preconceived opinions we are in fact adopting other even more harmful preconceptions; and (3) that the method of universal doubt which I have proposed cannot help us to discover any truths at all.

204 The first of these objections is based on the fact that the author of this book has not realized that the term 'preconceived opinion' applies not to all the notions which are in our mind (which I admit it is impossible for us to get rid of) but only to all the opinions which we have continued to accept as a result of previous judgements that we have made. And since making or not making a judgement is an act of will (as I have explained in the appropriate place[2]) it is evident that it is something in our power. For, after all, in order to get rid of every kind of preconceived opinion, all we need to do is resolve not to affirm or deny anything which we have previously affirmed or denied until we have examined it afresh. But this does not entail that we cease to retain all the same notions in our memory. Nevertheless, I did say that there was some difficulty in expelling from our belief everything we have previously accepted. One reason for this is that before we can decide to doubt, we need some reason for doubting; and that is why in my First Meditation I put forward the principal reasons for doubt. Another reason is that no matter how much we have resolved not to assert or deny anything, we easily forget our resolution afterwards if we have not strongly impressed it on our memory; and this is why I suggested that we should think about it very carefully.

The second objection involves a supposition which is manifestly false. For although I said that we should go so far as to force ourselves to deny the things which we had previously affirmed with too much confidence, I 205 expressly stipulated that we should do so only during the period when our attention was occupied in looking for something more certain than whatever might be denied in this way. And it is evident that during this period one could not possibly adopt any preconceptions that might be harmful.

The third objection is mere carping. Although it is true that doubt does not on its own suffice to establish any truth, it is still useful to prepare the mind in order to establish the truth at a later date; and this was my sole aim in employing it.

1 See below, pp. 274f.   2 Med. IV, above pp. 39ff.

Your friends note six objections against the Second Meditation. The first is this. The author of the *Counter-Objections* claims that when I say 'I am thinking, therefore I exist' I presuppose the major premiss 'Whatever thinks exists', and hence I have already adopted a preconceived opinion. Here he once more misuses the term 'preconceived opinion'. For although we can apply the term to the proposition in question when it is put forward without attention and believed to be true only because we remember that we judged it to be true previously, we cannot say that it is always a preconceived opinion. For when we examine it, it appears so evident to the understanding that we cannot but believe it, even though this may be the first time in our life that we have thought of it – in which case we would have no preconceived opinion about it. But the most important mistake our critic makes here is the supposition that knowledge of particular propositions must always be deduced from universal ones, following the same order as that of a syllogism in Dialectic.[1] Here he shows how little he knows of the way in which we should search for the truth. It is certain that if we are to 206 discover the truth we must always begin with particular notions in order to arrive at general ones later on (though we may also reverse the order and deduce other particular truths once we have discovered general ones). Thus when we teach a child the elements of geometry we will not be able to get him to understand the general proposition 'When equal quantities are taken from equal amounts the remaining amounts will be equal', or 'The whole is greater than its parts',[2] unless we show him examples in particular cases. It is by failing to take heed of this that our author has gone astray and produced all the invalid arguments with which he has stuffed his book. He has simply made up false major premisses whenever the mood takes him, as though I had used them to deduce the truths which I expounded.

The second objection which your friends note is that in order to know that I am thinking I must know what thought is; and yet, they say, I do not know this at all, since I have denied everything. But I have denied only preconceived opinions – not notions like these, which are known without any affirmation or denial.

The third objection is that thought cannot exist without an object, e.g. the body. Here we must avoid the ambiguity in the word 'thought', which can be taken to apply both to the thing which thinks and also to the activity performed by that thing. Now I deny that the thing which

---

1 By 'Dialectic' Descartes means scholastic logic.
2 These are two of the 'Axioms' which appear at the start of Euclid's *Elements of Geometry*.

thinks needs any object apart from itself in order to exercise its activity (though it may also extend the scope of this activity to material things when it examines them).

207   The fourth objection is that even though I have a thought of myself, I do not know if this thought is a corporeal action, or a self-moving atom, rather than an immaterial substance. Here the ambiguity in the word 'thought' is repeated, and apart from this I can see only a question without any basis to it, rather like the following: 'You judge that you are a man because you perceive in yourself all the things which lead you to give the name "men" to those who possess them; but how do you know that you are not an elephant rather than a man, for various other reasons which you do not perceive?' Similarly, after the substance which thinks has judged that it is intellectual, because it has noticed in itself all the properties of intellectual substances, and has not been able to detect any properties belonging to a body, the objector still continues to ask how it knows that it is not a body rather than an immaterial substance.

The fifth and sixth objections are similar to this. The fifth is that even if I find no extension in my thought, it does not follow that my thought is not extended, because my thought is not the standard which determines the truth of things. The sixth is that although my thought finds a distinction between thought and body, it is possible that this distinction may be false. Now we must be particularly careful to notice the ambiguity in the phrase 'my thought is not the standard which determines the truth of things'. If the claim is that my thought must not be the standard for others, obliging them to believe something just because I

208   think it is true, then I entirely agree. But this is quite irrelevant in the present context, since I never wanted to force anyone to follow my authority. On the contrary, I pointed out in several places that one should allow oneself to be convinced only by quite evident reasoning. Again, if we take the word 'thought' to apply indifferently to any kind of operation of the soul, it is certain that we can have many thoughts which do not provide any basis for inferring the truth about things which are outside us. But this is irrelevant in the present context, where we are dealing only with the thoughts that are clear and distinct perceptions and the judgements which each of us must make within himself as a result of these perceptions. This is why I say that, in the sense in which the phrase should be understood here, the thought of each person – i.e. the perception or knowledge which he has of something – should be for him the 'standard which determines the truth of the thing'; in other words, all the judgements he makes about this thing must conform to his perception if they are to be correct. Even with respect to the truths of faith, we

should perceive some reason which convinces us that they have been revealed by God, before deciding to believe them. Although ignorant people would do well to follow the judgement of the more competent on matters which are difficult to know, it is still necessary that it be their own perception which tells them they are ignorant; they must also perceive that those whose judgement they want to follow are not as ignorant as they are, or else they would be wrong to follow them and would be behaving more like automatons or beasts than men. Thus the most absurd and grotesque mistake that a philosopher can make is to want to make judgements which do not correspond to his perception of things. Yet I fail to see how our author could be cleared of having committed this blunder in most of his objections. For he is not prepared to allow each person to abide by his own perception, but claims that we should give more credence to the opinions or fantasies which he pleases to set before us, despite our complete lack of any proper perception of them.

209

Your friends have noted four objections against the Third Meditation: (1) that not everyone is aware of the idea of God within himself; (2) that if I did have this idea, I should grasp it; (3) that several people have read my arguments without being convinced by them; and (4) that from the fact that I know myself to be imperfect it does not follow that God exists. But if we take the word 'idea' in the way in which I quite explicitly stated I was taking it, and do not take refuge in ambiguity, like those who restrict this term to the images of material things formed in the imagination, then we will be unable to deny that we have some idea of God. The only way of denying this would be to say that we do not understand the meaning of the phrase 'the most perfect thing which we can conceive of'; for this is what everyone calls *God*. It is indeed going to extraordinary lengths in the desire to raise objections to say that one does not understand the meaning of one of the most ordinary phrases in common use. Besides, if someone says of himself that he does not have any idea of God, in the sense in which I take the term 'idea', he is making the most impious confession he could make. He is saying not only that he does not know God by natural reason, but also that neither faith nor any other means could give him any knowledge of God. For if one has no idea, i.e. no perception which corresponds to the meaning of the word 'God', it is no use saying that one believes that *God* exists. One might as well say that one believes that *nothing* exists, thus remaining in the abyss of impiety and the depths of ignorance.

210

The next point, namely that if I did have this idea I would grasp it, has no basis. Since the word 'grasp' implies some limitation, a finite mind cannot grasp God, who is infinite. But that does not prevent him having a perception of God, just as one can touch a mountain without being able to put one's arms round it.

The point about my arguments, namely that several people have read them without being convinced by them, can easily be rebutted, since there are others who have understood them and found them acceptable. If one single person honestly says that he has seen or understood something, we should believe him in preference to a thousand others who deny what he says simply because they have not been able to see or understand it. Similarly, in the case of the discovery of the antipodes, the report of a few sailors who had circumnavigated the earth was believed in preference to the views of those thousands of philosophers who did not believe the earth was round. In this connection my critics cite the *Elements* of Euclid, claiming they are easy for everyone to understand;

211 but I beg them to consider that among those regarded as the most learned exponents of scholastic philosophy there is not one in a hundred who understands them, and there is not one in ten thousand who understands all the demonstrations of Apollonius or Archimedes, although these demonstrations are as evident and certain as those of Euclid.

Lastly, when they say that, from the fact that I recognize some imperfection in myself, it does not follow that God exists, they do not prove anything. For I did not deduce the existence of God directly from this premiss alone, but added further considerations. Here they merely remind me of the ploy of the author of the *Counter-Objections* who has the habit of truncating my arguments, and reporting only parts of them, in order to make them seem imperfect.

All the points my critics note concerning the other three Meditations are ones which, so far as I can see, I have fully answered elsewhere. This applies to the following objections which they make: (1) that I was guilty of circularity in proving the existence of God by means of certain notions which are in us, yet saying afterwards that one cannot be certain of anything without prior knowledge that God exists; (2) that the knowledge of God's existence does not in any way help us to acquire knowledge of the truths of mathematics; and (3) that God may be a deceiver. On this topic see my reply to the Second Set of Objections, points labelled *Thirdly* and *Fourthly*, and the end of the second part of the Fourth Replies.[1]

But at the end my critics add a thought which, as far as I know, the

212 author of the *Counter-Objections* has not included in his book, although it is very similar to his objections. They say that many people of great intelligence think they clearly see that mathematical extension, which I lay down as the fundamental principle of my physics, is nothing other

---

1 See above pp. 100, 103–5, 171.

than my thought, and hence that it does not and cannot have any subsistence outside my mind, being merely an abstraction which I form from physical bodies. And they conclude that the whole of my physics 'must be imaginary and fictitious, as indeed the whole of pure mathematics is, whereas real physics dealing with the things created by God requires the kind of matter that is real, solid and not imaginary'. Here is the objection of objections and the epitome of the entire doctrine held by those 'people of great intelligence' who are cited here. All the things that we can understand and conceive are, on their account, only imaginings and fictions of our mind which cannot have any subsistence. And it follows from this that nothing that we can in any way understand, conceive, or imagine should be accepted as true; in other words we must entirely close the door to reason and content ourselves with being monkeys or parrots rather than men, if we are to deserve a place among these great minds. For if the things we can conceive must be regarded as false merely because we can conceive them, all that is left is for us to be obliged to accept as true only things which we do not conceive. We shall have to construct our doctrines out of these things, imitating others without knowing why, like monkeys, and uttering words whose sense we do not in any way understand, like parrots. But at least I can console myself with the thought that my critics here link my physics with pure 213 mathematics, which I desire above all that it should resemble.

There are two further questions which they add at the end: how can the soul move the body if it is in no way material, and how can it receive the forms[1] of corporeal objects? These questions simply give me the opportunity to point out that the author of the *Counter-Objections* was being quite unfair when, under the pretext of objecting to my views, he put to me large numbers of such questions which do not require to be answered in order to prove what I asserted in my writings. The most ignorant people could, in a quarter of an hour, raise more questions of this kind than the wisest men could deal with in a lifetime; and this is why I have not bothered to answer any of them. These questions presuppose amongst other things an explanation of the union between the soul and the body, which I have not yet dealt with at all. But I will say, for your benefit at least, that the whole problem contained in such questions arises simply from a supposition that is false and cannot in any way be proved, namely that, if the soul and the body are two substances whose nature is different, this prevents them from being able to act on each other. And yet, those who admit the existence of real accidents like heat, weight and so on, have no doubt that these accidents can act on the body; but there is much more of a difference between

1 French *espèces*: see note on *species* above p. 174.

them and it, i.e. between accidents and a substance, than there is between two substances.

For the rest, since I have my pen in my hand, I will go on to point out
214   two ambiguities which I have found in this book of *Counter-Objections*, because they are the kinds of ambiguity which, in my view, could most easily trap the less attentive reader. My aim in dealing with them is to show you that if I had found any other point that I believed to deserve an answer, I would not have neglected to deal with it.

215   The first ambiguity is on page 63,[1] and arises as follows. I said in one place that while the soul is in doubt about the existence of all material things, it knows itself *praecise tantum* – 'in the strict sense only'[2] – as an immaterial substance; and seven or eight lines further down I showed that by the words 'in the strict sense only' I do not at all mean an entire exclusion or negation, but only an abstraction from material things; for I said that in spite of this we are not sure that there is nothing corporeal in the soul, even though we do not recognize anything corporeal in it. Here my critic is so unfair to me as to try to persuade the reader that when I used the phrase 'in the strict sense only' I meant to exclude the body, and that I thus contradicted myself afterwards when I said that I did not mean to exclude it. He subsequently accuses me of committing a logical blunder in assuming something in the Sixth Meditation which I had not previously proved. But I will offer no reply to this, since it is easy to recognize the falsity of this accusation, which occurs all too often throughout his book. This sort of thing could make me suspect that the
216   author was not acting in good faith did I not know his nature and believe that he was in fact the first to be trapped by such a false supposition.

The other ambiguity is on page 84,[3] where he wants *distinguishing* and

1 A reference to Gassendi's *Counter-Objections*. The relevant passage is quoted in AT IXa 214–15:

After saying 'Therefore I am in the strict sense only a thing that thinks', you then say that you 'do not know, and are not here disputing whether you are that structure of limbs which is called the human body, or some thin vapour which permeates the limbs – a fire, air, breath', etc. But two things follow from this. First, when we come to your proof in the Sixth Meditation you will be convicted of never having proved that you are not a structure of limbs or a thin vapour, etc. For you cannot assume this as something proved or conceded. Secondly, your conclusion 'Therefore I am in the strict sense only a thing which thinks' is unjustifiable. What does the term 'only' mean? Does it not have a restrictive force, limiting you only to a thing that thinks and excluding other things such as a structure of limbs, a thin vapour, etc?

See also Gassendi's original objection (above p. 185) and Descartes' reply (p. 247).

2 Med. II, above p. 18.

3 The relevant passage from the *Counter-Objections* is quoted in AT IXa, 216:

You say that you did not abstract the concept of the wax from the concept of its accidents . . . But are not these your very words: 'I distinguish the wax from its outward *abstracting* to be the same thing. But there is a great difference between the two. In *distinguishing* a substance from its accidents we must consider both the one and the other, and this is very useful in helping us to gain knowledge of a substance. But if we merely separate the substance from its accidents by *abstraction*, i.e. consider it all on its own without thinking of the accidents, this prevents our being able to gain sound knowledge of it, because it is by means of the accidents that the nature of the substance is revealed.

These, Sir, are all the points I thought I should make in replying to this large volume of *Counter-Objections*. For although I might perhaps please the author's friends more if I were to reply to all his counter-objections one after the other, I do not think I would give my own friends equal satisfaction; for they would then have cause to blame me for having spent time on such a needless enterprise, and for devoting my leisure to the service of those who might want to waste theirs by putting pointless questions to me. But I thank you for the trouble you have taken. And so I take my leave.

217

forms – take the clothes off, as it were, and consider it naked'? What else is it to abstract the concept of one thing from the concept of another but to consider it apart from its accidents? . . . You say that you wanted to show 'how the substance of the wax is revealed by means of its accidents' . . . But how did you reveal the wax if not by looking first at its accidents or clothes, as it were, and then taking them off and considering the wax in its nakedness?

See also Gassendi's original objection (above pp. 189f) and Descartes' reply (above p. 248).

413

After a very careful reading of your *Meditations* and of your replies to the objections so far raised, we find there are still some difficulties remaining, which it is only fair to ask you to remove.

The *first* point is that from the fact that we are thinking it does not seem to be entirely certain that we exist.[2] For in order to be certain that you are thinking you must know what thought or thinking is, and what your existence is; but since you do not yet know what these things are, how can you know that you are thinking or that you exist? Thus neither when you say 'I am thinking' nor when you add 'therefore, I exist' do you really know what you are saying. Indeed, you do not even know that you are saying or thinking anything, since this seems to require that you should know that you know what you are saying; and this in turn requires that you be aware of knowing that you know what you are saying, and so on *ad infinitum*. Hence it is clear that you cannot know whether you exist or even whether you are thinking.

To come to the *second* difficulty, when you say you are thinking and that you exist, someone might maintain that you are mistaken, and are not thinking but are merely in motion, and that you are nothing else but corporeal motion. For no one has yet been able to grasp that demonstration of yours by which you think you have proved that what you call thought cannot be a kind of corporeal motion. Have you used your method of analysis to separate off all the motions of that rarefied matter of yours? Is this what makes you so certain? And can you therefore show us (for we will give our closest attention and our powers of perception are, we think, reasonably keen) that it is self-contradictory that our thoughts should be reducible to these corporeal motions?

The *third* difficulty is very like the second. Several of the Church Fathers believed, along with the Platonists, that angels are corporeal, which led the Lateran Council to decide that they can be depicted; the Fathers took exactly the same view of the rational soul, some of them maintaining that it was passed on in procreation. But in spite of this, they still maintained that angels think, and that the soul thinks. They appear

---

1 Compiled by Mersenne; see above pp. 63f.　　2 Cf. Med. II, above pp. 16f.

to have believed that this could occur by means of corporeal motions, or even that angels were themselves corporeal motions; at any rate they drew no distinction between thought and such motions. This view can be confirmed by reference to the thoughts of apes, dogs and other animals. For dogs bark in their sleep as if they were chasing hares or robbers, and when they are awake they know that they are running, just as in their dreams they know that they are barking; yet, like you, we do not recognize any element in them which is distinct from their bodies. If you say that a dog does not know that it is running or thinking, then this is an assertion that cannot be proved; the dog might well make a similar judgement about us, and suppose that when we are running or thinking, we do not know that we are running or thinking. You do not see the dog's internal mode of operation any more than he sees yours; and there are plenty of distinguished men, both now and in the past, who have been prepared to allow that the beasts have reason. So far are we from accepting that all their operations can be satisfactorily explained by means of mechanics, without invoking any sensation, life or soul, that we are willing to wager anything you like that this is an impossible and ridiculous claim. Finally, there are plenty of people who will say that man himself lacks sensation and intellect, and can do everything by means of mechanical structures, without any mind, given that apes, dogs and elephants can perform all their operations by mechanical means. For if the limited reasoning power to be found in animals differs from human reason, the difference is merely one of degree and does not imply any essential difference.

The *fourth* difficulty concerns the kind of knowledge possessed by an atheist.[1] When the atheist asserts 'If equals are taken from equals the remainders will be equal' or 'The three angles of a rectilinear triangle are equal to two right angles' and numerous similar propositions, he maintains his knowledge is very certain and indeed – on your own criterion – utterly evident. For he cannot think of these propositions without believing them to be wholly certain. He maintains that this is so true that even if God does not exist and is not even possible (as he believes), he is just as certain of these truths as if God really existed. Moreover he maintains that no reason for doubt can be presented to him which could shake him in the slightest or make him at all uncertain. What reason can you produce? That God, if he exists, may deceive him? The atheist will reply that he cannot be deceived about these truths even by a God who exercises all his omnipotence to this end.

The *fifth* difficulty arises from this point, and it is based on your uncompromising assertion that no deception is to be found in God. Now

----

1 Cf. Second Replies, above p. 101.

very many theologians believe that the damned, both angels and men, are continually deceived by the idea of a tormenting fire which God has implanted in them; thus they most firmly believe, and think they see and perceive very clearly, that they are really being tormented by the fire, even though there is no such fire. May not God, then, deceive us with similar ideas, and continually delude us by sending such semblances or ideas into our souls? Thus we might think we clearly saw, and perceived with each of our senses, things which in fact have no existence outside us: there might be no heaven or earth, and we might have no arms or feet or eyes etc. God can do this without any wrong or injustice, since he is the supreme Lord of all things and has the absolute power to deal with his creatures as he wishes, especially when his actions may serve to humble the pride of men and punish them for their sins, either because of original sin or because of other causes which are hidden from us. All this seems to be confirmed by those passages in Scripture which establish that we can know nothing. Paul, for example, says in 1 Corinthians, Chapter 8, verse 2: 'If any man think that he knoweth anything, he knoweth nothing yet as he ought to know.' Again, in Ecclesiastes, Chapter 8, verse 17 we find: 'Then I understood that of all the works of God a man can find no reason for those that are done under the sun; and the more he labours to seek it, the less shall he find it; nay, though a wise man say that he knoweth it, yet shall he be unable to find it out.' The whole book makes it clear that the 'wise man' says what he does because of carefully considered reasons, not hastily or thoughtlessly; this is exceptionally clear when the issue of the mind, which you maintain is immortal, is discussed. For Chapter 3, verse 19 says that the death of man 'is as the death of beasts'. In case you should reply that this refers only to the body, the preacher adds that 'a man hath no pre-eminence above a beast'. And speaking explicitly of the spirit of man he says that there is no one who knows 'whether it goeth upward' (i.e. whether it is immortal), or whether, with the spirits of the beasts, it 'goeth downward' (i.e. perishes). You cannot claim that these are words put into the mouth of an unbeliever; if so, the writer would have had to have drawn our attention to this and refuted these assertions. Nor can you claim that you do not have to reply to these points because Scripture is the province of the theologians. For since you are a Christian, it behoves you to be ready to reply to every objection that can be raised against the faith and deal with it to the best of your powers – especially when it goes against a position you wish to establish.

The *sixth* difficulty arises in connection with the indifference that belongs to our judgement, or liberty. This indifference, you claim, does not belong to the perfection of the will but has to do merely with its imperfection; thus, according to you, indifference is removed whenever the mind clearly perceives what it should believe or do or refrain from doing.[1] But do you not see that by adopting this position you are 417 destroying God's freedom, since you are removing from his will the indifference as to whether he shall create this world rather than another world or no world at all? Yet it is an article of faith that God was from eternity indifferent as to whether he should create one world, or innumerable worlds, or none at all. But who doubts that God has always perceived with the clearest vision what he should do or refrain from doing? Thus, a very clear vision and perception of things does not remove indifference of choice; and if indifference cannot be a proper part of human freedom, neither will it find a place in divine freedom, since the essences of things are, like numbers, indivisible and immutable. Therefore indifference is involved in God's freedom of choice no less than it is in the case of human freedom of choice.

The *seventh* difficulty concerns the surface in which, or by means of which, you say all our sensations occur.[2] We do not understand how it can be that it is neither a part of the bodies which are perceived by the senses, nor a part of the air and its vapours; for you say it is no part of these things, not even the outermost layer. Nor do we grasp your assertion that there are no real accidents belonging to any body or substance – accidents which could by divine power exist apart from any subject, and which do really exist in the sacrament of the altar. However, there is no reason for our professors to be upset by your assertion until they see whether you propose to demonstrate it in the treatise on physics which you promise us; for they can hardly believe that this will provide us with such a clear account of the matter as to enable or require your view to be accepted in preference to the traditional view.

The *eighth* difficulty arises out of your reply to the Fifth Set of Objections. How can the truths of geometry or metaphysics, such as those you refer to, be immutable and eternal and yet not be independent of God?[3] What sort of causal dependence on God do they have? Could 418 he have brought it about that there has never been any such thing as the nature of a triangle? And how, may we ask, could he have made it untrue from eternity that twice four makes eight, or that a triangle has three angles? Either these truths depend solely on the intellect that is thinking of them, or on existing things, or else they are independent, since it seems that God could not have brought it about that any of these essences or truths were not as they were from all eternity.

Our *ninth* and most worrying difficulty is your assertion that we ought to mistrust the operations of the senses and that the reliability of the

1 Med. IV, above p. 40.   2 Cf. Fourth Replies, above pp. 174ff.   3 Above p. 261.

intellect is much greater than that of the senses.[1] But how can the intellect enjoy any certainty unless it has previously derived it from the senses when they are working as they should? How can it correct a mistake made by one of the senses unless some other sense first corrects the mistake? Owing to refraction, a stick which is in fact straight appears bent in water. What corrects the error? The intellect? Not at all; it is the sense of touch. And the same sort of thing must be taken to occur in other cases. Hence if you have recourse to all your senses when they are in good working order, and they all give the same report, you will achieve the greatest certainty of which man is naturally capable. But you will often fail to achieve it if you trust the operations of the mind; for the mind often goes astray in just those areas where it had previously supposed doubt to be impossible.

  These are the main questions that give us pause. After dealing with them, we ask you to provide in addition a reliable rule and some firm criteria which will make us utterly sure of the following point: when we understand something entirely apart from some other thing, in the way you describe, is it indeed certain that the one is so distinct from the other that they could subsist apart – at least through the power of God?[2] That is, how can we know for sure, clearly and distinctly, that when our in-tellect makes this distinction, the distinction does not arise solely from the intellect but arises from the nature of the things themselves? For when we contemplate the immensity of God while not thinking of his justice, or when we contemplate his existence when not thinking of the Son or the Holy Spirit, do we not have a complete perception of that existence, or of God as existing, entirely apart from the other Persons of the Trinity? So could not an unbeliever deny that these Persons belong to God on the same reasoning that leads you to deny that the mind or thought belongs to the body? If anyone concludes that the Son and the Holy Spirit are essentially distinct from God the Father or that they can be separated from him, this will be an unsound inference; and in the same way, no one will grant you that thought, or the human mind, is distinct from the body, despite the fact that you conceive one apart from the other and deny the one of the other, and despite your belief that this does not come about simply through an abstraction of your mind. If you can give a satisfactory answer to these points, then, so far as we can see, nothing at all remains that can displease our theologians.

Appendix

There now follow a number of points suggested by other critics. These are included to give you the opportunity to reply to them in conjunction

1 See above, Med. I, p. 17; Med. II, pp. 20f; Med. VI, p. 57.   2 Cf. Med. VI, above p. 54.

with the preceding objections, since they belong to the same argument. Some of your most learned and acute critics have asked for clarification on the following three points:

(1) How do I know for certain that I have a clear idea of my soul?

(2) How do I know for certain that this idea is wholly different from any other thing?

(3) How do I know for certain that this idea contains nothing of a corporeal nature?   420

The following argument has been put forward by another group of critics.

FROM A GROUP OF PHILOSOPHERS AND GEOMETERS TO M. DESCARTES

However much we ponder on the question of whether the idea of our mind (or a human mind), i.e. our knowledge and perception of it, contains anything corporeal, we cannot go so far as to assert that what we call thought cannot in any way belong to a body subject to some sort of motion. For since we see that there are some bodies that do not think, and others, namely human bodies and perhaps those of the brutes, which do think, will not you yourself convict us of sophistry and of making rash judgements if we infer from this that there are no bodies that think? We can hardly doubt that we would deserve your lasting ridicule if it was we who had originally devised this argument from ideas to establish the nature of the mind and the existence of God, and you had then condemned it by using your method of analysis. But you seem to be so preoccupied and prepossessed by this method that you seem to have dulled your mind with it, so that you are no longer free to see that the individual properties or operations of the soul which you find in yourself depend upon corporeal motions.

If you do not accept this, then you must untie the knot which in your view must be binding us with adamantine bonds and preventing our mind from soaring above every kind of body. The knot is this. We   421 perceive very well that three and two make five and that if you take equals from equals the remainders will be equal; we are convinced of these and numerous other matters, just as you find yourself to be. But why are we not similarly convinced on the basis of your ideas, or our own, that the soul of man is distinct from the body, or that God exists? You will say that you cannot graft this truth into us unless we are prepared to meditate along with you. Well, we have read what you have written seven times, and have lifted up our minds, as best we could, to the level of the angels, but we are still not convinced. We do not believe you will allege that our minds are in the grip of a brutish stupor and are wholly unfitted for metaphysical subjects, when we have had thirty years practice in them! Surely you will prefer to accept that your arguments derived from the ideas of the mind and of God do not have the kind of weight or strength that could or should conquer the minds of learned men who have tried with all their might to detach themselves from corporeal stuff. Indeed we think you will readily admit this if you re-read your *Meditations* in the spirit of analytical scrutiny which you would adopt if they had been put forward for your examination by an opponent.

Lastly, since we do not know what can be done by bodies and their motions, and since you confess that without a divine revelation no one can know everything which God has imparted or could impart to any object, how can you possibly have known that God has not implanted in certain bodies a power or property enabling them to doubt, think etc.?

These are our arguments, or if you prefer, our 'preconceived opinions'. If you can cure them, then, Sir, we swear by the ever-living God that we will all join in giving you our fullest thanks for freeing us from the thorns which are choking the seed you have sown! May almighty God in his supreme goodness bring this to pass, since we can see that it is to his glory alone that you have so auspiciously devoted all your efforts.

AUTHOR'S REPLIES TO THE SIXTH SET OF OBJECTIONS

1. It is true that no one can be certain that he is thinking or that he exists unless he knows what thought is and what existence is.[1] But this does not require reflective knowledge, or the kind of knowledge that is acquired by means of demonstrations; still less does it require knowledge of reflective knowledge, i.e. knowing that we know, and knowing that we know that we know, and so on *ad infinitum*. This kind of knowledge cannot possibly be obtained about anything. It is quite sufficient that we should know it by that internal awareness which always precedes reflective knowledge. This inner awareness of one's thought and existence is so innate in all men that, although we may pretend that we do not have it if we are overwhelmed by preconceived opinions and pay more attention to words than to their meanings, we cannot in fact fail to have it. Thus when anyone notices that he is thinking and that it follows from this that he exists, even though he may never before have asked what thought is or what existence is, he still cannot fail to have sufficient knowledge of them both to satisfy himself in this regard.

2. When someone notices that he is thinking, then, given that he understands what motion is, it is quite impossible that he should believe that he is mistaken and is 'not thinking but merely in motion'.[2] Since the idea or notion which he has of thought is quite different from his idea of corporeal motion, he must necessarily understand the one as different from the other. Because, however, he is accustomed to attribute many different properties to one and the same subject without being aware of any connection between them, he may possibly be inclined to doubt, or may even affirm, that he is one and the same being who thinks and who moves from place to place. Notice that if we have different ideas of two things, there are two ways in which they can be taken to be one and the same thing: either in virtue of the unity or identity of their nature, or else merely in respect of unity of composition. For example, the ideas which we have of shape and of motion are not the same, nor are our ideas of understanding and volition, nor are those of bones and flesh, nor are those of thought and of an extended thing. But nevertheless we clearly

423

1 Above p. 278.   2 *Ibid.*

285

perceive that the same substance which is such that it is capable of taking on a shape is also such that it is capable of being moved, and hence that that which has shape and that which is mobile are one and the same in virtue of a unity of nature. Similarly, the thing that understands and the thing that wills are one and the same in virtue of a unity of nature. But our perception is different in the case of the thing that we consider under the form of bone and that which we consider under the form of flesh; and hence we cannot take them as one and the same thing in virtue of a unity of nature but can regard them as the same only in respect of unity of composition – i.e. in so far as it is one and the same animal which has bones and flesh. But now the question is whether we perceive that a thinking thing and an extended thing are one and the same by a unity of nature. That is to say, do we find between thought and extension the same kind of affinity or connection that we find between shape and motion, or understanding and volition? Alternatively, when they are said 424 to be 'one and the same' is this not rather in respect of unity of composition, in so far as they are found in the same man, just as bones and flesh are found in the same animal? The latter view is the one I maintain, since I observe a distinction or difference in every respect between the nature of an extended thing and that of a thinking thing, which is no less than that to be found between bones and flesh.

However, you go on to say that no one has been able to grasp this demonstration of mine.[1] In case this appeal to authority may prejudice the truth, I am compelled to reply that even though not many people have yet examined the demonstration, there are nevertheless several who affirm that they understand it. One witness who has sailed to America and says that he has seen the antipodes deserves more credence than a thousand others who deny their existence merely because they have no knowledge of them. And similarly, those who give due consideration to the true force of an argument will have more respect for the authority of one person who says that he has understood a proof correctly, than they will accord to a thousand others who claim, without providing any argument to back up their case, that it cannot be understood by anyone. For the fact that such people fail to understand the argument themselves does not prevent anyone else's understanding it; indeed, the very fact that they infer its general unintelligibility from their own failure to understand it shows that their reasoning is careless, and that they do not deserve to have their views accepted.

Lastly, my critics ask whether I have used my method of analysis to separate off all the motions of that rarefied matter of mine. Is this (they ask) what makes me certain? And can I therefore show my critics, who

1 Above p. 278.

are most attentive and (they think) reasonably perceptive men, that it is self-contradictory that our thought should be reduced to corporeal motions?[1] By 'reduced' I take it that they mean that our thought and corporeal motions are one and the same. My reply is that I am very certain of this point, but I cannot guarantee that others can be convinced of it, however attentive they may be, and however keen, in their own judgement, their powers of perception may be. I cannot guarantee that they will be persuaded, at least so long as they focus their attention not on things which are objects of pure understanding but only on things which can be imagined. This mistake has obviously been made by those who have imagined that the distinction between thought and motion is to be understood by making divisions within some kind of rarefied matter. The only way of understanding the distinction is to realize that the notions of a thinking thing and an extended or mobile thing are completely different, and independent of each other; and it is self-contradictory to suppose that things that we clearly understand as different and independent could not be separated, at least by God. Thus, however often we find them in one and the same subject – e.g. when we find thought and corporeal motion in the same man – we should not therefore think that they are one and the same in virtue of a unity of nature, but should regard them as the same only in respect of unity of composition.

3. The view here advanced in connection with the Platonists and their followers[2] has now been rejected by the entire Catholic Church and is commonly dismissed by all philosophers. The Lateran Council did conclude that angels could be depicted, but did not, in so doing, grant that they were corporeal. And even if they really were believed to be corporeal, it would certainly not be intelligible to suppose their minds to be inseparable from their bodies, any more than it is in the case of men. Again, even if the human soul were supposed to be passed on in procreation, it could not be concluded from this that it was corporeal, but only that it was derived from the soul of the parents, just as the body grows from the parents' body. As for dogs and apes, even were I to concede that they have thought, it would not in any way follow from this that the human mind is not distinct from the body; the conclusion would rather be that in other animals, too, the mind is distinct from the body. This was the view taken by those same Platonists whose authority my critics were extolling a moment ago, as is clear from the fact that they followed the Pythagoreans in believing in the transmigration of souls. But in fact the brutes possess no thought whatsoever; I not only stated this, as my critics here imply, but proved it by very strong arguments which no

1 *Ibid.*   2 Above pp. 278f.

one has refuted up till now. Yet those who assert, as if they were present in the animals' hearts, that 'dogs when awake know that they are running, and in their dreams know that they are barking',[1] are simply saying something without proving it. My critics go on to say that they do not believe that the ways in which the beasts operate can be explained 'by means of mechanics without invoking any sensation, life or soul' (I take this to mean 'without invoking thought'; for I accept that the brutes have what is commonly called 'life', and a corporeal soul and organic sensation); moreover, they are 'ready to wager any amount that this is an impossible and ridiculous claim'. But these remarks should not be taken to constitute an argument, for the same could be said of any other claim, however true it might be. Indeed the use of wagers in debate is generally resorted to only when there is a lack of arguments to prove the case; and since once upon a time distinguished people used to laugh at claims about the antipodes in just such a fashion, I do not think that a claim should be immediately dismissed as false just because some people laugh at it.

My critics add in conclusion: 'There are plenty of people who will say that man himself lacks sensation and intellect, and can do everything by means of mechanical structures, without any mind, given that apes, dogs and elephants can perform all their operations by mechanical means.'[2] This is surely not an argument that proves anything, except perhaps that some people have such a confused conception of everything and cling so tenaciously to their preconceived opinions (which they understand only in a verbal way) that rather than change them they will deny of themselves what they cannot fail to experience within themselves all the time. We cannot fail constantly to experience within ourselves that we are thinking. It may be shown that animate brutes can perform all their operations without any thought, but this does not entitle anyone to infer that he does not himself think. Such an inference would be made only by someone who has previously been convinced that he operates in exactly the same way as the brutes, simply because he has attributed thought to them; he then remains so stubbornly attached to the sentence 'Men and the brutes operate in the same way' that when it is pointed out to him that the brutes do not think, he actually prefers to deny his own thought, of which he cannot fail to be aware, rather than change his opinion that he operates in the same way as the brutes. But I find it hard to accept that there are many people of this sort. It will be found that the great majority, given the premiss that thought is not distinct from corporeal motion, take a much more rational line and maintain that thought is the same in the brutes as it is in us, since they observe all kinds of corporeal motions in them, just as in us. And they will add that 'the difference,

427

---

1 Above p. 279.   2 *Ibid.*

which is merely one of degree, does not imply any essential difference';[1] from this they will be quite justified in concluding that, although there may be a smaller degree of reason in the beasts than there is in us, the beasts possess minds which are of exactly the same type as ours.

4. As for the kind of knowledge possessed by the atheist,[2] it is easy to demonstrate that it is not immutable and certain. As I have stated previously, the less power the atheist attributes to the author of his being, the more reason he will have to suspect that his nature may be so imperfect as to allow him to be deceived even in matters which seem utterly evident to him.[3] And he will never be able to be free of this doubt until he recognizes that he has been created by a true God who cannot be a deceiver.

5. The assertion that it is self-contradictory that men should be deceived by God[4] is clearly demonstrated from the fact that the form of deception is non-being, towards which the supreme being cannot tend. On this point all theologians are agreed, and the entire certainty of the Christian faith depends on it. For why should we believe what God has revealed to us if we thought that we were from time to time deceived by him? And although the theologians commonly say that the damned are tormented by the fires of hell, they do not therefore believe that they are 'deceived by the false idea of a tormenting fire which God has implanted in them'; rather they think that the damned are tormented by a real fire, since 'just as the incorporeal spirit of a living man is naturally confined within the body, so after death it can easily be confined in corporeal fire, through the power of God', etc. See the Master of the Sentences, Book IV Distinction 44.[5]

As for the passages cited from Scripture, I do not regard it as my job to comment on them, except when they seem to be in conflict with an opinion that is peculiar to me. For when the Scriptures are invoked against opinions which are common to all Christians, such as the opinions attacked here (e.g. that something can be known and that human souls are not like those of animals), I should be afraid of being accused of arrogance if I did not choose to be content with the replies already discovered by others, rather than thinking up new answers of my own. For I have never become involved in theological studies except in so far as they contributed to my private instruction, nor am I conscious of having so much divine grace within me that I feel a vocation for such sacred studies. So I hereby declare that in future I will refuse to comment on questions of this kind; but I will make an exception just this once, to avoid giving anyone an excuse to think that I am keeping silent because I cannot give an adequate explanation of the passages cited.

1 *Ibid.*   2 Above p. 279.   3 Cf. Med. 1, above p. 14.   4 Above pp. 279f.
5 The 'Magister Sententiarum' was the twelfth-century theologian Peter Lombard, whose *Sentences* became a standard theological textbook.

First, then, I maintain that the passage from St Paul[1] 1 Corinthians, Chapter 8, verse 2, should be understood to refer only to knowledge which is not conjoined with love, i.e. to the knowledge possessed by atheists; for if anyone knows God as he should, he cannot fail to adore him or to have love. This is proved by the words that come just before those cited, 'Knowledge puffeth up, but love edifieth', and also by the words which immediately follow: 'If anyone loveth God, the same (i.e. God) is known by him.' Thus the apostle does not mean that we cannot possess any knowledge, for he admits that those who love God know him, i.e. have knowledge of him. He merely says that those who do not have love, and hence do not have sufficient knowledge of God, do not know things as they ought to know them, even though they may think they have some knowledge in other matters; for we must begin with

430 knowledge of God, and our knowledge of all other things must then be subordinated to this single initial piece of knowledge, as I explained in my *Meditations*.[2] Thus this very passage which is invoked against me so openly confirms my own opinion on the subject that I do not think that those who disagree with me can possibly give a correct explanation of it. If anyone maintains that the phrase 'the same' refers not to God but to the man who is known and approved of God, then a passage from another apostle, namely St John, in the First Epistle, Chapter 2, wholly supports my interpretation. Verse 2 reads as follows: 'And hereby we do know that we know him, if we keep his commandments.'[3] Again, Chapter 4, verse 7 reads: 'Everyone that loveth is born of God and knoweth God.'

The same reasoning applies to the passages cited from Ecclesiastes.[4] It should be noted that in this book Solomon is not adopting the role of an unbeliever but speaking in his own right, as a sinner who had previously turned away from God and is now repenting. He says that while he merely employed human wisdom and did not refer it to God, he was unable to find anything that was wholly satisfying, or which did not contain vanity. Because of this he warns us in various passages that we should turn to God, and he makes this explicit in Chapter 11, verse 9: 'Know thou that for all these things God will bring thee to judgement'; the message is continued in what follows up to the end of the book. More specifically, in Chapter 8, verse 17, the words 'then I understood that of all the works of God man can find no reason for those that are done under the sun' are to be taken to refer not to any man, but to the man described in the preceding verse: 'There is a man that neither by day or night taketh

431 sleep with his eyes.' It is as if the prophet wanted to warn us here that

1 Above p. 280.   2 Cf. Med. IV, above p. 37.
3 The verse in question is in fact verse 3.   4 Above p. 280.

those who are too assiduous in their studies are not suited to the pursuit of truth; and those who know me will certainly find it hard to suppose that this saying applies to me. But we should pay special attention to the phrase 'those things that are done under the sun'. This phrase frequently recurs in the book, and always refers to natural things, leaving out their subordination to God; this is because God is above all things, and hence is not included in those which are *under* the sun. Thus the true sense of the passage cited is that man cannot achieve correct knowledge of natural things so long as he does not know God, which is just what I too have asserted. Finally, in Chapter 3, verse 19, the statements 'The death of man is as the death of the beasts' and 'Man hath no pre-eminence above a beast' are obviously intended to apply only to the body; for the passage mentions only things which belong to the body. Immediately afterwards we find a separate comment about the soul: 'Who knoweth if the spirit of the sons of Adam goeth upward and if the spirit of the beasts goeth downward?' In other words, who knows whether human souls are destined to enjoy celestial bliss, so long as man relies on human reasoning and does not turn to God? Now I have certainly tried to prove by natural reason that the human soul is not corporeal, but I grant that only faith can enable us to know whether it will ascend above.

6. As for the freedom of the will,[1] the way in which it exists in God is quite different from the way in which it exists in us. It is self-contradictory to suppose that the will of God was not indifferent from eternity with respect to everything which has happened or will ever happen; for it is impossible to imagine that anything is thought of in the divine intellect as good or true, or worthy of belief or action or omission, prior to the decision of the divine will to make it so. I am not speaking here of temporal priority: I mean that there is not even any priority of order, or nature, or of 'rationally determined reason' as they call it, such that God's idea of the good impelled him to choose one thing rather than another. For example, God did not will the creation of the world in time because he saw that it would be better this way than if he had created it from eternity; nor did he will that the three angles of a triangle should be equal to two right angles because he recognized that it could not be otherwise, and so on. On the contrary, it is because he willed to create the world in time that it is better this way than if he had created it from eternity; and it is because he willed that the three angles of a triangle should necessarily equal two right angles that this is true and cannot be otherwise; and so on in other cases. There is no problem in the fact that the merit of the saints may be said to be the cause of their obtaining eternal life; for it is not the cause of this reward in the sense that it

432

---

1 Above pp. 280f.

determines God to will anything, but is merely the cause of an effect of which God willed from eternity that it should be the cause. Thus the supreme indifference to be found in God is the supreme indication of his omnipotence. But as for man, since he finds that the nature of all goodness and truth is already determined by God, and his will cannot tend towards anything else, it is evident that he will embrace what is good and true all the more willingly, and hence more freely, in proportion as he sees it more clearly. He is never indifferent except when he does not know which of the two alternatives is the better or truer, or at least when he does not see this clearly enough to rule out any possibility of doubt. Hence the indifference which belongs to human freedom is very different from that which belongs to divine freedom. The fact that the essences of things are said to be indivisible[1] is not relevant here. For, firstly, no essence can belong univocally to both God and his creatures; and, secondly, indifference does not belong to the essence of human freedom, since not only are we free when ignorance of what is right makes us indifferent, but we are also free – indeed at our freest – when a clear perception impels us to pursue some object.

7. My conception of the surface by which I think our senses are affected[2] is exactly the same as the normal conception which all mathematicians and philosophers have (or should have), when they distinguish a surface from a body and suppose it to be wholly lacking in depth. But the term 'surface' is used in two senses by mathematicians. In one sense they use the term of a body whose length and breadth alone they are studying and which is considered quite apart from any depth it may have, even though the possession of some degree of depth is not ruled out; alternatively, they use the term simply for a mode of body, in which case all depth is completely denied. So to avoid this ambiguity I stated that I was talking of the surface which is merely a mode and hence cannot be a part of a body. For a body is a substance, and a mode cannot be a part of a substance. But I did not deny that the surface is the boundary of a body; on the contrary it can quite properly be called the boundary of the contained body as much as of the containing one, in the sense in which bodies are said to be contiguous when their boundaries are together. For when two bodies are in mutual contact there is a single boundary common to both which is a part of neither; it is the same mode of each body, and it can remain even though the bodies are removed, provided only that other bodies of exactly the same size and shape take their places. Indeed, the kind of place characterized by the Aristotelians as 'the surface of the surrounding body' can be understood to be a surface in no other sense but this, namely as something which is not a

1 Above p. 281.   2 *Ibid.*

substance but a mode. For the place where a tower is does not change even though the air which surrounds it is replaced, or even if another body is substituted for the tower; and hence the surface, which is here taken to be the place, is not a part either of the surrounding air or of the tower.[1]

In order to demolish the doctrine of the reality of accidents, I do not think we need to look for any arguments beyond those I have already deployed. First, since all sense-perception occurs through contact, only the surface of a body can be the object of sense-perception; yet if there were real accidents they would have to be something different from the surface, which is nothing but a mode; and hence, if there are any real accidents, they cannot be perceived by the senses. But surely the only reason why people have thought that accidents exist is that they have supposed that they are perceived by the senses. Secondly, it is completely contradictory that there should be real accidents, since whatever is real can exist separately from any other subject; yet anything that can exist separately in this way is a substance, not an accident. The claim that real accidents cannot be separated from their subjects 'naturally', but only by the power of God, is irrelevant. For to occur 'naturally' is nothing other than to occur through the ordinary power of God, which in no way differs from his extraordinary power – the effect on the real world is exactly the same. Hence if everything which can naturally exist without a subject is a substance, anything that can exist without a substance even through the power of God, however extraordinary, should also be termed a substance. I do admit that one substance can be attributed to another substance; yet when this happens it is not the substance itself which has the form of an accident, but only the mode of attribution. Thus when clothing is the attribute of a man, it is not the clothing itself which is the accident, but merely 'being clothed'. But the principal argument which induced philosophers to posit real accidents was that they thought that sense-perception could not be explained without them, and this is why I promised to give a very detailed account of sense-perception in my writings on physics, taking each sense in turn. Not that I want any of my results to be taken on trust; but I thought that the explanation of vision which I had already given in the *Optics* would make it easy for the judicious reader to guess what I was capable of accomplishing with regard to the remaining senses.[2]

8. If anyone attends to the immeasurable greatness of God he will find it manifestly clear that there can be nothing whatsoever which does not depend on him[3] This applies not just to everything that subsists, but to

435

---

1 Cf. *Principles*, Part II, art. 15: vol. I, p. 229.   2 Cf. *Optics*, Disc. 6: vol. I, pp. 167ff.
3 Cf. above p. 281.

all order, every law, and every reason for anything's being true or good. If this were not so, then, as noted a little earlier, God would not have been completely indifferent with respect to the creation of what he did in fact create. If some reason for something's being good had existed prior to his preordination, this would have determined God to prefer those things which it was best to do. But on the contrary, just because he resolved to prefer those things which are now to be done, for this very reason, in the words of Genesis, 'they are very good'; in other words, the reason for their goodness depends on the fact that he exercised his will to make them so. There is no need to ask what category of causality is applicable to the dependence of this goodness upon God, or to the dependence on him of other truths, both mathematical and metaphysical. For since the various kinds of cause were enumerated by thinkers who did not, perhaps, attend to this type of causality, it is hardly surprising that they gave no name to it. But in fact they did give it a name, for it can be called efficient causality, in the sense that a king may be called the efficient cause of a law, although the law itself is not a thing which has physical existence, but is merely what they call a 'moral entity'. Again, there is no need to ask how God could have brought it about from eternity that it was not true that twice four make eight, and so on; for I admit this is unintelligible to us. Yet on the other hand I do understand, quite correctly, that there cannot be any class of entity that does not depend on God; I also understand that it would have been easy for God to ordain certain things such that we men cannot understand the possibility of their being otherwise than they are. And therefore it would be irrational for us to doubt what we do understand correctly just because there is something which we do not understand and which, so far as we can see, there is no reason why we should understand. Hence we should not suppose that eternal truths 'depend on the human intellect or on other existing things';[1] they depend on God alone, who, as the supreme legislator, has ordained them from eternity.

9. If we are to get a clear view of what sort of certainty attaches to the senses, we must distinguish three grades of sensory response. The first is limited to the immediate stimulation of the bodily organs by external objects; this can consist in nothing but the motion of the particles of the organs, and any change of shape and position resulting from this motion. The second grade comprises all the immediate effects produced in the mind as a result of its being united with a bodily organ which is affected in this way. Such effects include the perceptions of pain, pleasure, thirst, hunger, colours, sound, taste, smell, heat, cold and the like, which arise from the union and as it were the intermingling of mind and body, as

1 Cf. above p. 281.

explained in the Sixth Meditation.[1] The third grade includes all the judgements about things outside us which we have been accustomed to make from our earliest years – judgements which are occasioned by the movements of these bodily organs.

For example, when I see a stick, it should not be supposed that certain 'intentional forms' fly off the stick towards the eye,[2] but simply that rays of light are reflected off the stick and set up certain movements in the optic nerve and, via the optic nerve, in the brain, as I have explained at some length in the *Optics*.[3] This movement in the brain, which is common to us and the brutes, is the first grade of sensory response. This leads to the second grade, which extends to the mere perception of the colour and light reflected from the stick; it arises from the fact that the mind is so intimately conjoined with the body that it is affected by the movements which occur in it. Nothing more than this should be referred to the sensory faculty, if we wish to distinguish it carefully from the intellect. But suppose that, as a result of being affected by this sensation of colour, I judge that a stick, located outside me, is coloured; and suppose that on the basis of the extension of the colour and its boundaries together with its position in relation to the parts of the brain, I make a rational calculation about the size, shape and distance of the stick: although such reasoning is commonly assigned to the senses (which is why I have here referred it to the third grade of sensory response), it is   438 clear that it depends solely on the intellect. I demonstrated in the *Optics* how size, distance and shape can be perceived by reasoning alone, which works out any one feature from the other features. The only difference is that when we now make a judgement for the first time because of some new observation, then we attribute it to the intellect; but when from our earliest years we have made judgements, or even rational inferences, about the things which affect our senses, then, even though these judgements were made in exactly the same way as those we make now, we refer them to the senses. The reason for this is that we make the calculation and judgement at great speed because of habit, or rather we remember the judgements we have long made about similar objects; and so we do not distinguish these operations from simple sense-perception.

It is clear from this that when we say 'The reliability of the intellect is much greater than that of the senses',[4] this means merely that when we are grown up the judgements which we make as a result of various new observations are more reliable than those which we formed without any reflection in our early childhood; and this is undoubtedly true. It is clear that we are not here dealing with the first and second grades of sensory

1 Above pp. 56ff.   2 Cf. footnote, p. 174.   3 See Vol 1, pp. 169f.
4 Above pp. 281f.

response, because no falsity can occur in them. Hence when people say that a stick in water 'appears bent because of refraction', this is the same as saying that it appears to us in a way which would lead a child to judge that it was bent – and which may even lead us to make the same judgement, following the preconceived opinions which we have become accustomed to accept from our earliest years. But I cannot grant my critics' further comment that this error is corrected 'not by the intellect but by the sense of touch'.[1] As a result of touching it, we may judge that the stick is straight, and the kind of judgement involved may be the kind we have been accustomed to make since childhood, and which is therefore referred to as the 'sense' of touch. But the sense alone does not suffice to correct the visual error: in addition we need to have some degree of reason which tells us that in this case we should believe the judgement based on touch rather than that elicited by vision. And since we did not have this power of reasoning in our infancy, it must be attributed not to the senses but to the intellect. Thus even in the very example my critics produce, it is the intellect alone which corrects the error of the senses; and it is not possible to produce any case in which error results from our trusting the operation of the mind more than the senses.

10. My critics' remaining comments[2] are put forward as doubts rather than as objections, and I am not so confident of my powers as to venture to guarantee that I shall be able to give a satisfactory explanation of matters which I see still give rise to doubt in the minds of many learned and highly intelligent men. But nevertheless, so as not to desert the cause, I will do what I can and give a frank account of how it happened that I managed to free myself entirely from these same doubts. In so doing, I shall be delighted if my comments are perhaps of some help to others; and if they are not, I shall at least not feel myself to have made any rash promises.

When, on the basis of the arguments set out in these Meditations, I first drew the conclusion that the human mind is really distinct from the body, better known than the body, and so on, I was compelled to accept these results because everything in the reasoning was coherent and was inferred from quite evident principles in accordance with the rules of logic. But I confess that for all that I was not entirely convinced; I was in the same plight as astronomers who have established by argument that the sun is several times larger than the earth, and yet still cannot prevent themselves judging that it is smaller, when they actually look at it. However, I went on from here, and proceeded to apply the same fundamental principles to the consideration of physical things. First I attended to the ideas or notions of each particular thing which I found

1 Above p. 282. 2 *Ibid.*

within myself, and I carefully distinguished them one from the other so that all my judgements should match them. I observed as a result that nothing whatever belongs to the concept of body except the fact that it is something which has length, breadth and depth and is capable of various shapes and motions; moreover, these shapes and motions are merely modes which no power whatever can cause to exist apart from body. But colours, smells, tastes and so on, are, I observed, merely certain sensations which exist in my thought, and are as different from bodies as pain is different from the shape and motion of the weapon which produces it. And lastly, I observed that heaviness and hardness and the power to heat or to attract, or to purge, and all the other qualities which we experience in bodies, consist solely in the motion of bodies, or its absence, and the configuration and situation of their parts.

Since these opinions were completely different from those which I had 441 previously held regarding physical things, I next began to consider what had led me to take a different view before. The principal cause, I discovered, was this. From infancy I had made a variety of judgements about physical things in so far as they contributed to preserving the life which I was embarking on; and subsequently I retained the same opinions I had originally formed of these things. But at that age the mind employed the bodily organs less correctly than it now does, and was more firmly attached to them; hence it had no thoughts apart from them and perceived things only in a confused manner. Although it was aware of its own nature and had within itself an idea of thought as well as an idea of extension, it never exercised its intellect on anything without at the same time picturing something in the imagination. It therefore took thought and extension to be one and the same thing, and referred to the body all the notions which it had concerning things related to the intellect. Now I had never freed myself from these preconceived opinions in later life, and hence there was nothing that I knew with sufficient distinctness, and there was nothing I did not suppose to be corporeal; however, in the case of those very things that I supposed to be corporeal, the ideas or concepts which I formed were frequently such as to refer to minds rather than bodies.

For example, I conceived of gravity[1] as if it were some sort of real quality, which inhered in solid bodies; and although I called it a 'quality', thereby referring it to the bodies in which it inhered, by adding that it was 'real' I was in fact thinking that it was a substance. In the same way clothing, regarded in itself, is a substance, even though when referred to the man who wears it, it is a quality. Or again, the mind, even though it is 442 in fact a substance, can nonetheless be said to be a quality of the body to

---

1 Lat. *gravitas*, literally 'heaviness'.

which it is joined. And although I imagined gravity to be scattered throughout the whole body that is heavy, I still did not attribute to it the extension which constitutes the nature of a body. For the true extension of a body is such as to exclude any interpenetration of the parts, whereas I thought that there was the same amount of gravity in a ten foot piece of wood as in one foot lump of gold or other metal – indeed I thought that the whole of the gravity could be contracted to a mathematical point. Moreover, I saw that the gravity, while remaining coextensive with the heavy body, could exercise all its force in any one part of the body; for if the body were hung from a rope attached to any part of it, it would still pull the rope down with all its force, just as if all the gravity existed in the part actually touching the rope instead of being scattered through the remaining parts. This is exactly the way in which I now understand the mind to be coextensive with the body – the whole mind in the whole body and the whole mind in any one of its parts. But what makes it especially clear that my idea of gravity was taken largely from the idea I had of the mind is the fact that I thought that gravity carried bodies towards the centre of the earth as if it had some knowledge of the centre within itself. For this surely could not happen without knowledge, and there can be no knowledge except in a mind. Nevertheless I continued to apply to gravity various other attributes which cannot be understood to apply to a mind in this way – for example its being divisible, measurable and so on.

443   But later on I made the observations which led me to make a careful distinction between the idea of the mind and the ideas of body and corporeal motion; and I found that all those other ideas of 'real qualities' or 'substantial forms' which I had previously held were ones which I had put together or constructed from those basic ideas. And thus I very easily freed myself from all the doubts that my critics here put forward. First of all, I did not doubt that I 'had a clear idea of my mind', since I had a close inner awareness of it. Nor did I doubt that 'this idea was quite different from the ideas of other things', and that 'it contained nothing of a corporeal nature'.[1] For I had also looked for true ideas of all these 'other things', and I appeared to have some general acquaintance with all of them; yet everything I found in them was completely different from my idea of the mind. Moreover, I found that the distinction between things such as mind and body, which appeared distinct even though I attentively thought about both of them, is much greater than the distinction between things which are such that when we think of both of them we do not see how one can exist apart from the other (even though we may be able to understand one without thinking of the other). For example, we can

1 Above p. 283.

understand the immeasurable greatness of God even though we do not attend to his justice; but if we attend to both, it is quite self-contradictory to suppose that he is immeasurably great and yet not just. Again, it is possible to have true knowledge of the existence of God even though we lack knowledge of the Persons of the Holy Trinity, since the latter can be perceived only by a mind which faith has illuminated; yet when we do perceive them, I deny that it is intelligible to suppose that there is a real distinction between them, at least as far as the divine essence is   444 concerned, although such a distinction may be admitted as far as their mutual relationship is concerned.

Finally, I was not afraid of being so preoccupied with my method of analysis that I might have made the mistake suggested by my critics: seeing that there are 'certain bodies which do not think' (or, rather, clearly understanding that certain bodies can exist without thought), I preferred, they claim, to assert that thought does not belong to the nature of the body rather than to notice that there are certain bodies, namely human ones, which do think, and to infer that thought is a mode of the body.[1] In fact I have never seen or perceived that human bodies think; all I have seen is that there are human beings, who possess both thought and a body. This happens as a result of a thinking thing's being combined with a corporeal thing: I perceived this from the fact that when I examined a thinking thing on its own, I discovered nothing in it which belonged to body, and similarly when I considered corporeal nature on its own I discovered no thought in it. On the contrary, when I examined all the modes of body and mind, I did not observe a single mode the concept of which did not depend on the concept of the thing of which it was a mode. Also, the fact that we often see two things joined together does not license the inference that they are one and the same; but the fact that we sometimes observe one of them apart from the other entirely justifies the inference that they are different. Nor should the power of God deter us from making this inference. For it is a conceptual contradiction to suppose that two things which we clearly perceive as different should become one and the same (that is intrinsically one and   445 the same, as opposed to by combination); this is no less a contradiction than to suppose that two things which are in no way distinct should be separated. Hence, if God has implanted the power of thought in certain bodies (as he in fact has done in the case of human bodies), then he can remove this power from them, and hence it still remains really distinct from them.

It is true that, before freeing myself from the preconceived opinions acquired from the senses, I did perceive correctly that two and three

1 Cf. p. 283.

make five, and that if equals are taken from equals the remainders are equal, and many things of this kind; and yet I did not think that the soul of man is distinct from his body.[1] But I do not find this surprising. For I can easily see why it happened that, when still an infant, I never made any false judgements about propositions of this sort, which everyone accepts; the reason was that I had no occasion to employ these propositions, since children do not learn to count two and three until they are capable of judging whether they make five. But, by contrast, I had from my earliest years conceived of my mind and body as a unity of some sort (for I had a confused awareness that I was composed of mind and body). It happens in almost every case of imperfect knowledge that many things are apprehended together as a unity, though they will later have to be distinguished by a more careful examination.

What does greatly surprise me is that learned men who have 'practised metaphysical studies for thirty years' and have read my *Meditations* 'seven times' consider that if I re-read them in the spirit of analytical 446 scrutiny which I would adopt if they had been put forward by an opponent, I would not believe that the arguments contained there had the kind of 'weight or strength' that ought to lead everyone to assent to them.[2] It is surprising that my critics should say this even though they themselves cannot point to any flaw whatsoever in these arguments of mine. They certainly give me more credit than they should, or than should be given to anyone, if they think that the kind of 'analysis' I employ is one which enables true demonstrations to be overthrown and false ones to be so disguised and tricked out that no one is capable of refuting them. On the contrary, I declare that the only method I have sought is one which will enable the certainty of true arguments to be known and the flaws in false ones to be detected. Hence I am struck not so much by the fact that there are learned men who do not yet accept my conclusions as by the fact that, after a careful and repeated re-reading of my arguments they can point to no false assumptions or invalid inferences in what I have written. As to their reluctance to accept the conclusions, that can easily be attributed to the inveterate habit of making different judgements on these matters; they are just like the astronomers who, as noted earlier, do not find it easy to picture the sun as being bigger than the earth although they can demonstrate this by most reliable arguments. But the only possible reason that I can see why neither these critics, nor, as far as I know, any others, have so far been able to fault my arguments is that they possess complete truth and certainty; in particular, they are deduced step by step, not from principles which are obscure and unknown, but, in the first place, from total doubt

1 Above p. 283.   2 Above pp. 283f.

about all things, and, in the second place, from principles which appear to be utterly evident and certain to the mind, once it has been set free from preconceived opinions. It follows from this that there cannot be any mistakes in my arguments which would not be noticed without difficulty by anyone of even moderate intelligence. Hence I think I can justly conclude that if these learned gentlemen cannot yet accept my conclusions after several close readings, their authority does not so much weaken what I have written as strengthen it, since after such a careful and repeated examination, they have failed to note any errors or fallacies in my demonstrations.

447

SEVENTH SET OF OBJECTIONS WITH THE AUTHOR'S
REPLIES

or

'An essay on First Philosophy'
together with the author's comments[1]

[Bourdin]

A   You ask me many questions, distinguished Sir, regarding your new
method for investigating the truth, and you beg – indeed you insistently
B   demand – that I should give my reply. But I shall keep silent and refuse to
humour you unless you agree to the following. First, let us throughout
our discussion completely ignore the contributions of those who have
written or spoken on this subject. Further, will you please frame your
questions in such a way as to avoid appearing to ask about the views of
others, or their intentions, or the results of their work, or whether or not
their opinions were correct. I ask you to behave as if no one had ever had
any views or written or spoken anything on these matters, and to ask
only the questions which seem to you to present some difficulty as you
meditate and pursue your new method of philosophizing. This will
enable us to search for the truth and to do so in a way which will keep
safe and intact those laws of friendship and respect which should govern
the dealings of learned men. Since you signify your agreement, and
promise to follow this suggestion, I shall respond appropriately. And so
we may proceed.

[Descartes]

COMMENTS

A   'You ask me many questions'. I received this essay from its author after I
had earnestly asked him 'either to publish or at least send me' the
comments which I heard he had written on my *Meditations on First*
452   *Philosophy*, 'so that they might be added to the other objections to the

---

1   The 'essay' comprising the objections is by Bourdin; the interspersed 'comments' are by
Descartes. See Translator's preface, above p. 64. The marginal letters (which appeared in
the original 1642 edition) are designed to help the reader correlate Descartes' comments
with Bourdin's objections.

[Descartes]

Meditations which others had produced'.[1] Hence I could not refuse to include his work here. I cannot doubt that I am the person addressed in the above passage, even though I certainly do not remember ever having asked the writer for his opinion of my method of investigating the truth. On the contrary, when, some eighteen months ago, I saw a preliminary attack of his against me which, in my judgement, did not attempt to discover the truth but foisted on me views which I had never written or thought, I did not hide the fact that I would in future regard anything which he as an individual produced as unworthy of a reply. But since he is a member of a society which is very famous for its learning and piety,[2] and whose members are all in such close union with each other that it is rare that anything is done by one of them which is not approved by all, I confess that I did not only 'beg' but also 'insistently demand' that some members of the society should examine what I had written and be kind enough to point out to me anything which departed from the truth. I also added many reasons which I hoped would make them agree to my request, and I said that, because of this hope,

If either this author or any other member of the society should in future write anything concerning my opinions, I should value it very highly. And whatever name it bore, I would be certain that it was not composed by one member but that several of the most learned and prudent members of the Society had examined and corrected it; and therefore it would be sure to contain no quibbles or sophisms or abuse or empty verbiage, but only arguments of the strongest and   453
most solid kind. I could also be confident that no points which could legitimately be brought against me would be omitted, and hence that this one work of criticism would free me from all my errors. Moreover, if anything I had published was not refuted in this work, I would believe that it was incapable of being refuted by anyone, and that it was entirely true and certain.[3]

Now I would take the same view of the present essay, and believe that it was written at the instigation of the Society as a whole, if only I were certain that it contained no quibbles or sophisms or abuse or empty verbiage. But if this is not the case, I shall think it a sin to suspect that this work was produced by men of such sanctity. In this matter I do not trust my own judgement, and so I will here state my views frankly and openly, not because I want the reader in any way to take my word on this matter, but simply because I want to give him an opportunity to examine the truth.

1 Descartes conveyed this request to Bourdin via a letter to Mersenne of 22 December 1641.
2 The Jesuits.
3 Descartes did not communicate directly with the Jesuits; the comments reported here are from a letter to Mersenne of 30 August 1640.

[Descartes]

B   'But I shall keep silent' etc. Here the writer promises that he will not
attack anyone's writings, but will merely reply to my questions. But I have
never asked him any questions – indeed I have never even spoken to the
man or set eyes on him. The questions which he pretends I have put to
him are for the most part constructed out of phrases to be found in my
Meditations, and thus it is quite clear that the *Meditations* are his sole
target. He may have honourable and pious motives for pretending that
this is not so, but I cannot but suspect that he thinks that adopting this
454   pretence will leave him all the freer to foist any view he likes on to me; for
it will be impossible to show that he is misrepresenting what I wrote if he
claims that he is not attacking my writings. What is more, I suspect that
he is trying to avoid giving his readers cause to consult my writings, as
would perhaps happen if he actually mentioned them. He apparently
prefers to represent me as so foolish and ignorant that his readers will be
deterred from looking at anything I have produced. So what he does is to
take fragments from my *Meditations* and ineptly piece them together so
as to make a mask which will not so much cover as distort my features.
But I hereby pull off the mask and throw it away, because in the first
place I am not used to play-acting, and in the second place it is quite out
of place here, when I am debating a very serious issue with a man who
belongs to a religious order.

[Bourdin]
First question:
whether things that are doubtful should be regarded
as false, and if so, how

Your first question is about the legitimacy of your rule for investigating
the truth, *viz.* 'that we should regard as false whatever contains even a
minimal element of doubt'.[1] If I am to reply, I must ask you some
questions:
   (1) What is the 'minimal element of doubt' you refer to?
   (2) What is meant by 'regarding something as false'?
   (3) To what extent should we 'regard something as false'?

455   1. *What is the 'minimal element of doubt'?*
As far as doubt is concerned, what is the 'minimal element' you speak of?
'I can answer briefly', you may say. 'Firstly, if there is anything whose
C   existence or whose nature I can doubt, not rashly but for powerful
                    1 Cf. Med. II, above p. 16.

[Bourdin]
reasons, then it contains some element of doubt. But, secondly, there is also an element of doubt in things concerning which, though they may seem clear to me, some evil demon may deceive me; for he may wish to trick me and bring it about by his cunning devices that something may appear clear and certain though it is in fact false. Now items in the first category contain a considerable element of doubt, whereas those in the second contain a small element of doubt which although "minimal" is sufficient to justify the label "doubtful" and to make the doubt a real one. If you want an example, then the existence of the earth, and the sky, and of colours, and the belief that you have a head and eyes and a body and a mind, are matters which are doubtful in terms of the first category of doubt; while to the second category belong such beliefs as that two and three make five, or that the whole is greater than one of its parts, and so on.'

Brilliant! But if this is so, what, may I ask, will there be that is left free of doubt? What will be immune from the fear with which that crafty demon threatens us? 'Nothing', you may reply, 'absolutely nothing, until D
we have established for certain, on the basis of the most solid metaphysical principles, that God exists and cannot be a deceiver; for the one rule here is that if I lack knowledge of whether God exists and whether, if he exists, he can be a deceiver, I do not see that I can ever be wholly certain of anything.[1] But let me make my meaning thoroughly clear to you. Until I know that God exists, and is a truthful God who will curb that evil demon, then I can – and indeed should – continue to fear that the demon is tricking me and is forcing what is false on to me under the guise of truth, as though it were clear and certain. But when I have gained a thorough understanding that God exists and can neither be deceived nor deceive, I know he will necessarily prevent the demon imposing on me 456
concerning things which I clearly and distinctly understand. And I shall then be able to say that if there are any such things, if I do perceive anything clearly and distinctly, then these things are true and certain. And so I will have my rule of truth and certainty, *viz.* that everything which I very clearly and distinctly perceive is true.'[2] I have no further questions to raise here, and so I come to the second point.

2. What is meant by 'regarding something as false'?
Since on your view it is doubtful whether you have eyes, a head or a body, and you must therefore consider all this as false, I should like to know exactly what you mean by this. Is it a matter of saying and believing 'it is false that I have eyes, a head and a body'? Must I 'turn my will in

1 Cf. Med. III, above p. 25.   2 Cf. Med. III, above p. 24.

[Bourdin]

completely the opposite direction',[1] believing and saying 'I do not have eyes, a head, or a body'? In a word, must I say, believe and maintain the
E opposite of that which is doubtful? 'Exactly', you reply. Fine. But I still need some answers. Is it not certain that two and three make five? And should I therefore believe and maintain that two and three do not make five? 'Yes, you must believe it and maintain it', you reply. But I now go further. It is not certain that while I speak these words, I am awake and not dreaming. Should I therefore say and believe that while I am speaking, I am not awake but dreaming? 'Yes', you say, 'believe it and say it.' To avoid being tedious, let me finally come to the point. If someone doubts whether he is awake or asleep, it is not certain that what appears clear and certain to him is in fact clear and certain. Should I therefore say and believe that if something appears clear and certain to one who doubts whether he is awake or asleep, then it is not clear and certain, but obscure and false? Why do you hesitate? You cannot possibly go too far in your distrustful attitude.[2] Has it never happened to you, as it has to many people, that things seemed clear and certain to you while you were dreaming, but that afterwards you discovered that they were doubtful or false? It is indeed 'prudent never to trust completely
457 F those who have deceived you even once'.[3] 'But', you reply, 'matters of the utmost certainty are quite different. They are such that they cannot appear doubtful even to those who are dreaming or mad.' But are you really serious in what you say? Can you pretend that matters of the utmost certainty cannot appear doubtful even to dreamers or madmen? What are these utterly certain matters? If things which are ridiculous or absurd sometimes appear certain, even utterly certain, to people who are asleep or insane, then why should not things which are certain, even utterly certain, appear false and doubtful? I know a man who once, when falling asleep, heard the clock strike four, and counted the strokes as 'one, one, one, one'. It then seemed to him that there was something absurd about this, and he shouted out: 'That clock must be going mad; it has struck one o'clock four times!' Is there really anything so absurd or irrational that it could not come into the mind of someone who is asleep or raving? There are no limits to what a dreamer may not 'prove' or believe, and indeed congratulate himself on, as if he had managed to invent some splendid thought. But to avoid fighting you on many fronts at once, let me come to your maxim 'If something appears certain to someone who is in doubt whether he is dreaming or awake, then it *is* certain – indeed so certain that it can be laid down as a basic principle of a scientific and metaphysical system of the highest certainty and exactness.'

1 The phrase is lifted from Med. 1, above p. 15.   2 *Ibid.*   3 Med. 1, above p. 12.

[Bourdin]
You have not at any point managed to make me consider this maxim to be as certain as the proposition that two and three make five; you have not shown it to be so certain that no one can possibly have any kind of doubt about it, or be deceived about it by an evil demon. And if I persist in this view, I have no fear that anyone will regard me as obstinate. So on the basis of your rule, I reach the following result: it is not certain that what appears as certain to a person who is in doubt whether he is awake or asleep, is in fact certain; and hence what appears certain to someone who is in doubt whether he is awake or asleep can and should be regarded as entirely false. Alternatively, if you have some other special rule which you have devised, please communicate it to me. I now come to my third question.

3. *To what extent should we 'regard something as false'?*   458
Since it does not seem certain that two and three make five, and since the above rule obliges me to say and believe that two and three do not make five, may I ask whether I should constantly believe this, to the extent of convincing myself that it is certain and cannot be otherwise? You are amazed at my question. This is not surprising to me, since I am amazed at it myself. But you must still answer it, if you expect me to answer in turn. Do you mean to regard it as certain that two and three do not make five? Do you mean this to be certain, and to appear as certain to everyone – so certain that it is safe even from the tricks of the evil demon?

You laugh and say 'How could any sane man arrive at that idea?' But what is the alternative? Will our statement be doubtful and uncertain, just like the statement that two and three do make five? If so, if the statement that two and three do not make five is doubtful, then following your rule I will believe and state that it is false and I will assert the opposite: I will assert that two and three do make five. I shall behave in the same way when it comes to my other beliefs; and since it does not seem to be certain that any body exists, I shall say 'No body exists'; and since the statement that no body exists is not certain, I shall then turn my will in completely the opposite direction and say 'Bodies do exist'. And so bodies will both exist and not exist at the same time.

'That is right', you say. 'Doubting is just this – going round in a circle,   G advancing and retreating, affirming and denying, banging in the nail and then pulling it out to bang it in again.'

Splendid. But what am I to do when it comes to making use of those statements which were doubtful? What shall I do concerning the statement that two and three make five, or the statement that bodies do exist? Shall I affirm them, or deny them?

[Bourdin]

'Neither affirm, nor deny them', you say. 'Employ neither statement, but regard them both as false; and do not expect such shaky propositions 459 to yield anything which is not itself shaky, doubtful and uncertain.'

Since there is nothing left for me to ask, I shall now answer in my turn by providing a brief summary of your position.

(1) We can doubt all things, especially material things, so long as we have no foundations for the sciences other than those we have had up till now.[1]

(2) To consider something as false is to withhold our assent from it as if it were an evident falsehood, and to turn our will in completely the opposite direction, adopting an opinion of it that is appropriate to something false and imaginary.[2]

(3) What is doubtful should be regarded as false to the extent of regarding its opposite as being equally doubtful and false.

[Descartes]

COMMENTS

It would be embarrassing for me to be over-zealous and produce an extended commentary on all these claims; for although they are expressed virtually in my own words, I do not recognize them as mine. I will merely ask my readers to recall what I wrote in the First Meditation, at the start of the Second and Third Meditations and in the Synopsis. If they do this, they will recognize that my critic has lifted almost everything which is included above from these sources, but that he has so mixed up and distorted and misinterpreted the material that although everything in the original is very rational, this version makes it seem for the most part to be quite absurd.

C   'For powerful reasons'.[3] I said at the end of the First Meditation that we may doubt all those things which we have not yet perceived with 460 sufficient clarity, since our doubt is based on 'powerful and well thought-out reasons'.[4] But I said this because at that point I was dealing merely with the kind of extreme doubt which, as I frequently stressed, is metaphysical and exaggerated and in no way to be transferred to practical life.[5] It was doubt of this type to which I was referring when I said that everything that could give rise to the slightest suspicion should

1 Cf. Synopsis, above p. 9.   2 Cf. Med. I, above p. 15.
3 To determine which of Bourdin's remarks Descartes is addressing, here and throughout the discussion, simply refer to the relevant marginal letter. Thus letter C appears above on p. 304, etc.
4 Above pp. 14f.
5 Med. I, p. 15; Med. III, p. 25; Med. VI, p. 61; Synopsis, p. 11.

[Descartes]

be regarded as a sound reason for doubt. But my friendly and ingenuous critic here puts forward as an example of the things that I said we could doubt 'for powerful reasons' the question of whether there is an earth, or whether I have a body, and so on; the effect is that the reader, if he knows nothing of my 'metaphysical' doubt and refers the doubt to practical life, may think that I am not of sound mind.

'"Nothing," you reply, "absolutely nothing".' I have explained, in D several places, the sense in which this 'nothing' is to be understood. It is this. So long as we attend to a truth which we perceive very clearly, we cannot doubt it. But when, as often happens, we are not attending to any truth in this way, then even though we remember that we have previously perceived many things very clearly, nevertheless there will be nothing which we may not justly doubt so long as we do not know that whatever we clearly perceive is true.[1] But my careful critic here takes 'nothing' quite differently. From the fact that at one point I said that there was nothing that we might not doubt – namely in the First Meditation, in which I was supposing that I was not attending to anything that I clearly perceived – he draws the conclusion that I am unable to know anything certain, even in the following Meditations. This is to suggest that the reasons which may from time to time give us cause to doubt something are not legitimate or sound unless they prove that the same thing must be permanently in doubt.

'Must I say, believe, and maintain the opposite of what is doubtful?' E When I said that doubtful matters should for a time be treated as false, or 461 rejected as false, I merely meant that when investigating the truths that have metaphysical certainty we should regard doubtful matters as not having any more basis than those which are quite false. I made this so clear that I do not think anyone of sound mind could interpret what I said in any other way; surely only someone who would not blush to be called a quibbler could pretend that it was my intention to believe the opposite of what is doubtful, let alone to believe this 'to the extent of convincing myself that it is certain and cannot be otherwise'.[2] And although my critic does not go so far as to insist on the interpretation just quoted, but merely raises it in the form of a question, I am surprised that a man of such sanctity has been willing to imitate those disgraceful detractors who often try to slander an author with impunity by giving an account of his work which they intend others to believe and then adding that they 'do not believe it themselves'.

'But matters of the utmost certainty are quite different. They are such F that they cannot appear doubtful even to those who are dreaming or

1 Cf. Second Replies, p. 100; Fourth Replies, p. 171.   2 Cf. p. 307.

[Descartes]

mad.' I do not know what kind of analysis has enabled my supremely subtle critic to deduce this from my writings, for I do not remember ever having had any such thought, even in a dream. Admittedly he might have inferred from what I wrote that everything that anyone clearly and distinctly perceives is true, although the person in question may from time to time doubt whether he is dreaming or awake, and may even, if you like, be dreaming or mad. For no matter who the perceiver is, nothing can be clearly and distinctly perceived without its being just as
462   we perceive it to be, i.e. without being true. But because it requires some care to make a proper distinction between what is clearly and distinctly perceived and what merely seems or appears to be, I am not surprised that my worthy critic should here mistake the one for the other.

G   'Doubting is just this, going round in a circle' etc. What I said was that doubtful items should not be regarded as having any more basis than those which are wholly false;[1] but this was so as to enable us to dismiss them completely from our thought, and not so as to allow us to affirm first one thing and then its opposite. But my critic has seized every possible opportunity to quibble. Incidentally, it is worth noting that at the end, when he says he is providing a brief summary of my position, he does not attribute to me any of the doctrines which he criticizes or ridicules either in his earlier comments or in what follows. This is presumably to let us know that he has foisted these doctrines on me merely as a joke, without seriously believing that I held them.

[Bourdin]
                          REPLY[2]

Reply 1. Consider the rule that in the investigation of the truth, whatever contains even a minimal element of doubt should be regarded as false. If this means that when we try to find what is certain we should not in any way rely on those things which are not certain or which contain any element of doubt, then the rule is a valid one; indeed, it is widely accepted and extremely common among philosophers of all kinds.

Reply 2. The said rule might be interpreted as follows. When we are trying to find what is certain, we should reject things which are not certain, or which are in any way doubtful, to the extent of not making any use of them and considering them as non-existent – or rather not considering them at all but completely dismissing them from our mind. This rule, too, is a valid and reliable one; indeed, it is a well-worn maxim

---

1 Cf. Med. 1, above p. 15.
2 Bourdin's 'reply' is addressed to the question he himself raised, above p. 304.

[Bourdin]

even among beginners, and is so closely related to the preceding rule that   463
it scarcely differs from it.

Reply 3. Suppose the said rule is taken as follows. When we are trying to find what is certain we should reject whatever is doubtful in the sense of supposing that it is in fact non-existent and that its opposite really obtains; and we should employ this supposition as a firm basis for our inquiry, treating the doubtful items as non-existent and relying on their non-existence. Now this rule is an invalid and fallacious one which conflicts with sound philosophy. For in order to find out what is true and certain, it makes a supposition which is doubtful and uncertain; or it supposes as certain that which may in fact be wholly otherwise, by treating doubtful items as not really existing when it is possible that they do exist.

Reply 4. If anyone were to understand the rule in the sense just described and wanted to use it in order to discover what is true and certain, he would be wasting his time and effort and would be working without any reward, since he would no more achieve his goal than its opposite. Do you want an example? Suppose someone is inquiring whether it is possible that he is a body, or is corporeal, and he makes use, among other things, of the following principle: 'It is not certain that any body exists; therefore, in accordance with the rule just adopted, I shall   H
maintain and assert that no body exists.' He will then go on as follows. 'No body exists; but I am and exist, as has been properly established from other sources; therefore I cannot be a body.' A splendid argument; but see how the same initial premiss will enable him to derive the opposite conclusion. 'It is not certain', he says, 'that any body exists; hence, in accordance with the rule I shall maintain and assert that no body exists. But what sort of claim is the statement that no body exists? It is surely a doubtful and uncertain one, for who can establish its truth, or on what basis? The result is clear. The statement that no body exists is doubtful; hence in accordance with the rule I shall say "Some body exists." For I am and exist; hence I may possibly be a body if nothing else rules this out.' So you see I can be a body and I cannot be a body. Have I satisfied you? Only too well, I fear, if I may judge from the questions that   464
follow. And so I will come to your second question.

[Descartes]

COMMENTS

In his first two replies here, my critic gives his approval to all the views, whether explicitly stated in my writings or derivable from them, which I

[Descartes]

hold concerning the topic under discussion. But he adds that my position is 'extremely common and well-worn even among beginners'. In his third and fourth replies, however, he criticizes a view which he wants people to think I hold, even though it is so absurd that it could not possibly enter the mind of a sane man. This is very clever of him: his aim is to impose on those who have either not read my *Meditations* or else not read them attentively enough to have accurate knowledge of their contents, and influence them by his authority into thinking I hold ridiculous views. And in the case of any others who do not believe this, he hopes at least to convince them that I have not produced anything which is not 'extremely common and well-worn even among beginners'. I would certainly not argue with the last statement. For I have never sought any praise for the novelty of my opinions. On the contrary, I consider my opinions to be the oldest opinions of all, since they are the truest. My principal aim has always been to draw attention to certain very simple truths which are innate in our minds, so that as soon as they are pointed out to others, they will consider that they have always known them. It is easy to recognize that my critic is attacking my views precisely because he thinks they are sound and original; for if he really believed that they were as absurd as he pretends, he would surely have judged them worthy of contempt and silence rather than such a lengthy and contrived refutation.

465
H

'Therefore, in accordance with the rule just adopted, I shall maintain and assert the opposite.' I should like to know when and in what statutes my critic found this law written down. He has certainly laid quite enough stress on it in his remarks above, but equally, in my comments on the sentence 'Must I say, believe and maintain the opposite of what is doubtful?',[1] I have made it clear enough that the rule is not my own. Moreover, I do not think he will be able to go on maintaining that the rule is mine if he is questioned on the matter. Under heading (3) above, he presented me as saying with regard to things which are doubtful, that we should 'neither affirm nor deny them; employ neither statement but regard them both as false'.[2] But a little later, in his summary of my position, he has it that we should 'withhold our assent from something doubtful as if it were an evident falsehood, and turn our will in completely the opposite direction, adopting an opinion of it that is appropriate to something false and imaginary'.[3] Now this is quite different from 'maintaining and saying the opposite' in the sense of regarding the opposite as true in the way he supposes me to be doing here. When in the First Meditation I said that I wanted for a time to try to convince myself of the opposite of the views which I had rashly held before, I immediately

1 Above p. 309.   2 Above p. 308.   3 *Ibid.*

[Descartes]

added that my reason for wanting to do this was as it were to counter-balance the weight of preconceived opinion so that I should not incline to one side more than the other.[1] I did not mean that I should regard either side as true, or set this principle up as the basis of a system of supremely certain knowledge, as my critic elsewhere unfairly maintains. So I should like to know what purpose he had in mind in introducing this law of his. If it was to foist it on to me, then his honesty leaves something to be desired; for it is clear from what he himself says that he is quite well aware that the rule is not mine. No one could possibly think that both alternatives should be regarded as false (which he said was my view), and at the same time maintain and assert that one of the two opposites was true (as this rule of his has it). But if he merely introduced the rule to amuse himself, so as to have something to attack, then I am amazed that his ingenuity has been unable to devise anything more plausible or subtle. I am also amazed that he has the leisure to produce such a verbose refutation of an opinion which is so absurd that it would not even strike a seven year old child as plausible; for we must remember that up till now his attacks have been limited to this foolish rule. Lastly, I am amazed at the power of his imagination; for even though he is doing battle only with a totally empty mirage which his own brain has produced, he has throughout adopted the same attitude, and used the same words, as if I myself had been his adversary, and he had seen me fighting him face to face.

466

[Bourdin]

Second question:
whether renouncing everything that is doubtful
is a good method of philosophizing

Your second question is whether it is a good method of philosophizing to renounce everything which is in any way doubtful. Unless you disclose your method at greater length, you have no reason to expect an answer from me. But you do in fact expound the method as follows.

'In order to philosophize', you say, 'in order to examine whether there is anything certain, or supremely certain, and if so what, I proceed as follows. Since everything I have previously believed or known is doubtful and uncertain, I consider it as false and completely reject it. I convince myself that there exists neither earth, nor sky, nor any of the things which I previously believed to be in the world; indeed, I suppose that there is

J
467

1 Above p. 15.

[Bourdin]

not a world at all, or any body or mind – in a word, that there is nothing. Then, after completing this general dismissal of my beliefs and declaring that there is nothing, I embark in earnest on my own philosophy; using it as a guide, I follow the trail of truth and certainty with care and caution, just as if there were some supremely powerful and cunning demon who wished to lead me into error. To avoid being deceived I look round carefully and decide to accept only things of the kind which provide no possible scope whatever for that rascally demon to impose on me, no matter how hard he tries – the kinds of fact that not even I can make myself refuse to acknowledge, or bring myself to deny. So I reflect and turn things over and over in my mind until some fact of this sort occurs to me; and when I come across it I use it as an Archimedean point on which to construct other truths, and in this way I arrive step by step at further facts that are wholly certain and thoroughly scrutinized.'[1]

This is quite excellent, and I might easily reply that on the surface the method seems to me to be an outstandingly brilliant one; but since you expect me to give a careful reply, and I cannot give one until I have tried and tested this method of yours by actual practice, let us set out on this safe and well-trodden road ourselves, and discover where it eventually leads us. Since you know every bend and defile and detour on the way, and have for a long time trained yourself to follow it, I ask you to be my guide. You now have either a companion or a pupil ready to accompany you, so tell me please, what are your orders? Although for me the road is new and frightening, since I am not accustomed to the darkness, I am happy to set out because the prospect of the truth is a powerful lure. I hear you: you command me to do whatever I see you doing, and to tread in your footsteps. This is a splendid way of giving your orders and guidance, and I am delighted with your response. I am all ears.

468   §1. AN APPROACH TO THE METHOD IS REVEALED

'First of all', you say, 'after going over my previous opinions, I am finally compelled to admit that there is not one of my former beliefs about which a doubt may not properly be raised; and this is not a flippant or ill-considered conclusion but is based on powerful and well thought-out reasons. So in future I must withhold my assent from these former beliefs just as carefully as I would from obvious falsehoods if I want to discover any certainty. In view of this I think it will be a good plan to turn my will in completely the opposite direction and deceive myself by pretend-

1 None of this is exact quotation, but it is reminiscent of, and sometimes a distortion of, material to be found at the end of Med. 1 and beginning of Med. 11.

[Bourdin]

ing for a time that these former opinions are utterly false and imaginary. I shall do this until the weight of preconceived opinion is counter-balanced and the distorting influence of habit no longer prevents my judgement from perceiving things correctly. I will suppose therefore, that some malicious demon of the utmost power and cunning has employed all his energies in order to deceive me. I shall think that the sky, the air, the earth, colours, shapes, sounds and all external things are merely the delusions of dreams which he has devised to ensnare my judgement. I shall convince myself that there is nothing at all in the world, no sky, no earth, no minds or bodies. I repeat: no minds, and no bodies; this is the K
chief point here. I shall consider myself as having no hands, no eyes, no flesh or blood or senses, but as falsely believing that I have all these things. I shall stubbornly and firmly persist in this meditation.'[1]

Here, with your permission, let us pause a little to gather our strength 469
afresh. The novelty of your enterprise disturbs me somewhat. Are you telling me to renounce all my former beliefs?

'Yes I am', you say, 'All of them'.

All of them? This implies no exceptions. L

'All of them', you repeat.

I am reluctant to obey and yet I will. But it is extremely hard, and, to tell the truth, I have some scruples in complying; and unless you remove my scruples I fear that we shall not succeed in making our planned entry into your method. You acknowledge that all your former beliefs are doubtful, and you claim that you are compelled to admit this. But why M
not let me feel the same constraints so that I am compelled to admit it too? What compels you, may I ask? I heard you say just now that you had 'powerful and well thought-out reasons'. But what are they? And if they are powerful, why renounce them? Why not keep them? If, on the other hand, they are doubtful and completely suspect, how have they managed to force or compel you?

'Here they are, out in the open', you say. 'I make a habit of sending them out in front like skirmishers to begin the battle. The senses sometimes deceive us; we sometimes dream. Some people periodically go mad and think they see things which they really are not seeing at all and which exist nowhere.'

Is that all? When you promised me 'powerful and well thought-out reasons', I expected ones which were certain and free from all doubt – reasons of the kind which are demanded by this little pamphlet of yours which we are examining, since it invokes such a high standard of care as

---

1 Extracts from Med. 1, above pp. 14f. But the two sentences at letter K ('I shall convince myself . . . chief point here') are Bourdin's own insertion.

[Bourdin]
to rule out the faintest shadow of doubt. But are your reasons of this
sort? Are they any more than hesitant suspicions? 'The senses sometimes
deceive us', 'Sometimes we dream', 'Some people go mad.' How do you
establish these claims beyond any doubt with the kind of certainty
demanded by that rule of yours which you continue to brandish – 'we
must take great care not to admit anything as true which we cannot
470   prove to be so'? Has there been a time when you were able to make any
of the following statements with certainty: 'At this moment the senses are
indubitably deceiving me; this I know for sure'; 'Now I am dreaming'; 'I
was dreaming a moment ago'; 'This man is delirious and quite sincerely
thinks he sees things which he is not seeing at all'? If you say that there
have been such occasions, make sure to prove it; make sure that the evil
demon which you referred to was not perhaps tricking you. There is a
serious risk that even while you are saying 'The senses sometimes deceive
us', even though you regard this as a powerful and well thought-out
consideration, the rascal of a demon is cocking a snook at you because he
has tricked you all along. If, on the other hand, you say that there have
N   not been any such occasions, why do you assert with such confidence that
we sometimes dream? Why not follow your first law and reason as
follows: 'It is not wholly certain that the senses have sometimes deceived
us, or that we have sometimes dreamed, or that people have sometimes
gone mad; hence I will assert and insist that the senses never deceive us,
we never dream and no one goes mad.'
     'But I suspect that these things do happen', you reply.
     Here is my worry. Wherever I have trodden, I have found these
'powerful reasons' of yours to be feeble and to resemble fleeting
suspicions, and this is why I have been reluctant to press on. In short, I
am suspicious.
     'But I am just as suspicious myself', you reply. 'Mere suspicion is all
that is needed here. It is enough to say "I do not know whether I am
awake or asleep", or "I do not know whether the senses are deceiving me
or not".'
     If I may say so, it is not enough for me. I just do not see how you move
from 'I do not know whether I am awake or dreaming' to 'I sometimes
dream.' What if I never dream? What if I always do? What if you are not
even capable of dreaming, and the demon is hooting with laughter
because he has managed to persuade you that you sometimes dream and
are deceived, when this in fact never happens? Believe me: since bringing
that demon into the argument, since reducing your 'powerful and well
thought-out reasons' to a mere 'perhaps', you have conjured up an evil
O   which has produced no benefits for you at all. What if the cunning demon

[Bourdin]

is presenting all these matters to you as doubtful and shaky when in fact   471
they are firm and certain? What if he intends thereby to drive you into a
pit, once you have stripped yourself by renouncing all these beliefs?
Would it not be more sensible if, before divesting yourself, you were to
put forward a reliable rule to ensure that the beliefs which you do
renounce are ones which you are right to renounce? This general
renunciation of all former beliefs is surely a considerable enterprise and   P
one of the greatest importance, and if you take my advice you will first
summon your thoughts to the council chamber for a serious discussion.

   'No', you reply. 'I cannot possibly go too far in my distrustful attitude,
and I know that no danger or error will result from my plan.'[1]

   What are you saying? You *know*? Is this certain and beyond all doubt?   Q
Is this the sole surviving timber from the great shipwreck that is to be
hung up as an offering in the temple of truth? Or, since you are opening a
new school of philosophy and thinking of your disciples, is it that you
want this inscription to be placed over the door in gold letters: 'I cannot
go too far in my distrustful attitude'? Will the students who enter your
precincts be told to lay aside the old belief that 'Two and three make five',
but to retain the maxim 'I cannot go too far in my distrustful attitude'?
But what will you say if one of your new students happens to complain?
What if it sticks in his throat when he is ordered to abandon the old belief
that two and three make five, which no one has ever called into doubt,
just because it is possible that some demon may be deceiving him, and yet
he is ordered to retain this doubtful maxim that is full of flaws – 'I cannot   R
go too far in my distrustful attitude' – as if this was something which
gave the demon no scope for imposing on him? What is your answer
here? Will you guarantee that I need have no fear or apprehension or
worry about the evil demon? Even if you give me every possible
reassurance I shall still be very afraid of overdoing my distrustful attitude   S
if I renounce and forswear as false such long-standing and virtually
innate beliefs as 'A syllogism in Barbara[2] has a valid conclusion', or 'I am   472
something composed of body and mind.' And to judge by your expression and your voice, not even you, who are leading the way and offering
yourself as a guide for the rest of us, are immune from fear. Come then;
tell me straightforwardly and honestly, as is your custom. Do you really
have no scruples about renouncing such long-standing beliefs as the   T
following: 'I have a clear and distinct idea of God'; 'Everything that I
clearly and distinctly perceive is true'; or 'Thinking, nutrition and   V
sensation do not in any way belong to the body but belong to the mind'?

---

1 Cf.p. 15, above.
2 A syllogism of the form 'All M is P; all S is M; therefore, all S is P'.

[Bourdin]

I could list a hundred other such questions. My inquiries here are quite serious and I ask you to reply. In leaving the old philosophy and embarking on the new, can you sincerely shake off, reject and forswear these beliefs? Can you assert and maintain the opposite, *viz.* 'Now I do not have a clear and distinct idea of God'; 'I have been wrong to believe up till now that thinking, sensation and nutrition belong to the mind and not in any way to the body'? But what have I done? How quickly I have forgotten what I promised! At the beginning I pledged myself to you entirely as your companion and disciple, and yet here I am hesitating at the very start of our journey, full of scruples and obstinacy. Forgive me; I have sinned greatly, and have merely displayed my weakness of mind. I should have left all fear aside and plunged intrepidly into the darkness of renunciation; but I have hesitated and drawn back. If you show forbearance, I will make amends and will wipe out my evil deeds by a full and free rejection of all my former beliefs. I renounce and forswear all my former opinions. Excuse me for not calling the heavens and earth to witness my vow, since you claim that they do not exist. Nothing exists, then, absolutely nothing. Lead the way and I shall follow. You are an easy guide to follow, for you readily agree to go first.

[Descartes]

COMMENTS

J 473 'Since what I have previously known is doubtful'. Here my critic has put 'known' instead of 'thought I knew'. The statement 'I knew' is incompatible with the statement 'It is doubtful', though he has undoubtedly failed to notice this. We must not attribute this to malice, for if malice had been involved he would not have touched on the point so briefly but would have pretended that the contradiction was of my making and would have produced a prolonged torrent of criticism.

K 'I repeat, no minds and no bodies'. He says this to enable him to indulge in a protracted piece of quibbling later on. At the outset, when I was supposing that I had not yet sufficiently perceived the nature of the mind, I included it in the list of doubtful things; but later on, when I realized that a thing that thinks cannot but exist, I used the term 'mind' to refer to this thinking thing, and said that the mind existed. But my critic proceeds as if I had forgotten my earlier denial of all this (when I was taking the mind to be something unknown to me); he talks as if I had taken the view that what I denied at the earlier stage (because I found it doubtful), must be denied for ever, as if it was impossible that such beliefs could be rendered certain and evident to me. It should be noted

[Descartes]

that throughout he treats doubt and certainty not as relations of our thought to objects, but as properties of the objects which inhere in them for all time. This means that if we have once realized that something is doubtful, it can never be rendered certain. But we should attribute all this to his good nature, and not to malice.

'All of them'. Here he is indulging in a fatuous quibble about the word   L 'all', just as he did earlier with the word 'nothing'.

'You are compelled to admit this'. Here this is an equally fatuous play   M on the word 'compelled'. There may be reasons which are strong enough to compel us to doubt, even though these reasons are themselves doubt-ful, and hence are not to be retained later on, as I have just pointed out.   474 The reasons are strong so long as we have no others which produce cer-tainty by removing the doubt. Now since I found no such countervailing reasons in the First Meditation, despite meditating and searching for them, I therefore said that the reasons for doubt which I had found were 'powerful and well thought-out'. But this is beyond the grasp of our critic, for he goes on to say 'When you promised me powerful reasons, I expected certain ones, ones of the kind demanded by this little pamphlet of yours' – as if the imaginary pamphlet he has put together can be related to what I said in the First Meditation. A little later on he says, 'Has there been a time when you were able to say with certainty that at this moment the senses are indubitably deceiving me, and I know this for sure?'[1] But he does not see that here again he has produced a contradic-tion, by talking of regarding a thing as indubitable and at the same time doubting it. What a good fellow he is!

'Why do you assert with such confidence that we sometimes dream?'   N Here again he goes astray, though without any malicious intent. There is nothing at all that I asserted 'with confidence' in the First Meditation: it is full of doubt throughout. Yet it is the sole source for all the statements he discusses. He might just as well have found there the statements 'We never dream' and 'We sometimes dream.' When, shortly afterwards, he says 'I just do not see how you move from "I do not know whether I am awake or dreaming" to "I sometimes dream"',' he is foisting on me, good-natured fellow that he is, a piece of reasoning that is worthy of himself alone.

'What if the cunning demon is presenting all these matters to you as   O doubtful and shaky when in fact they are firm and certain?' This remark makes it quite clear that, as I have pointed out above, my critic regards   475 doubt and certainty as being in the objects rather than our thought. Otherwise, how could he pretend that things are being presented to me as

1 Above p. 316.

[Descartes]

doubtful even though they are not doubtful but certain? For the mere fact that something is presented as doubtful automatically makes it doubtful. But perhaps the demon prevented him seeing the contradiction in his words. It is regrettable that the demon so often interferes with his thought processes.

P   'This general renunciation of all former beliefs is surely a considerable enterprise and one of the greatest importance.' I myself made this point emphatically enough at the end of my reply to the Fourth Set of Objections and in the Preface to the *Meditations*,[1] and for this very reason I suggested that they should be read only by those of a fairly robust intellect. I also made the point quite explicitly on pages 16 and 17 of the *Discourse on the Method*, published in French in 1637, where I described two types of intellect;[2] I said that those in either of the two categories should at all costs avoid the general renunciation of beliefs. If my critic happens to fall into one of these categories, he should not impute his own mistakes to me.

Q   'What are you saying? You *know*,' etc. When I said 'I knew' that there was no danger in my renouncing my beliefs I added 'because the task now in hand does not involve action but merely the acquisition of knowledge'.[3] This makes it clear that in that passage I was merely speaking of 'knowing' in the practical sense which suffices for the conduct of life. I frequently stressed that there is a very great difference between this type of knowledge and the metaphysical knowledge that we are dealing with here – indeed I made the point so clear that I think only my critic could fail to see it.

476   'This doubtful maxim that is full of flaws – "I cannot go too far in my
R   distrustful attitude".' Here again there is a contradiction in what my critic says. For everyone knows that a distrustful person, as long as he remains in a state of distrust, and therefore does not affirm or deny anything, cannot be led into error even by an evil demon. But a man who adds two and three together can be deceived by such a demon, as is shown by the example my critic himself has produced concerning the man who counted one o'clock four times.[4]

S   'I shall still be very afraid of overdoing my distrustful attitude if I renounce these long-standing beliefs.' Although my critic here attempts at length to convince us that we should not carry our distrust too far, it is worth noting that he does not produce even the smallest hint of an argument to prove this, beyond his fear or distrust of the maxim that we should distrust everything. But here once again there is a contradiction.

1 Above pp. 172, 8.   2 *Discourse*, part 2; see vol. 1, p. 118.   3 Med. 1, above p. 15.
4 Above p. 306.

[Descartes]

For from the fact that he is so afraid, but does not know for certain that he should not distrust himself, it follows that he should indeed distrust himself.

'Do you really have no scruples about renouncing such long-standing   T
beliefs as "I have a clear and distinct idea of God" or "Whatever I clearly and distinctly believe is true"?' My critic calls these beliefs 'long-standing' because he is afraid that they may be taken to be original ideas that I was the first to notice. But I am prepared to let that go. He also wants to introduce a doubt concerning God, but only in passing; his aim here is perhaps to avoid being accused of slandering me by those who know that when renouncing my former beliefs I was especially careful to make an exception of all matters concerning faith, and morals in general. Finally, he fails to see that the renunciation of beliefs applies only to those who have not yet perceived anything clearly and distinctly. The sceptics, for example, for whom such a renunciation is commonplace,   477
have never, *qua* sceptics, perceived anything clearly. For the very fact that they had perceived something clearly would mean that they had ceased to doubt it, and so ceased to be sceptics. As far as everyone else is concerned, until making such a renunciation there is virtually no one who ever perceives anything clearly, i.e. with the clarity which is required for metaphysical certainty; and for this reason the renunciation of beliefs is of great value to those who are capable of such clear knowledge and yet do not yet possess it. But as has become clear in the event, our critic will not find the exercise to be of such value – indeed I think he should studiously avoid it.

'Or will you renounce the belief that "thinking, nutrition and sensation   V
do not in any way belong to the body but belong to the mind"?' My critic reports this belief as if it were mine, and implies at the same time that it is so certain that it could not possibly be called into doubt by anyone. But one of the most notable points in my *Meditations* is that I refer nutrition to the body alone, not to the mind or to that part of man which thinks.[1] This one error proves three things clearly: first, my critic wholly fails to understand the *Meditations*, although he has undertaken to refute them; second, he has been confused by the fact that in the Second Meditation I referred nutrition to the soul in the course of quoting the common opinion;[2] and in the third place he himself regards as indubitable many beliefs which should not be accepted without examination. At the end, however, he finally reaches a conclusion which is wholly true when he says that in all these matters he has 'merely displayed his weakness of mind'.[3]

1 Cf. above Med. II, p. 18: Med. VI, p. 58.   2 Above p. 17.   3 Above p. 318.

[Bourdin]

§2. WE PREPARE TO FIND THE WAY INTO THE METHOD

X 'After renouncing all my former beliefs', you say, 'I begin to philosophize
as follows: I am; I am thinking. I am, so long as I am thinking. This
478 proposition, "I exist", is necessarily true whenever it is put forward by
me or conceived in my mind.'[1]

This is excellent, my distinguished friend! You have found your
'Archimedean point',[2] and without doubt you can now move the world if
you so wish. Look: the whole earth is already shaking. But since, I gather,
you are cutting everything back to the bone, so that your method may
include only what fits and is coherent and necessary, may I ask why you
Y refer to the *mind* (I mean in the phrase 'whenever it is conceived in my
mind')? Did you not banish both mind and body? But perhaps this phrase
slipped in by accident. And if it is so hard, even for an expert, to forget
altogether the things we have been accustomed to accept since childhood,
then even a raw beginner like myself need not despair, should I happen to
stumble. But please continue.

'I will therefore go back', you say, 'and meditate on what I originally
believed myself to be, before I embarked on this present train of thought.
I will then subtract anything capable of being weakened, even minimally, by the arguments now introduced, so that what is left at the end
may be exactly and only what is certain and unshakeable.'[3]

Before you proceed, shall I venture to ask you a question? Since you
have solemnly renounced all your former beliefs as doubtful and false,
why do you want to look at them again, as if you hoped to salvage
something certain from the rags and tatters? What if your 'original beliefs
about yourself' were wrong? Indeed, given that everything which you
recently abjured was doubtful and uncertain (otherwise why did you
abjure it?), how can it be that these beliefs should now cease to be
doubtful and uncertain — unless your renunciation of your beliefs was
like Circe's drug or some cleansing solution?[4] But I prefer to admire and
479 respect your plan. People who show their friends round palaces and
castles often enter through a private side-door rather than the main
entrance. So I shall follow you even through underground passages, so
long as I can hope to reach the truth eventually.

'What then did I formerly think I was?', you ask. 'A man'.[5]

---

1 Cf. above p. 17.   2 Cf. above p. 16.   3 Above p. 17.
4 Circe's drug changed men into animals. Bourdin wants to know how renouncing a belief
can change its nature, or alter it from dirty (doubtful) to clean (certain).
5 Above p. 17.

[Bourdin]

Permit me here to admire your skill once again. In order to discover what is certain, you make use of what is doubtful. To bring us out into the light, you order us down into the darkness. Do you want me to reflect   Z on what I originally believed myself to be? Do you want me to put on once more the ragged old cloak which I renounced some time ago, and say again 'I am a man'? But what if Pythagoras or one of his disciples were present, and told you that he used to be a cockerel? This is not to mention madmen, fanatics or other sorts of raving or deranged people. However, you are a skilled and experienced guide who knows all the twists and turns of the way, and so I shall not despair.

'What is a man?', you go on to ask.

If you want me to answer, let me first ask a question. Which man are you asking about, and what exactly are you asking when you ask what a man is? Do you mean the man I formerly imagined I was and believed myself to be – the man I now maintain I am not, since renouncing my beliefs, thanks to you? If this is the man you are asking about, the man whom I used to have such a mistaken conception of, then he is some kind of compound of soul and body. Is my answer adequate? I think so, in view of your next question.[1]

[Descartes]

COMMENTS

'I begin to philosophize as follows: "I am; I am thinking. I am, so long as   X I am thinking".' Note that my critic here admits that I have made my first   480 step in philosophizing, and for the first time established a proposition as firm, by recognizing my own existence. This shows that when he elsewhere pretends that my first step was a positive or definite renunciation of all my beliefs, he is saying the opposite of what he really believes. I will not comment further on the subtlety with which he portrays me as beginning to philosophize with the words 'I am; I am thinking etc.' For even if I say nothing, his sincerity can be recognized throughout.

'Why do you refer to the mind (in the phrase "whenever it is conceived   Y in my mind")? Did you not banish both mind and body?' I have already pointed out how my critic seizes on the word 'mind' to construct his quibbles. But 'it is conceived in the mind' here means simply 'it is thought of'; and hence he is incorrect in supposing that I am referring to the 'mind' *qua* part of a man. Moreover, even though I have previously rejected body and mind, together with everything else, as being doubtful or not yet clearly perceived by me, this does not prevent my re-adopting

1 See below p. 325.

[Descartes]
these items later on, if it happens that I perceive them clearly. But our critic does not grasp this, since he thinks that doubt is something that inheres in the object doubted, and is inseparable from it. For shortly afterwards he asks 'How can it be that these same beliefs' (i.e. those which were previously doubtful) 'should now cease to be doubtful and uncertain?' He wants me solemnly to forswear these beliefs and he 'admires my skill in making use of what is doubtful in order to discover what is certain', etc. This is to suggest that I made it a basic principle of my philosophy that everything doubtful should be regarded as false for all time.

Z 'Do you want me to reflect on what I originally believed myself to be?
481 Do you want me to put on once more the ragged cloak', etc.? Here I shall employ an everyday example to explain to my critic the rationale for my procedure, so as to prevent him misunderstanding it, or having the gall to pretend he does not understand it, in future. Suppose he had a basket full of apples and, being worried that some of the apples were rotten, wanted to take out the rotten ones to prevent the rot spreading. How would he proceed? Would he not begin by tipping the whole lot out of the basket? And would not the next step be to cast his eye over each apple in turn, and pick up and put back in the basket only those he saw to be sound, leaving the others? In just the same way, those who have never philosophized correctly have various opinions in their minds which they have begun to store up since childhood, and which they therefore have reason to believe may in many cases be false. They then attempt to separate the false beliefs from the others, so as to prevent their contaminating the rest and making the whole lot uncertain. Now the best way they can accomplish this is to reject all their beliefs together in one go, as if they were all uncertain and false. They can then go over each belief in turn and re-adopt only those which they recognize to be true and indubitable. Thus I was right to begin by rejecting all my beliefs; and later on, noticing that there was nothing which I could know more certainly or more evidently than that I existed so long as I was thinking, I was right to make this my first assertion. Finally, I was right to go on to ask what I had originally believed myself to be; my purpose was not to continue to believe all my former opinions concerning myself, but to re-adopt any beliefs which I perceived to be true, reject any that were false, and reserve for subsequent examination any that were uncertain. This makes it clear that my critic's remarks about my 'skill' in making what is uncertain yield certainties and my 'method of dreaming' (as he
482 calls it below)[1] are quite beside the point. And what he goes on to say

1 Cf. above p. 323, and below p. 335.

[Descartes]

about Pythagoras and the cockerel, and facetious comments in the two following paragraphs concerning other people's views on the nature of the body and soul, are similarly quite irrelevant. It was not my intention to make a survey of all the views anyone else had ever held on these matters, nor was there any reason why I should have done so. I confined myself to what I had originally believed quite spontaneously and with nature as my guide, and to the commonly held views of others, irrespective of truth or falsity; for my purpose in making the survey was not to adopt these beliefs, but merely to examine them.

[Bourdin]

§3. WHAT IS A BODY?

'What is a body?', you ask. 'What did I formerly understand by "a body"?'

Do not be offended if I keep a constant look out and if at every step I am afraid of falling into a trap. May I inquire what body you are asking about? Is it the body which I formerly conceived of as consisting of various definite properties? Yet according to your latest renunciation, I must suppose that this conception was incorrect. Or is it some other body that you mean, if such there can be? But how do I know? I am in doubt as to whether there can be such a body or not. But if your question concerns the former type of body, then I can answer without difficulty: 'by a body I understood whatever has a determinable shape and a definable location and can occupy space in such a way as to exclude any other body; it can be perceived by the senses, and can be moved by whatever else comes into contact with it'.[1] This was my previous conception of a body, which led me to call a 'body' whatever possessed the properties just listed; but I did not go on to infer that nothing but this could be, or be called, 'a body'. It is one thing to say 'by a body I understood this or that', and another to say 'by a body I understood *nothing but* this or that'. If, however, your question concerns some other kind of body, then I shall reply by following the views of contemporary philosophers (since it is not so much my own opinions that you are asking for, as what anyone may happen to believe). By a body I understand whatever has a definable location, like a stone, or whatever is confined within that location in such a way that it is wholly present throughout the entire location and wholly present in any one part of it, like the indivisible constituents of a quantity or a stone or whatever. This is what some recent writers have proposed, on analogy with the indivisibility of angels or souls; and their doctrine

483

---

1 Med. II, above p. 17.

[Bourdin]

has found some favour, at least in their own eyes, as we can see in the case of Oviedo.[1] They assert further that a body is that which is extended, either actually, like a stone, or virtually, like the indivisible constituents just mentioned; further, it may be divisible into several parts, like a stone, or may be incapable of division like the aforementioned indivisible constituents. It can also be moved by another body, as in the case of a stone which is propelled upwards, or can move by itself, like a stone

AA   falling downwards. Again it can have sensations, as a dog does, or think, as an ape does, or imagine, as a mule does. Previously on coming across anything which moved (either on its own or because of something else), or which had sensation or imagination or thought, then, in the absence of any reason to the contrary, I called it a 'body' – and indeed I still do so.

'But this is quite wrong', you say. 'For according to my judgement the power of self-movement, like the power of sensation or thought, was quite foreign to the nature of a body.'[2]

According to your judgement? Since you say so, I believe you: thoughts are free. But in taking this view you were also conceding that everyone else is free to choose his own view and I cannot believe that you are the sort of person who can have wanted to be the arbiter of all thoughts, rejecting some and approving others. So unless you had some simple and reliable rule which you omitted to mention when you ordered us to renounce all our beliefs, I shall make use of the freedom that nature has given us. You talk about your 'former judgements'; well, I also had my own 'former judgements'. I judged one way and you another; we may

484   both have been wrong. But certainly there must have been an element of doubt in both our views, given that you and I were required, when we embarked on the method, to divest ourselves of our old opinions. So, to cut short the dispute, if you want to define a 'body' in the special sense employed in the first definition given above, then I have no objection; indeed, I readily accept this account, provided you remember that your definition does not cover every 'body' in the general sense, but only a specific kind of body, as conceived by you. You have left out other sorts of body whose existence, or possibility, is, in the opinion of the learned, a matter of dispute; we certainly cannot decide for certain whether they are capable of existing or not – or at least not with the kind of certainty that you require. Thus it is still doubtful and uncertain whether the definition

1 Francisco de Oviedo (1601–51), a Spanish Jesuit who taught at Madrid. His *Integer Cursus Philosophicus* ('Complete Course in Philosophy') was published in France in 1640.
2 Above p. 17.

[Bourdin]

of body so far arrived at is correct or not. But go ahead, if you wish, and I shall follow gladly. Indeed, to follow you will be happiness itself for me, so attracted am I by this new and unheard of hope of deriving certain results from what is uncertain.

[Descartes]

COMMENTS

'Have sensations, as a dog does, or think, as an ape does, or imagine, as a   AA
mule does'. Here my critic is laying the ground for a battle about terminology. To enable him to show that I was wrong in locating the difference between the mind and the body in the fact that the former thinks, whereas the latter does not think but is extended, he says that he uses the term 'body' to include everything that has sensations or imagines or thinks. Well, let him even use the term 'mule' or 'ape' for these things, if he likes. If he can ever succeed in getting the new terms accepted into ordinary usage, then I shall agree to use them in his sense. But in the meantime, he has no right to complain that I use the recognized terms.

[Bourdin]

§4. WHAT IS THE SOUL?   485

'What is the soul?', you ask. 'What did I formerly understand by "soul"? Either I did not think about its nature, or I imagined it to be something tenuous like a wind or fire or ether, which permeated my more solid parts. And it was to this soul that I referred nutrition and movement and sense-perception and thinking.'[1]
    A very full statement. But you will, I suppose, permit me to ask you some questions here. When you ask about the soul,[2] are you asking us to give our former opinions, the beliefs we have long held about it?
    'Yes', you reply.   BB
    But do you think that our former views were correct, so that your method is unnecessary? Has everyone kept to the right road despite all the mists of doubt? The opinions of philosophers concerning the soul are so various and so conflicting that I cannot sufficiently admire the skill which you confidently believe will enable you to distil a reliable and wholesome medicine from such a murky sediment. Yet we can produce a

1 Cf. Med. II, above p. 17.
2 Lat. *animus*. Traditionally this term was used to denote the rational soul or intellect, while *anima* was used for the soul *simpliciter*. Bourdin, however, appears to use the two terms interchangeably.

[Bourdin]
healing drug even from the venom of a viper. Do you then wish me to add
to your own views on the soul by introducing the actual or possible
opinions of others? You do not require me to say whether they are
correct or not; it is enough that those who hold such opinions think that
they could never be made to abandon them by any argument, no matter
how powerful. Some people, then, will say that 'soul' is the name for a
specific kind of body. Why are you amazed? This is their view; and they,
at least, consider that it has some plausibility. They describe it as a body,
and that includes whatever is extended, has three dimensions and is
divisible into definite parts. And when, in the case of a horse, for
486   example, they see something extended and divisible, i.e. flesh, bones and
that external structure which impinges upon our senses, they conclude,
with strong arguments to back them up, that in addition to this structure
there is something internal, something tenuous, which permeates the
outer structure and extends through it; this something has three dimensions and is divisible, so that when a foot is cut off, part of the internal
element is also lost. They thus take the horse to be composed of two
extended, three-dimensional and divisible things – two bodies – which, in
view of the difference between them, we distinguish by employing
different names. One component, namely the external one, retains the
name 'body', while the internal element is called the 'soul'. As far as
sense-perception, imagination and thought are concerned, those who
hold the view under discussion think that the power of perceiving
through the senses, thinking and imagining, resides in the soul, or inner
body, although some relation to the external body, without which
sense-perception cannot occur, is also involved. There are various
different views and suggestions on this, which I have no need to go over
individually, but at least some people will be found to take the view that
all souls are exactly as described above.

'Away with this impiety', you reply.

Impious it certainly is. But why then do you raise the question? How
will you deal with atheists, or with those men of the flesh whose very
thought is so fixed on filth that their senses are aware of nothing but body
CC   and flesh? Since your method is intended to establish and demonstrate
that the soul of man is incorporeal and spiritual, you should certainly not
presuppose your desired result; rather, you should expect to have
opponents who will deny it, or who, if only for the sake of arguing, will
repeat the views described above. Suppose, then, that one of these
adversaries presents himself, and when you ask 'What is the soul?' replies
'The soul is something corporeal – something tenuous and rarefied which
487   permeates the external body and is the principle responsible for all

[Bourdin]

sensory awareness, imagination and thought. There are thus three grades of being whose existence we are investigating: first the body; second, the corporeal, or the soul; and third, the mind or spirit. And these three grades of being may be referred to by the terms *body*, *soul* and *mind* respectively.' Suppose, I repeat, that someone answers your question in this way. Will this reply be adequate? But I do not wish to anticipate the results to which your skill will lead us; my role is to follow you. And so you move on to the next stage.

[Descartes]

COMMENTS

'Yes', you reply. Here, as almost everywhere else, my critic represents me   BB
as answering him with comments that are wholly at variance with my true views. But it would be too tedious to list all his fabrications.

'Since your method is intended to demonstrate that the soul of man is   CC
incorporeal, you should certainly not presuppose your desired result.' My critic here dishonestly pretends that I presupposed what I ought to have proved; but this is not true. All the fabrications of this kind which he constructs so freely and which cannot be supported with any but the thinnest of arguments, deserve no response, except to say that they are false. As for what should be termed 'body', or 'soul' or 'mind', my discussion made no reference whatever to this. I gave an account of two things, namely that which thinks and that which is extended, and I proved that everything else may be referred to these two. I also established by my arguments that they are two substances which are really distinct one from the other. However, I did call one of the substances 'mind' and the other 'body'; if my critic does not like these terms, he may employ others, and I shall not complain.

[Bourdin]
§5. WE ATTEMPT TO FIND A WAY INTO THE METHOD   488

'Good', you say; 'the foundations have been successfully laid. I am, so long as I think. This is certain and unshakeable. Now I can start to build, but I must take great care that the evil demon does not impose on me. I am. But what am I? Undoubtedly I am one of the things I formerly   DD
believed myself to be. I believed myself to be a man, and I believed that a man possesses a body and a soul. Am I then a body? Or am I a mind? A body is an extended thing, with a definite location, impenetrable and

[Bourdin]
visible. Are any of these properties to be found in me? Extension? How
could this be found in me, since it does not exist at all? I renounced it at
the outset. What about tangibility and visibility? I might think that I can
be seen or that I can touch myself, and yet in fact I am neither seen nor
EE   touched: I decided this when I made my renunciation of beliefs. What
then am I? I concentrate, I think, I turn things over and over in my mind,
but nothing occurs to me. I am tired of going over the same ground. I find
in myself none of the attributes which belong to a body. I am not a body.
And yet I exist, and I know that I exist; and so long as I know that I exist
FF   I am not aware of anything belonging to the body. Am I therefore a
mind? What attributes did I formerly believe to belong to the mind? Is
any of them to be found in me? I formerly supposed thinking to belong to
the mind. But wait: I am thinking. Eureka, eureka! I exist, I am thinking.
I exist so long as I am thinking; I am a thinking thing, I am a mind,
intellect, reason.[1] Here then is my method, the method that has enabled
me to advance so successfully. Follow me, if you please.'
   O fortunate man, to emerge from such darkness into the light almost at
one single leap! But please give me your hand and steady my tottering
steps as I tread in your footprints. I shall follow you, word for word, but,
acknowledging my limitations, I shall go a little slower. 'I am, I am
thinking. But what am I? Am I any of the things which I formerly
believed myself to be?' But was I right in my former beliefs? That is
489 uncertain. I have renounced all doubtful matters, and I am considering
GG   them as false. So I was not correct in my beliefs.
   'On the contrary', you shout. 'Here you may tread firmly.'
   Tread firmly? But everything is unstable. What if I am something else?
   'You are too scrupulous', you reply. 'Either you are a body, or a mind.'
   Very well — though I am still tottering. Please take my hand, for I
hardly dare to step forward. What if I am a soul, I ask you? What if I am
something else? I do not know.
   'No matter', you say. 'You are either a body or a mind.'
HH   So be it. Either I am a body or a mind. But surely I am the former? I
will undoubtedly turn out to be a body if I find in myself anything which I
formerly believed to belong to the body. And yet I fear that my beliefs
may not have been correct.
   'Courage! Fear nothing!', you reply.
   With your encouragement, then, I venture to proceed. I had formerly
supposed that thinking was something belonging to the body. But wait: I
am thinking. Eureka, eureka. I am, I am thinking. I am a thinking thing, I
am something corporeal; I am extension, something divisible, words

---

1 This paragraph is loosely based on Med. II, above p. 18.

[Bourdin]
whose meaning I have been ignorant of until now.[1] Why are you angry?
Why do you push away the hand I am holding out to you? I have reached
the bank and am standing on the same shore as you, thanks to you and
the renunciation of beliefs which you have ordained.

'This is all wrong', you say.

Why? What have I done wrong?

'Your former belief that thinking is something belonging to the body   JJ
was incorrect. You should have believed that it is something belonging to
the mind.'

But why did you not warn me at the outset? When you saw that I was
all keyed up and ready to renounce my former beliefs, why did you not
tell me to keep this one belief, to take from you a special certificate
bearing the words 'Thinking is something that belongs to the mind'? Well,
I must take all the credit for warning you to stress this maxim when
dealing with your next batch of beginners: take care to remind them not
to renounce it along with such former beliefs as 'Two and three make
five.' Yet I cannot readily guarantee that they will obey you. Each person   490
has his own views, and you will not find many disciples to accept the
maxim as uncomplainingly as the disciples of Pythagoras who were
satisfied with 'these our master's words'. Suppose some of your followers
deny the maxim or stubbornly persist in their former opinion: what will
you do? But without calling others in, I will put the point to you. You
promise us that you will establish by strong arguments that the human
soul is not corporeal but wholly spiritual; yet if you have presupposed as
the basic premiss of your proofs the maxim 'Thinking is a property of the
mind, or of a wholly spiritual and incorporeal thing', will it not seem that
you have presupposed, in slightly different words, the very result that was
originally in question? If anyone believes that 'thinking is a property of a
spiritual and incorporeal thing', and knows and is conscious that he is
thinking (for surely no one requires instruction to discover that rich vein
of thought within him), then could he really be so stupid as to be capable
of doubting that there is something within him that is spiritual and
wholly incorporeal? In case you think I am throwing in this objection just
for the sake of it, there are many people, and serious philosophers at that,
who claim that the brutes think, and hence regard thought as an attribute
which, though not common to all bodies, is common to all extended
souls of the kind which the brutes possess; and this implies that it is
certainly not a property that uniquely and necessarily belongs to a mind
or spiritual substance! What, I ask you, will such philosophers say, when
they are ordered to renounce this opinion and adopt yours, just to please

1 Bourdin parodies Descartes' words at Med. II, above p. 18.

[Bourdin]

you? And when you demand acceptance of your view, are you not asking a favour, or begging the question? But why should I continue to argue the point? If I have made a false step, should I go back and try again?

[Descartes]

491   COMMENTS

DD 'But what am I? Undoubtedly I am one of the things I formerly believed myself to be.' Here, as in countless other cases, my critic makes it his practice to foist a certain position on me without any pretence of accuracy.

EE 'I decided this when I made my renunciation of beliefs.' Here again he is inaccurately foisting on me a view which I do not hold. I never drew any conclusions from the fact that I had renounced a belief. Indeed, I expressly indicated that this was not the case when I said 'It may perhaps be the case that these things which I am supposing to be nothing, because they are unknown to me, are in reality identical with the "I" of which I am aware,' etc.[1]

FF 'Am I therefore a mind?' Again, it is false that I asked whether I was a mind; for I had not yet explained what I understood by the term 'mind'. What I did do was to inquire whether there were in me any of the features which I had previously been in the habit of attributing to the soul as previously described by me. Now I did not find within me all the attributes which I had formerly referred to the soul; the only one I found was thought, and hence I did not say I was a soul but merely that I was a thinking thing. In applying the term 'mind' or 'intellect' or 'reason' to this thinking thing, I did not intend to endow the term 'mind' with any more weighty significance than the phrase 'thinking thing'; I did not suppose I was making some further discovery at which I could exclaim with the words 'eureka, eureka', as my critic here jeeringly and impertinently suggests. On the contrary, I expressly went on to say that up till now I had been ignorant of the meaning of the words 'mind', 'intellect', etc. This puts it beyond doubt that by these words I understood exactly and only what is conveyed by the term 'thinking thing'.

492 GG 'I was not correct in my former belief. "On the contrary", you shout.' Again, the implication is utterly false. At no point did I ever suppose that my previous beliefs were true; I merely examined them to see whether they were true.

HH 'Either I am a body or a mind.' Again, it is false that I ever asserted this.

1 Above p. 18.

[Descartes]

'Your former belief that thinking was something belonging to the body JJ
was incorrect. You should have believed that it is something belonging to
the mind.' It is also false that I made this claim. As far as I am concerned,
my critic is quite at liberty to say, if he wishes, that the term 'body' is
more appropriate for a thing that thinks than the term 'mind'; he will
have to argue this out with the grammarians, not with me. But if he
pretends that I meant anything more by the term 'mind' than I did by the
term 'thinking thing', then a firm denial on my part is in order. And this
also applies to the passage a little later on where he says, 'If you have
presupposed that thinking is a property of the mind, or of a wholly
spiritual and incorporeal thing, then are you not asking a favour, or
begging the question?'[1] I deny that I in any way presupposed that the
mind is incorporeal; though later on, in the Sixth Meditation, I did in fact
demonstrate as much.

However, it is tiresome for me to have to intervene so frequently to
prove that my critic has falsified my position. From now on I shall
conceal my feelings and be a silent spectator of his tricks, right up to the
end. Yet it is embarrassing to see a Reverend Father so obsessed with the
desire to quibble that he is driven to play the buffoon. In presenting
himself as hesitant, slow and of meagre intellect, he seems eager to
imitate not so much the clowns of Roman comedy like Epidicus and
Parmenon as the cheap comedian of the modern stage who aims to   493
attempt to raise a laugh by his own ineptitude.

[Bourdin]

§6. A SECOND ATTEMPT TO FIND
A WAY INTO THE METHOD

'Very well, try again', you say, 'provided you follow closely in my steps.'

I shall walk exactly where you tread. Start again, I beg you.

'I am thinking', you say.

So am I.

'I exist', you continue, 'so long as I am thinking.'

The same is true of me.

'But what am I?', you now ask.

A wise question! This is what I am after, and I will gladly join in asking
what I am.

You go on 'What did I formerly believe myself to be?[2] What was my
former view of myself?'

Please do not repeat yourself. I have heard all this already. Yet help me,
I beg you. I cannot see where to tread amid such darkness.

1 Cf. above pp. 331f.   2 Cf. Med. II, above p. 17.

[Bourdin]

'Repeat after me', you say. 'Tread where I tread. What did I formerly believe myself to be?'

KK   'Formerly?' Was there a former time? Did I have former beliefs?

'Now you have gone astray', you object.

No; you yourself, if I may say so, have gone astray in mentioning 'former' beliefs. I have renounced all my former beliefs; 'formerly' has become nothing; it no longer exists. But you are a kindly guide; you take my hand and pull me along.

'I am thinking', you say. 'I exist.'

Yes; I am thinking, I exist. I am holding onto this, but it is all that I have. Beyond this there is nothing, there has never been anything.

494   'Bravo!', you say. 'But what did you formerly believe about yourself?'

I think you want to test me here, and to see whether I have spent fifteen days or a whole month on the beginner's exercise of renouncing beliefs. But although I have only spent an hour here with you, my mental concentration has been enormous, and a brief but intensive effort is surely equivalent to a longer but less concentrated one. So I have, in effect, spent a month – even a year, if you wish. Here you are then: I am thinking; I exist. There is nothing further. I have renounced everything.

'But recollect', you say; 'try to remember.'

What do you mean by 'recollect'? Granted, I think that I have thought in the past. But does the mere fact that I *think* that I have thought entail that I have in fact always thought in the past?

'You are too timid', you reply. 'You are frightened of a shadow. Start again: I am thinking.'

Unhappy man that I am! The darkness closes in on me, and now I cannot even clearly discern the 'I am thinking' that was so clearly apparent to me a moment ago. I am dreaming that I am thinking. So I am not thinking.

'No', you reply. 'If someone is dreaming, then he is thinking.'

I see a ray of light. Dreaming is thinking, and thinking is dreaming.

'Certainly not', you say. 'Thinking extends more widely than dreaming. He who is dreaming is thinking; but he who is thinking is not dreaming all the time, but may be thinking while awake.'

But is this right? Are you dreaming it, or are you really thinking it? If you are dreaming that thinking extends more widely, does it follow that it really does so? If you wish, I am ready to dream that dreaming extends more widely than thinking. But how do you know that thinking extends more widely, if there is no thinking, but only dreaming? Suppose that whenever you have thought that you were thinking while awake, you were not really thinking while awake, but merely dreaming that you were

[Bourdin]
thinking while awake? What if dreaming is a single operation which enables you sometimes to dream that you are dreaming, and at other times to dream that you are thinking while awake? What will you do now? Since you are silent, are you prepared to listen to me? We should look for another ford; this one is so unreliable and treacherous that I am utterly amazed that you have just tried to show me the way across without testing it before. So do not ask me what I formerly believed myself to be, but what I dream that I dreamed myself to be. If you ask me this, I shall answer. But to prevent the sleep-talk of dreamers from confusing our conversation, I shall use the language of those who are awake, provided you remember that from now on 'thinking' means no more than 'dreaming', and provided you rely on your thoughts no more than a dreamer relies on his dreams. Indeed, you must now entitle your method the 'method of dreaming', and your technique must be governed by the supreme principle that 'in order to reason aright, we must dream'. I think you must approve of my advice, for you go on as follows.

'What then did I formerly think that I was?'[1]

Here once again is the rock that I bumped into a moment ago. We must both take care. So, may I inquire why, before asking this question, you did not first state the implied premiss 'I am one of the things that I formerly believed myself to be', or 'I am what I formerly believed myself to be'?

'There is no need', you reply.

Excuse me, but there is every need, or else what is the point of all the work you put in to find out what you formerly believed yourself to be? Suppose it is possible that you are not any of the things you formerly believed yourself to be? Suppose, as in the case of Pythagoras, you are something else? Will it not then be pointless for you to ask what you formerly believed yourself to be?

'But the premiss "I am one of the things that I formerly believed myself to be" is an old belief that I have now renounced', you reply.

It certainly is, if you have renounced all your beliefs. But what can you do? Either you must grind to a halt at this point, or you must make use of this premiss.

'No', you say. 'We must try again and use a different route. Well then: I am either a body or a mind. Am I a body?'

Please stop. How do you know you are either a body or a mind, since you have renounced both body and mind? What if you are neither a body nor a mind but a soul, or something else? How am I to know the answer? This is the very point we are investigating, and if I knew or was aware of

495

LL

496

1 Cf. Med. II, above p. 17.

[Bourdin]
the answer, I should not be finding things such hard work. I would not like you to think that it was merely for the sake of an outing or a stroll that I came to these shores of renunciation which are so full of terror and darkness. It is only the hope of certainty that attracts me, or drives me on.

'Let us start again, then', you say. 'I am either a body, or else something that is a non-body, something incorporeal.'

You are now taking another, quite different, route. But is what you say certain?

'Very certain and necessary', you reply.

But why did you renounce it? Was I not right to worry that we should have retained some beliefs, and that you might have carried your distrustful attitude too far? But let us admit that what you say is certain. What now?

'Am I a body?', you continue. 'Do I find in myself any of the things which I formerly believed to belong to a body?'

Here is another stumbling block. We shall certainly trip over it unless you make explicit the striking and remarkable presupposition involved: 'My former beliefs regarding what pertains to a body were correct' or 'Nothing belongs to a body apart from what I formerly understood to belong to it.'

'Why this?' you ask.

Because if your former view of the body left anything out, or if your beliefs about it were wrong (for 'being human you must not consider that anything human is foreign to your nature'),[1] then all this labour of yours will have been utterly pointless, and you will have every reason to fear

MM   ending up in the position of the peasant I heard of recently. The fellow had just seen a wolf for the first time, though from a long way off, and stopped to ask his master, a well-born young man whom he was following, about what he had seen: 'What is it?' he asked. 'It is undoubtedly an animal – it moves and walks. But what animal can it be? It must be one of those I know already. What are they? Ox, horse, goat and donkey. Is it an ox? No; it does not have horns. Is it a horse? No; its tail is not big enough. Is it a goat? A goat has a beard, but this animal

497   does not, so it is not a goat. So it must be a donkey, since it is not an ox or a horse or a goat!' Why do you laugh? Wait for the end of the story. 'Come now', said the young master, 'you may just as well conclude that it is a horse as a donkey. Look: is it an ox? No; it does not have horns. Is it a donkey? Certainly not: I see no ass's ears. Is it a goat? No; it has no beard. So it is a horse.' The peasant was a little upset by this new analysis, and exclaimed 'Wait: it is not an animal. For the animals I know are the

1 A reference to Terence, *Heauton Timorumenos*, I, i, 25.

[Bourdin]
ox, the horse, the goat and the donkey. It is not an ox, or a horse, or a
goat, or a donkey. And so' (jumping up and down in triumph) 'it is not
an animal; and hence it is something that is a non-animal!' What a sturdy
philosopher we have here, trained not in the Lyceum but in the cow-pen!
Do you want to make the same blunder as he does?

'Enough', you say. 'I see the point. The false presupposition in the
peasant's mind (though he did not state it explicitly) was "I am
acquainted with all the animals there are", or "There are no animals
apart from those I know". But what has this to do with our enterprise?'

The two cases are as alike as peas in a pod. Admit it: there is a
concealed premiss in your mind which you have failed to mention, *viz.* 'I
know everything which relates, or can possibly relate, to the body' or
'Nothing belongs to the body apart from what I formerly understood to
belong to it.' But suppose that your previous knowledge did not include
everything that belongs to the body; suppose you left out even one thing;
suppose that you attributed to the mind something which really belongs
to the body or to a corporeal thing like the soul; suppose you were wrong
in separating thought, sensation and imagination from the body or the
corporeal soul: if you have the least suspicion that you may have
committed any of these errors, should you not be worried about ending
up like the peasant, so that any conclusion you draw may be invalid?
Even though you try to drag me along with you I will obstinately stay put
and not move a single pace forward unless you remove this difficulty.

'Let us go back and try to find a third way in', you reply. 'Let us try
every entrance, every pathway; every detour and every bypass.'

Very well, but on condition that if any doubt arises we do not merely   498
snip at it, but chop it right back. Lead on, please; but I will insist on
radical pruning. You go on as follows.

§7. A THIRD ATTEMPT TO FIND A WAY IN

'I am thinking', you say.   NN

I deny it; you are dreaming that you are thinking.

'I call that "thinking"', you reply.

You are wrong to do so. I, at least, call a spade a spade. You are
dreaming, I grant you that. Proceed.

'I exist, so long as I am thinking', you say.

Very well. Since you want to put it that way, I will not argue.

'This is certain and evident', you continue.

No: you merely dream that it is certain and evident.

'But at least it is certain and evident to the dreamer', you insist.

[Bourdin]

No: it only seems or appears certain, but it is not really so.

'But I do not doubt it', you insist. 'I am conscious of it, and the demon cannot deceive me here, however hard he tries.'

I deny this. You are dreaming that you are conscious of it, that you do not doubt it, that it is evident to you. There is a wide difference between, on the one hand, something's *seeming* certain and evident to someone who is dreaming (or even awake) and, on the other hand, something's *being* certain and evident to one who is dreaming or awake. This is an impasse: we cannot go any further. We must look for another approach, if we are not to live out our lives in a dream. You must give us something to go on: if there is to be a harvest, the seed must first be sown. But proceed, since you are so certain.

'What did I formerly believe myself to be?', you ask.

Abandon 'formerly': that road is blocked! How often have I told you that these old pathways are blocked off? You exist so long as you are thinking, and you are certain that you exist so long as you are thinking. I repeat: 'so long as you are thinking'. The past is wholly doubtful and uncertain; the present is all you have left. Yet still you persevere. Ill fortune cannot break you, and I must admire you for this.

OO   You go on as follows: 'I am, I am thinking, I am a thinking thing; there is in this "me" not one, not a single one, of the things that belong to the body or to a corporeal thing.'

I deny this. Prove it.

'Since the time when I renounced everything, no body exists, no soul, no mind – in a word, nothing. And therefore, if I exist, as I am certain that I do, I am not a body or anything corporeal.'

How glad I am to see you revive, and begin to reason once more and slowly recover your old form! Step forward then; this way we shall find a quicker way out of the labyrinth, and since you are free with your arguments, I shall be even freer. I deny both your antecedent and your consequent, and I also deny that the antecedent entails the consequent. Please do not be amazed; there is a solid basis for what I say. I deny that your antecedent entails the consequent because you could just as well prove the opposite result, as follows: 'Since the time when I renounced everything, no mind exists, no soul, no body – in a word, nothing. And therefore if I exist, as I am certain that I do, I am not a mind.' Here is the rotten kernel of your argument, and you will recognize just how bad it is from what follows. Meanwhile, consider whether next time you would do better to draw the following conclusion from your antecedent: 'Therefore if I exist, as I do, I am nothing.' Surely, either you were wrong to assert the antecedent, or else your assertion of it is vitiated by the

Seventh Set of Objections with Replies

[Bourdin]

subsequent introduction of the conditional 'if I exist'. Hence I deny the antecedent 'since the time when I renounced everything, no body exists, no soul, no mind, nor anything else'. And I am quite right to deny it. Your renunciation of everything is either a mistake or else it does not include absolutely everything (how could it, since in making the renunciation, you yourself must necessarily exist?). Let me now answer you more precisely. When you say 'Nothing exists, no body, no soul, no mind', etc. you have two alternatives. First, you could exclude yourself when you assert the proposition 'Nothing exists', etc. and take it to mean 'Nothing exists except for me.' You must necessarily do this if this 500 proposition of yours is to stand and continue to do so; for this is exactly what we are commonly told in logic in connection with propositions like 'Every proposition written in this book is false' or 'I am lying', and many more, which must exclude themselves from what they assert. Alternatively, you could include yourself and be prepared not to exist while you make your renunciation and say 'Nothing exists', etc. If you take the first alternative, then the proposition 'Since the time when I renounced everything, nothing exists', etc. cannot stand. For you exist, and are something, and necessarily you are either a body or a soul or a mind or something else. If you take the second alternative, you are in error — indeed your error is twofold. First, you are attempting the impossible and trying to be nothing when you are something; and second, you are refuting your own proposition in your consequent when you say 'Hence if I exist, as I do', etc. For how can it be that you exist, if nothing exists? And so long as you maintain that nothing exists, how can you maintain that you exist? And if you maintain that you exist, will you not be refuting the claim which you just made that nothing exists, etc.? Thus your antecedent is false, and your consequent is false. But you now fight back.

'When I say "nothing exists"', you reply, 'I am not certain that I am a body or a soul or a mind or anything else. Indeed, I am not certain that any other body or soul or mind exists. Hence, in accordance with the law of renunciation which states that doubtful matters should be considered as false, I shall say and maintain that there is no body or soul or mind or anything else. Hence, if I exist, as I do, I am not a body.'

This is quite splendid. But please allow me to shake out your statements one by one and measure and weigh them in turn. I take the antecedent first: 'Nothing exists; I am not certain that I am a body or a soul or a mind or anything else.' Now this may be taken in two distinct ways. It could be taken determinately, meaning that you are not certain that you are a body or mind or any other specific thing. I accept the

[Bourdin]

501 antecedent in this form, since this is precisely the question you are raising. But it could also be taken indeterminately, as meaning that you are not certain that you are a body, soul, mind, or anything else at all. And I deny the antecedent in this form. For you exist, you are something, and you are necessarily either a body or a soul or a mind or something else; and hence you cannot seriously call this into doubt, however much the demon may plague you. I now come to the consequent 'Hence in accordance with the law of renunciation I shall say that there is no body or soul or mind or anything else'. Again, the consequent may be taken in two ways. If it is taken determinately, as meaning that the body, or the soul, or the mind, or any other specific thing, does not exist, then I accept the consequent. But if it is taken indeterminately, to mean that in a general sense neither body nor soul nor mind nor anything else exists, then I deny it. In the same way your final conclusion, 'Hence if I exist, as I do, I am not a body', may be taken in two ways: if it is taken determinately I accept it, but if it is taken indeterminately I deny it. Look how generous I am: I have doubled all your propositions. And yet you do not despair, but fall back and regroup your forces. How happy you make me!

PP 'I know I exist', you say. 'The next question is what is this "I" that I know? If the "I" is understood strictly as we have been taking it, then it is quite certain that knowledge of it does not depend on things of whose existence I am as yet unaware.'[1]

What more do you have to say? Is that all? I was expecting you to produce some further inference, as you did just now. Perhaps you were afraid that the outcome would be no better than before. It is just like you to be so cautious; but let me take up your points one by one. You know you exist. Agreed. You then ask what is this 'I' that you know. Quite right; I will ask the same question since this is what we have been after for some time. The knowledge of this 'I' that you are asking about does not depend on things of whose existence you are still unaware. What am I to say? Your drift is not yet clear enough, and I do not really see the point of this statement of yours. But if you insist on asking 'What is this "I" that I know?', then I shall ask a question. Why do you ask, if you know?

'I know that I exist', you reply, 'not what I am.'

502 Fine. But how will you discover the nature of the 'I' that exists if not from what you formerly knew or will know later on? Surely you will not have recourse to what you formerly knew, since all this is full of doubt and has been renounced. Therefore you must be relying on what you do

1 Med. II, above p. 18.

[Bourdin]
not yet know but will know later on. This suggestion seems to upset you greatly, but I do not see why.

'I do not yet know that these things exist', you say.

Keep up your hopes! You will find out at some time or other.

'But what am I to do meanwhile?', you ask.

Keep waiting. But I shall not leave you in suspense for long. I shall make a distinction as before. If you mean that you do not have any determinate and clear knowledge of what you are, then I agree. But if you mean that you do not have some indeterminate and confused knowledge of what you are, this I deny. For you know you are something, and that you are necessarily either a body or a soul or a mind or something else. But what then? Afterwards you will know yourself clearly and determinately. What will you do now? This one distinction between 'determinately' and 'indeterminately' will block your progress for a whole century. You must pray for another route, if there is one left. But have courage; I have not yet thrown down my weapons. Substantial and novel undertakings are often beset with substantial and novel difficulties.

'There is still one way left', you reply. 'But if there is even the smallest obstacle in the way, then that will be the end. I shall retreat, and these shores of renunciation will never see me wandering here again. Do you want to explore this last avenue with me?'

Very well, but on condition that since this is your last attempt, you are ready to see me expend my last remaining energy. Lead on!

§8. A FOURTH ATTEMPT TO FIND A WAY IN,
WHICH IS ABANDONED AS HOPELESS

'I exist', you say.   QQ

I deny it.

'I am thinking', you continue.

I deny it.

'What do you deny?', you ask.   503

I deny that you exist, that you are thinking. I am quite well aware of what I did when I said 'Nothing exists.' It was a splendid achievement; at a stroke I chopped off everything. Nothing exists: you do not exist, you are not thinking.

'But I beg you to listen', you say. 'I am certain of it, I am conscious of it; this is my consciousness – that I exist, that I am thinking.'

Even if you put your hand on your heart, even if you swear and implore, I shall deny it. Nothing exists; you do not exist; you are not thinking; you are not conscious. Here, then, is the problem, which I will

[Bourdin]

now set before you so that you can see it clearly and try to avoid it. If the proposition 'Nothing exists' is true, then the proposition 'You do not exist and you are not thinking' is necessarily also true. But you insist that the proposition 'Nothing exists' is true. Therefore the proposition 'You do not exist and you are not thinking' is also true.

'This is excessively rigorous', you say. 'You must be a little less strict.'

Since you ask me, I will grant your request, and more. You exist, I allow it; you are thinking, I grant you this. You may even add that you are a thinking thing, or a 'thinking substance' since you are so fond of high-sounding phrases. I am happy with this, and I congratulate you; but you may go no further. Yet you insist on going on, and you summon up your last reserves of strength.

'I am a thinking substance', you say. 'I know that I exist as a thinking substance, and I know that a thinking substance exists. I also have a clear and distinct concept of this thinking substance, and yet I am unaware of the existence of any body or of any of the features that belong to the concept of a corporeal substance. More than that, body does not exist at all; there is no corporeal thing; I have renounced everything. Hence the knowledge of my existence or the existence of a thinking thing does not depend on the knowledge of bodily existence, or an existing body. Therefore since I exist, and exist as a thinking substance, and body does not exist, I am not a body. Hence I am a mind. These then are the arguments that compel my assent, since there is nothing in them that is not both coherent and derived from evident principles in accordance with the laws of logic.'

504   What a fine swan-song! But why did you not talk like this before, and clearly and unambiguously abandon your programme of renunciation? I have good reason to bring a complaint against you for allowing us to wander out here for so long and taking us through this trackless and impassable terrain when you could have brought us to our goal with one single step. I could even be very angry and burst out in a fury against you were you not a good friend; for you have not dealt so honestly and affably with me as you did before, but have reserved something for your own private stores without sharing it with me. You are amazed, but I shall not keep

RR   you guessing for long: here is my chief complaint. A little time ago, just a few steps back, you were asking me 'What is this "I" that I know?' But it now turns out that not only do you know what you are, but you have a clear and distinct concept of what you are. Either you were concealing something and pretending ignorance out of cunning, or you have some underground cache of truth and certainty which you are hiding from me. Yet if you point out this hidden source to me, I shall be more inclined to

[Bourdin]

question you about it, than to complain. Where, may I ask, did you get this clear and distinct concept of a thinking substance? Whether the clarity and evidence comes from the words involved or from the thing itself, I shall beg you again and again to give me just one glimpse of this concept that is so clear and distinct, so that I may revive at the sight of it – especially since it is virtually from this concept alone that we expect to derive the truth which we are working so hard to discover.

'Here you are then', you say. 'I know for certain that I exist, that I am thinking, that I exist as a thinking substance.'

Please pause here while I brace myself to grasp such a difficult concept. I too know and am well aware that I exist, that I am thinking, that I exist as a thinking substance. Now you may continue, if you will.

'No; it's all over', you say. 'When I thought that I existed as a thinking substance, I formed the clear and distinct concept of a thinking substance.'

Wonderful! What a sharp and subtle person you are! In one single   505 instant you manage to penetrate and go right through everything that exists and does not exist, and can exist and cannot exist. You form a clear and distinct concept of a thinking substance when you clearly and distinctly conceive that a thinking substance exists. Does this mean that if you clearly know (as you surely do, given your brilliant intellect) that no mountain exists without a valley, then without more ado you possess a clear and distinct concept of a mountain without a valley? Being ignorant of the technique involved, I am amazed at this new achievement. Please reveal your skill and show me how this concept can be clear and distinct.

'Listen then', you say. 'I have a clear and distinct conception of the existence of a thinking substance, and I have no conception of anything corporeal, or spiritual, or of anything else but a thinking substance – this and this alone. Therefore the concept of a thinking substance which I have is clear and distinct.'

I hear you, finally, and unless I am mistaken I understand you. This concept of yours is clear because you have certain knowledge of it, and it is distinct because you are aware of nothing else. Have I put my finger on it? I think so, for you go on as follows: 'This is quite sufficient', you say, 'to enable me to affirm that in so far as I know myself, I am nothing other than a thinking thing.'

More than sufficient. If I have clearly grasped what you mean, the concept of a thinking substance which you form is clear and distinct in so far as it represents to you that a thinking substance exists, without your having to attend to the body or the soul or the mind, or anything else apart from the existence of this substance. And hence you say that you, in

[Bourdin]

so far as you know yourself, are nothing other than a thinking substance, and not a body or soul or mind or anything else; thus if you exist in a way which exactly corresponds to your knowledge of yourself, you are only a thinking substance, and no more. I suppose you are pleased with yourself and congratulating yourself, thinking that in producing this unusually long summary I am trying to play for time, avoid the battle and leave your line of troops unbroken and unchallenged? But my intention is quite different. Do you want me, by uttering a single remark, to scatter the entire army you have amassed, including the reserves in their serried ranks which you have cautiously kept back for the final struggle? In fact I shall let fly with three comments, not one, so that not even a single messenger will be left to tell the tale of defeat.

Here is my first comment. The inference from knowledge to existence is not a valid one. Meditate on this for two weeks at least, and your meditation will bear fruit which you will not be sorry to have, if you then cast your eye on the table below. A thinking substance is one which understands or wills or doubts or dreams or imagines or has sensory perceptions; and hence all cognitive acts such as understanding, willing, imagining and having sensory perceptions come under the common definition of thought, or perception, or consciousness. And we call the substance in which they inhere a 'thinking thing'.

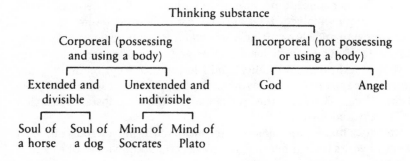

My second point is to remind you of the distinction between determinately and indeterminately, distinctly and confusedly, explicitly and implicitly. This too you should turn over and over in your mind, say for a week. It will be worth your while if you apply each of these distinctions to your own propositions and make all the appropriate divisions and differentiations. I would be happy to do it myself if I were not afraid of boring you. Now for my third point: an over-ambitious inference fails to establish anything at all. On this occasion, no time for

[Bourdin]

meditation is allowed. The crisis is upon you. Come, consider your argument once more, and watch me to see if I cannot make some progress in the same direction. 'I am a thinking thing; I know that I am a   507
thinking substance and that a thinking substance exists. Nevertheless I do not yet know that a mind exists. In fact no mind does exist; nothing exists, since I have renounced all my beliefs. Therefore the knowledge of my existence, or of the existence of a thinking substance, does not depend on knowledge of the existence of a mind, or of an existing mind. So since I exist, and exist as a thinking thing, and mind does not exist, I am not a mind. Therefore I am a body.' Why do you not speak? Why do you draw back? I at any rate have not yet abandoned all hope. Now at last it is your turn to follow me. Come, keep up your spirits: I propose to deploy the traditional form and method of conducting our reasoning which is familiar to all the ancients – indeed to absolutely everyone. Please let me do this and do not take it amiss, for I have put up with your method. It may be that my method will open up a way for us, as often happens when the situation is so complex that it has been given up as hopeless. And if it does not succeed, then at least we shall be able to use it, as we retire, to indicate the faults in your method, if there are any. Here then is your argument recast in formal terms.

§9. WE MAKE A SAFE RETREAT EMPLOYING THE TRADITIONAL FORM OF REASONING

Nothing that is such that I can doubt whether it exists does in fact exist.   55
Every body is such that I can doubt whether it exists.
Therefore no body does in fact exist.

I do not want to go back over old ground, but is not the major premiss your own? The minor is yours as well, so the conclusion is yours too. So I will go on.

No body does in fact exist.

To proceed:

Nothing that in fact exists is a body.
I (I that am a thinking substance) do in fact exist.
Therefore I (I that am a thinking substance) am not a body.   508

Why do you smile? Why does a new springtime of hope blossom on your countenance? I think you are pleased with the traditional form of reasoning, and the results it has brought us. But now your smile will turn to a bitter smile. Substitute 'mind' for 'body' in the above argument and you may validly infer 'Therefore I (I that am a thinking substance) am not a mind'. This is how it goes.

[Bourdin]

Nothing which is such that I can doubt whether it exists does in fact exist.

Every mind is such that I can doubt whether it exists.

Therefore no mind does in fact exist.

No mind does in fact exist.

Therefore nothing that in fact exists is a mind.

Nothing that in fact exists is a mind.

I (I that am a thinking substance) do in fact exist.

Therefore I (I that am a thinking substance) am not a mind.

TT

What now? The form of argument is sound and valid: it never goes wrong, it never produces a false conclusion unless one of the premisses happens to be false. And hence any fault you find in the conclusion must necessarily arise not from the form of argument but from some false assumption in the premisses. Now do you really think the assumption that was the starting point of your entire journey was correct, *viz.* 'Nothing which is such that I can doubt whether it is true or exists is in fact true or does in fact exist'? Is this certain? Have you examined it sufficiently to be able to place a firm and unconstrained reliance on it? Please tell me why you deny the statement 'I have a body'? Undoubtedly you deny it because it seems doubtful to you. But is not the statement 'I do not have a body' equally doubtful? Could anyone really base his entire doctrine and system of knowledge on a proposition which he would be sensible to regard as false – especially when he plans to set his system up as the dominant one, and impose it on others? But I have said enough. This is the final impasse, the end of our wanderings; from now on there is nothing I can hope for. So I will now go back to your question 'Is renouncing everything that is doubtful a good method of philosophizing?',[1] and will give you the free, frank and straightforward answers you expect of me.[2]

509

[Descartes]

COMMENTS

Up till now the Reverend Father has been having some fun at my expense. But in what follows he appears to adopt quite a different role and attack me in earnest. For the time being, then, I will merely record my brief observations on his humorous efforts.

KK

'Formerly? Was there a former time?' 'I am dreaming that I am thinking, so I am not thinking.' These and similar remarks are witticisms that are wholly appropriate to the character my critic has assumed. The

1 See above p. 313.   2 Bourdin's 'answers' appear below, pp. 358ff.

[Descartes]

same goes for the solemn question 'Does thinking extend more widely than dreaming?', the proposed title 'the method of dreaming', and the principle 'In order to reason aright we must dream.'[1] But I do not think I in fact provided even the smallest target for this kind of mockery, since I expressly indicated that in talking about the beliefs I had renounced I was not affirming that they were true but merely that they seemed to be so. And so when I raised the question of what I had formerly supposed myself to be, I was merely asking what it seemed to me that I had formerly thought. And when I said that I was thinking, I did not inquire whether I was awake or asleep while I was thinking. I am surprised that he dubs my method 'the method of dreaming', when it seems, to say the least, to have jolted him out of his slumbers.

My critic's next piece of reasoning is also well suited to the role he has assumed. He thinks that, if I am to ask what I formally considered myself to be, I should state the implied premiss 'I am one of the things I formerly believed myself to be', or 'I am what I formerly believed myself to be.' And shortly afterwards he insists that in order to raise the question of whether I am a body I should make explicit the 'striking and remarkable presupposition involved', *viz.* 'My former beliefs regarding what pertains to a body were correct', or 'Nothing belongs to a body beyond what I formerly understood to belong to it.'[2] Remarks which are manifestly absurd are well suited to provoke laughter; but it is clear that it was both possible and useful for me to raise the question of what I formerly believed myself to be, and of whether I was a body, despite the fact that I did not know whether I was any of the things I had previously believed myself to be, or that my former beliefs were correct. The point of raising the question was to enable me to examine what I was with the aid of the new perceptions I was now on the verge of achieving; or, if nothing else, I should at least realize that this line of inquiry would not enable me to discover anything.

My critic continues to play his comic role outstandingly well when he tells the story of the peasant. But what is most laughable here is that he thinks the story applies to my words, when in fact it applies only to his own. A moment ago he was censuring me for not stating the premiss 'My former beliefs regarding what pertains to a body were correct', or 'Nothing belongs to a body apart from what I formally understood to belong to it.' And yet now he takes this very proposition which he was just complaining I had not stated (and which he drew entirely from his own imagination) and attacks it, as if I had really put it forward, comparing it with the absurd piece of reasoning produced by his

1 Above pp. 344f.   2 Above p. 336.

[Descartes]

peasant.[1] In fact I never based my assertion that a thinking thing is not a
511   body on the premiss that my former beliefs about the nature of body
were correct; it was based on the fact that while confining my use of the
term 'body' to designating a thing of which I had sufficient knowledge,
viz. an extended substance, I recognized a thinking thing to be quite
different from this.

NN   Here we have, yet again, the subtle dialogue my critic has already
produced several times before: '"I am thinking." I deny it – you are
dreaming. "This is certain and evident". I deny it – you are dreaming; it
only appears certain and evident, but it is not really so.' These comments
are amusing enough, if only because they would be so inappropriate if
they were intended to be serious. But it may be that beginners will be led
astray here into thinking that if someone doubts whether he is awake or
dreaming, then nothing can be certain and evident to him, but things can
only seem or appear so. To prevent this, I would like people to remember
what I pointed out above, at letter F, namely that if something is clearly
perceived, then no matter who the perceiver is, it is true, and does not
merely seem or appear to be true.[2] There are, however, few people who
correctly distinguish between what they in fact perceive and what they
think they perceive; for not many people are accustomed to clear and
distinct perceptions.

OO   So far our critic has not managed to depict anything in the way of a
memorable battle. He has merely set up some paltry obstacles in his own
path, shaken his fist at them for a short time, and then sounded the
retreat without more ado and marched off elsewhere. But now he
embarks on a mighty struggle against an enemy who is supremely worthy
of his little drama, namely the ghost of myself – a ghost which is not
visible to anyone else but which has been formed out of his own brain.
And to make sure that the ghost should look completely insubstantial, he
512   has constructed it from nothingness itself! But he joins battle with it in all
seriousness; he argues till he is sweating with effort; he makes a truce, he
calls in logic to help him, he renews the fight; he 'shakes my statements
out one by one and measures and weighs them in turn'.[3] And, then, not
daring to meet the blows of his valiant foe with his shield, he dodges
them, throws in a distinction, and finally, by means of the diversion
'determinately and indeterminately' escapes in full flight. What a delight-
ful spectacle, especially once we appreciate the cause of this heroic battle.
He must have read somewhere in my writings that any true opinions
which we have before we begin to philosophize seriously are mixed up
with many others that are either false or at least doubtful. And hence, in

1 Above pp. 336f.   2 Cf. above pp. 309f.   3 Above p. 339.

[Descartes]

order to separate out the true ones, it is best to begin by rejecting all our opinions and renouncing every single one; this will make it easier, afterwards, to recognize those which were true (or discover new truths), so that we end up by admitting only what is true. Now this is just the same as if I had said that if we have a basket or tub full of apples and want to make sure that there are no rotten ones, we should first tip them all out, leaving none at all inside, and then pick up again (or get from elsewhere) only those apples in which no flaw can be detected. But my critic does not grasp this profound piece of theory, or rather pretends he does not grasp it, and he stands amazed – especially at the statement 'There is nothing that should not be renounced.' Indeed, after thinking hard and long about this 'nothing',[1] he has become so obsessed with it that he finds it hard to get it out of his mind, even though by this time he is fighting most of his battles against himself.

After this successful battle, and elated with his supposed victory, my critic attacks a new enemy – one which he again believes to be my ghost (for it is always there in his imagination) but which he now constructs out of fresh material, namely the words 'I know I exist; the next question is, what is this "I" . . .' Now he is not so well acquainted with this new target as he was with the previous one, and so his attack is more cautious and he does not come into close range. The first missile he throws is 'Why do you ask, if you know?' He thinks the enemy will shield himself as follows: 'I know that I exist, not what I am'; and so he immediately launches his longer and more pointed spear: 'How will you discover the nature of this "I" that exists, if not from what you formerly knew or will know later on? Surely you will not have recourse to what you formerly knew, since all this is full of doubt and has been renounced. Therefore you must be relying on what you do not yet know but will know later on.' He thinks the wretched ghost will be very upset and all but overcome by this blow, and imagines it crying out 'I do not yet know that these things exist.' Then he turns from anger to pity and consoles the ghost with the words 'Keep up your hopes! You will find out at some time or other.' He then has the ghost replying in querulous and supplicating tones 'But what am I to do in the meantime?' And he answers in the haughty tones of a conqueror: 'Keep waiting.'[2] But being a merciful man, he does not leave the ghost in suspense for long. Instead, he rushes back to the diversion 'determinately, indeterminately; clearly, confusedly', and seeing that no one challenges him here, he triumphs by default. All this is excellent; it is the kind of joke that depends on someone pretending to be a fool when his looks and style of dress made us expect great seriousness

PP 513

1 Above p. 339.   2 Above p. 341.

[Descartes]

and wisdom. To make this point clearer, let us regard our critic as a man
of seriousness and learning who wants to attack my method of seeking
514   out the truth. The method tells us to reject everything that is uncertain,
and start from knowledge of our own existence, progressing from there
to an examination of our nature, or that thing which we already know to
exist. Now my critic attempts to show that this route provides no access
to further knowledge and he uses the following argument: 'Given that
you know merely that you exist, and not what you are, you cannot learn
this from what you formerly knew, since you have renounced everything;
hence you must be relying on what you do not yet know.' A three year
old child could supply the answer to this: there is nothing to prevent our
learning from what we formerly knew, since even though these beliefs
were renounced because they were doubtful, we shall be able to re-adopt
them afterwards when we establish their truth. Moreover, even if we
were to concede that nothing can be learnt from our former knowledge,
there is another route still open, *viz.* the things that we have not so far
known but will succeed in coming to know by effort and concentration.
But here my critic imagines an enemy who not only concedes that the
former route is closed, but actually blocks off the latter one himself by
saying 'I do not know that these things exist.' This is to imply that we can
never acquire fresh knowledge of what exists, and also that our
ignorance of what exists precludes any knowledge of essences. This really
is utterly stupid. But even here there is an allusion to my own words, for I
wrote that the knowledge I already have of something I know to exist
cannot possibly depend on the knowledge of things of whose existence I
am as yet unaware.[1] I made this remark about the present, but my critic
absurdly transfers it to the future, just as if he were to infer from the fact
that we cannot see those who are not yet born, but will be born this year,
515   that we will never be able to see them. It is transparently clear that the
already acquired knowledge of a thing which is recognized as existing
does not depend on the knowledge of that which we have not yet
recognized as existing; for the very fact that something is perceived to
belong to an existing thing necessarily implies that it is perceived to exist.
But it is quite different in the case of the future, since nothing prevents
knowledge of the thing which I know to exist being augmented by
knowledge of other things which I do not yet know to exist, but which I
will recognize afterwards, when I perceive that they belong to the thing in
question. However, my critic goes on to say 'Keep up your hopes; you
will find out some time or other'; and then, 'I will not keep you in
suspense for long.' Here he leads us to expect either that he will

1 Cf. p. 18 above.

[Descartes]
demonstrate that no further knowledge is attainable by the proposed
route, or else that he will open up another route, on the supposition
(which is in fact foolish) that the original one has been closed by his
opponent. But all he goes on to say is 'You know what you are
indeterminately and confusedly, not determinately and clearly.' The most
straightforward inference from this is that a route to further knowledge *is*
open to us, because we shall later be able, through meditation and
concentration, to achieve a clear and determinate perception of what we
now know only indeterminately and confusedly. The conclusion which
he draws, however, is that 'This one distinction between "determinately"
and "indeterminately" will block our progress for a whole century',[1] and
hence that we must search for another route. I think that producing all
these observations is the best plan my critic could possibly have devised
in order to maintain his pretence of complete mental ineptitude and
stupidity.

'"I exist"; I deny it. "I am thinking"; I deny it', etc. Here my critic   QQ 5
attacks the poor old ghost again, and supposing that he has dispatched it
at the first blow he boastfully shouts out 'What a splendid achievement;
at a stroke I have chopped off everything!' But since the ghost lives only
in my critic's brain and cannot die till he does, it revives despite all the
'chopping off'; and putting its hand on its heart it swears that it exists
and is thinking. My critic is mollified by this new kind of pleading, and
spares its life. He allows it to collect its strength for the last time and
produce some more fatuous observations; he does not refute these,
however, but makes a treaty of friendship and passes on to other
fatuities.

First, he raises the following complaint: 'A little time ago, just a few   RR
steps back, you were asking me "What is this 'I'?" But now it turns out
that not only do you know what you are, but you have a clear and
distinct concept of it.' He then begs to be shown 'just one glimpse of this
concept that is so clear and distinct' so that he may revive at the sight of
it. Then he pretends that he has been afforded such a glimpse, thus: 'Here
you are then: I know for certain that I exist and am thinking, and that I
exist as a thinking substance.' He then proves that this will not do, by
means of the following example: 'If you know that no mountain exists
without a valley, do you therefore possess a clear and distinct concept of
a mountain without a valley?' He explains the point as follows: 'This
concept of yours is clear because you have certain knowledge of it, and it
is distinct because you are aware of nothing else ... and hence the
concept of a thinking substance which you form is clear and distinct in so

1 Above p. 341.

[Descartes]

far as it represents to you that a thinking substance exists, without your
having to attend to the body or the soul or the mind or anything else
517   apart from the existence of this substance.' Finally he resumes his warlike
frame of mind and thinks he sees a mighty army including 'reserves in
their serried ranks', which he proposes, like the braggart Pyrgopolynices[1]
to scatter 'as the wind blows the leaves or scatters clumps of thatch' so
that 'not even a single messenger will be left to tell the tale'. His first blast
is the comment that 'the inference from knowledge to existence is not a
valid one', and he produces, like a fluttering flag of victory, a diagram
which contains a completely arbitrary classification of thinking
substance.[2] His second blast is the distinction between 'determinately and
indeterminately, distinctly and confusedly, explicitly and implicitly'. His
third blast is that 'an over-ambitious inference fails to establish anything
at all'. Finally he produces the following exposition: 'I know I exist as a
thinking substance, but I do not yet know that a mind exists. Hence the
knowledge of my existence does not depend on knowledge of an existing
mind. So since I exist, and a mind does not exist, I am not a mind.
Therefore I am a body.'[3] Hearing this, the ghost has no answer; it
retreats, gives up hope, and allows itself to be taken prisoner and led in
triumph. There is much here that deserves to be laughed at now and for
evermore, but rather than point this out I prefer to respect the actor's
costume that my critic has assumed; and indeed I do not think it is right
for me to spend all this time laughing at such ill-considered comments. So
I shall confine my remarks to those criticisms which some readers might
perhaps suppose I had accepted if I were to ignore them completely,
though in fact they are utterly unfounded.

518   I turn first to the suggestion that I claimed to possess a clear and
distinct concept of myself before providing a sufficient explanation of
how I had acquired it, and at a time when 'just a few steps back' I had
been asking what I was,[4] as he puts it. This complaint is quite unjustified.
For in between asking the question and answering it I went through all
the properties of a thinking thing, namely understanding, willing,
imagining, remembering, having sensory perceptions etc.; and I also
listed all the other commonly accepted properties which do not belong to
it, in order to distinguish the latter from the former – a task we could not
hope to perform until our preconceived opinions had been removed. I
admit, however, that those who do not abandon their preconceived
opinions will find it hard to acquire a clear and distinct concept of
anything; for it is obvious that the concepts which we had in our

1 Character in Plautus' comedy *Miles Gloriosus*; the quotation is from Act 1, Scene 1, line
18.   2 Above p. 344.   3 Above p. 345.   4 Above p. 342.

[Descartes]

childhood were not clear and distinct, and hence, if not set aside, they will affect any other concepts which we acquire later and make them obscure and confused. Thus when my critic asks for a glimpse of 'that clear and distinct concept, so that he may revive at the sight of it' he is being fatuous, and the same applies to his subsequent presentation of me as affording him the desired glimpse with the words 'I know for certain that I exist', etc.[1] But when he tries to refute his own fatuity by asking whether I have a clear and distinct concept of a mountain without a valley simply because I know for certain that no mountain exists without a valley, he is confusing himself with his own sophism. For the premiss as stated merely implies that I clearly and distinctly perceive that no mountain exists without a valley, not that I have a concept of a mountain without a valley. Since there is no such concept, we do not have to possess it in order to perceive that no mountain exists without a valley. But presumably my critic has such a 'brilliant intellect'[2] that he cannot   519 refute the fatuities he himself has constructed except by producing fresh ones.

When he goes on to say 'I conceive of myself as a thinking substance and I have no conception of anything corporeal or spiritual', etc.,[3] I accept this, as far as the corporeal is concerned, for I had previously explained that by the term 'body' or 'corporeal thing' I meant merely that which is extended, or that which contains extension as part of its concept. But his inclusion of the spiritual is a foolish addition; and the same goes for the many other places where he represents me as saying 'I am a thinking thing, but I am not a body or a soul or a mind', etc. In fact I deny of a thinking thing only those items such that I know that no thought is contained in their concept; and I never wrote or thought that this applies to the soul or the mind.

He goes on to say that he grasps what I have in mind, *viz.* that I take the concept of myself to be clear because I have certain knowledge of it, and I consider it to be distinct because I am aware of nothing else.[4] But here he is pretending to be very slow-witted. It is one thing to perceive something clearly, and another to know it for certain: there are many things that we now know for certain, either through faith or because we clearly perceived them on an earlier occasion, but which we do not now perceive clearly. Moreover, awareness of other things in no way prevents the awareness we do have of something from being distinct. I have never written a single word which could justify this kind of absurd interpretation.

The claim that 'the inference from knowledge to existence is not a valid   520

1 Above p. 343.   2 *Ibid.*   3 *Ibid.*   4 *Ibid.*

[Descartes]

one'[1] is plainly false. Admittedly the fact that we know the essence of something does not entail that it exists, nor does it follow from the fact that we think we know something that it exists, if there is a possibility of our being mistaken. But the inference from knowledge to existence is still quite valid, since it is plainly impossible for us to know something unless it really is exactly as we know it to be – i.e. existing, if we perceive that it exists, or of such and such a nature, if it is merely its nature that we know.

It is also false, or at least asserted without the slightest supporting reason, that some thinking substance is divisible.[2] This is the claim made in the table where he sets out various types of thinking substance as if he had got his information from some oracle. In fact we cannot understand thought to possess any extension or divisibility, and it is wholly absurd to put this forward as a true claim when it has neither been revealed by God nor established by our intellect. And I cannot refrain from pointing out here that this doctrine of the divisibility of thinking substance seems to me exceedingly dangerous and entirely at variance with the Christian religion. For as long as anyone accepts it he will never be persuaded by the force of reasoning to acknowledge the real distinction between the human soul and the body.

The contrast between 'determinately and indeterminately, distinctly and confusedly, explicitly and implicitly'[3] has no meaning at all when it is simply set down without any further explanation, as it is here. It seems to be merely a piece of pedantry which my critic is apparently trying to use to persuade his disciples that he has some good thoughts, when in fact he has nothing worthwhile to say.

My critic's other dictum, *viz.* 'An over-ambitious inference fails to establish anything at all',[4] should not be accepted without making a distinction. By the term 'over-ambitious' he may mean merely something which is beyond what we were looking for; thus in a passage below he criticizes the arguments by which I demonstrated the existence of God because he thinks they establish more than the laws of prudence require or than any mortal demands.[5] But in that case his dictum is quite false and foolish, for the more conclusions we can draw, provided they are sound, the better; and there cannot be any laws of prudence which can ever conflict with this. Alternatively, he might mean by the term 'over-ambitious' not just something more than we were looking for, but something which is incontrovertibly false; and in this case his dictum is true. But the Reverend Father is quite wrong in trying to foist anything of this sort onto me. What I wrote was that 'the knowledge of those things that I know to exist does not depend on the knowledge of things of

1 Above p. 344.   2 See diagram, p. 344.   3 *Ibid.*   4 *Ibid.*   5 Below p. 361.

[Descartes]

whose existence I am as yet unaware; now I know that a thinking thing exists, but I do not yet know that any body exists; therefore the knowledge of a thinking thing does not depend on knowledge of the body'.[1] But here none of my conclusions were 'over-ambitious', since they were all valid. As for the line of thought which my critic offers, *viz.* 'I know that a thinking thing exists, and I do not yet know that a mind exists; in fact no mind exists, nothing exists, since I have renounced all my beliefs'[2] – this is quite fatuous and false. For I cannot affirm or deny anything of the mind unless I know what I understand by the term 522 'mind'; and of all the ways in which this term is normally understood, there is none, on my understanding, that does not contain some reference to thought. Hence it is self-contradictory for anyone to know that a thinking thing exists and not to know that a mind exists, or that there exists some element of what is signified by the term 'mind'. Hence the comment that 'in fact no mind exists, nothing exists, since I have renounced all my beliefs' is so absurd as not to deserve a reply. For after making my renunciation, I acknowledged the existence of a thinking thing, and hence I simultaneously acknowledged the existence of a mind (at least in so far as this term signifies a thinking thing); accordingly, from this time on the existence of the mind ceased to be something that I renounced.

Finally, when he is about to deploy syllogisms in his formal presentation,[3] and he extols them as 'a method of conducting our reasoning' which is to be contrasted with my own, his apparent intention is to persuade people that I do not approve of syllogistic patterns of argument, and hence that my method is not a rational one. But this is false, as is clear enough from my writings where I have always been prepared to use syllogisms when the occasion required it.

Here he constructs a syllogism from false premisses which he claims SS are my own. But this I emphatically deny. As far as the major premiss is concerned, *viz.* 'Nothing which is such that I can doubt whether it exists does in fact exist',[4] it is so absurd that I have no fear of his being able to persuade anyone that it came from me, unless he can simultaneously persuade people that I am not in my right mind. Indeed, I am lost in admiration at his sound judgement, good faith, hope and confidence in undertaking this task. For in the First Meditation I was not yet concerned 523 with establishing any truths, but was merely setting about eradicating my preconceived opinions. I showed that these opinions, which I had been accustomed to believe quite unreservedly, could be called into doubt, and hence that I should withhold my assent from them just as carefully as I

1 Cf. Med. II, above pp. 18f (not an exact quotation).
2 Above p. 345. 3 *Ibid.* 4 Above p. 346.

[Descartes]
would from obvious falsehoods, if they were not to be a possible
hindrance to me in my search for truth. I then went on as follows:

> But it is not enough merely to have noticed this; I must make an effort to
> remember it. My habitual *opinions* keep coming back and, despite my wishes,
> they capture my belief, which is, as it were, bound over to them as a result of long
> occupation and the law of custom. I shall never get out of the habit of confidently
> assenting to these opinions so long as I suppose them to be what in fact they are,
> namely highly probable opinions – opinions which, despite the fact that they are
> *in a sense doubtful*, as has just been shown, it is still much more reasonable to
> believe than to deny. In view of this I think it will be a good plan to *turn my will
> in completely the opposite direction* and deceive myself, by pretending for a time
> that these former opinions are *utterly false and imaginary*. I shall do this until the
> weight of preconceived opinion is counter-balanced, and the distorting influence
> of habit no longer prevents my judgement from perceiving things correctly.[1]

Now my critic has ignored most of this passage and extracted the
following phrases: 'opinions which are in a sense doubtful', 'turn my
will in completely the opposite direction' and 'pretend that they are
utterly false and imaginary'. What is more, for the word 'pretend' he has
substituted 'maintain and believe', and indeed 'believe' to the extent of
taking the 'opposite of what is doubtful' and affirming it as true.[2] He will
524   have it that this is the maxim or reliable rule to which I constantly
adhere, not just for uprooting my preconceived opinions, but for
establishing the foundations of a supremely certain and exact metaphysics. To begin with he suggests this hesitantly and ambiguously,
namely in Sections 2 and 3 of his 'First Question'.[3] But in Section 3, after
assuming that this rule requires him to believe that two and three do not
make five, he asks 'whether he should constantly believe this, to the
extent of convincing himself that it cannot be otherwise'. Having asked
this utterly absurd question, he then represents me as producing various
evasive and superfluous comments and finally replying 'Neither affirm
nor deny it; employ neither statement but regard them both as false.'[4]
Now his attributing this reply to me makes it quite clear that he did
understand perfectly well that I do not in fact believe as true the opposite
of what is doubtful, and that no one, on my view, can possibly employ
this proposition as the major premiss of any syllogism which is supposed
to yield a certain conclusion. For there is a clear contradiction between
'neither affirming nor denying', i.e. employing neither statement, and
'affirming one of them as true', i.e. employing one of them. But he
gradually forgets the reply which he had reported as my own, and goes
on not only to affirm the opposite but to insist on it again and again;

1 Above p. 15.   2 Cf. above p. 306.   3 Above pp. 305–7.   4 p. 308.

[Descartes]

indeed, it seems that this entire discussion is virtually confined to this one point of criticism, and that the twelve faults which he foists onto me in his concluding sections[1] are all based on this and this alone.

From all this, one conclusion quite evidently and demonstrably follows about what my critic is doing, not only here, where he takes the major premiss 'Nothing that is such that I can doubt whether it exists does in fact exist' and asserts that it is my own maxim, but also in all the other 525 places where he attributes this sort of thing to me. The conclusion, unless I am wholly ignorant of what is meant by the verb 'to lie', is that he is inexcusably lying – saying what he does not believe and knows to be false. Although I am very reluctant to use such a distasteful term, the defence of the truth which I have undertaken requires of me that I should not refuse to call something by the proper word, when my critic is so unashamedly and openly guilty of the deed. Throughout this whole discussion he does virtually nothing else but repeat this foolish lie in a hundred different ways, and try to persuade and bludgeon the reader into accepting it. In view of this, I think his only possible excuse is that he has asserted the same thing so emphatically and so often that he has gradually managed to convince himself that it is true, and no longer recognizes it as the lie that he himself invented. I now turn to the minor premiss: 'Every body is such that I can doubt whether it exists', or 'Every mind is such that I can doubt whether it exists.'[2] If this is taken unrestrictedly to apply to any occasion whatsoever (and this is how it must be taken if his conclusion is to follow), then, like the major premiss, it is false, and I deny that it represents my own view. For immediately after the beginning of the Second Meditation, when I perceived with certainty that a thinking thing existed – that thinking thing which in common usage is termed a 'mind' – I could no longer doubt that it existed. Equally, once I had recognized the existence of body, in the Sixth Meditation, no further doubt was possible about this. What a formidable intellect my critic possesses! He has managed with supreme ingenuity to devise false premisses such that a false conclusion follows from them in a valid pattern of argument. But I do not understand why he here presents me as 'smiling bitterly',[3] since I have in fact been able to find some cause 526 for pleasure in his discussion – not great pleasure, it is true, but genuine and solid satisfaction for all that. The reason is that in criticizing all these claims that are not mine, but which he has foisted on me, he clearly shows that he has left no stone unturned in his attempts to find something worth criticizing in my book, and yet for all that he has been quite unable to find anything at all.

1 Below pp. 358ff.   2 Above pp. 345f.   3. p. 345

[Descartes]

TT   But any smiling that *he* has done has certainly not been sincere, as is
shown both by the grim attack with which he concludes this section and
especially by the 'replies' that now follow, in which he is not only
sombre and straight-faced but positively cruel. The explanation is
presumably as follows. Although he has no cause to hate me, he has
found nothing to criticize in my book except for the one absurd maxim
which he has deliberately and knowingly foisted onto me and which, a
moment ago, I was unable to describe in any more pleasant terms than as
a plain lie. Nevertheless, he thinks that he has completely convinced his
readers that I do accept this maxim, not through the force of his
arguments, since he does not have any, but because of the remarkable
self-assurance with which he makes his statements. For people will never
think that a man who makes a special profession of piety and Christian
charity could be shameless enough to make such confident statements
concerning something he knows to be false. He also relies on the
perseverence and frequency with which he repeats the same thing, for it
frequently happens that even when we know that something is false, we
get used to hearing it, and thus gradually get into the habit of regarding it
as true. Confident assertion and frequent repetition are the two ploys that
are often more effective than the most weighty arguments when dealing
with ordinary people or those who do not examine things carefully. So
now he arrogantly taunts his defeated foe and lectures me like a strict
schoolmaster telling off a pupil, accusing me in the twelve replies that
527   follow of more sins than are contained in the ten commandments. But we
should excuse the Reverend Father, since he seems to have lost control of
himself. Just as those who have drunk too much often see double, he is so
fired with charitable zeal that he manages to discover twelve faults to
charge me with, all arising out of the one maxim which he has foisted on
me so perversely and dishonestly. Were it not embarrassing to state it
openly and unambiguously, I should have to say that these charges were
simply slander and abuse; but since I think it is now my turn to have
some fun, I shall merely call them hallucinations, and I will ask my
readers to remember that every single word the Reverend Father utters in
the following replies is the result of his suffering from a hallucination.

[Bourdin]

REPLY[1]

Reply 1. The method is faulty in its principles, which are either

---

1 To the question 'Is renouncing everything a good method of philosophizing?' see above
pp. 313, 346.

[Bourdin]

non-existent or unlimited. Other systems which aim to derive certain results from certain starting points lay down clear, evident and innate principles such as 'The whole is greater than one of its parts', 'Nothing comes from nothing' and countless others of this sort; and by relying on these they are able to rise aloft and strive after the truth without danger. But your method is quite different, since it aims to derive something not from something but from nothing. It chops off, renounces and forswears all former beliefs without exception; it requires the will to be turned in completely the opposite direction, and, to avoid the impression that it has no wings to rise aloft, it puts on artificial wings of wax and adopts new principles which are the complete opposite of those formerly held. Thus it divests itself of all old preconceived opinions in order to put on new ones; it lays aside what is certain in order to take up what is doubtful; it equips itself with wings, but they are made of wax; it soars aloft only to   528 fall; and finally, it struggles to derive something from nothing, only to end up producing nothing at all.

Reply 2. The method is faulty in the implements it uses, for as long as it destroys the old without providing any replacements, it has no implements at all. Other systems have formal logic, syllogisms and reliable patterns of argument, which they use like Ariadne's thread to guide them out of the labyrinth; with these instruments they can safely and easily unravel the most complicated problems. But your new method denigrates the traditional forms of argument, and instead grows pale with a new terror – the imaginary fear of the demon which it has conjured up. It fears it may be dreaming; it has doubts about whether it is mad. If you propose any syllogism, it will be scared of the major premiss, whatever it may be. 'The evil demon may be deceiving us', it says. What about the minor premiss? It will tremble and call it doubtful. 'What if I am dreaming? How often have things seemed certain and clear to me while dreaming, and yet afterwards turned out to be false, once the dream was over!' Finally, what about the conclusion? It will run away from all conclusions as if they were traps and snares. 'People who are raving, or children, or madmen may believe that they are producing a splendidly rational argument when in fact their powers of reason and judgement are seriously deficient. So what if the same thing is now happening to me? What if the demon is tricking and deluding me? He is malicious, and I do not yet know that God exists and that the demon is being curbed by him.' What will you do about this? What will you do when your method obstinately maintains that any conclusion you draw is doubtful unless you previously know for certain that you are not dreaming or mad, and that there is a God, a truthful God, who has the evil demon under

[Bourdin]
control? You may produce your syllogism 'To say that something is contained in the nature or concept of anything is the same as saying that it is really true of that thing; now existence is contained in the nature and concept of God', etc.[1] But what if your method repudiates both the content and the form of this argument and other arguments of this kind? Whatever argument you press, the reply will be 'Wait until I know there is a God and see the demon curbed.' You may say that by failing to produce any syllogisms your method at least has the advantage of

529　avoiding any fallacies. A splendid notion this – to cut a child's nose off so that it will not suffer from catarrh! Is it not better to wipe its nose, as mothers do? In short, I have just one point to make: if you take away all form, nothing remains but the formless, or the deformed.

　　Reply 3. The method goes astray by failing to reach its goal, for it does not attain any certainty. Indeed, it cannot do so, since it has itself blocked off all the roads to the truth. You yourself have seen and experienced this during the long odyssey when you wandered around and exhausted both yourself and me, your companion. You maintained that you were a mind, or that you had a mind, but you were quite unable to establish this since you got stuck on rugged slopes and in dense thickets more times than I can remember. Yet it will be useful to go over the problems again, to reinforce the present reply. Here then are the chief ways in which your method cuts its own throat or cuts off all hope of attaining the light of truth. (1) You do not know whether you are dreaming or awake, and hence you can place no more confidence in your thoughts and reasonings (that is, if you have any, and are not merely dreaming you have them) than a dreamer can place in the thoughts he has while asleep. Hence everything is doubtful and shaky, and your very inferences are uncertain. I shall not produce any examples; you may yourself proceed to run through the storehouse of your memory, and if you find anything which is not infected with this rot, then bring it out, and I shall congratulate you. (2) Until I know that there exists a God who will curb the evil demon, I must continue to doubt everything and consider every proposition as suspect. Or at any rate – to revert to the ordinary style of philosophy and the traditional method of reasoning – we must first of all determine whether any propositions are immune from doubt, and if so which propositions they are; and we must then instruct the beginner to keep hold of these. So everything is doubtful, just as we found under point (1), and hence we have nothing left which will be the slightest use for investigating the truth. (3) If anything contains even the smallest element of doubt, we must turn our will in completely the opposite

1 See Second Replies, above p. 117.

[Bourdin]
direction and believe that it is false; indeed, we must believe the opposite   530
and employ it as a principle in our inquiry. But this cuts off every
pathway to the truth. What can you possibly hope to get from such
propositions as 'I do not have a head', 'There is no body and no mind',
and countless others of this sort? You cannot reply that this renunciation
of yours is not perpetual but is like a suspension of the law sittings for a
fixed time, a month or a fortnight, to allow everyone the freedom to
devote himself to the task with all the more effort. For even if we concede
that the renunciation is only for a fixed period, this is the very period
when you are searching for the truth, the time when you are actually
using, or misusing, the beliefs you have renounced, just as if all truth
depended on them, or as if they were the necessary base on which it
rested. 'But I am employing the technique of renunciation to strengthen
my foundations and columns, as architects do', you reply. 'Do they not
construct temporary scaffolding to use while they are raising the column
and fixing it in place – scaffolding which they dismantle and remove once
it has discharged its function so admirably? Why should I not imitate
them?' You may indeed imitate them, as far as I am concerned, but be
careful that your foundations and columns are not supported by your
temporary scaffolding in such a way that they collapse once it is removed.
This is precisely the point at which it seems to me that your method is
vulnerable to criticism. It lays down false foundations and then relies on
them in such a way that once they are removed, it too becomes liable to
be shifted.

Reply 4. The method goes astray by being excessive. That is, it
attempts more than the laws of prudence demand of it, more, indeed,
than any mortal demands. Admittedly there are people who are looking
for a demonstration of the existence of God and the immortality of the
human mind. But you will not find anyone up till now who has been
dissatisfied if propositions like 'God exists and the world is governed by
him', or 'The souls of men are spiritual and immortal', are known with as
much certainty as 'Two and three make five', or 'I have a head and a
body.' So all these efforts to search for some higher grade of certainty are
superfluous. Moreover, just as in practical concerns there are well-   531
defined limits of certainty which are quite sufficient to enable people to
manage their affairs sensibly and safely, so in the area of meditation and
speculation there are definite limits. Anyone who attains these limits has
certainty – indeed he is so certain that if people try to push the limits
further to encompass some desperate or lost cause, he sensibly and safely
halts, declaring 'No more: do not attempt too much!' 'And yet', you
reply, 'to push the limits further, and cross the sea which no one in past

[Bourdin]

ages has ever tried to cross, is an achievement that deserves no ordinary praise.' Yes, it deserves high praise indeed – provided you can cross the sea without shipwreck. So I come to the next point.

Reply 5. The method is faulty because it is deficient. That is, in pushing too hard it achieves nothing at all. Here you yourself are the only witness and judge I need. What results have you obtained with all your magnificent apparatus? What has your solemn renunciation brought you – a renunciation so general and unstinting that you have not even spared yourself, apart from the cliché 'I am thinking; I am; I am a thinking thing'? The cliché is so familiar, even to the mass of mankind, that you will find no one since the foundation of the world who has had even the slightest doubt about it, let alone anyone who has seriously asked for a proof that he is, that he exists, that he is a thinking thing. So you deserve no thanks, nor will you get any, unless someone happens to recognize your wholehearted good-will towards the human race and applauds your efforts, as indeed I do, because of my friendship and special concern for you.

Reply 6. The method commits the common fault which it accuses other systems of committing. It is astonished that everyone should say and maintain with such confidence 'I have a head, I have eyes', etc., and yet is not equally astonished at itself when it claims with just as much confidence 'I do not have a head', etc.

Reply 7. The method commits a fault peculiar to itself. The rest of mankind regard the assertion 'I have a head; body and mind exist' as 532 certain up to a point – sufficiently certain. But your peculiar strategy regards the opposite assertion, 'I do not have a head; there is no body or mind', as not just certain, but so certain than an exact metaphysics can be based on it. Indeed, your method places so much weight on this crutch that if you remove it, it will fall flat on its face.

Reply 8. It goes astray through negligence. That is, it fails to observe that doubt is a two-edged sword, and while avoiding one edge, it cuts itself on the other. Since it regards the statement 'Some body exists' as doubtful, it removes it and sets up the opposite statement 'No body exists'; but by imprudently adopting this doubtful statement and relying on it as if it were certain, it ends up by cutting itself.

Reply 9. It goes astray wilfully. For knowingly, voluntarily and advisedly it blinds itself, and by deliberately renouncing what it needs in order to investigate the truth, it allows itself to be deluded by its own analysis; thus it not only produces results it did not intend, but also those which it most fears.

Reply 10. It sins by commission, by returning to former beliefs which it

[Bourdin]
had proscribed by solemn edict, and by reassuming opinions that were renounced, thus violating the law of renunciation. Think back, and you will see this well enough.

Reply 11. It sins by omission. For having laid it down as a fundamental principle that we should 'take great care not to admit as true anything we cannot prove to be true', it proceeds to violate the principle more than once. It assumes with impunity, and regards as completely certain and true, unproved statements such as 'The senses sometimes deceive us', 'We are all dreaming', 'Some people go mad', and so on.

Reply 12. What the method contains is either unsound or nothing new, and for the most part it is superfluous.

(i) You may say that your renunciation of what is doubtful is meant to be a 'metaphysical abstraction', as they call it; that is, what is doubtful is considered simply as doubtful and hence, when we are looking for $\quad$ 533 something certain, our mind is withdrawn from these matters and we place no more reliance in them than we do in what is false. If this is the case, then what your method says is *sound*, but nothing *new*, and the renunciation will not be anything new either, but a traditional device which all philosophers without exception have adopted.

(ii) If the renunciation of what is doubtful means that doubtful matters must be dismissed in the sense that we are to suppose and maintain that they are false, treating them as false, or their opposites as true, then this is something *new*, but it is utterly *unsound*, and so your renunciation will be novel, but illegitimate.

(iii) You may claim that your method can achieve the following result by weighty and powerful arguments: 'I am a thinking thing, and in so far as I am a thinking thing, I am neither mind, nor soul, nor body, but something so separate from these things that I can understand myself without understanding these things, just as an animal, or sentient thing, can be understood without our understanding that it is a thing that neighs or bellows', etc. This claim is *sound*, but nothing *new*: you will find lecture rooms everywhere echoing with this doctrine, which is put forward in various different ways by everyone who considers that some animated creatures think; indeed, if thought includes sensation, so that everything that has sensations and sees and hears also thinks, then the doctrine is held by everyone who believes that the brutes have sensations, i.e. everyone without exception.

(iv) If you say that your method proves by powerful and well thought-out arguments that you really exist as a thinking thing or substance, and that while you exist, the mind and the body and the soul do not really exist, then you are saying something *new* but quite

[Bourdin]

unsound. For your claim is just as suspect as saying that an animal exists, but that no lion, or fox, or whatever, exists.

(v) By 'thinking' you may mean that you understand and will and imagine and have sensations, and that you think in such a way that you can contemplate and consider your thought by a reflexive act. This would mean that when you think, you know and consider that you are thinking 534 (and this is really what it is to be conscious and to have conscious awareness of some activity). Such consciousness, you claim, is a property of a faculty or thing that is superior to matter and is wholly spiritual, and it is in this sense that you are a mind or a spirit. This claim is one you have not made before, but which should have been made; indeed, I often wanted to suggest it when I saw your method struggling ineffectively to bring it forth. But the claim, although *sound,* is nothing *new,* since we all heard it from our teachers long ago, and they heard it from their teachers, and so on, I would think, right back to Adam.

If this, then, is your claim, then what superfluous results your method has produced! What redundancy! What verbal excesses! What elaborate techniques designed to secure your glory and prestige! What was the point of all that talk about the deception of the senses, the delusions of dreamers, and the visions of madmen? What was the point of that renunciation of yours, which was so strict that it refused to leave us with anything more than a shred of existence? Why those interminable wanderings to distant shores, far away from the senses, amid ghosts and shadows? How does all this finally help to establish the existence of God – as if God's existence could not stand up unless everything is turned upside down? Why so many massive shiftings of opinion, leading us to reject our old views, adopt new ones, and then abandon the new ones only to reassume the old ones again? Perhaps it is simply that these new mysteries require new ceremonies, just as each of the pagan gods once used to have his or her own individual rites! But why does your method not lay aside all ambiguities and tell us the truth simply, clearly and briefly in one sentence: 'I think, I am conscious of thinking, therefore I am a mind'?

(vi) Finally, you may mean that understanding, willing, imagining, and having sensory awareness – i.e. thinking – are properties of a mind in such a way that no animals whatever, except for man, can think or 535 imagine or have sensations, or see, or hear. This is indeed something *new,* but it is quite *unsound.* It will turn out to be an arbitrary and unacceptable claim, unless perhaps (and this is the only hope left) you are keeping something hidden in reserve that you can bring on stage and display to the gaping audience at the crucial moment. But we have been waiting for this for so long that it is now quite hopeless.

[Bourdin]

Final reply. I think you are now fearful for your method which, understandably enough, you love and embrace and kiss like your own child. You are afraid that after convicting it of so many faults and revealing, as you can see, that it is full of holes and leaking everywhere, I shall condemn it to be thrown on the rubbish heap. But be of good courage; I am a friend! I shall disappoint and overcome your fearful expectations, by sitting quietly and waiting. I know you, and the keenness and perspicacity of your intellect: if you are given time for meditation, and allowed to consult your faithful technique of analysis in some secluded retreat, you will shake the dust off your method, wash off all the grime, and display it to our sight clean and polished once again. Meanwhile, accept my comments and give me your attention while I go on to reply to your remaining questions. I shall include many topics which for the sake of brevity I have so far touched on only lightly, namely issues relating to the mind, clear and distinct concepts, truth and falsity, and so on. But you yourself can pick up the points which we deliberately failed to deal with earlier. To proceed then:

Third question
can the method be repaired?

Your third question is . . .[1]

[Descartes]

The Reverend Father did not send me any more material, and when he was asked for the remainder, he replied that he was too busy to write it. But I have made it an article of faith not to leave out one syllable of what he wrote.

COMMENTS

536

If the author of this monstrous verdict on my method for investigating the truth (such as it is), had been someone unknown, I should have considered that merely recording it without comment would have been sufficient to reveal its falsity and absurdity. But in fact the author is so highly placed that it will be hard for anyone to believe that he is either out of his mind or else extraordinarily untruthful, slanderous and shameless. So to prevent his authority having some power to counteract the manifest truth, I ask my readers to remember that in his earlier remarks, before the twelve replies printed above, he had proved little or

---

1 As Descartes explains in the short note that follows, Bourdin's objections break off at this point.

[Descartes]

nothing against me, but had merely made use of foolish quibbles in order to foist on me opinions that were so laughable as to require no refutation. Not that he attempts to prove anything in his final replies: he merely makes the false supposition that he has previously made good all the charges of which he pretends I am guilty. To see just how fair-minded his verdict is, the reader should remember that in his previous accusations he adopted a bantering tone, but now, in his final verdict, he is wholly serious and grim. What is more, in the first twelve replies he condemns me out of hand and unhesitatingly, whereas in his final reply he deliberates and makes distinctions – 'If this is what is meant, the method contains nothing new; if that is what is meant, it is unsound', etc. Yet in fact throughout all the replies he is attacking one and the same target viewed from different angles. This single target turns out to be a figment of his own imagination, and I shall now explain just how tedious and absurd it is by means of a simile.

Throughout my writings I have made it clear that my method imitates that of the architect. When an architect wants to build a house which is stable on ground where there is a sandy topsoil over underlying rock, or clay, or some other firm base, he begins by digging out a set of trenches from which he removes the sand, and anything resting on or mixed in with the sand, so that he can lay his foundations on firm soil. In the same way, I began by taking everything that was doubtful and throwing it out, like sand; and then, when I noticed that it is impossible to doubt that a doubting or thinking substance exists, I took this as the bedrock on which I could lay the foundations of my philosophy. My critic, by contrast, is like a jobbing bricklayer who, because he wants to be regarded as a professional expert in his town, has a grudge against an architect who happens to be building a chapel there, and looks for every opportunity to criticize his work. But being so ignorant that he cannot grasp the point of anything the architect does, he only dares to attack the first and most obvious stages of the work. Thus he notices that the architect started by digging a trench, and removing not just the sand and loose soil but bits of wood and stone and anything else that is mixed up with the sand, so that he could get down to a firm base on which to lay the foundations of the chapel. He has also heard the architect answering questions about the reason for digging trenches and explaining that the topsoil on which we stand is not always firm enough to bear the weight of a large building; sand, he went on to explain, is particularly unstable because it not only sinks when a heavy weight is placed on it, but is also quite often shifted by running water, which leads to the unexpected collapse of anything built on top of it; and finally, when this kind of

[Descartes]

subsidence occurs in mines, the miners often say that it is caused by goblins or demons who dwell underground. Hearing all this, the envious bricklayer seizes the opportunity to pretend that the architect believes that digging out a trench is all there is to building a chapel: 'He thinks that building a chapel consists in digging a trench', he cries, 'or in uncovering the bedrock at the base of the trench, or in building something over the trench in such a way that the trench stays empty!' And he goes on to suggest that the architect is so foolish as to fear that the earth he stands on will give way under his feet or be undermined by goblins. Now he may manage to convince a few children or others who are so ignorant of architecture that they think that digging trenches in order to lay the foundations of a building is something new and strange. Such people may be ready to listen to someone whom they know and whom they regard as an honest man who knows his job, and they may believe what he says about an architect whom they do not know and who, so far as they have heard, has only dug trenches and never actually built anything. After convincing a few people in this way, the poor fellow becomes so delighted with his story that he hopes he will persuade the whole world of it. By now the architect has filled all the trenches with stones, and built his chapel securely on a base of very solid material, so that it stands there for everyone to see; but our critic still sticks to his plan and hopes to persuade everyone of his absurd story. To this end he stands in the high street every day and presents a comic account of the architect's doings for the benefit of the passing crowd. This is how it goes.

538

He begins by representing the architect as giving orders for trenches to be dug and for the removal not only of all the sand but of everything mixed up with or resting on the sand – even boulders or four-square blocks of stone; in a word, *everything* must be removed and *nothing* whatever left. He lays great stress on the words 'nothing', 'everything', 'even the boulders and blocks of stone'; and at the same time he pretends that he wants to go down into the trenches and get the architect to teach him his skill. 'Please be my guide', he says. 'You now have either a companion or a pupil, so tell me, what are your orders? Although for me the road is new and frightening, since I am not accustomed to the darkness, I am happy to set out. I hear you: you command me to do whatever I see you doing and to tread in your footsteps. This is a splendid way of giving your orders and guidance, and I am delighted with your response. I am all ears.'[1]

539

In scene two he pretends that he is afraid of the goblins lurking down

1 Cf. above p. 314.

[Descartes]

in the trenches, and tries to get a laugh from the spectators. 'Will you guarantee that I need have no fear or apprehension or worry about the evil demon? Even if you give me every possible reassurance I am still exceedingly afraid of coming down here.'[1] And, a little later on: 'What have I done? How quickly I have forgotten what I promised! At the beginning I pledged myself to you entirely as your companion and disciple, and yet here I am hesitating at the very start of our journey, full of scruples and obstinacy. Forgive me; I have greatly sinned and have merely displayed my weakness of mind. I should have left all fear aside and plunged intrepidly into the darkness of the trench; but I have hesitated and drawn back.'[2]

In scene three, he represents the architect as showing him the stone or rock at the bottom of the trench – the rock on which he intends that his entire building shall rest. But he picks up the rock with a sneer. 'This is excellent, my distinguished friend: you have found your Archimedean point, and without doubt you can now move the world if you so wish. Look: the whole earth is already shaking. But since, I gather, you are cutting everything back to the bone, so that your method may include only what fits and is coherent and necessary, may I ask you why you keep this stone? Did you not order us to throw out the stones with the sand? But perhaps it slipped in by accident. And if it is so hard, even for an expert, to forget altogether the things we have been accustomed to accept since childhood, then even a raw beginner like myself need not despair, should I happen to stumble.'[3] And later on, when the architect sees some rough stones, which had been thrown out of the trench with the sand, and collects them so that he can use them in the building, his opponent makes a joke of this. 'Before you proceed, shall I venture to ask you a question? Since you have solemnly rejected all these rough stones as being insufficiently firm, why do you now look at them again, as if you hoped to salvage something solid from this rubble? . . . Indeed, given that everything you previously rejected was shaky and unstable (otherwise why did you reject it?), how can it be that this material should cease to be shaky and unstable?' And, a little later: 'Permit me to admire your skill once again. In order to put down stable foundations, you make use of what is unstable. To bring us into the light, you order us down into the darkness', etc.[4] And then he launches into a long and foolish discussion on the titles and duties of the architect and the bricklayer, whose only relevance or point is to confuse the meaning of the terms so that it is less easy to distinguish one from the other.

In the fourth scene, both characters are standing at the bottom of the

1 Cf. above p. 317.   2 Cf. above p. 318.   3 Cf. above p. 322.   4 Cf. pp. 322f.

[Descartes]
trench. The architect tries to start building the foundations of his chapel, but without success. For as soon as he tries to put down a block of stone, the bricklayer at once reminds him that he gave orders for all the stones to be thrown out, and that his present action is therefore inconsistent with the rules of this method. The architect is floored by this reminder, as if it had all the force of an Archimedean demonstration, and is compelled to stop working. And whenever he goes on to pick up any stones or bricks or mortar, or whatever, the bricklayer jumps in with 'You have 541 rejected everything! You have kept nothing back!' And by repeating the two words 'everything' and 'nothing' as if they were magic spells, he destroys all the architect's work. The speech he delivers is so like what we find above in Sections 5 to 9[1] that there is no need to repeat it here.

In the fifth and final scene, he sees that he has collected a sufficiently large crowd round him and adopts a new style, exchanging his comic banter for the grim delivery of the tragic actor. He wipes off his clown's make-up, assumes a stern expression and a censorious tone and proceeds to enumerate and condemn all the architect's faults, i.e. those which he somehow supposes that he has exposed in the earlier scenes! I shall now set down his entire verdict exactly as delivered in that final scene where he performs in front of the crowd, so as to show how closely my own critic has followed the example of our imaginary bricklayer. Pretending that the architect has asked him to pronounce judgement on his procedure, he gives his verdict as follows.

'Firstly, the procedure is faulty in its foundations, which are either non-existent or unlimited. Other systems of house-building lay down very firm foundations such as stone blocks, bricks, quarried stones, and numerous other materials of this sort, and by using these as a base they are able to make their buildings as high as they wish. But your method is quite different, since it aims to construct something not from something but from nothing. It demolishes, digs up and rejects all old foundations without exception; it requires the will to be turned in completely the opposite direction, and to avoid the impression that it has no wings, it puts on artificial wings of wax and lays down new foundations which are the complete opposite of the old ones. Thus it avoids the old, shaky foundations only to go for equally shaky new ones; it overturns what is stable in order to set up what is unstable; it equips itself with wings, but 542 they are made of wax; it builds a structure up to the skies only to see it collapse; and finally, it struggles to produce something from nothing only to end up producing nothing at all.'[2]

1 Above pp. 329–32, 333–46.
2 See above pp. 358f for the passage which Descartes here parodies.

[Descartes]

The mere fact that the architect has already built his chapel shows that all this is simply a ridiculous slander. The finished chapel makes it clear that the architect laid down very firm foundations and destroyed nothing which did not deserve to be destroyed; he never departed from the maxims of others unless he had something better; he built up his structure to a great height without any risk of a collapse; and, finally, he started not from nothing but from very solid materials, and from these he built not nothing but a solid chapel, destined to last for many years to the glory of God. Now in just the same way, my own achievements, about which my critic suffers from such strange delusions, are plain to see simply from the *Meditations* which I published. Incidentally, we should not blame the story-teller from whom I got the bricklayer's speech for making him talk about the 'wings' of architecture and using other unsuitable metaphors; he probably did this on purpose, to indicate the mental confusion that the speaker must have been in to say such things. Besides, all these metaphors are just as unsuitable for discussing my method of searching for the truth, yet this is the use to which my critic puts them.

His second reply is this: 'The architect's procedure is faulty in the implements it uses, for so long as it destroys the old without providing any replacements, it has no implements at all. Other systems have measuring rods, spirit-levels and plumb-lines which they use like Ariadne's thread to guide them out of the labyrinth; with these instruments they can easily and properly position even the most shapeless of rocks. But your method denigrates the traditional techniques and instead grows pale with a new terror – the imaginary fear of the goblins which it has conjured up. It fears that the earth may subside; it has doubts about whether the sand will shift. If you erect a column, it will be scared of the pedestal and the base, no matter what kind you use. "The goblins may push it over." What about the shaft? It will tremble and call it weak. "What if it is only made of plaster, not marble? How often have things seemed solid and firm but then, when we tested them, turned out to be fragile?" Finally, what about the capital? It will run away from all capitals as if they were traps and snares. "Bad architects have often constructed buildings which they thought were firm but which have collapsed of their own accord. What if this should happen in the present case? What if the goblins are undermining the soil? They are malicious, and I do not yet know that the pedestal is so firm that the goblins cannot shift it." What will you do about this? What will you do when your method obstinately maintains that any capital is unstable unless you previously know for certain that the column is not made of fragile

[Descartes]

material and that it rests not on sand but on firm rock – rock which no goblins will ever be able to shift? What if your method repudiates both the material and the form of the column?' (And here, with jeering insolence he holds out a model of one of the columns which the architect had set up in his chapel.) 'Whatever arguments you press, the reply will be "Wait till I know that there is rock underneath and that no goblins will undermine it." You may reply that failing to set up any columns at least has the advantage of avoiding the possibility that any are badly made. A splendid notion this – to cut off a child's nose so that it will not suffer from catarrh.' The rest is too dreary to repeat, so I will simply ask the reader to compare the above points one by one with the corresponding criticisms that my critic has produced.[1]

This reply, like the previous one, is shown to be a most shameless falsehood by the very fact that the chapel has been built and that we find 544 many perfectly firm columns standing inside it, including the very one of which the bricklayer held up a model, claiming that the architect had repudiated it. In the same way, my own writings establish quite firmly that I do not disapprove of syllogisms or denigrate the traditional form of argument which employs them; indeed, I used syllogisms throughout my writings, when I needed to. Amongst others, the very syllogism whose matter and form my critic pretends that I repudiate, is one which he copied down from my own writings; for I use it at the end of my Replies to the Second Set of Objections, proposition 1, where I demonstrate the existence of God.[2] I cannot see the purpose behind this pretence of his, unless it is perhaps to suggest that everything which I put forward as true and certain is in conflict with my renunciation of the doubtful, which he tries to present as the sum total of what is meant by my method. This is exactly the same – and just as childish and silly – as our bricklayer's pretence that the digging of the ditch for laying the foundations was the sum total of the architect's technique, and his complaint that anything subsequently constructed was in conflict with the initial excavation.

Reply 3. 'The technique goes astray by failing to reach its goal, for it does not succeed in constructing anything stable. Indeed, it cannot do so, since it has itself blocked off all the roads to completing its task. You yourself have seen and experienced this during the long odyssey when you wandered around and exhausted both yourself and me, your companion. You maintained that you were an architect, or that you had the skills of an architect, but you were quite unable to establish this since you got stuck on rugged slopes and in dense thickets more times than I can remember. Yet it will be useful to go over the problems again to

1 Cf. pp. 359f. 2 Above p. 360; cf. Second Replies, p. 117.

[Descartes]

545 reinforce the present reply. Here, then, are the chief ways in which your method cuts its own throat or cuts off all hope of producing a building. (1) You do not know whether there is sand or rock beneath the topsoil, and hence you can place no more confidence in the rock (that is, if you do ever manage to stand on rock) than you can place in sand. Hence everything is doubtful and shaky and your very walls are unstable. I shall not produce any examples; you may yourself proceed to run through the storehouse of your memory, and if you find anything which is not infected with this rot, then bring it out, and I shall congratulate you. (2) Until I find firm ground which I know for certain does not have shifting sand beneath it or any goblins who may undermine it, I must reject everything and consider all building materials as suspect. Or at any rate – to revert to the ordinary and traditional architectural technique – we must first of all determine whether there are any materials which should not be rejected, and if so what they are; and we must instruct our diggers to keep these materials in their trenches. So everything is doubtful, just as we found under point (1), and hence there is nothing which is of the slightest use for constructing a building. (3) If there is anything that could possibly be shifted, even slightly, then we must turn our will in completely the opposite direction and believe that it has already collapsed; indeed we must believe that it is necessary to re-excavate, and use the empty trench as our foundation. But this cuts off every pathway which could lead to successful building. What can you possibly hope to get from such propositions as "There is now no earth here, no sand and no stone", and countless others of this sort. You cannot reply that this excavation of yours is not permanent but is for a fixed period, like a suspension of the law sittings, until we reach a specified depth corresponding to the depth of sand in the relevant area. For even if we concede that the excavation is limited to a specified period, this is the very period when you suppose that you are building, the period when you are using, or misusing, the emptiness of the trench just as if the whole building depended on it, or as if it was the necessary base on which the building rested. "But I am employing the digging technique to strengthen my foundations and columns, as other architects do", you reply. "Do they

546 not construct temporary scaffolding to use while they are raising the column?'"; and so on as above.[1]

Here none of the bricklayer's complaints against the architect are more ridiculous than the complaints which my critic has devised against me. In rejecting what is doubtful I no more cut myself off from knowledge of the truth than the architect's excavation precluded the subsequent building

1 Cf. above pp. 360f.

[Descartes]

of the chapel, as is shown by all the truths I was able to demonstrate later on. At the very least my critic should have tried to point out something false or uncertain in my demonstrations; but since he does not do so, and is incapable of doing so, we must accept that he is suffering from an inexcusable delusion. I never made any greater effort to prove that I, a thinking thing, am a mind than the man in the story makes to prove that he is an architect; but my critic, by contrast, expends great labour and effort without proving anything – except that he has no mind at all, or at any rate not a sound one. Furthermore, from the fact that metaphysical doubt goes so far as to make us suppose that we do not know whether we are dreaming or awake, it does not follow that we cannot discover anything certain, any more than, from the fact that when the architect starts digging he does not yet know whether he is going to find rock or clay or whatever beneath the sand, it follows that it is impossible for him to find rock, or to rely on it once he has found it. Again, until we know that God exists, we have reason to doubt everything (i.e. everything such that we do not have a clear perception of it before our minds, as I have often explained); but it does not follow that nothing is of any use for pursuing the truth, any more than, from the fact that the architect ordered everything to be thrown out of the trench until firm ground was struck, it followed that the rejected material contained no boulders or other sound rocks which might afterwards be thought useful for laying the foundations. When the poor bricklayer said that the ordinary and traditional architectural technique required that such rocks should not be thrown out of the trench, but that the diggers should be told to keep them, this was as silly a mistake as our critic makes when he says that 'we must first of all determine whether any propositions are immune from doubt, and if so, which propositions they are'. For how can we establish these propositions if we are supposing that we do not yet know any? He is also wrong in saying that this is a maxim of ordinary traditional philosophy, for no such maxim is in fact to be found there. Again, when the bricklayer pretended that the architect wanted to use the empty trench as a foundation, and that his entire building depended on it, this was as silly as the quite obviously deluded claim of my critic that I 'employ the opposite of what is doubtful as a principle of inquiry' and that I use or misuse the beliefs I have renounced as if all truth depended on them and as if they were the necessary base on which it rested.[1] He has here forgotten the words that he had earlier reported as mine, viz. 'Neither affirm nor deny it; employ neither statement but regard both as false.'[2] Finally, when the bricklayer compares the digging of a trench in

1 Above p. 361. 2 Above p. 308; cf. p. 356.

[Descartes]

order to lay the foundations with the temporary scaffolding used to set up a column, he shows that he was as ignorant and inexperienced as my own critic, who uses exactly the same comparison to describe the renunciation of what is doubtful.

Reply 4. 'The technique goes astray by being excessive. That is, it attempts more than the laws of prudence demand of it, more, indeed than any mortal demands. Admittedly, there are people who ask for solid houses to be built for them. But you will not find anyone, up till now, who has been dissatisfied if the house in which he lives is as firm as the earth which supports us. So all these efforts to search for a superior level of firmness are superfluous. Moreover, just as where walking is concerned there are well-defined limits of soil-stability which are quite sufficient to enable people to walk safely, so in the building of houses there are definite limits such that anyone who attains them is certain'; and so on, as above.[1]

Although the bricklayer's complaint against the architect here is unfair, my critic's corresponding complaint against me is much more unfair. It is true that in house-construction there are well-defined limits which fall short of the complete stability of the ground beneath us, but which it is not normally worth exceeding. These vary depending on the size of the building and the load it imposes; a humble dwelling can be safely built on sand, for sand is just as capable of supporting a small house as rock is of supporting a high tower. But it is wholly false that in laying down our foundations in philosophy there are corresponding limits which fall short of complete certainty, but which we can sensibly and safely accept without taking doubt any further. For since truth is essentially indivisible, it may happen that a claim which we do not recognize as possessing complete certainty may in fact be quite false, however probable it may appear. To make the foundations of all knowledge rest on a claim that we recognize as being possibly false would not be a sensible way to philosophize. If someone proceeds in this way, how can he answer the sceptics who go beyond all the boundaries of doubt? How will he refute them? Will he regard them as desperate lost souls? Fine; but how will they regard him in the meantime? Moreover we should not suppose that sceptical philosophy is extinct. It is vigorously alive today, and almost all those who regard themselves as more intellectually gifted than others, and find nothing to satisfy them in philosophy as it is ordinarily practised, take refuge in scepticism because they cannot see any alternative with greater claims to truth. Yet it is just such people who are particularly insistent in their demands for a

1 Cf. above p. 361.

[Descartes]

demonstration of the existence of God and the immortality of the human mind. Hence my critic's comments here set a very bad example, especially in view of his reputation for learning. What he says shows that he does not think that the errors of the atheistic sceptics can be refuted, and hence he is giving them all the support and encouragement he can. No sceptic nowadays has any doubt in practice about whether he has a head, or whether two and three make five, and so on. What the sceptics say is that they merely treat such claims as true because they appear to be so, but they do not accept them as certain, because no reliable arguments require them to do so. But they do not see the existence of God and the immortality of the human mind as having the same appearance of truth, and hence they are unwilling to treat these claims as true for practical purposes unless and until they have seen them proved by means of arguments more reliable than any of those which lead them to accept whatever is apparently true. Now since I have provided a reliable proof of these matters, and this is something that no one, so far as I know, has done before, I think my critic's attack is the greatest and most unfair slander that could possibly be devised; for throughout his discussion he repeatedly and emphatically attributes to me the one error which is the hallmark of the sceptics, namely excessive doubt. He is remarkably unstinting when he comes to catalogue my faults. He says that 'to push the limits further, and cross the sea which no one in past ages has ever tried to cross, is an achievement that deserves no ordinary praise'; yet although (as I shall show in a moment) he has no reason to suspect that I have failed to achieve this with respect to the very problem he discusses, he goes on to list the achievement among my faults, with the words 'it deserves high praise indeed, provided you can cross the sea without shipwreck'.[1] He obviously wants my readers to believe that I came to grief or committed some error in this enterprise, but he does not really believe this himself, or have any reason to suspect it. If he had been able to think up the least reason to suspect that I had made some error anywhere on my journey, where I led the mind from knowledge of its own existence to knowledge of the existence of God and to the distinction between mind and body, then he would surely have included it somewhere in the course of a discussion which is so long and verbose and so lacking in arguments. Surely he would have preferred to do this rather than do what he in fact did, namely keep changing the subject whenever the argument required this issue to be discussed, and fatuously represent me as holding forth about whether a thinking thing was a mind. It follows that he did not in fact have any reason to suspect that I

550

---

1 Above pp. 361f.

[Descartes]

had gone astray in any of my assertions, or in the arguments by means of which I became the first philosopher ever to overturn the doubt of the sceptics. He admits that this deserves the highest praise, and yet he has the face to censure me on this very count, and to foist on me that very doubt which, rather than singling me out, he might more justly have attributed to all the other human beings who have never managed to refute it.

Reply 5. 'The technique is faulty because it is deficient. That is, in pushing too hard it achieves nothing at all. Here you yourself are the only witness and judge I need. What results have you obtained with all your magnificent apparatus? What has your solemn excavation brought you – an excavation so general and unstinting that you have not even spared the most solid boulders – apart from the well-worn rock referred to in the cliché "The rock which is discovered underneath all the sand is solid and firm." This cliché is so familiar even to the mass of mankind'; and so on as above.[1]

551

Here I was expecting our bricklayer – and my critic too – to prove something. But the bricklayer confines himself to asking what results the architect achieved wih his digging, apart from uncovering a rock, and ignores the fact that he has built his chapel on this foundation. And similarly my critic merely asks what I have achieved by my renunciation of what is doubtful, apart from the cliché 'I am thinking, I exist.' Presumably he regards it as nothing that I demonstrated the existence of God and many other things from this starting point. He says I am the only witness he needs – presumably he means the only witness to his remarkable impudence. The same goes for the other equally false assertions he makes elsewhere, when he says 'Everyone without exception believes them', or 'Lecture-rooms everywhere echo with these doctrines', or 'We all heard as much from our teachers, and they heard it from theirs, and so on back to Adam.'[2] These assertions are no more to be trusted than the oaths of people who try to persuade us of something incredible and false: the more false and incredible they think their claim is, the more they tend to double and redouble their oaths.

Reply 6. 'The technique commits the common fault which it accuses other systems of committing. It is astonished that everyone should say and maintain with such confidence "The sand on which we stand is firm enough; the ground on which we stand is not shifting" etc.; and yet it is not equally astonished at itself when it says with just as much confidence "We must throw out the sand"', etc.[3]

---

1 Cf. above p. 362.   2 Above pp. 363f.   3 Cf. above p. 362.

[Descartes]

This is no sillier than what my critic says in his corresponding criticism.

Reply 7. 'The technique commits a fault peculiar to itself. The rest of 552
mankind regard the ground on which we stand, the sand and the stones,
as firm up to a point – sufficiently firm. But your peculiar strategy regards
the opposite of ground, namely the trench from which the sand, stones
and the rest have been removed, as not only something firm but as so firm
that this most solid chapel can be built on it. Indeed, your method places
so much weight on this crutch that if you remove it, it will fall flat on its
face.'[1]

Here the speaker is completely deluded, just as my critic is when he
forgets the words 'Neither affirm it nor deny it', etc.

Reply 8. 'It goes astray through negligence. That is, it fails to observe
that the instability of the ground is a two-edged sword, and while
avoiding one edge it cuts itself on the other. Since it regards sand as not
being firm enough ground, it removes it and produces the opposite,
namely an empty trench; but by imprudently relying on this as if it were
something stable, it ends up cutting itself.'[2]

Here again, he should have remembered the words 'Neither affirm it
nor deny it.' And the figure of the double-edged sword better fits the
wisdom of our poor bricklayer than it does that of my critic.

Reply 9. 'It goes astray wilfully. For knowingly, voluntarily and
advisedly it blinds itself, and by deliberately rejecting what it needs to
build a house, it allows itself to be deluded by its own rule; thus it not
only produces results it did not intend, but those it most fears.'[3]

How much truth there is in this, and in the corresponding charge
against me, is shown in the architect's case by his success in building the
chapel, and in my case by the truths which I managed to demonstrate.

Reply 10. 'It sins by commission by returning to old materials which it 553
had proscribed by solemn edict, and by picking up rejected stones against
the laws of trench-digging. Think back and you will see this well
enough.'[4]

My critic imitates this absurdity when he forgets the words 'Neither
affirm nor deny.' Otherwise, how could he have had the face to pretend
that what he had earlier said 'should neither be affirmed nor denied' is
now proscribed by solemn edict?

Reply 11. 'It sins by omission. For having laid it down as a solemn
principle that "we should take great care not to admit as true anything
we cannot prove to be true", it proceeds to violate the principle more
than once. It assumes with impunity, and regards as completely certain

1 *Ibid.*   2 *Ibid.*   3 *Ibid.*   4 *Ibid.*

[Descartes]
and true, such unproved statements as "Sandy soil is not sufficiently firm to support a building"', and so on.[1]

Here the speaker is plainly as deluded as my critic: he applies to the excavation of trenches what properly relates to the construction of buildings, just as my critic applies to the renunciation of the doubtful what properly relates to the construction of a philosophy. The maxim 'We should not admit anything as true unless we can prove it is true' is perfectly correct when it is a question of establishing or affirming some proposition; but when it is merely a matter of renouncing a belief (or digging out a trench), then mere suspicion is all that is required.

Reply 12. 'What the technique contains is either unsound or nothing new, and for the most part it is superfluous.

(i) 'You may say that your rejection of sandy soil is meant to be the normal excavation process which other architects employ when they reject sand only in so far as it is not sufficiently firm for supporting the weight of a building. If this is the case, then your technique is *sound*, but it is nothing *new*, and your excavation process will be nothing new either, but a traditional device which all architects without exception have employed.[2]

554   (ii) 'If the excavation of sand means that all the sand must be thrown out in the sense that we are supposed to remove it all and keep nothing back, using none of it, or rather using its opposite, namely the empty space which it previously occupied, as something solid and firm, then this is something *new* but it is utterly *unsound*, and so your principle of excavation will be novel but illegitimate.[3]

(iii) 'You may claim that your technique can achieve the following result by weighty and powerful arguments. "I am qualified in architecture and I practise it, but in virtue of this I am neither an architect nor a bricklayer nor a builder's mate, but something so separate from these things that I can understand myself without understanding any of these things, just as an animal, or sentient thing, can be understood without our understanding that it is a thing that neighs or bellows", etc. This claim is sound, but nothing new: you will find street-corners everywhere echoing with this doctrine, which is put forward in various different ways by everyone who considers that there are people qualified in architecture; indeed, if architecture includes wall-building, so that those who mix mortar and cut stones and haul around building materials are regarded as knowing architecture, then this doctrine is held by everyone who believes that workmen perform these tasks, i.e. everyone without exception.[4]

1 Cf. above p. 363.   2 *Ibid.*   3 *Ibid.*   4 *Ibid.*

[Descartes]

(iv) 'If you say that your method proves by powerful and well thought-out arguments that you really exist and are qualified in architecture, and that while you exist, no architect or bricklayer or builder's mate really exists, then you are saying something *new* but quite *unsound*. For your claim is just as suspect as saying that an animal exists but that no lion, or fox, or whatever, exists.[1]

(v) 'By "building" you may mean that you employ architecture in the construction of buildings and build in such a way that you can contemplate and consider your building activities by a reflexive act. This would mean that when you build, you know and consider that you are 555 building (and this is really what it is to be conscious and to have conscious awareness of some activity). Such consciousness, you may claim, is a property of architecture, or of the art which is superior to the skill of a builder's mate, and it is in this sense that you are an architect. This is a claim that you have not made before, but which you should have made; indeed, I often wanted to suggest it to you when I saw your method struggling ineffectively to bring it forth. But the claim, although *sound*, is nothing *new*, since we all heard it from our teachers long ago, and they heard it from their teachers, and so on, I would think, right back to Adam.

'If this, then, is your claim, what superfluous results your method has produced! What redundancy! What verbal excesses! What elaborate techniques designed to secure your glory and prestige! What was the point of all that talk about instability of the sand, subsidence and goblins, and your other empty scare-tactics? What was the point of that excavating of yours, which went so deep that it refused to leave us with any more than a mere patch of earth to build on? Why all those interminable wanderings to distant shores, far away from the senses, amid ghosts and shadows? How does all this finally help to set up a solid chapel – as if a chapel could not stand up unless everything else were turned upside down? Why so much massive shifting of materials, leading us to throw away the old ones, take up the new, and then abandon the new only to take up the old again? Perhaps it is simply that these new mysteries require new ceremonies, just as while we are in a temple or in the presence of the mighty we should not behave as if we were in a tavern or a hovel! But why does your method not lay aside all ambiguities and tell us the truth simply, clearly and briefly, in one sentence: "I build, I am conscious of building, therefore I am an architect."?[2]

(vi) 'Finally, you may mean that you construct houses, design and plan 556 bedrooms, storerooms, porches, doors, windows, pillars and so on, and

1 Cf. above pp. 363f.   2 Cf. above p. 364.

[Descartes]

then give orders to the suppliers and manufacturers, bricklayers, tilers, labourers and other workmen, and supervise their work. And you may claim that this is the special function of the architect in the sense that no other craftsmen can discharge it. This is indeed something *new*, but it is quite *unsound*. It will turn out to be an arbitrary and unacceptable claim, unless perhaps (and this is the only hope left) you are keeping something hidden in reserve which you can bring on stage and display to the gaping crowd at the crucial moment. But we have been waiting for this for so long that it is quite hopeless.'[1]

Final reply. 'I think you are now fearful for your method which, understandably enough, you love and embrace and kiss like your own child. You are afraid that after convicting it of so many faults and revealing, as you can see, that it is full of holes and leaking everywhere, I shall condemn it to be thrown on the rubbish heap. But be of good courage; I am a friend! I shall disappoint and overcome your fearful expectations by sitting quietly and waiting. I know you, and the keenness and perspicacity of your intellect: if you are given time for meditation, and allowed to consult your faithful rule in some secluded retreat, you will shake the dust off your architectural technique, wash off all the grime, and display it to our sight clean and polished once again. Meanwhile, accept my comments, and give me your attention while I go on to reply to your remaining questions. I shall include many topics which for the sake of brevity I have so far touched on only lightly, namely problems relating to arches, the openings for windows, pillars, porches and so on.'[2] But here we have the programme for a new comedy.

557 CAN THE ARCHITECTURAL TECHNIQUE BE RECONSTRUCTED?

'Your third question is . . .' When the speaker embarked on this speech,[3] some of his friends saw that the excessive envy and hatred which afflicted him had now reached the proportions of a disease, and instead of letting him continue to rant and rave on in the streets, took him straight to a doctor.

For my part, I would not venture to suspect that my critic suffered a similar fate. But I will simply proceed to point out how closely he has imitated the poor bricklayer in all his criticisms. First of all he has copied him in playing the part of a judge – a very upright one, of course – who is scrupulously and meticulously careful not to pass any rash judgements. After condemning me no less than eleven times on the one charge of rejecting what is doubtful in order to establish what is certain (or digging

1 Cf. above p. 364.   2 Cf. above p. 365.   3 *Ibid.*

[Descartes]

trenches in order to lay the foundations of my building), he comes back
to the charge for the twelfth and last time, and examines it as follows:[1]

(i) He says that if I meant by my method what he in fact knows I did
mean by it (as is clear from the words 'Neither affirm nor deny', which
he himself attributes to me), then my method is indeed *sound*, but
'nothing *new*'.

(ii) He says that I may have meant it in another way – the way that
forms the basis of the eleven faults he listed earlier; but he knows that
this is quite remote from my intention, since he represents me in Section 3
of his 'first question' as reacting to it with amazement and saying 'How
could any sane man arrive at that idea?'[2] Yet he says that on this
interpretation my method is *new* but quite *unsound*. Surely no one in the   558
whole history of abuse has ever told such shameless lies, or shown such
disregard for all truth and plausibility; what is more, surely no one has
ever been so exceedingly careless and forgetful! For in his elaborate and
carefully planned discussion my critic has returned time and time again
to attack the very doctrine which he admitted at the start to be so
abhorrent to the very author charged with holding it that the author
regarded it as incapable of entering the mind of a sane man!

As for the topics that follow in both our bricklayer's speech and that of
my critic (numbers (iii), (iv) and (v)), they are quite irrelevant, and were
never raised either by me or by the architect. It seems probable that the
bricklayer first thought them up because he did not dare to attack any of
the architect's achievements, for fear of making his own ignorance all too
apparent, and yet he wanted to give the impression of not limiting his
criticism entirely to the technique of excavation. My critic has apparently
copied the ignorant bricklayer here for similar reasons.

(iii) In saying that a thinking thing can be understood without our
having any understanding of a mind or soul or body, my critic is
philosophizing just as ineptly as the bricklayer was when he said that a
person qualified in architecture can be understood to be no more an
architect than a bricklayer or a builder's mate, and can be understood
separately from any of these things.

(iv) To say that a thinking thing can exist although no mind exists is
just as silly as saying that a person qualified in architecture can exist
although no architect exists (provided, that is, the word 'mind' is taken in
the ordinary sense, in the way in which I explained I was taking it).
Again, for a thinking thing to exist without a body is no more of a   559

---

1 See above pp. 363f for Bourdin's six criticisms under this heading, and pp. 378–80 above
  for Descartes' parody of them.
2 Above p. 307.

[Descartes]

contradiction than for an architectural expert to exist without there being any bricklayers or builders' mates.

(v) My critic says that to enable a substance to be superior to matter and wholly spiritual (and he insists on using the term 'mind' only in this restricted sense), it is not sufficient for it to think: it is further required that it should think that it is thinking, by means of a reflexive act, or that it should have awareness of its own thought.[1] This is as deluded as our bricklayer's saying that a person who is skilled in architecture must employ a reflexive act to ponder on the fact that he has this skill before he can be an architect. It may in fact be that all architects frequently reflect on the fact that they have this skill, or at least are capable of so reflecting. But it is obvious that an architect does not need to perform this reflexive act in order to be an architect. And equally, this kind of pondering or reflecting is not required in order for a thinking substance to be superior to matter. The initial thought by means of which we become aware of something does not differ from the second thought by means of which we become aware that we were aware of it, any more than this second thought differs from the third thought by means of which we become aware that we were aware that we were aware. And if it is conceded that a corporeal thing has the first kind of thought, then there is not the slightest reason to deny that it can have the second. Accordingly, it must be stressed that my critic commits a much more dangerous error in this respect than does the poor bricklayer. He removes the true and most clearly intelligible feature which differentiates corporeal things from incorporeal ones, *viz.* that the latter think, but not the former; and in its place he substitutes a feature which cannot in any way be regarded as essential, namely that incorporeal things reflect on their thinking, but corporeal ones do not. Hence he does everything he can to hinder our 560 understanding of the real distinction between the human mind and the body.

(vi) In championing the cause of brute animals and wanting to attribute thought to them just as much as to human beings,[2] my critic behaves even less excusably than the bricklayer, who attempts to arrogate to himself and his like the skill of the architect.

Finally, it is quite clear throughout that both my critic and the bricklayer have behaved in a similar fashion: they have not thought up objections that have any truth or plausibility but have merely employed whatever bogus charges they could devise in order to disparage their enemy by representing him as foolish or ignorant before an audience that neither knows the man accused nor takes the trouble to make any careful

1 Cf. above p. 364.   2 *Ibid.*

[Descartes]

inquiries about the truth of the charges. How appropriate it is that our report of the bricklayer's speech had him expressing his insane envy by praising the architect's excavation as a magnificent device but despising the rock uncovered by this technique, and the chapel built upon the rock, as things of no account! But in spite of all this, our report shows him expressing his thanks, 'out of friendship and the particular goodwill he felt', etc. Again, our report has the bricklayer producing this splendid peroration: 'What superfluous results your method has produced! What redundancy! What verbal excess! What elaborate techniques designed to secure you glory and prestige!' And a little later: 'I think you are now fearful for your method which, understandably enough, you love and embrace . . . Be of good courage; I am a friend!'[1] All this describes our bricklayer's disease of envy so graphically that I think no poet could have produced a more lifelike account. Yet it is remarkable that our critic 561 imitates all this so effectively that he himself does not realize what he is doing, and does not perform that reflexive act of thinking which a moment ago he was putting forward as the mark that distinguishes mankind from the brutes. For surely he would not be commenting on the excessive verbosity of my own writings if he was aware of the far greater verbal excess of which he is himself guilty. He confines himself to the method of doubt which I presented and – I cannot say criticizes it, since he produces no critical arguments, but simply barks at it, if I may use a somewhat harsh expression, since no other phrase occurs to me which express the truth more aptly; and after all this he ends up producing vastly more words than I took to present the doubt in the first place. He would hardly have referred to 'verbal excess' if he had been aware of the prolix and superfluous and empty loquacity of which he has been guilty throughout his discussion, notwithstanding his claim at the end that he has tried to be brief. But since he says in conclusion that he is my friend, and since I want to be as friendly towards him as possible, I shall follow the example of the bricklayer's friends who carried him off to the doctor, and entrust my critic to the care of his superior.[2]

1 Above p. 365.
2 Bourdin's religious superior was Father Dinet, the head of the Jesuits in France. See the letter that follows, and Translator's preface, above pp. 64f.

LETTER TO FATHER DINET
To the Very Reverend Father Dinet, S.J., Provincial of France,
from René Descartes

563
I recently wrote to the Reverend Father Mersenne about the essay which I had heard that Father Bourdin[1] had written against me, and I indicated that I was very keen for him to publish it or at least send it to me so that I could have it published along with the remaining sets of objections which others had sent me. But when I asked him to get permission for this either from Father Bourdin, or indeed from Your Reverence, since I thought this the fairest course, he replied that he had already passed my letter on to you, and that you had not only been pleased with it but had also given him every indication of your singular concern, warmth and good-will towards me. And immediately afterwards I saw the proof of this myself, when the essay in question was sent to me. This leads me to express my utmost thanks to you, and also encourages me to tell you quite openly
564 what I think of the essay, and to ask your advice about my projected studies.

When I held Father Bourdin's essay in my hands for the first time I was as happy as if I was clutching some great treasure. For my dearest wish is to test the certainty of my opinions by having them examined by distinguished men, in the hope that they will be unable to discover any element of falsity in them; and failing that, my next wish is to be advised of my mistakes so that I can put them right. In a healthy body there is such communication and harmony between all the parts that the individual members do not have to rely merely on their own private resources of strength, but can call on a kind of communal vigour, belonging to the whole organism, which assists the operation of each part. And similarly, knowing what a close linking of minds normally obtains among members of your Society, I thought that what I had before me was not just one man's essay but the balanced and careful assessment that your entire Society had formed of my views.

When I read the essay, however, I was astounded to realize that I

---

1 The name is supplied here and elsewhere for the reader's convenience. In the original Descartes always refers to his critic obliquely as 'R.P.' ('the Revd Father'). The 'essay' referred to is the work published as the Seventh Set of Objections. For publication details of this and the letter to Dinet, see Preface above pp. 64f.

would have to revise my view completely. For if it had come from an author governed by the same spirit which animates your whole Society, then I would have found within it more – or at least no less – kindness, gentleness and modesty than I have found in the comments of those laymen who have written to me about my work. But instead, anyone comparing it with other people's objections to my *Meditations* would be sure to think that it was these other critics' work that had been composed by those in holy orders, and to regard this essay as having been written with such bitterness as would be unseemly even for a layman, let alone one whose vows require him to be more virtuous than ordinary men. Moreover, I would have expected the work of a religious man to shine with the love of God and the burning desire to promote his glory; but instead I found this essay attacking the principles from which I deduced the existence of God and the distinction between the human soul and the body, and, what is more, attacking them with great enthusiasm, in the face of reason and truth, and with all the bogus authority and fictitious invention that could be mustered. Again, I would have expected to find learning, sound reasoning and intelligence; but instead I found no learning at all (unless we count familiarity with the kind of Latin used by the plebs of ancient Rome as learning), no reasoning (except what was either invalid or false), and a sharpness of intellect more suited to a bricklayer than a Jesuit priest. I will not mention good sense and the other virtues for which your Society is so distinguished, since they are conspicuous by their absence – indeed, there is not even the slightest whiff of them to be detected anywhere in the essay. But I would at least have expected some reverence for the truth, some integrity and honesty; yet, as is clear from the comments which I added,[1] no imaginable slander is further removed from all semblance of truth than are all the charges against me which are to be found in this essay. Moreover, just as, if one part of the body is greatly out of step with those common principles that regulate the whole, this shows that it is in the grip of some disease peculiar to that organ, so the essay which the Reverend Father has produced makes it quite clear that he does not enjoy the health and good sense which are to be found elsewhere in your Society. Now we do not think less of the head, or the whole person, just because there may be malign humours infecting his foot or finger, against his will and through no fault of his own; on the contrary, we praise his resolution and courage when he agrees to undergo a painful cure. No one has ever despised Caius Marius for having varicose veins in his legs; on the contrary he is more often praised for his courage in undergoing surgery than for his seven consulships and all his victories over his enemies. In the same way,

565

566

1 See Seventh Set of Objections and Replies, above pp. 302, 308 etc.

since I know the devout and paternal affection with which you treat all your members, the fact that this essay seems to me to be so bad makes me appreciate all the more your integrity and concern in ordering it to be sent to me, and increases even more my respect and veneration for your whole Society. But since Father Bourdin had the essay sent to me under his own name, I do not want to seem too hasty in believing that he did not do so of his own accord; and so I will now explain the reason which leads me to believe that this is the case, as well as giving an account of everything that has so far passed between us . . .[1]

(572)   It would have greatly assisted the Reverend Father's plan if he could have prevented his essay from being published, and merely given a private reading to a few friends. This would have made it easy for him to make sure it was not seen by anyone who could recognize all the fabrications; and the others would have listened to him that much more, thinking that he was my friend and hence was unwilling to publish the essay for fear of damaging my reputation. In the meantime he would not have suffered any risk of his audience's being too small; for if he had managed to convince only his fellow members of your College in Paris, as he hoped to do, their view would easily have spread to all your other members throughout the world, and from them to almost all those influenced by the authority of your Society. I should not have been surprised if this had in fact happened. For given that each of you is so busy with his own studies, it is impossible for each individual to examine the vast numbers of new books that are published every day. I would imagine that you wait for the verdict of whichever member of your

573   Society first undertakes to read a given book, and that you then base your decision as to whether to read it or not on his judgement. Indeed, I think I have experienced the effects of this policy already in connection with the treatise on meteorology[2] that I published. For since, if I am not mistaken, it provides a truer and more precise explanation of the area of philosophy[3] with which it deals than is to be found in anyone else's writings, I can see no reason why the philosophers who give annual courses on meteorology in all your colleges should not refer to my account, other than that they may have believed Father Bourdin's unjust verdict on me and thus never read the book.

---

1 There follows an account of Bourdin's earlier attacks on Descartes during the year 1640 and of Descartes' complaints against him to the head of the Jesuit College at Paris.

2 One of the essays published with the *Discourse* in 1637; see vol. 1, p. 109.

3 It should be remembered here, and in what follows, that 'philosophy' for Descartes and his contemporaries included natural philosophy, i.e. what we should nowadays call 'science'.

But as long as he merely attacked my views on physics or mathematics, I was not too concerned. But in his essay he undertakes to subvert the metaphysical principles by means of which I demonstrated the existence of God and the real distinction between the human soul and the body; and what is more he tries to do so not with arguments but with lies and slander. Now knowledge of these truths is so important that no decent person could object to my vigorously defending what I wrote. And it will not be difficult to do this, for since Father Bourdin confines his objections to the claim that the doubts I raise are excessive, I simply need to show that this is an unjust and trumped-up charge. To do this, I do not need to refer to all the passages in my *Meditations* where I refuted and eliminated these doubts more carefully and, if I am not mistaken, more scrupulously than any other author whose writings we possess. It will be enough for me to remind the reader of what I explicitly stated at the beginning of my Reply to the Third Set of Objections, namely that, in every case, I put forward these arguments for doubting not to convince people of them but, on the contrary, in order to refute them, just as a medical writer must provide a description of a disease if he wants to explain how it can be cured.[1] And who, may I ask, has ever been so presumptuous, or such a shameless slanderer, as to censure Hippocrates or Galen for describing the causes which generally give rise to diseases, and then to infer that their doctrines contain nothing more than a method of falling ill? 574

Those who know that the Reverend Father has in fact been as bold and shameless as this would not readily accept that he acted on his own initiative in this matter, unless I were to come forward and declare that his previous writings against me were not approved by your Society and that this most recent essay was sent to me on your instructions. The best place in which I can make this known is in this letter, and so I think it is quite appropriate for me to have it published, along with my comments on Father Bourdin's essay.[2]

But in the hope of deriving some personal benefit from the publication of this letter, I will now say something of the philosophy which I am writing at the moment,[3] and which I have decided, unless any obstacle arises, to publish in a year or two. I published some specimen essays[4] of this philosophy in the year 1637, and I tried to do everything I could to protect myself from the envy and hostility which, although quite undeserved, I realized would fall on me as a result. This was the reason 575

1 Above p. 121.
2 This was in fact done, for the letter to Dinet appears immediately after the 'essay' and 'comments' (i.e. the Seventh Set of Objections and Replies) in the 1642 edition.
3 I.e. the *Principles of Philosophy* which eventually appeared in 1644.
4 The three essays published with the *Discourse*. See vol. 1, p. 109.

why I did not want my name to appear on the title page;[1] it was not, as some may have thought, that I was diffident about, or ashamed of, any of the arguments in the book. The desire to avoid envy was also the reason for my stating explicitly on page 66 of the *Discourse on the Method*,[2] that I did not intend that my philosophy should be published in my lifetime. I should still be sticking to this decision today, if it had done at least something to keep me free of the envy and hostility of others, as I had every reason to hope it would. But in fact quite the opposite happened, and my specimen essays met with the following fate. Although it was not possible for many people to understand them, there were several very intelligent and learned readers who did bother to look at them in detail and found them to contain many truths which had not been common knowledge before. The reputation of the work thus grew, and led many people to become convinced straightaway that I was capable of providing explanations in philosophy that possessed incontrovertible certainty. As a result, the great majority of people wanted me to go ahead and publish my entire philosophical system. This majority included all lovers of the truth: not just those outside the Schools who can conduct their philosophical inquiries without restrictions, but a large number of professional teachers, especially the younger generation and those who rely more on their native wit than on some undeserved reputation for learning. But there remained a minority, namely those who prefer to appear learned rather than to acquire genuine learning, and who suppose that they have some reputation in the academic world because they have mastered the technique of acrimonious debate over scholastic controversies; and these people were afraid that once the truth was discovered all these controversies would collapse and that their own speciality would become wholly despised. Thus, fearing that if my philosophy were to be published the truth would be uncovered, but

576   not daring to say openly that they were anxious for it not to appear, they seethed with hatred towards me. It was quite easy for me to distinguish my supporters from my opponents. For those who wanted my philosophical system to be published remembered very well that I had decided not to publish it in my lifetime, and several of them said that they were unhappy about my preferring to bestow it on future generations rather than on my own contemporaries. But all honest men saw my reason for doing so, and continued to show their affection for me, realizing that I had no lack of zeal to serve the public good. But those who feared publication failed to remember what I had said, or else refused to believe it; on the contrary, they actually supposed that I had

---

1 The *Discourse* and the three essays that follow it were published anonymously.
2 See vol. 1, p. 145.

promised to publish the work. Hence they called me the 'famous promiser' and compared me to those who pretend for years that they are writing a book and indulge in empty boasts about their 'forthcoming publication'. Indeed, Father Bourdin himself says that he has been waiting for me to produce this for so long that it is now 'quite hopeless'.[1] But it is quite ridiculous for him to think that we can have been 'waiting for so long' for a person who is still comparatively young to produce something which others have not managed to provide these many centuries. It is also foolish of him, if he is trying to attack me, to concede that I am the sort of genius who can be expected to produce in a few years (so that anything more is a 'long wait') what I would not expect him to produce in six hundred years, were we both to live that long. Opponents of this sort, then, were quite convinced that the philosophical system of which they were so frightened was already complete, and that I had decided to publish it straightaway. So they began to attack not only the views set out in the books I had already published, but also the philosophy whose contents they did not yet know. They assailed it with many slanders, some surreptitious, some open and public, with the aim either of scaring me into withholding publication or else of destroying my philosophy immediately on publication and, as it were, smothering it at birth. At first I tried to laugh this off, and the more fiercely I saw them attacking me, the higher opinion of me I supposed they must have. But I have seen my attackers growing in number every day, and, as often happens, the enthusiasm with which they have looked for every chance to damage me has far exceeded the enthusiasm of any of my supporters to defend me. So I have begun to fear that their undercover efforts to discredit me may meet with some success, and that they may be more of a nuisance to me if I stick to my plan of not publishing my philosophy than if I confront them openly; for by setting before them in its entirety the work of which they are so afraid, I can at least ensure that they will have nothing further to be frightened of. I have therefore decided to submit to the public the sum total of my few reflections on philosophy, and to fight for the widest possible acceptance of my views, if indeed they are true. Because of this, I shall not present them in the same order and style which I adopted when I wrote about many of these matters before – namely in the Treatise of which I gave an outline in my *Discourse on the Method*,[2] but instead I shall use a style more suited to the current practice in the Schools. That is, I shall deal with each topic in turn, in short articles, and shall present the topics in such an order that the proof of what comes later depends solely on what has come earlier, so that everything is connected together in a single structure. In this way I hope I can provide

577

1 Cf. above p. 380.
2 The treatise referred to is *The World*; see vol. 1, pp. 79ff and 131ff.

such a clear account of the truth of all the issues normally discussed in philosophy,[1] that anyone who is seeking the truth may be able to find it in my book without any difficulty.

578   Now the class of those who seek the truth includes all young people when they first get down to learning philosophy. It also includes all of us, of whatever age, when we are meditating on philosophical issues in privacy and solitude, and are making our inquiries solely for our personal benefit. In addition, there are all the royal patrons and rulers and others who found universities and colleges, and set up endowments for the teaching of philosophy. Such patrons desire that, so far as is possible, only true philosophy shall be taught in their institutions, and if they allow doubtful and contentious opinions to be aired, the intention is not that their subjects should get into the habit of disputing everything, and so become more argumentative, refractory and stubborn, and thus less obedient to their superiors and more likely to stir up sedition; their hope is, rather, that the truth will be discovered, since most of them are convinced that it will eventually emerge out of all these debates and arguments. And even if long experience has taught them that the truth is rarely discovered in this way, their zeal for the truth is such that they think that even the smallest hope of discovering it should not be neglected. For there has never been a nation so savage or barbarous or so opposed to the right use of reason (which alone makes us human beings) as to want its teachers to propagate opinions which are at variance with the known truth. There is no doubt that the truth is always to be preferred to any opinion that conflicts with it, however long-standing and widely accepted that opinion may be; and all teachers should therefore be obliged to seek for the truth with all their might, and to teach it, once it has been discovered.

    But people may not believe that the truth will be found in the new philosophy which I have undertaken to publish. For it may hardly seem likely that one person has managed to see more than hundreds of thousands of highly intelligent men who have followed the opinions that 579 are commonly accepted in the Schools. Well-trodden and familiar pathways are always safer than new and unknown ones, and this maxim is particularly relevant because of theology. For the experience of many years has taught us that the traditional and common philosophy is consistent with theology, but it is uncertain whether this will be true of the new philosophy. For this reason some people maintain that the new philosophy should be prohibited and suppressed at the earliest opportunity, in case it should attract large numbers of inexperienced people who are avid

---

1 See note 3 above p. 386.

for novelty, and thus gradually spread and gain momentum, disturbing the peace and tranquility of the Schools and the universities and even bringing new heresies into the Church.

As far as I am concerned, my reply to this is that I make no special claims for myself, and would not venture to assert that my vision is better than anyone else's. What has perhaps helped me is that I have no great confidence in my own intelligence, and so I have followed only those paths that are easy and straightforward. It is hardly surprising that, by keeping to such simple routes, a person can make more progress than others of greatly superior intelligence, who follow rugged and impenetrable pathways.

Let me add that I do not want people to take my word for the truth of the philosophy I have promised to publish; its truth should be judged on the basis of the specimen essays I have already produced.[1] For in those essays I dealt with not one or two but many hundreds of problems which no one before me had ever explained in such a fashion. And although many people have looked askance at my writings in the past and tried to refute them by every possible means, no one, so far as I know, has been able to find in them anything that is not true. If we survey all the past ages in which earlier philosophies flourished and make a list of all the problems solved by those philosophies, they will be found to be both fewer and less important than the problems solved by means of my own philosophy. Indeed, I maintain that for every single problem ever solved   580 by means of the principles distinctive of peripatetic philosophy,[2] I can demonstrate that the supposed solution is invalid and false. Let us put this to the test: I invite my readers to come forward, not with a complete list – for I do not think it is worth the trouble for me to spend too much time on this – but with a few selected examples, and I will stand by my promise. To prevent possible quibbling, I must point out that in speaking of the 'principles distinctive of peripatetic philosophy' I am excluding those problems where the solution has been derived either (i) merely from the common experience of all mankind, or (ii) from the consideration of shapes and motions (which is the province of the mathematicians), or (iii) in the case of metaphysics, from those common notions[3] which, like the items under (i) and (ii), I do indeed accept, as is clear from my *Meditations*.

I shall add something that may seem paradoxical. Everything in peripatetic philosophy, regarded as a distinctive school that is different from others, is quite new, whereas everything in my philosophy is old.

---

[1] See note 4, above p. 387.   [2] I.e. Aristotelian philosophy.
[3] For examples of 'common notions' see pp. 116f above.

For as far as principles are concerned, I only accept those which in the past have always been common ground among all philosophers without exception, and which are therefore the most ancient of all. Moreover, the conclusions I go on to deduce are already contained and implicit in these principles, and I show this so clearly as to make it apparent that they too are very ancient, in so far as they are naturally implanted in the human mind. By contrast, the principles of the commonly accepted philosophy – at least at the time when they were invented by Aristotle and others – were quite new, and we should not suppose that they are any better now than they were then. Moreover, everything deduced from them is controversial and liable to be changed by individual philosophers 581 depending on the fashion in the Schools, and hence it is exceedingly new, since it is still being revised every day.

As far as theology is concerned, since one truth can never be in conflict with another, it would be impious to fear that any truths discovered in philosophy could be in conflict with the truths of faith. Indeed, I insist that there is nothing relating to religion which cannot be equally well or even better explained by means of my principles than can be done by means of those which are commonly accepted. I think I gave a very striking example of this at the end of my Replies to the Fourth Set of Objections, where I dealt with a topic where it is notoriously difficult to reconcile philosophy with theology.[1] I am ready to do the same for any other topic, if need be, and also to show that there are in fact many points in the commonly accepted philosophy which are in conflict with theological certainties, although this is generally concealed by philosophers or else not noticed because people are so used to accepting the points in question.

There is also no need to fear that my opinions may attract large numbers of inexperienced people who are avid for novelty, and thus gain too large a following. On the contrary, since experience shows that my views find favour principally among those who are more experienced, and who are attracted not by novelty but simply by the truth, they cannot possibly gain too wide a following.

Again, there is no need to fear that my opinions will disturb the peace of the Schools. On the contrary, philosophers already take sides against each other on so many controversies that they could hardly be more at 582 war than they are now. Indeed, the best way of establishing peace between them, and curbing the heresies that spring up every day out of these debates, is to secure the acceptance of true opinions, such as I have proved mine to be. For the clear perception of these truths will eliminate everything that could fuel doubt and controversy.

1 *Viz.* transubstantiation in the Eucharist, above pp. 172f.

It is clear from all this that there is really no reason why certain persons should be so anxious to prevent the rest of mankind from coming to know these truths. The only explanation is that they think these truths are all too evident and certain, and they are afraid that the truth will undermine the reputation for learning which they have tried to acquire by mastering other less probable doctrines. Thus the very envy which they feel towards me is considerable evidence of the truth of my philosophy. But I do not wish to appear to be boasting about the alleged envy which I excite, with only Father Bourdin's essay to cite as evidence, and so I shall now tell you something of the events which occurred lately in one of the most recently founded universities here in Holland . . .[1]

He [Voetius] has three reasons for condemning the new philosophy. (596) The first is that 'it is opposed to the traditional philosophy'. Here I will not repeat what I said about my philosophy being the oldest of all, and about there being nothing in the ordinary philosophy, in so far as it differs from mine, that is not quite new. I shall merely ask if someone can have a correct understanding of the philosophy which he wants to condemn if he is so stupid (or, if he prefers, malicious) as to try to get that philosophy suspected of being magical merely because it concentrates on figures and shapes. Or again, why, may I ask, is it the custom in the Schools to hold debates? Undoubtedly the object is to search for the truth and make it manifest. For if the truth were already in our possession, the debates would cease, as we can see in the case of geometry, where it is not the custom to hold debates. But if the manifest truth, which has been sought out and for so long desired, should now be laid before us – even by an angel – would it not have to be rejected on the argument under discussion, because it would be seen as 'new' by those accustomed to the

---

1 There follows an account of the bitter dispute at the University of Utrecht between Henricus Regius (1598–1679), who championed the Cartesian philosophy, and Descartes' implacable enemy Gisbertus Voetius (1589–1676) who was Rector of the University. Descartes describes how Voetius managed to get the academic senate to issue a formal condemnation of the 'new' (i.e. Cartesian) philosophy, in March 1642. He then quotes the senate's decree, which ends as follows:

The professors reject this new philosophy for three reasons. First, it is opposed to the traditional philosophy which universities throughout the world have hitherto taught on the best advice, and it undermines its foundations. Second, it turns away the young from this sound and traditional philosophy and prevents them reaching the heights of erudition; for once they have begun to rely on the new philosophy and its supposed solutions, they are unable to understand the technical terms which are commonly used in the books of traditional authors and in the lectures and debates of their professors. And, lastly, various false and absurd opinions either follow from the new philosophy or can be rashly deduced by the young – opinions which are in conflict with other disciplines and faculties and above all with orthodox theology. (AT VII, 592f)

debates in the Schools? To this Voetius[1] may reply that the debates in the
Schools are not concerned with the first principles, yet it is these which
597   are overturned by the claims of my philosophy. But why, in that case,
does he permit them to be overturned so easily? Why does he not defend
them by rational argument? And is not their uncertainty sufficiently
proved by the fact that no one has so far been able to use them as a basis
for constructing any reliable results?

The second reason for condemnation is that 'once the young have
begun to rely on the new philosophy and its supposed solutions they are
unable to understand the technical terms which are commonly used
in the books of traditional authors'. As if philosophy, which was
instituted to provide knowledge of the truth, should have to teach a
terminology which it does not need! One might just as well condemn
grammar and rhetoric, since it is more their function to deal with words,
and yet they are so far from teaching traditional terminology that they
condemn it as barbarous! So if Voetius were to say that these subjects
'turn away the young from sound philosophy and prevent them reaching
the heights of erudition' this claim would be no more ridiculous than the
corresponding charge he makes against my philosophy. It is not my
philosophy that should be required to produce an explanation of these
technical terms; one must demand such an explanation from the books of
those who use such terminology.

The third reason for condemnation has two parts, of which the first is
clearly ridiculous, and the second vicious and false. In the first place, any
doctrine, however true and obvious, is highly liable to have 'various false
and absurd opinions rashly deduced from it by the young'; but the
further claim that opinions can in fact be deduced from my philosophy
which 'are in conflict with orthodox theology' is vicious and false. I will
not use the counter-argument that I do not regard my accuser's theology
as orthodox, for I have never despised anyone for having different views
598   from my own, especially in matters of faith. I know that faith is the gift of
God, and in fact I have respect and affection for many theologians and
preachers who profess the same religion as my accuser. But I have often
declared that I have no desire to meddle in any theological disputes; and
since, even in philosophy, I deal only with matters that are known very
clearly by natural reason, these cannot be in conflict with anyone's
theology (unless that theology manifestly clashes with the light of reason,
which, I am sure, will not be said by anyone to be true of the theology
that he himself professes) . . .

---

1 The name is supplied for the reader's convenience. In the original Descartes avoids
   referring to Voetius by name, by using circumlocutions such as 'the Reverend Rector'.

For my own part, I neither seek popularity nor have any other desire (599) than to defend the truth to the best of my ability for the benefit of all people of learning and integrity and for the satisfaction of my own conscience. And I hope to bring those futile quibbles, and other ploys which my opponents habitually employ, so clearly out into the open that no one will use them in future unless he is not ashamed to be known publicly as a slanderer and a hater of the truth. Up till now, those who are not wholly shameless have to a considerable extent been kept in check by a request I made when I first began to publish: I asked anyone 600 who had any criticisms to offer of any of the claims I made in my writings to be kind enough to write and tell me, and I promised that I would send him a reply.[1] This made people realize that they could not go round voicing their criticisms to others unless they had indicated them to me; for if they did so, that very action would justly open them to a charge of malicious slander. But many ignored my request, and although they could not in fact find anything in my writings which they could show to be false, and despite the fact that in some cases they had not read my work at all, they nevertheless maliciously attacked it in private. Indeed, some were so enthusiastic that they wrote entire volumes of criticism, not for publication but – and I think this is much worse – for private circulation among the gullible. These books were stuffed partly with invalid arguments (though the flaws were disguised with many verbal ambiguities), and partly with arguments which were valid but which were directed against opinions that had been inaccurately foisted onto me. But I now beg and urge all these critics to publish what they have written. Experience has taught me that this will be better than if they send their criticisms to me personally, as I originally requested. For were I to decide that their comments did not deserve an answer, they might either falsely boast that I had been unable to find a reply, or else complain that I had arrogantly ignored them. Another risk is that if I were to publish any of the comments sent to me, some might complain that I had done them a wrong by adding my own replies. For they might feel (as someone recently told me in connection with his own criticisms) that this would deprive them of a benefit they would have enjoyed had they arranged to publish their criticisms themselves – the benefit of having the full attention of a wide readership for some months, until I managed to produce a reply.[2] I shall certainly not grudge them this benefit; indeed I 601 do not promise to produce any replies at all unless I find their arguments to be of such a quality that it does not seem to me that the general reader could answer them for himself. But as for quibbles and abuse and other

1 *Discourse*, part 6; see vol. 1, p. 149.
2 Descartes has Gassendi in mind here; see Author's note, above pp. 268f.

such attacks which are irrelevant to the subject-matter of my books, I shall regard them as supporting my case rather than attacking it. For I do not think anyone will employ such tactics in a debate of this kind unless he is keen to win more points by rhetorical tricks than he can prove by rational argument; and this shows that he is not after the truth but is prepared to attack it, and hence that he is not a person of honesty and integrity.

I do not doubt, however, that there are many decent and god-fearing men who may regard my views as suspect, first, because they see others criticizing them, and, secondly, simply because my views are described as 'new', and not many people have so far understood them. And if people were asked to deliberate on my views, it would perhaps not be easy to find a jury in which those who considered that my views should be rejected did not greatly outnumber those who ventured to approve of them. For reason and prudence suggest that if we have to make a judgement in a case where our perception is not wholly clear, our verdict should accord with the results which have been found to obtain in similar cases. In the past, so many people have produced new opinions in philosophy which have later been recognized to be no better, and in many cases more dangerous, than the ordinary accepted views, that if anyone who does not yet have a clear perception of my views is asked to give his opinion of them, it would be perfectly fair for him to say that they should be rejected. So no matter how true my views may be, I could still have reason to fear that they might be condemned by your whole Society, and by all groups of teachers everywhere, just as they were in the
602 case of the university senate which I have described above; or at least I might well be concerned about this if I were not confident that, in your singular kindness and wisdom, you will take my views under your protection. But since you are in charge of that section of the Society which can read my work with particular ease since a substantial proportion of it is written in French, I am convinced that you are particularly well placed to help in this matter.[1] Indeed, I ask no other favour of you here than that you should examine my work yourself, or, if weightier business prevents you, that you should delegate the job not to Father Bourdin alone but to other more intellectually gifted members. In the law courts, when two or three reliable witnesses affirm they have seen something, more reliance is placed on their word alone than on that of a vast crowd of dissenting witnesses who may have been led to think the reverse by pure guesswork. And similarly, I ask you to give credence only to those who declare that they have a perfect understanding of the subject

---

1 Dinet was head of the Jesuits in France.

on which they are to pass judgement. Finally, if you have any reasons which might oblige me to revise my future plans, I beg you not to shrink from informing me of them.

In the brief set of *Meditations* which I published are to be found all the principles of the philosophy on which I am working. And in the *Optics* and the *Meteorology* I deduced many specific results from these principles which illustrate the method of reasoning which I employ. Hence, although I have not yet revealed the whole of my philosophy, I think that the samples I have already produced make it easy to understand what it will be like. I think I was quite justified in preferring to publish certain 603 specimen essays to begin with, rather than setting out the entire system before there was a demand for it. For although, to be frank, I have no doubts about its truth, I know how easy it is for it to be condemned by many sensible people, once a few envious critics have attacked it by making allegations about its 'novelty'. And so I am not sure that there really is a general demand for my philosophy, and I do not want to force it on an unwilling public. This is why I have given everyone so much advance warning that I am working on it, why many private individuals are eagerly waiting for it, and why one group of teachers has already judged that it should be rejected – though since I know they were incited to do this by their quarrelsome and foolish Rector,[1] I am not very impressed. But if other groups were to be against publication, and had a more justifiable case to put forward, then I would put their wishes before those of any private individuals. Indeed, I emphatically declare that I will never knowingly do anything against the advice of the prudent or against the wishes of the powerful. And since I have no doubt that, whichever side your Society comes down on, the weight of that decision must tip the scales, you will be doing me a great kindness if you will inform me of the verdict that you and your members reach. For just as throughout my past life I have always had a particular respect and esteem for your Society, so in the present undertaking, which I consider to be of some considerable importance, I will not embark on any course which does not meet with your approval. And so I take my leave.

1 See above p. 393.

The Search for Truth

Translators' preface

The Search for Truth by means of the Natural Light (*La Recherche de la Vérité par la lumière naturelle*) is an incomplete work which was not published during Descartes' lifetime. In the inventory of Descartes' papers, made after his death in Stockholm, the work is listed as 'thirteen pages of a Dialogue with the title "The Search for Truth by means of the Natural Light"'.[1] The work first appeared, in a Latin translation, in the collection of Descartes' posthumous works (*Opuscula posthuma*) edited by P. and J. Blaeu and published at Amsterdam in 1701.

The original French manuscript has been lost. Leibniz obtained a copy made by Tschirnhaus in 1676, and a part of this copy – roughly the first half of the published Latin translation – was discovered among Leibniz's papers in the Royal Public Library at Hanover. Adam and Tannery's edition comprises this French text, completed by the Latin translation of the Amsterdam edition.

The date of composition of the dialogue is a matter of conjecture.[2] In his biography of Descartes, Baillet takes it to date from the last years of Descartes' life. Some scholars have suggested that it dates from Descartes' earlier years. And others have put forward the hypothesis that Descartes wrote it during the summer of 1641, while he was living in the castle of Endegeest and his thoughts were occupied with the central arguments of the *Meditations* and the objections of his scholastic critics, both of which find expression, though in a somewhat crude form, in the dialogue. Of the three characters appearing in the dialogue, Epistemon ('Knowledgeable') represents someone well versed in classical and scholastic philosophy, and Polyander ('Everyman') the person of untutored common sense; Eudoxus (literally 'Famous', but the Greek root also suggests one of sound judgement) is the mouthpiece for Descartes' own views.

D.M.
R.S.

---

1 The inventory is reproduced in AT x, 5–12.
2 For a full discussion of the issue see AT x, 529ff and F. Alquié (ed.), *Oeuvres philosophiques de Descartes*, vol. II, pp. 1102ff.

THE SEARCH FOR TRUTH
BY MEANS OF THE NATURAL LIGHT

This light alone, without any help from religion or philosophy, determines what opinions a good man should hold on any matter that may occupy his thoughts, and penetrates into the secrets of the most recondite sciences.

A good man is not required to have read every book or diligently mastered everything taught in the Schools. It would, indeed, be a kind of defect in his education if he had spent too much time on book-learning. Having many other things to do in the course of his life, he must judiciously measure out his time so as to reserve the better part of it for performing good actions – the actions which his own reason would have to teach him if he learned everything from it alone. But he came into the world in ignorance, and since the knowledge which he had as a child was based solely on the weak foundation of the senses and the authority of his teachers, it was virtually inevitable that his imagination should be filled with innumerable false thoughts before reason could guide his conduct. So later on he needs to have very great natural talent, or else the instruction of a wise teacher, in order to rid himself of the bad doctrines that have filled his mind, to lay the foundations for a solid science, and to discover all the ways in which he can raise his knowledge to the highest level that it can possibly attain.

I intend in this work to explain these matters. I shall bring to light the true riches of our souls, opening up to each of us the means whereby we can find within ourselves, without any help from anyone else, all the knowledge we may need for the conduct of life, and the means of using it in order to acquire all the most abstruse items of knowledge that human reason is capable of possessing.

But in case the grandeur of my plan should immediately fill your minds with so much wonder as to leave no room for belief, I must tell you that what I am undertaking is not so difficult as one might imagine. For the items of knowledge that lie within reach of the human mind are all linked together by a bond so marvellous, and can be derived from each other by means of inferences so necessary, that their discovery does not require much skill or intelligence – provided we begin with the simplest and know how to move stage by stage to the most sublime. In what follows I shall try to explain this by means of a chain of reasoning which is so clear and accessible to all that anybody who has not reached the same conclusions earlier will blame his failure to do so simply on the fact that he did not cast his eyes in the right direction and fix his thoughts on the matters that I considered. And I shall not deserve any more glory for having made these discoveries than a passer-by would deserve for having accidentally stumbled upon some rich treasure for which many persons had previously conducted a diligent but unsuccessful search.

I am surprised, indeed, that amongst so many exceptional minds, much better equipped than I to carry out this task, none have had the patience to pick their way through the difficulties. Instead they have nearly all acted like travellers who leave the main path to take a shortcut, only to find themselves lost amongst briars and precipices.

But I do not wish to consider what others have known or not known. I am content to observe that even if all the knowledge that can be desired were contained in books, the good things in them would be mingled with so many useless things, and scattered haphazardly through such a pile of massive tomes, that we should need more time for reading them than our present life allows, and more intelligence for picking out the useful material than would be required for discovering it on our own. 498

This makes me hope that you will be happy to find here an easier path. I hope too that the truths I set forth will not be any less well received for their not being derived from Aristotle or Plato, and that they will have currency in the world in the same way as money, whose value is no less when it comes from the purse of a peasant than when it comes from a bank. Moreover I have done my best to make these truths equally useful to everybody. I could find no style better suited to this end than that of a conversation in which several friends, frankly and without ceremony, disclose the best of their thoughts to each other. Thus let us imagine that Eudoxus, a man of moderate intellect but possessing a judgement which is not corrupted by any false beliefs and a reason which retains all the purity of its nature, is visited in his country home by two friends whose minds are among the most outstanding and inquiring of our time. One of them, Polyander, has never studied at all, while the other, Epistemon, has 499 a detailed knowledge of everything that can be learned in the Schools. Leaving to your imagination their other conversations as well as their surroundings (from which, however, I shall frequently have them take examples in order to make their thoughts clearer), I shall now present them introducing the topic which will occupy them throughout these two books.

Polyander I consider you very fortunate to have found all those fine things in the Greek and Latin literature. Indeed, it seems to me that if I had studied as much as you, I should have been as different from my present self as the angels are from you. I cannot forgive the folly of my parents for believing that the pursuit of learning enfeebles the spirit, and for sending me to court and into the army at such an early age, and I shall regret my ignorance for the rest of my life if I do not learn anything through my association with you.

Epistemon The best thing I can tell you on this topic is that the desire for knowledge, which is common to all men, is an illness which cannot be cured, for curiosity grows with learning. But because the defects in the soul trouble a person only in so far as he becomes aware of them, you

500   have an advantage over us in that, unlike us, you do not notice all the many things which you lack.

Eudoxus Is it possible, Epistemon, that you, with all your learning, are persuaded that nature can contain a malady so universal without also providing a remedy for it? For my part, just as I think that each land has enough fruits and rivers to satisfy the hunger and thirst of all its inhabitants, so too I think that enough truth can be known in each subject to satisfy amply the curiosity of orderly souls. The body of a person suffering from dropsy is no further removed from its proper condition than is the mind of someone who is perpetually tormented by an insatiable curiosity.

Epistemon I have, indeed, heard that our desire cannot naturally extend to matters which appear to us to be impossible, and that it ought not to extend to those which are evil or useless. But there are so many things to be known which seem to us possible and which are not only good and pleasant but also very necessary for the conduct of our actions; and I cannot believe that anyone ever knows so much that he cannot have good reasons to desire to know more.

501   *Eudoxus* What will you say of me, then, if I assure you that I no longer feel any passion to learn anything at all. I am as happy with what little knowledge I have as ever Diogenes was in his barrel, and this without having any need for his philosophy.[1] For my neighbours' knowledge does not limit mine in the way that their fields form the boundaries of my small property. And my mind, having at its disposal all the truths it comes across, does not dream there are others to discover. Instead it enjoys the same tranquillity as would a king if his country were so isolated and cut off from others that he imagined there was nothing beyond his frontiers but infertile deserts and uninhabitable mountains.

---

1 Diogenes of Sinope (fourth cent. B.C.), one of the founders of the Cynic school of philosophy, was celebrated in antiquity for residing in a large earthenware tub.

Epistemon If anyone else were to speak to me in this manner, I should consider him to be very vain or else to be lacking in curiosity. But you escape the charge of vanity because you have chosen to retire to this remote place and because you are so unconcerned about being well known; and in view of the time you formerly spent in travelling, in associating with learned men, and in investigating all the most complex discoveries in every science, we can be sure that you do not lack curiosity. So all I can say is that I consider you extremely happy, and I am convinced that you must therefore be in possession of knowledge which is far more perfect than that enjoyed by others.

Eudoxus I thank you for the good opinion you hold of me. But I would not presume so much upon your courtesy as to expect you simply to take my word for what I have said. One must never advance propositions so 502 remote from common opinion without at the same time being able to point out some of their consequences. That is why I invite you both to stay here this summer, so that I may have time to show you a part of what I know. For I venture to hope not only that you will admit that I have some reason for being content with my knowledge, but, in addition, that you for your part will be fully satisfied with the things you have learned.

Epistemon I have no hesitation in accepting a kindness which I was myself going to beg of you.

Polyander For my part, I shall be pleased to be present at this discussion, though I do not think myself capable of deriving any profit from it.

Eudoxus On the contrary, Polyander, I think it is you who will gain the greater benefit from it, since you are unprejudiced; and it will be far easier for me to set on the right track someone who is neutral than to guide Epistemon, who will often take up the opposite position. But to give you a more distinct conception of the sort of doctrine I propose to teach, I should like you to notice how the sciences differ from those simple forms of knowledge which can be acquired without any process of reasoning, such as languages, history, geography and in general any subject which rests on experience alone. I readily grant that one man could not live long enough to acquire first-hand experience of everything in the world; but I am no less convinced that it would be folly to desire 503 this. A good man is not required to know Greek or Latin any more than the languages of Switzerland or Brittany, or the history of the Empire any more than that of the smallest state in Europe. He ought simply to take care to employ his leisure in good and useful occupations, and equip his memory only with the most necessary knowledge. As to the sciences – which are simply a matter of our making reliable judgements on the basis of knowledge we already possess – some are drawn from ordinary facts about which everyone has heard, and others from observations which are unusual and highly contrived. I admit, too, that we could not possibly discuss each of the latter in detail. For we should need first of all to have examined all the herbs and stones that come from the Indies, to have beheld the Phoenix, and in short to have knowledge of all the marvels of nature. But I believe I shall adequately fulfil my promise if I explain to you the truths which can be deduced from the ordinary facts known to each of us, and so make you capable of discovering for yourselves all the others, when you care to take the trouble to look for them.

Polyander I think that this is all we can possibly desire. I should be happy if you would merely prove a certain number of propositions which are so well known that no one is ignorant of them, such as those concerning the Deity, the rational soul, the virtues and their rewards, etc. I compare these propositions to those ancient families which everyone recognizes as being very illustrious even though their titles to nobility lie buried in the ruins of antiquity. For I have no doubt at all that those who first brought mankind to believe these truths were able to prove them with very strong arguments. But ever since that time, these proofs have been repeated so rarely that no one knows them any longer. These truths are so important, however, that prudence obliges us to believe them blindly at the risk of being mistaken, rather than to wait until the next world in order to get clear about them.

Epistemon For my part, I am a little more curious, and I should like you to go on to clarify for me some special difficulties which I find in every science, and chiefly those concerning human contrivances, apparitions, illusions, and in short all the marvellous effects attributed to magic. For I think it is useful to know about them, not in order to make use of them, but in order to prevent our judgement from being beguiled by wonder at something of which it is ignorant.

Eudoxus I shall try to satisfy both of you. In order to establish an order that we can follow to the end, first of all, Polyander, I should like us to have a discussion, just the two of us, about all the things in the world, considering them as they are in themselves. I want Epistemon to interrupt as little as possible, because his objections would often force us to depart from our subject. Afterwards we shall all consider these things afresh, but under a different aspect, namely in so far as they are related to us and can be described as true or false, and good or bad. It is here that Epistemon will have a chance to set forth all the difficulties which will have occurred to him during the preceding conversations.

Polyander Tell us the order, then, that you will follow in your explanations.

Eudoxus We must begin with the rational soul, for all our knowledge resides in it; and after considering its nature and effects, we shall proceed to its author. When we have come to know who he is, and how he has created all things that exist in the world, we shall be able to see what is most certain regarding the other creatures, and we shall examine in what way our senses receive their objects and how our thoughts are made true or false. Then I shall lay before your eyes the works of men involving corporeal things. After causing you to wonder at the most powerful machines, the most unusual automatons, the most impressive illusions and the most subtle tricks that human ingenuity can devise, I shall reveal to you the secrets behind them, which are so simple and straightforward that you will no longer have reason to wonder at anything made by the hands of men. I shall then pass to the works of nature, and after showing you the cause of all her changes, the variety of her qualities, and how the souls of plants and of animals differ from ours, I shall present for your 506 consideration the entire edifice of the things that are perceivable by the senses. After giving an account of celestial phenomena and what we can judge with certainty about them, I shall pass on to the soundest conjectures concerning matters which cannot be definitely settled by men, in order to explain the relation of things perceivable by the senses to things perceivable by the intellect, the relation of both sorts of things to the Creator, the immortality of his creatures, and their state of being after the end of time. Then we shall come to the second part of this discussion, where we deal with each science in particular, picking out the most solid elements in each of them and proposing the method for carrying them much further forward than has hitherto been achieved – a method which enables someone of average intelligence to discover for himself everything that the most subtle minds can devise. Having thus prepared our understanding to make perfect judgements about the truth, we must also learn to control our will by distinguishing good things from bad, and by observing the true difference between virtues and vices. That done, I trust that your passion for knowledge will not be so intense, and that it will seem to you that everything I have said has been satisfactorily proved – so much so that you will believe that a man with a good mind, even one brought up in a desert and never illuminated by any light but the light of nature, could not have opinions different from ours if he carefully weighed all the same reasons. Now, to enter upon this discussion, we must ask the following questions: What are the first things that people know? What part of the soul does this knowledge reside in? And why is it 507 so imperfect to begin with?

Epistemon It seems to me that all this can be explained very clearly if we compare the imagination of a child to a *tabula rasa* on which our ideas are to be traced, these ideas being like portraits drawn from nature. Our senses, inclinations, teachers and intellect are the different artists who may work at this task, and among them the least competent are the first to take part, namely our imperfect senses, blind instincts and foolish nurses. The most competent is the intellect, which comes last; and it must serve an apprenticeship of many years, following the example of its masters for a long time before daring to correct any of their errors. In my opinion, this is one of the chief causes of the difficulties we have in acquiring knowledge. For our senses see nothing beyond the more coarse and ordinary things and our natural inclinations are entirely corrupt; and as to our teachers, although undoubtedly you might find very perfect ones among them, they cannot force our judgement to acccept their reasonings until our intellect has done the work (which only it can do) of examining them. But the intellect is like an excellent painter who is called 508 upon to put the finishing touches to a bad picture sketched out by a young apprentice. It would be futile for him to employ the rules of his art in correcting the picture little by little, a bit here and a bit there, and in adding with his own hand all that is lacking in it, if, despite his best efforts, he could never remove every major fault, since the drawing was badly sketched from the beginning, the figures badly placed, and the proportions badly observed.

Eudoxus Your comparison nicely illustrates the first obstacle facing us; but you do not describe the means we must use if we wish to avoid it. Now it seems to me that your painter would do far better to make a fresh start on the picture; rather than wasting time in correcting all the lines he finds on the canvas, he should wipe them off it with a sponge. Similarly, as soon as a man reaches what we call the age of discretion he should resolve once and for all to remove from his imagination all traces of the imperfect ideas which have been engraved there up till that time. Then he should begin in earnest to form new ideas, applying all the strength of his intellect so effectively that if he does not bring these ideas to perfection, at least he will not be able to blame the weakness of the senses or the 509 irregularities of nature.

Epistemon That would be an excellent remedy if it were easy to apply. But you are not ignorant of the fact that the opinions first received in our imagination remain so deeply imprinted there that our will cannot erase them on its own, but can do so only by calling on the assistance of powerful reasons.

Eudoxus I should like to try and impart some of these reasons to you. But if you wish to derive any profit from this conversation, you must now give me your attention, and let me converse a bit with Polyander; this will enable me to begin by overturning all the knowledge acquired up to the present. For, since this knowledge is not enough to satisfy him, it must be faulty: I would compare it to a badly constructed house, whose foundations are not firm. I know of no better way to repair it than to knock it all down, and build a new one in its place. For I do not wish to be one of those jobbing builders who devote themselves solely to refurbishing old buildings because they consider themselves incapable of undertaking the construction of new ones. But, Polyander, while engaged upon this work of demolition we can use the same method to dig the foundations which ought to serve our purpose, and to prepare the best and most solid materials which will be needed for building up these foundations. So please join me in considering which, of all the truths men can know, are 510 the most certain and the easiest to become acquainted with.

Polyander Is there anyone who can doubt that things that are perceivable by the senses – by which I mean those which can be seen and touched – are much more certain than all the others? I for one would be quite astonished if you were to make me see just as clearly any of the things which are said about God or the soul.

Eudoxus That is just what I hope to do. I find it strange that men are so credulous as to base their knowledge on the certitude of the senses, when everyone knows that they are sometimes deceptive, and that we have good reason always to distrust those who have deceived us even once.

Polyander I am well aware that the senses are sometimes deceptive if they are in poor condition, as when all food seems bitter to a sick person; or if their objects are too far away, as when we look at the stars, which never appear so large to us as they really are; or, in general, whenever they do not act freely in accordance with their natural constitution. But such defects of the senses are all quite easy to recognize, and do not prevent me from being quite sure at present that I am seeing you, that we are walking in this garden, that the sun is shining on us, and in a word, that everything which ordinarily appears to my senses is genuine.

Eudoxus So if I wish to make you fear that the senses are deceptive on 511 occasions when you are unaware of the deception, it is not enough for me to tell you that the senses deceive you on certain occasions when you perceive the deception. I shall have to go further, and ask if you have never seen one of those melancholic individuals who think themselves to be vases, or take some part of their body to be enormous; they will swear that what they see and touch is just as they imagine it to be. To be sure, a good man would be indignant if you told him that his beliefs cannot have any more rational basis than theirs, since he relies, like them, on what the senses and imagination represent to him. But you cannot take it amiss if I ask whether you are not, like all men, liable to fall asleep, and whether you cannot think, while asleep, that you are seeing me, that you are walking in this garden, that the sun is shining – in brief, all the things of which you now believe you are utterly certain. Have you never heard this expression of astonishment in comedies: 'Am I awake or asleep?' How can you be certain that your life is not a continuous dream, and that everything you think you learn through your senses is not false now, just as much as when you are asleep? In particular, how can you be certain of this when you have learned that you were created by a superior being who, being all-powerful, would have found it no more difficult to create us just as I am describing, than to create us as you think you are?

Polyander There, surely, we have arguments sufficient to overturn all the teachings of Epistemon, if he is reflective enough to give his attention to them. For myself, however, I fear that I should simply go wool-gathering if I tried to consider such abstract matters, for I am a man who has never engaged in study or accustomed himself to turning his mind so far away from things that are perceivable by the senses.

Epistemon I agree that it is very dangerous to proceed too far in this line of thinking. Such general doubts would lead us straight into the ignorance of Socrates or the uncertainty of the Pyrrhonists.[1] These are deep waters, where I think we may lose our footing.

Eudoxus I confess that it would be dangerous for someone who does not know a ford to venture across it without a guide, and many have lost their lives in doing so. But you have nothing to fear if you follow me. Indeed, just such fears have prevented most men of letters from acquiring a body of knowledge which was firm and certain enough to deserve the name 'science'.[2] Supposing that there was no firmer basis for their opinions other than things perceivable by the senses, they have built upon sand instead of digging further down to find rock or clay. So we must not let the matter rest here, especially since even if you did not wish to give further consideration to the arguments I have stated, the arguments have already done what I desired: their chief effect has been to touch your imagination so as to make you fear them. For this indicates that your knowledge is not so infallible as to prevent your fearing that these arguments will undermine its foundations by making you doubt every-thing. Consequently it indicates that you already have these doubts, and so I have achieved my aim, which was to overturn all your learning by showing you its uncertainty. But in case you should now lack the courage to proceed any further, I would advise you that these doubts, which alarmed you at the start, are like phantoms and empty images which

512

513

---

1 Socrates attributed his reputation as the wisest man in Athens to the fact that he alone recognized that he knew nothing. Pyrrhonism was a strong version of scepticism which advocated complete suspension of judgement (named after Pyrrhon of Elis, born *c.* 365 B.C.).
2 Cf. above p. 101.

appear at night in the uncertain glimmer of a weak light: if you flee from them, your fear will follow you, but if you approach as if to touch them, you will find nothing but air and shadow and you will be more confident the next time such an encounter may occur.

Polyander I should like, then, to follow your suggestion and set forth 514 these difficulties in the strongest form possible. I shall apply my mind to the task of doubting whether I have not been dreaming all my life, and whether all the ideas I thought capable of entering my mind only by way of the senses were not in fact formed by themselves, just as similar ideas are formed whenever I am asleep, and I know that my eyes are shut, my ears closed, and in short, that none of my senses help to form them. Thus I shall be uncertain not only about whether you are in the world and whether there is an earth or a sun; but also about whether I have eyes, ears, a body, and even whether I am speaking to you and you are speaking to me. In short, I shall doubt everything.[1]

Eudoxus There you are, all prepared, and at the very stage to which I had intended to bring you. The time has now come for you to consider closely the conclusions which I wish to draw at this point. Now, you see that you can reasonably have doubts about everything that you know only by means of the senses. But can you ever have doubts about your doubt, and remain doubtful whether you are doubting or not?

Polyander I must confess that your question strikes me with amazement. The modicum of insight I possess (which gives me a moderate amount of good sense) makes me see with some astonishment that I am forced to confess that I know nothing with any certainty, that I am doubtful about everything and certain of nothing. But what do you want 515 to infer from this? I do not see that this universal amazement can be of any use, nor do I see how this sort of doubt can be a principle which gets us very far. For you arranged this conversation with quite the opposite end in view – to free us from our doubts and make clear to us truths which we should know and which even Epistemon, for all his learning, might not know.

Eudoxus Just give me your attention and I shall conduct you further than you think. For from this universal doubt, as from a fixed and immovable point, I propose to derive the knowledge of God, of yourself, and of everything in the universe.

Polyander You are promising a great deal indeed; and if things turn out as you promise, it will be worth our while to grant your initial demands. Keep your word and we shall be quite content to do so.

Eudoxus You cannot deny that you have such doubts; rather it is

1 Here the French manuscript ends; what follows is translated from the Latin of the Amsterdam edition (1701).

certain that you have them, so certain in fact that you cannot doubt your doubting. Therefore it is also true that you who are doubting exist; this is so true that you can no longer have any doubts about it.

Polyander I quite agree with you on that point, because if I did not exist, I would not be able to doubt.

Eudoxus You exist, therefore, and you know that you exist, and you know this just because you are doubting.

Polyander All of this is quite true.

Eudoxus But, so that you are not deflected from the course I suggested, let us proceed gradually, and as I said, you will find that you are making greater progress than you think. Let us go through the argument again. You exist, and you know that you exist, and you know this because you know that you are doubting. But what are you – you who have doubts about everything but cannot doubt that you yourself exist?

Polyander The answer to that is not at all difficult, and I can see perfectly well why you chose me rather than Epistemon to answer your questions: you did not want to ask anything which could not be answered very easily. So I shall say I am a *man*.

Eudoxus You are not paying attention to my question, and the reply you give me, however simple it may seem to you, would plunge you into very difficult and complicated problems, were I to press you even a little. If, for example, I were to ask even Epistemon himself what a man is, and he gave the stock reply of the scholastics, that a man is a 'rational 516 animal', and if, in order to explain these two terms (which are just as obscure as the former), he were to take us further, through all the levels which are called 'metaphysical', we should be dragged into a maze from which it would be impossible to escape. For two other questions arise from this one. First, what is an *animal*? Second, what is *rational*? If, in order to explain what an animal is, he were to reply that it is a 'living and sentient being', that a living being is an 'animate body', and that a body is a 'corporeal substance', you see immediately that the questions, like the branches of a family tree, would rapidly increase and multiply. Quite clearly, the result of all these admirable questions would be pure verbiage, which would elucidate nothing and leave us in our original state of ignorance.

Epistemon I am sorry you despise the tree of Porphyry,[1] which the learned have always admired, and it annoys me that you would try to convey to Polyander what he is in a different way from the one which has

---

1 Porphyry, one of the founders of Neoplatonism (born *c.* 237 A.D.), proposed a 'family tree' of genera and species under which things may be classified. Thus the genus, substance (the 'trunk' of the tree), branches into the two species, corporeal and incorporeal, each of which divides into a further pair, etc. – for example, corporeal into living and non-living, living into sentient and non-sentient, etc. Cf. above p. 344.

long been universally accepted in the Schools. To this day no better or more appropriate way has been found for explaining what we are than displaying all the levels which make up our whole nature, for in this way, by passing up and down through all these levels, we can learn what our nature has in common with the natures of all other things, and in what respects it differs from them. And this is the highest point to which our knowledge can reach.

Eudoxus I have never had any intention of condemning the method of explanation ordinarily employed in the Schools, nor shall I ever wish to. For it is to that method that I owe the little I know, and my use of it has helped me to recognize the uncertainty of all the things I have learned there. So, even if my teachers taught me nothing that was certain, I owe them my thanks none the less, since it was due to their instruction that I came to realize this. Indeed, the fact that everything they taught me was quite doubtful gives me greater reason now to be thankful than would have been the case had their teaching been in closer accord with reason; for in the latter case I might have been content with the smattering of reason which I found in it, and that might have made me less conscientious in searching carefully for the truth. What I told Polyander serves not so much to point out to him the confusion and uncertainty into which his answer plunges you as to make him more attentive in future to my questions. Thus I am addressing my remarks to him; and to keep us from wandering any further from our path, I ask him once more what he is – he who can have doubts about everything but cannot have doubts about himself.

Polyander I thought I had satisfied you when I said that I am a *man*, but I quite see that I misread the situation: I can see that my answer does not satisfy you, and I must admit that it no longer seems adequate to me, especially when I think of the confusion and uncertainty into which, as you have shown me, it can plunge us if we want to make the answer clearer and understand it better. Indeed, whatever Epistemon may say, it strikes me that there is a great deal of obscurity in these metaphysical levels. If, for example, we say that a body is a 'corporeal substance', without making clear what a corporeal substance is, these two words do not tell us any more than does the word 'body'. In the same way, if we assert that to be living is to be an 'animate body', without first explaining what a body is and what it is to be animate – and likewise with all the other metaphysical levels – we are uttering words and putting them as it were in a certain order, but we are not really saying anything. The words do not convey anything that can be conceived, or form any distinct idea in our mind. When, in reply to your question, I said that I was a *man*, I was not actually thinking of all the scholastic entities which I knew

517

nothing about and had never heard of, and which, so far as I am concerned, subsist only in the imagination of those who have invented them. I was thinking, rather, about the things we see, touch, perceive with our senses, and experience within ourselves – in a word, about things which even the most simple-minded of men know just as well as the greatest philosopher in the world. Undoubtedly I am a certain whole made up of two arms, two legs, one head, and all the other parts which make up what we call the human body, and which besides is nourished, walks, perceives by the senses, and thinks.

Eudoxus I saw at once from your answer that you had not properly understood my question, and that you answered more questions than I had asked. Now, in the list of things which you were doubting earlier on, you had already included arms, legs, head, and all the other parts which make up the mechanism of the human body. It was not my intention to question you about these things, the existence of which you are not certain of. Tell me, then, what you are, strictly speaking, in so far as you are doubting. This was the sole point on which I had decided to question you, because beyond this you can know nothing for certain.

518   *Polyander* I now see that I was mistaken in my answer, and that I went much further than was appropriate, since I did not quite grasp your intention. This will make me more careful in future, and it makes me marvel now at the precision of your method, as you guide us step by step along simple and easy paths towards knowledge of the things you want to teach us. But we have reason to say that it was a happy mistake I made, since, thanks to it, I know very well that what I am, in so far as I am doubting, is certainly not what I call my body. Indeed, I do not even know whether I have a body; you have shown me that it is possible to doubt it. I might add that I cannot deny absolutely that I have a body. Yet even if we keep all these suppositions intact, this will not prevent me from being certain that I exist. On the contrary, these suppositions simply strengthen the certainty of my conviction that I exist and am not a body. Otherwise, if I had doubts about my body, I would also have doubts about myself, and I cannot have doubts about that. I am absolutely convinced that I exist, so convinced that it is totally impossible for me to doubt it.

Eudoxus Splendidly put! So admirably are you acquitting yourself here that I could not put the point better myself. All I need do, I see, is to leave you to get on with the job on your own, after taking care to set you on your course. Provided we have proper direction, all we need for discovering the truth on the most difficult issues is, I think, common sense, to give it its ordinary name. Since, as I had hoped, you have a decent supply of that, I am simply going to point out to you the way you should take in future. Just keep going and, relying on your own resources, draw the conclusions which follow from that first principle.

Polyander This principle seems so fertile, and suggests to me so many things at once that I think I would have an enormous job arranging them in order. Just now you advised me to ponder on what I am, I who am doubting, and not to confuse this with what I once believed myself to be. This single piece of advice has flooded my mind with light and all at once scattered the darkness; so much so that by the light of this torch I see more sharply within myself that which is hidden within me, and I am more convinced that I possess something non-tangible than I ever was that I possessed a body.

Eudoxus I am quite delighted with this sudden enthusiasm, though Epistemon may not be quite so pleased. You have not freed him from his mistake, and you have not placed before his eyes a fraction of the things 519 you say are contained in this principle. So he will always be wondering why he should not believe or at any rate fear that everything which this light presents to you is like a will-o'-the-wisp which dies out and vanishes as soon as you try to get near it, and that you will soon slip back into the darkness you were in before, that is, into your original state of ignorance. It would certainly be an extraordinary occurrence if you, who have never spent much time studying or delving into the works of the philosophers, should so suddenly and so effortlessly end up a learned man. Therefore we should not be surprised that Epistemon thinks the way he does.

Epistemon I admit I took Polyander's reaction to be a sort of burst of enthusiasm. Polyander has never given much thought to the grand truths which philosophy conveys, and I thought he was so transported by his reflection on the most insignificant of these truths that he could not refrain from displaying his intense excitement to you. But those who, like you,[1] have been plodding this path for a long time, expending much oil and effort in reading and re-reading the writings of the ancients, unravelling the thorniest knots in philosophy, are no longer surprised by such bursts of enthusiasm. They make no more of it than they do of the vain hopes of some who have just begun to learn mathematics. No sooner have such novices been given the line and the circle, and shown what a straight line is and what a curved, than they believe that they are going to discover how to square the circle and duplicate the cube.[2] But we have frequently refuted the views of the Pyrrhonists, and the fruits which 520 they themselves have derived from their philosophical method have been

---

1 AT suggest that 'you' (*tui*) is a misprint for 'me' (*mei*).
2 Two of the problems of Greek mathematics – both unsolvable: the former, to construct a circle with the same area as a given square; the latter, to construct a cube which is twice the volume of a given cube.

so meagre that they have been wandering about aimlessly all their lives. Unable to free themselves from the doubts which they themselves introduced into philosophy, they have put their efforts exclusively into learning to doubt. So, with all due respect to Polyander, I doubt whether he himself can derive anything better from it.

Eudoxus I quite see that in directing your words to Polyander you want to spare me. Nevertheless it is perfectly obvious that your jests are directed at me. But let Polyander speak, and we shall then see which of us has the last laugh.

Polyander I shall do so gladly. But I fear that the dispute between you two will become heated, and that while you are pursuing the matter at all too exalted a level, I shall not understand any of it, and shall lose all the fruits I am going to reap (I promise myself) when I proceed to retrace my first steps. So I ask Epistemon to let me indulge this hope so long as it pleases Eudoxus to lead me by the hand along the path on which he set me.

Eudoxus Very well; when you consider yourself simply in so far as you are doubting, you realize that you are not a body, and that so considered, none of the parts which make up the mechanism of the human body are to be found within you, that is, you have no arms, legs, head, eyes, ears or any sense organs. But see whether you can reject in the same way all the other things which you previously understood to be implied in your former notion of a man. As you rightly remarked, it was a fortunate error you made when your answer went beyond the bounds of my question. For it makes it easy for you to get to know what you are: all you need do is to separate from yourself and reject everything which you clearly see does not belong to you, and admit only what necessarily belongs to you – so necessarily that you are as certain and convinced of it as you are of your existing and doubting.

Polyander I am grateful to you for setting me on my way in the manner you did; for I no longer knew where I was. I said previously that I was a whole put together with arms, legs, a head and all the parts which make up what is called 'the human body', and in addition that I walk, am nourished, perceive by the senses, and think. In order to think of myself simply as I know myself to be, it was also necessary for me to set aside all the parts or components which make up the mechanism of the human body, that is, to think of myself as lacking arms, legs, head – in a word, as lacking a body. And yet it is true that whatever it is within me that is doubting, it is not what I call my body. Therefore it is also true that I, in so far as I am doubting, am not that which is nourished or walks; for neither of these actions can be performed without a body. I cannot even say that I, in so far as I am doubting, am capable of perceiving by the

521

senses. For as feet are needed for walking, so eyes are needed for seeing, and ears for hearing; yet since I have none of these organs – because I have no body – I cannot say I perceive by the senses. Furthermore, in the past I have thought while dreaming that I perceived by the senses many things which I did not really perceive. And since I have decided to admit nothing here unless its truth is such that I can have no doubts about it, I cannot say that I am a sentient being, i.e. one which sees with its eyes and hears with its ears. For it is possible in the way just described that I believe I am perceiving by the senses, even though I have no senses.

Eudoxus I cannot but stop you here, not to lead you off the road but to encourage you and make you consider what good sense can achieve if given proper direction. For is there anything in what you have said which is not exact, which is not validly argued, which is not correctly deduced from what has gone before? All these points have been stated and worked out not by means of logic, or a rule or pattern of argument, but simply by the light of reason and good sense. When this light operates on its own, it is less liable to go wrong than when it anxiously strives to follow the numerous different rules, the inventions of human ingenuity and idleness, which serve more to corrupt it than render it more perfect. Epistemon himself seems to agree with us on this point; for his silence indicates that he agrees entirely with what you have been saying. Go on, then, Polyander, and show him how far we can get with good sense, and also what conclusions can be derived from our first principle.

Polyander Of all the attributes I once claimed as my own there is only one left worth examining, and that is thought. I find that it alone is such that I cannot detach it from myself. For if it is true that I am doubting (I cannot doubt that), it is equally true that I am thinking, for what is doubting if not thinking in a certain kind of way? Indeed, if I did not think at all, I could not know whether I doubted or even existed. But I exist, and I know what I am, and I know these facts *because* I am doubting, i.e. because I am thinking. It could even happen that, if I were to cease thinking for a moment, I would also completely cease to exist. So the one thing which I cannot separate from myself, and which I know for certain that I am, and which I can now assert with certainty without fear of being mistaken, that one thing, I say, is that I am a thinking thing.

Eudoxus Epistemon, what do you think of what Polyander has just been saying? Do you find anything in his whole argument which is defective, or anything inconsistent? Would you have thought that an uneducated man who had never bothered to study could reason with such precision, and be so consistent in all his arguments? If I am not mistaken, you must, as a result of this, begin to see that if you simply know how to make proper use of your own doubt, you can use it to deduce

522

facts which are known with complete certainty – facts which are even more certain and more useful than those which we commonly build upon that great principle, as the basis to which they are all reduced, the fixed point on which they all terminate, namely, 'It is impossible that one and the same thing should exist and at the same time not exist.' Perhaps I shall have occasion to demonstrate the usefulness of doubt to you. But let us not interrupt the thread of Polyander's remarks, or stray from the argument. So see whether you have anything to say or any objection to make.

Epistemon Since you are asking me, even needling me, to take sides, I am going to show you what Logic can do when roused, and I shall raise such stiff obstacles that not only Polyander but even you will find it exceedingly difficult to get round them. So rather than going any further, let us stop here and take the trouble to make a rigorous examination of your fundamental principles and conclusions. With the aid of the true Logic and on the basis of your own principles, I shall demonstrate that nothing Polyander has said has a legitimate basis or leads to any firm conclusions. You say that you exist and you know you exist, and you know this because you are doubting and because you are thinking. But do you really know what doubting or what thinking is? Since you do not want to admit anything about which you are not certain or of which you do not have perfect knowledge, how can you be so sure that you exist, on the slender basis of such obscure facts as these? You should really have taught Polyander first of all what doubt is, what thought is, what existence is, so that his reasoning might have the strength of a demonstration, and that he might understand himself before trying to make himself intelligible to others.

Polyander That is quite beyond me; so I shall give up the struggle and leave you and Epistemon to unravel this knot together.

Eudoxus I shall undertake the task with pleasure on this occasion, but only on condition that you act as judge in our dispute, for I dare not hope that Epistemon will give in to my arguments. Someone who, like him, is stuffed full of opinions and taken up with any number of preconceptions 523 finds it difficult to submit himself exclusively to the natural light, for he has long been in the habit of yielding to authority rather than lending his ear to the dictates of his own reason. He would rather question others and ponder on what the ancients have written than consult his own thoughts about what judgement he should make. From childhood he has taken for reason what rested only on the authority of his teachers; so now he puts forward his own authority as reason, and is anxious that others should submit to him in the way that he himself once submitted to others. But I shall have cause to be content, and shall regard myself as having more than adequately answered the objections which Epistemon put to you, if only you agree with what I shall say, and your own reason convinces you of it.

Epistemon I am not so pigheaded or so difficult to persuade and satisfy as you think. And although I had reason to lack confidence in Polyander, I am positively eager to submit our dispute to his arbitration. As soon as he comes down on your side, I promise to admit defeat. But he must take care not to let himself be deceived or to make the mistake for which he reproaches[1] others, i.e. to regard his esteem for you as a convincing reason for believing what you say.

Eudoxus If he relied on such a feeble basis for belief, he would surely be neglecting his own interests, and, I vouch, he will look after himself in this matter. But let us get back to our subject. I quite share your view, Epistemon, that we must know what doubt is, what thought is, what existence is, before being convinced of the truth of this inference, 'I am doubting, therefore I exist', or what amounts to the same thing, 'I am thinking, therefore I exist'. But do not imagine that in order to know what these are, we have to rack our brains trying to find the 'proximate genus' and the 'essential differentia' which go to make up their true definition. We can leave that to someone who wants to be a professor or to debate in the Schools. But someone who wants to examine things for himself, and to base his judgements about them on his own conceptions, must surely have enough mental capacity to have adequate knowledge of what doubt, thought and existence are, whenever he attends to the question, without having to be taught the difference between them. Besides, there are, in my view, some things which are made more obscure by our attempts to define them: since they are very simple and clear, they 524 are perceived and known just on their own, and there is no better way of knowing and perceiving them. Perhaps some of the most serious errors in the sciences are those committed by those who try to define what should only be conceived, and who cannot distinguish between what is clear and what is obscure, nor tell the difference between something which needs and merits a definition if it is to be known and something which is best known just on its own. But doubt, thought and existence can be regarded as belonging to the class of things which have this sort of clarity and which are known just on their own.

I would never have believed that there has ever existed anyone so dull that he had to be told what existence is before being able to conclude and assert that he exists. The same applies to doubt and thought. Furthermore, the only way we can learn such things is by

---

1 Lat. *exprobat* ('he reproaches') may be a misprint for *exprobras* ('you reproach').

ourselves: what convinces us of them is simply our own experience or awareness – that awareness or internal testimony which everyone experiences within himself when he ponders on such matters. Thus it would be pointless trying to define, for someone totally blind, what it is to be white: in order to know what that is, all that is needed is to have one's eyes open and to see white. In the same way, in order to know what doubt and thought are, all one need do is to doubt or to think. That tells us all it is possible to know about them, and explains more about them than even the most precise definitions. So it is true that Polyander must have known these things before being able to draw the conclusions which he did. But, since we chose him as judge, let us ask him if he has ever been ignorant of what doubt or thought or existence is.

Polyander I am quite delighted, I must admit, to hear you arguing about something which you could learn only from me. I am pleased to see that on this occasion at any rate you must acknowledge me as your teacher and regard yourselves as my pupils. So to put both of you out of your misery, I shall solve your problem at a stroke (it is totally unexpected events which we say happen 'at a stroke'). I can say for sure that I have never doubted what doubt is, though I only began to recognize it, or rather to give my attention to it, when Epistemon tried to cast doubt on it. As soon as you showed me what little certainty we can have in the existence of things which we can know only by means of the senses, I began to doubt them. This was enough to bring my doubt home to me and to make me certain of it. Thus I can state that as soon as I began to doubt, I began to have knowledge which was certain. But my doubt and my certainty did not relate to the same objects: my doubt applied only to things which existed outside me, whereas my certainty related to myself and my doubting. So Eudoxus was right when he said that there are things we cannot know about unless we see them. In order, then, to know what doubt and thought are, all we need do is to doubt and to think. The same applies to existence: to know what that is, all we need do is to understand the meaning of the word, for that tells us at once what the thing is which the word stands for, in so far as we can know it. There is no need here for a definition, which would confuse rather than clarify the issue.

Epistemon Since Polyander is satisfied, I too shall agree, and I shall not press the argument any further. But, after two hours of discussion, I cannot see that he has made much progress. All Polyander has learnt with the aid of this marvellous method which you are making such a song about is the fact that he is doubting, that he is thinking, and that he is a thinking thing. Marvellous indeed! So many words for such a meagre result. Four words could have done the trick, and we should all have agreed about it. As for myself, if I were required to spend so much time and engage in such a long discussion in order to learn such an insignificant fact, I would be very reluctant to make the effort. Our teachers have so much more to tell us, and they do so with much more assurance. Nothing holds them back; they deal with everything themselves, and decide each point. Nothing deflects them from their purpose; nothing takes them by surprise. When they feel themselves pressed too hard on some point, an equivocation or a distinction gets them out of their difficulties. You can be sure that their method will always be preferred to yours, which casts doubt on everything, and has such a fear of tripping up that it is constantly dithering and making no headway.

Eudoxus It was never my intention to prescribe to anyone the method which he should follow in his search for truth, but simply to describe the method which I used myself: if it should be thought to be defective, it would be rejected; if good and useful, others would use it too. I left it up   526
to each individual to use it or reject it entirely as he saw fit. If someone should now say that it has not got me very far, this is a matter for experience to determine. Provided you continue to give me your attention, I am sure you will admit that we cannot be too careful in establishing our first principles, and that once these are established, the consequences will be able to be deduced more easily, and will take us further, than we dared hope was possible. All the mistakes made in the sciences happen, in my view, simply because at the beginning we make judgements too hastily, and accept as our first principles matters which are obscure and of which we do not have a clear and distinct notion. That this is true is shown by the slight progress we have made in the sciences whose first principles are certain and known by everyone. By contrast, in the case of sciences, whose principles are obscure and uncertain, those who are prepared to state their views honestly must admit that, for all the time they have spent reading many a vast tome, they have ended up realizing that they know nothing and have learnt nothing. So, my dear Epistemon, you should not be surprised that I wish to lead Polyander along a more certain path than the one I was led along myself, and that I am so careful and precise as to take nothing to be true if I am not as sure of it as I am of the certain fact that I exist, and am thinking, and am a thinking thing.

Epistemon You seem to me to be like an acrobat who always lands on his feet, so constantly do you go back to your 'first principle'. But if you go on in this way, your progress will be slow and limited. How are we always to find truths such that we can be as firmly convinced of them as we are of our own existence?

Eudoxus That is not as difficult as you think. For all truths follow logically from one another, and are mutually interconnected. The whole secret is to begin with the first and simplest truths, and then to proceed gradually and as it were step by step to the most remote and most complex truths. Now can anyone doubt that what I have laid down as the first principle is the first of all the facts we can get to know if we proceed more methodically? It is certain that we cannot doubt this, even if we doubt the truth of everything in the universe. Since, then, we are sure that we have made the right beginning, we must see to it that we do not go wrong from now on. We must take great care to admit as true nothing which is open to even the slightest doubt. With this in view, I say we should let Polyander speak on his own. The only master he follows is common sense, and his reason has not been marred by any false preconceptions. So it is hardly likely that he will be deceived; if he were, he would soon realize it, and would have no trouble getting back onto the road. So let us hear what he has to say; let him tell us about the things which, so he told us, he saw to be contained in our[1] first principle.

Polyander So many things are contained in the idea of a thinking thing that it would take whole days to unfold them. We shall be dealing for the moment only with the most important things, and with those which help to make the notion of a thinking thing more distinct, and which will help us to avoid confusing it with notions which have nothing to do with it. By a 'thinking thing' I mean . . .[2]

---

1 The Amsterdam edition (1701) has 'your' (*vestro*), but the sense requires 'our' (*nostro*). One might, alternatively, give this sentence to Epistemon.
2 The Amsterdam edition inserts here the sentence, 'The rest is missing.'

Index

objective reality/being 10, 28f, 32, 67,
74ff, 97, 113f, 116, 199f, 201ff
obscurity/confusion 103f, 105, 108, 116,
163f, 229
'ontological' argument 46f, 70ff, 82f, 85,
91, 106ff, 117f, 224–7, 263
Optics 173, 293n, 295, 397
Opuscula posthuma 399
organs, bodily 161
Oviedo, Francisco de 326

pain/pleasure 52f, 56, 231, 239, 294
painter, intellect compared with 406
Pandora 211f, 255
Pappus 5
Pegasus 226
perception(s) (*see also* ideas), clear and
distinct *see* clear and distinct
perception(s)
sensory/sense- *see* sensory/sense-
perception
perfect being, idea of 10, 31, 35, 78, 84f,
88, 207ff
perfect body, idea of 84, 89, 99
perfection(s) 28f, 99, 116, 118, 168
degree(s) of 88
idea(s) of 88f, 168, 207f
of God 28, 32, 34, 46f, 71, 84f, 100
of man 58, 88
of universe 39, 42f
peripatetic philosophy/philosophers 125,
292, 391f
Petit, Pierre 7n
phantom limb 53, 61
philosophy, Aristotelian/peripatetic 125,
292, 391f
Descartes' 'new' 387ff
and geometry 5
and theology 3ff, 390ff
scholastic 222, 274, 388ff, 410f
physics 14, 39, 175, 215, 274f
pineal gland 59n
place 292
Plato 121, 228, 401
Platonists 278, 287
pleasure *see* pain/pleasure
Porphyrian universals 100
Porphyry, tree of 344, 410
possibility 107
Praxiteles 250
preconceived opinions 5, 9, 12, 15, 47,
77f, 104, 111, 116, 241f, 264, 270f,
296ff, 299f, 313, 324, 352f, 355
preservation (in being) 33f, 79, 116ff, 148,
169
primary notion(s) 97, 100, 111

Principles of Philosophy x, 33n, 293n,
387n
Pyrrhonists 408, 413
Pythagoras 228, 263, 323, 325, 335
Pythagoreans 287

qualities, real 173, 176, 298
sensible/perceived by the senses 30, 52,
153, 173ff
quantity 44, 143, 174

real distinction 54, 72, 86, 95, 114, 119f,
140, 155f, 160, 247, 282
reality (*see also* being), degrees of 30f, 117,
130
modal 174, 251
objective vs formal (of ideas) 10, 28f, 32,
67, 74ff, 97, 113f, 116, 199f, 201f
of causes and effects 28
potential 32
reason, and animals 96, 189, 279, 287f
and the mind 18
and the senses 52, 144, 231
reasoning 125f, 130, 134, 189, 295f
Regius, Henricus 393n
remembering *see* memory
revelation, divine 105, 252
Rodis-Lewis, G. 2n
Rules for the Direction of the Mind x,
10n

scepticism 94, 374f
sceptics 94, 321, 375
scholastic philosophy/philosophers 222,
274, 388ff, 410f
science 408
sciences 403f, 419
scientia 101n
Scotus, Duns 72f, 85
Search for Truth, The 101n
self, and the body 56, 87f, 181ff, 235ff,
244f, 335ff, 412ff
as combination of mind and body 61
creation/preservation of 209
essence/nature of 18ff, 22, 54, 87f, 93,
139ff, 157, 181ff, 192f, 233, 235–7,
244f
existence of *see cogito* argument
idea of 129, 199, 234f, 258
knowledge of 17–20, 22f, 54, 141ff,
157, 185ff, 191f, 247
origin of existence of 33, 68, 77ff, 146f,
209f
self-evident propositions 115
self-movement, power of 17f

Printed in the USA
CPSIA information can be obtained
at www.ICGtesting.com
LVHW050853200823
755707LV00007B/13

9 780521 288088